AUGUSTINE

CITY OF GOD

II

LCL 412

AUGUSTINE

THE CITY OF GOD
AGAINST THE PAGANS

BOOKS IV–VII

WITH AN ENGLISH TRANSLATION BY

WILLIAM M. GREEN

HARVARD UNIVERSITY PRESS
CAMBRIDGE, MASSACHUSETTS
LONDON, ENGLAND

First published 1963
Reprinted 1978, 1995

ISBN 0-674-99453-1

Printed in Great Britain by St Edmundsbury Press Ltd,
Bury St Edmunds, Suffolk, on acid-free paper.
Bound by Hunter & Foulis Ltd, Edinburgh, Scotland.

CONTENTS

INTRODUCTION   vii

CITY OF GOD
    BOOK IV   1
    BOOK V   131
    BOOK VI   279
    BOOK VII   369

INTRODUCTION

The reader of the first volume has already become familiar with the general plan of the City of God.[1] In this volume Book IV begins with a recapitulation of the earlier books, and proceeds to the question whether the old gods deserve any credit for the greatness of Rome. Augustine resolves this question into two: (1) Should the extent of Roman rule, gained as it was by wars, be counted as a good, or as an evil? (2) Was the conquest of the empire really achieved with the help of the Roman gods? Then for a description of those gods Augustine turns to Varro, who had written a sort of encyclopedia of religious antiquities which everyone accepted as authoritative. Book V continues the argument to show that the extent of the empire was due neither to Fate nor to luck, but to the providence of the one true God.

Book VI begins a new section of five books, written avowedly to answer the pagan claim that the old gods should be worshipped for the sake of a future life. The future life was, in fact, a subject of concern to the pagans of the later Empire, and many cults held out promises concerning it, especially cults from

[1] Pages lxxvi–lxxxii, also 2–5. For a detailed analysis of the whole work and its frequent " digressions," see the article of Deferrari and Keeler listed in my bibliography, p. xxxiv.

INTRODUCTION

the East, such as those of Isis, Mithra and Cybele. Augustine, however, pays little attention to these,[1] but resumes the attack on the gods of Rome as they were described by Varro. He gives us a complete analysis of Varro's *Antiquities*, then of his three kinds of theology, and of his assignment of petty functions to a host of petty gods.

Book VII continues with a study of the " select " gods which are described in Varro's sixteenth book. These are twenty of the best-known deities of Rome, most of them identified with Greek counterparts, and thus involved in the absurd and scandalous tales of mythology. But the myths, Varro declares, are to be understood as referring to parts of the universe, or to physical phenomena. Jupiter, as the Stoics teach, is the World-soul, and the other gods are his parts. The gods of the state are thus made to serve as the base of a physical, or " natural " theology. The book closes with a story of the discovery of the supposed books of Numa, Rome's second king, re- nowned as the founder of her religion. If these books had been published, Augustine suggests, they might have disclosed the demonic origin and character of the whole system.

In reading these four books one is confronted with certain problems, two of which have been the subject of prolonged discussion. First, what is Augustine's

---

[1] Augustine mentions Cybele (*Berecynthia mater*), the Dea Caelestis of Carthage, the Egyptian deities Hermes Trisme- gistus, Isis and Osiris, and the Eleusinian and Samothracian mysteries, but no mention of the future life is made in con- nection with them. A closer approach to the subject is found in the discussion of Platonic theology in Book X.

INTRODUCTION

appraisal of Rome, her achievement in history, and her way of life? And second, how far is the portrayal of Roman religion here found relevant to the issues of Augustine's time? These topics will be discussed as far as seems useful to provide the reader with a background for the better understanding of Books IV–VII.

I

The circumstances which led Augustine to write the *City of God* provoked him to denounce not only Rome's gods, but also her morals and her ideals as expressed in literature. The gods, the pagans said, had blessed Rome with victory and prosperity, so long as they were properly worshipped. But now the gods were deserted and Rome had collapsed in disaster. Augustine denied the assertion, claiming that the present misfortunes were no greater than those of pagan times. We may suspect that the claim was not very convincing to the homeless refugees from the pillaged city. Pagans and Christians alike believed that a god should protect his worshippers. So Augustine made a further reply: the victories and the prosperity which the gods are supposed to have granted the Romans are worthless in comparison with the rewards of the Christian life. Indeed, when pagan prosperity is attended by luxury and pride and cruelty, as it was in Rome, the result is evil in itself, the exact antithesis of the Christian way of life. This thought has already appeared in the earlier books. " Why," Augustine demands of his adversaries, " when afflicted by adversities, do

you complain against the Christian era, unless because you wish to maintain your luxury untroubled, and to abandon yourselves to the most damnable practices? "[1] Sallust is quoted to show that the prosperity which followed the destruction of Carthage in 146 B.C. brought an increase of evils, although similar evils were not unknown in earlier times.[2] Cicero, too, is a witness to the corruption of the state in his time, a corruption which made it unworthy of the name *res publica*, having lost the essential quality of justice. But this, Augustine argues, was never really present in Rome, for it exists only in the republic whose founder is Christ.[3]

Augustine now further develops his attack on Rome by a study of Roman rule, the means by which it was attained, and the question whether it was a worthy object for pursuit. " You cannot show that men are happy," he argues, " who live always amid the disasters of war. The dark shadow of fear and the lust for blood are always with them. How then is it rational, how can it be wise, to see something to boast of in the area and greatness of an empire? "[4] In fact, " if justice is left out, what are kingdoms except great robber bands? "[5] The implication is that in all earthly kingdoms, and especially in Rome, justice had been left out. The testimony of Sallust and Cicero supported that view, and Augustine had gone further, with the sweeping claim that only in Christ's kingdom could true justice be found. Rome, it is pointed out, was peopled from the first by slaves

---

[1] 1.30, in Volume I, p. 125. [2] 2.18, p. 203.
[3] 2.21, pp. 217, 225. [4] 4.3, p. 13, below.
[5] 4.4, p. 17.

and criminals who fled to the asylum which was
there provided. How then did Romulus' kingdom
differ from that of Spartacus, who called the slaves
of Italy to revolt, ruled them for years, and defeated
three Roman armies which were sent against him?[1]

Yet for all this assault on Rome and her empire,
Augustine does recognize some value in her achievements, and especially in the character of her outstanding men. Ennius in his epic had once declared:

The ancient ways maintain the Roman state.
Its ancient heroes too.

Cicero had quoted this with approval, in order to
contrast the vices and afflictions which in his day had
displaced the ancient virtues and prosperity.[2] The
virtues are left for later study, while Augustine goes
on with the problem of justice in war.

However great Rome's vices were, it cannot fairly
be said that all her wars were unjustly launched
against innocent victims. Rome, in fact, regularly
made the claim that her wars were defensive.
" Are good men," Augustine asks, " reluctant [that
is, professedly reluctant] to wage an unfair and wicked
war, and to challenge by unprovoked attack neighbours who are peaceful and doing no wrong, all in
order to extend their dominion? If that is their
sentiment, I certainly give my approval and applause."[3] But these supposedly defensive wars
usually resulted in annexations, and so helped the
empire to grow. " Hence if it was by waging just war
that the Romans were able to acquire so great an

[1] 4.5, p. 119; on the asylum of Romulus see 5.17, p. 223.
[2] 2.21, I, p. 223.   [3] 4.14, p. 57, below.

empire, should they not also worship as a goddess
External Aggression? . . . Aggression provided the
occasion for wars, and Victory brought them to a
happy conclusion." [1] Thus, on the question whether
Rome's conquests were justified by the necessity of
defensive wars Augustine adopts a cautious reserve.
If the claim is true, he is willing to approve. Then he
adds the ironic suggestion that along with the cult of
the goddess of Victory they should also worship
External Aggression, which gave them the necessary
pretext for just wars of conquest. The irony shows
that he is unimpressed by any claim of justice for the
wars by which Rome won her empire.

It is not till the fifth book that we reach a full-
length study of the Roman character, and the reasons
for Rome's greatness among the nations. As
Sallust described them, the fighters of the early
Republic were eager for praise, sought unbounded
glory, and suppressed all other desires. They held
it shameful for their country to be in servitude, and
glorious for it to rule and command. Hence they
fought first for independence, then for dominion.
These motives are extolled by their great poet, Virgil,
who goes on in his most famous lines to proclaim
Rome's mission to govern the nations.[2] At this point
Augustine makes his own generous admission of
Rome's greatness:

When splendid empires had long been known in
the East, God willed that an empire of the West

[1] 4.15, p. 59.
[2] 5.12, pp. 194–199. Cf. Sallust, *Catiline*, 7.6; Virgil,
Aeneid, 8.646–648; 1.279–285; 6.847–853.

should arise, later in time, but more splendid for its extent and greatness. To overcome the grievous vices of many nations, he granted supremacy to men who for the sake of honour, praise and glory served the country in which they were seeking their own glory, and did not hesitate to prefer her safety to their own. Thus for the sake of one vice, that is, the love of praise, they overcame the love of money and many other vices.[1]

But even this concession to greatness could not be left without insisting on the contrast between Roman and Christian ethics. Despite Cicero's view of glory and honour as incentives to endeavour, Horace recognized that both love of praise and love of power are vices.[2] For the Christian, love of praise must yield to love of truth. Apostles and martyrs have set the example of seeking, not the glory of men, but the glory that comes from God.[3]

Though the Romans were idolaters, and so excluded from eternal life, God nevertheless granted them a proper reward for their virtues. They were like the Pharisees who did their good deeds to be seen of men, and like the Pharisees, Augustine suggests, they have received their reward. They lived the life which leads to honour, power and glory, and so are honoured among almost all nations. Many nations obey their laws, and poets and historians are eager to glorify them in their writings.[4]

There is a further thing which the Romans achieved by their deeds of virtue. They provided examples

[1] 5.13, p. 207.   [2] *Ibid.*
[4] 5.14, p. 211.   [4] 5.15, p. 217.

INTRODUCTION

of heroism, not only for their fellow citizens of the earthly city, but for the citizens of the city of God, who would one day be called on to deny themselves, suffer and die. If Romans could do such things for love of Rome, what should they not be willing to do for the love of God? Thus God had a double purpose in granting prosperity to the Romans: they obtained the earthly reward which was just, and through them God provided examples which would spur his own people on to equal deeds for a greater reward.[1]

After a further comparison of different standards of behaviour, of the shameful notion of making virtues the handmaids of the desire for glory, and of the hidden ways of Providence, Augustine closes Book V with three chapters on the Christian emperors. If they deserve to be called happy, he says, it is not because of long life or prosperity, but because they attained perfection in the character that is appropriate to a Christian prince.[2] Constantine, to be sure, enjoyed every earthly blessing—a long reign, victory in wars, the privilege of founding a new city free from idolatry, and sons to inherit his kingdom. That was enough to prove that one need not be a worshipper of demons to receive such blessings.[3] Of Theodosius more could be said. His victory over Eugenius and his pagan supporters was gained more by prayer than by the sword. He was not vindictive toward his defeated foes, but spared their children, and urged them to become Christians. His laws

---

[1] 5.16, p. 219. In 5.18, pp. 225–235 Augustine recites a list of famous exploits, each affording a model for Christian heroism.
[2] 5.24, p. 261.　　　　[3] 5.25, p. 265.

were intended to help the church, and to overthrow idolatry. And finally, when convicted of wrong-doing in his severe treatment of the people of Thessalonica, he humbly submitted to the discipline of the church.[1]

The question now arises: does this eulogy of the Christian emperors require us to modify our view of the long attack on Rome and her claim to greatness? Has Rome now achieved a new greatness, since her rulers submit to Christ and to the discipline of his church? Augustine makes no such claim. Any exaltation of Rome would be quite out of keeping with the spirit and aim of the *City of God*. The question indeed points to a larger problem, that of Augustine's political views, especially regarding the actual relations between the church and the state. But in this book these views are not set forth; here he is concerned with the city of God in its long struggle with the earthly city. These two cities, or societies, are of course not identical with the visible church and the city of Rome, though the latter are generally taken as representing on earth the two spiritual cities. The two are mixed, or interlaced, while the struggle now goes on, and will remain mixed until the end of this age (*saeculum*). Augustine offers no plan, no hint of a Utopia, or political solution for the problems of this age, however much Christians may desire to find such a plan.

A modern critic of the City of God has written:

I venture to think that St. Augustine would have done more justice to his own thought if he had

[1] 5.26, pp. 267–273.

formally described the state, like our earthly life generally, as a battleground of good and evil. The earthly representative of the Kingdom of God is the Church. . . . But the state, and human society generally, is not a similar representative of the lower powers.[1]

The last statement is misleading. Rome, like Assyria and the other world powers, is taken as representative of the *terrena civitas*. The whole statement amounts to a criticism of Augustine's otherworldliness from the viewpoint of modern social consciousness. Perhaps, as Étienne Gilson says, men of our day hope to construct a third city midway between the two Augustine describes—a city that is temporal like Augustine's " earthly city," yet just, in a temporal way. But, as Gilson observes, such an idea seems never to have occurred to St. Augustine; at least he never spoke of it.[2]

II

What can be learned of Roman paganism in Augustine's time by reading this volume? Material is here in abundance, but to interpret and evaluate it correctly is difficult. Much of the material is taken from Varro, who had written his encyclopedia of

[1] E. R. Hardy, in Battenhouse, 279 (see bibliography, p. xxxiv).

[2] Gilson, " Foreword," lxxx. For an ample bibliography on Augustine's appraisal of Rome, see Maier, 215–219. For a further discussion of the " third city," see Marrou, 348–350.

Antiquities more than four hundred years before. Did Varro's words have any meaning or relevance to the people of Augustine's day? It has long been a commonplace to deny any such relevance. To quote Franz Cumont, for example:

> By means of compromises between old Oriental ideas and Greco-Latin thought, an ensemble of beliefs slowly took form (i.e., in the later Empire), the truth of which seemed to have been established by common consent. So when the atrophied parts of the Roman religion had been removed, foreign elements had combined to give it a new vigour, and in it themselves became modified. This hidden work of internal decomposition and reconstruction had unconsciously produced a religion very different from the one Augustus had attempted to restore. However, we would be tempted to believe that there had been no change in the Roman faith, were we to read certain authors that fought idolatry in those days. Saint Augustine, for instance, in his *City of God*, pleasantly pokes fun at the multitude of Italian gods that presided over the paltriest acts of life. But the useless, ridiculous deities of the old pontifical litanies no longer existed outside of the books of antiquaries. As a matter of fact, the Christian polemicist's authority in this instance was Varro. . . . It has frequently been shown that apologists find it difficult to follow the progress of the doctrines they oppose, and their blows often fall upon dead men.[1]

[1] Cumont, 202 f.

And now, half a century after Cumont, similar views are expressed by the author of an extended account of Augustine's pastoral career:

> À vrai dire, Augustin, dans ce livre [the *City of God*], ne combattait presque plus des adversaires vivants; il liquidait plutôt une enterprise en faillite qui, fait remarquable, prétendait se reserver tant de place. Cet ouvrage n'appartient plus précisément au pasteur; il a été écrit bien plus pour Charlemagne et pour Innocent III que pour les évêques des alentours de 400 et pour les nobles que rencontrait Marcellin dans son club.[1]

Not only had Varro, the man so often addressed as adversary, been dead at least 440 years (27 B.C.–A.D. 413, when Augustine began writing the *City of God*), but there remains also a question whether in his catalogue of the gods Varro had given a true account of the religion of his own day. This involves us in the difficult question of Varro's sources, and the methods he used in compiling his work. Since this is a subordinate point, it will be discussed first.

Augustine's excerpts from Varro's religious *Antiquities* are taken chiefly, if not exclusively, from Books I, XIV, XV and XVI, and especially from Book XIV. This book dealt with *di certi*, that is, with gods of whose names and functions Varro was able to speak with certainty. The names were assembled in classified lists, according to the fields in which the functions of each group lay. Many petty deities were included (*di minuti*, Augustine calls them), each

---

[1] Meer, 91. But compare the English translation, *Augustine the Bishop* (1961), 44, where this paragraph has been omitted.

concerned with a special function, or even with a single moment of a man's life.[1] Varro is quoted by Servius as saying that such lists were found in the *indigitamenta*, or books of the pontiffs where one might find both the names of the gods and explanations of the names. The names, he adds, were taken from the functions, such as " Harrower " from harrowing, " Sower " from sowing, and so forth.[2] The pontiffs, we are told, put special gods in charge of each act of life, and these Varro called *di certi*.[3]

It is clear, then, that Varro used the pontifical *indigitamenta* in compiling his lists of *di certi*, but a question has been raised whether the lists of Varro give a reliable view of the books of the pontiffs. Georg Wissowa in 1904 called attention to two lists of special deities, independently preserved, and by a comparison undertook to show how far Varro's lists differ from the true, original, pontifical lists. Servius quotes Fabius Pictor (a historian of about 200 B.C.) as saying that the priest (*flamen*) when sacrificing to Ceres and Tellus invoked twelve deities, all connected with the seasonal work of the grain farmer, from the first ploughing to the harvesting and storing of the grain, and its removal from storage. All are

---

[1] 6.3, p. 299 f.; 7.17, p. 435 f. The Romans seem to have had no name for these little gods, or spirits which were restricted to special, limited functions. The German word *Sondergötter* is often applied to them, or the Latin *di speciales*.

[2] Servius, *Georgics*, 1.21.

[3] Servius auctus, *Aeneid*, 2.141. Pontifices dicunt singulis actibus proprios deos praeesse. Hos Varro deos certos appellat. The *di certi*, however, included major deities as well. The distinction between *di certi* and *incerti* is made clear in 7.17, p. 435, below.

nouns of agent in *-tor*, beginning with Vervactor and ending with Conditor and Promitor. The other series of names is found in the acts of the Arval Brothers preserved in inscriptions of the years A.D. 183 and 224. There was a ritual for the removal and destruction of an ill-omened tree which grew on the roof of the temple, and several deities, this time feminine, presided over the steps of the ritual. Both examples, Wissowa notes, belong to public rather than to private cult; the special gods have roles subsidiary to that of some principal deity; the series of functions is limited and unified; the names are formed on a single pattern and are unmistakable in their meaning. Varro's lists are quite different. One list is very long and relates to the various moments of a man's life, from his conception to his burial; it is thus hardly suitable for any "pontifical litany." The names are of varied patterns and origins, major gods are listed along with the obscure, functions are assigned on the basis of etymological speculation (for which Varro's fondness is displayed in other works), with etymologies often obviously incorrect. Hence, it is argued, Varro's lists are not of priestly origin, but are a scholar's collection made from various sources, and all far removed from the realities of actual belief and worship.[1]

[1] Wissowa, "Echte und falsche Sondergötter," 312–314; see also Lindemann, 7–12. The most damaging point made against Varro by Wissowa and Lindemann is the charge that he invents etymologies, often obviously false, for gods of whom he knew nothing except the name, whereas true "Sondergötter" were named from their function and there could be no question of false etymology. It is concluded that the lists of *di certi* were largely filled with Varro's false ety-

In reply it is pointed out that the *indigitamenta* certainly included more than such lists of subsidiary deities as those of the two examples cited. They presented both names and explanations of the names (*rationes ipsorum nominum*). Nor were they limited to subsidiary deities, for we are told that the absence of Apollo's name from the *Pompiliana indigitamenta* was enough to prove that the god was unknown in Roman worship in the time of Numa;[1] evidently the priestly books contained the names of all the gods whose cult was recognized in Rome. Nor is it safe to assume that all minor deities were inventions of the priests and of no concern to the people, for, as Warde Fowler has pointed out, the priests would hardly have proceeded with such invention if the matter did not have some basis in the habits and thinking of the people. He cites the case of the

mologies, and hence worthless. Wissowa rejects as unsubstantiated Bickel's view that the errors arose in popular beliefs (*Hermes* 56, 123). But it is equally impossible to prove, and perhaps less credible, that Varro invented the etymologies and then ascribed to numerous gods functions which they never possessed in the opinion of their worshippers. There remains a third possibility: that the pontiffs, besides inventing new names as occasion required, would sometimes assign to older gods functions which they had not previously had, somehow suggested by their names, and explained by a spurious etymology. Finally, the responsibility for the invention may belong in various proportions to the people, the pontiffs and Varro.

[1] Arnobius, *Against the Nations*, 2.73. Non doctorum in litteris continetur Apollinis nomen Pompiliana indigitamenta nescire? The noun is from the verb *indigitare*, " to invoke," and can be used of the formula for invoking any deity. Compare Macrobius, *Saturnalia*, 1.17.5, Virgines Vestales ita indigitant: Apollo Medice, Apollo Paean.

rites used to protect a new mother from the forest
god Silvanus, in which three petty deities are invoked at the threshold of the house. The whole
bears the stamp of popular superstition. Yet if the
priestly books provided any complete catalogue of
Roman gods, these must have been included, since
the private rites of the family were under the supervision of the pontiffs, as well as the rites of the state
cult.[1]

It is impossible to say how far Varro's account of
religion corresponded with the cult of his own time,
or of any earlier time. Varro expressed the fear that
the gods were about to perish from neglect, a fate
from which he hoped to rescue them.[2] Evidently
much of what he gleaned from his sources was already
antiquated, and to be discovered only by library research. That research he undertook as a duty, and
embedded in his work all that could then be learned
about the Roman religion. His work was im-
mediately recognized as authoritative—as much so,
apparently, as the very books of the pontiffs would
have been.

We may now turn to the broader question of the
relevance of Augustine's polemic to the problems of
his day. Were his blows, as Cumont and others
suggest, falling on dead men?

First, it must be remembered that there was a
real controversy going on, one in which Augustine
felt himself deeply involved. The circumstances

---

[1] Fowler, 163 f. cites *City of God*, 6.9, p. 341, below. On
the pontiffs' supervision of sacra privata, see Wissowa, *RK*[2],
400.

[2] 6.2, p. 295 f.

which led to his writing the *City of God* have been
sketched in the first volume (pp. lix–lxii, lxxi–lxxv),
on the basis of letters and sermons from the years
411–412, and in these the pagans were being answered
with arguments similar to those afterward used in the
City of God. Pagans were insistent in their charges,
and many Christians wavered in their faith. These
were the men, very much alive, whom he constantly
challenges in his great work. Nor did his challenge
miss the mark, for when three books had been published the pagans were stung to make a reply.[1]
Whether this was ever published we do not know.
But it appears that Augustine felt the need of re-
inforcement for his argument in those three books.
Hence he persuaded his friend Orosius to write a
History against the Pagans the more thoroughly to
refute the claim that the disasters under Christian
rule were unprecedented in Rome's history. Julian
of Carthage added his plea to that of Augustine.[2]
All must have agreed that the debate with the pagans
was an urgent matter.

Before assenting to the notion that in the *City of
God* Augustine was dealing with adversaries long
dead, we should remark that the attack on Varro
occupies only a small part of the twenty-two books.
The last twelve are a defence of the Christian view
of history, where neither Varro nor his gods are under
attack. In the first ten books, where the gods are
the centre of attack, the pagan sources are varied,
including such later writings as those of Apuleius,
Porphyry, the Hermetic writings, and Chaldean and

[1] 5.26, p. 275.
[2] Orosius, *History*, Praefatio; see also Lacroix, 163–175.

INTRODUCTION

Sibylline Oracles.[1] Astrology, divination and magic come in for extended discussion. All these were prominent in Augustine's day, and are often mentioned in his letters, sermons and other writings.[2] It is hardly fair to say with Mandouze that " the question of paganism, or more precisely, of Roman religion, scarcely interested him." [3]

As for Varro, and the space that Augustine devotes to his " ridiculous " gods, the important fact is that Varro was recognized by pagans as well as by Christians as the chief authority on Roman religion. This Augustine constantly asserts, and defends his assertion by quoting from Cicero and others.[4] He could have mentioned the honours heaped on Varro during his lifetime—his appointment by Caesar to arrange for a great public library in Rome,[5] and the bronze statue set up by Asinius Pollio in the Atrium Libertatis, Varro being the only living man so honoured.[6] Throughout the succeeding generations Varro is constantly cited on a variety of subjects for which we would use an encyclopedia today. His name is regularly accompanied by a complimentary epithet, such as *certus auctor, doctissimus Romanorum, auctor diligentissimus*, or the like.[7] Especially notable

---

[1] Angus, 9–51.
[2] Compare the index in Madden, 133–135, and that to appear in Vol. VII of this translation.
[3] Mandouze, 194.   [4] 6.2, p. 293.
[5] Suetonius, *Caesar*, 4.4.2.
[6] Pliny, *Natural History*, 7.115.
[7] Valerius Maximus, 3.2.24; Seneca, *Natural Questions*, 5.16.4; *Dialogues*, 12.8.1; Quintilian, *Institutes*, 10.1.95; Apuleius, *Apology*, 42; Aulus Gellius, 4.9.1; Solinus, 1.17. For the later grammarians see Keil, *Grammatici Latini*, index.

are two pagan writers contemporary with Augustine, distinguished by their interest in the old Roman cult; these, like Augustine, treat Varro as their chief authority. Servius was writing his bulky commentary on Virgil about the end of the fourth century, and in it cites Varro hundreds of times, very frequently on matters of religion. He once remarks that Varro is first among the authorities in that subject.[1] In the same period Macrobius was setting forth the views of cultured pagans in matters of common interest. He cites Varro at least thirty-seven times, usually on topics related to religion.[2]

It must be admitted that the interest thus shown was basically antiquarian. The same could be said of Varro's interest. But in each case there was a real desire to preserve the past, and preserve it in a form acceptable to the present. There was a patriotic sentiment which led men to glorify Rome's past, hoping to preserve that glory forever. Many of the gods were perhaps forgotten and their cult neglected, but there remained a desire to maintain the old system with the best-known features of the cult and the patriotic spirit that attended it.[3] Varro was the outstanding spokesman for that desire. His encyclopedia was intended both as a reference book and as propaganda. Perhaps it served its purpose in the days of Augustus, but it was poorly designed for the defence of the gods four hundred years

[1] *Aeneïd*, 10.275.

[2] See Eyssenhardt's index of the Teubner Macrobius.

[3] This sentiment is well displayed in the *Relatio* of Symmachus which pleads for the restoration of the altar of Victory, and in the poem of Rutilianus Namatianus on his return to Gaul in 416.

later. Instead, it presented an admirable target for attack.

Varro had analysed the theology of his day in a manner which afforded a convenient approach to the leading issues of the fifth century, as Augustine saw them. Following the pontiff Scaevola, Varro says that there are three kinds of gods, those of the poets, the philosophers and the statesmen. To these correspond three kinds of theology, the mythical, the physical (or natural) and the civil. This three-fold division Augustine takes as the basis of his attack.

First, he asserts, the gods of mythology have corrupted the morals of the people and proved themselves to be demons. All men read the poets in childhood, and learn what the gods are like. Then they attend the theatre and find delight in the lascivious behaviour of the objects of their worship. All this is done, as the historians relate, at the insistence of the gods themselves.[1] Varro accordingly included the stage plays (*ludi scaenici*) among the "divine things," and so they become an obvious target for Christian attack.[2]

A modern critic writes: "No feature of the *De Civitate Dei* is calculated to make a deeper or more painful impression upon modern readers than Augustine's unreserved attack upon theatrical performances, or stage plays."[3] Such is the observation of a modern churchman, living in a society where the theatre is an accepted part of the Christian

[1] 1.32, I, p. 133; cf. 2.8, p. 169.
[2] 4.31, p. 117, below; 6.3, 5, pp. 299, 311, 315 below.
[3] Welldon, II, 658.

way of life. But the situation was very different in Augustine's day. The shows had always been connected with the festivals of the gods, their temples, altars and sacrifices.[1] In the time of Augustine an attempt was made, in 399, to suppress the sacrifices connected with the shows.[2] Whatever the effect of the law may have been, it made the theatre no more acceptable to Augustine. Although members of his flock still went to the shows, these were denounced as false Christians, destined not to share in the eternal lot of the saints.[3] The hatred of the church for the stage did not die with Augustine, but went on through mediaeval, and into modern times.[4]

That hatred was based both on the pagan associations of the theatre and on its moral effects. Augustine stresses the immorality of the myths, as these were presented on the stage. To support his argument he quotes both Plato and Cicero.[5] Moreover, Augustine insists, the Roman people as a whole had already passed judgement on their own stage

[1] The religious origin of both Greek and Roman stage performances is unquestioned, but whether the connection remained close till the end of paganism has been questioned. Recent studies, especially in archaeology, seem to support the Christian writers in their claims. See Hanson, *Roman Theater-Temples*, especially Chapters I and V.

[2] Codex Theodosianus, 16.10.3, translated in Huttmann, 228. Similar legislation had been enacted by the sons of Constantine, but the need of re-enactment shows that the pagan rites went on. Constantine allowed the construction of theatres with temples and priests (Huttmann, 100–103).

[3] 1.35, I, p. 137 f.

[4] See Welldon, II, 658–669, on " The Church and the Stage."

[5] Plato is cited 2.14, I, p. 187 f., also 8.13; Cicero 2.9, I, p. 171 f., 2.13, p. 185, 4.30, p. 113, below.

and on the gods there honoured, when they branded their actors with the stigma of *infamia*.[1] Though distinguished actors, such as Roscius of Cicero's day, were held in high esteem, the profession remained under legal disabilities from the earliest times till Justinian.[2]

The second aspect of pagan theology, the religion of the philosophers, was the most serious matter of controversy, at least on the intellectual level. Of the ten books which Augustine devoted to his attack on paganism, the last four deal with the *theologia naturalis*, the effort of the philosophers to defend the old gods. In Book VII the " select gods " of Varro's natural theology are considered, while the next three books take up the debate with the Neoplatonists, who were properly recognized as the most formidable adversaries.

Something has already been said of Book VII (page viii) and the Stoic interpretation of gods as parts of the universe. The universe for them was a living being, whose parts were filled with spirits.[3] Jupiter is either the world-soul, including all other gods in himself, or, alternatively, is the aether, while Juno

---

[1] 2.29, p. 263; cf. 2.11, 13, 27, pp. 177, 185, 257.

[2] Justinian, *Digest* 3.2.2.5; cf. *RE* 8, 2117 s.v. " Histrio " and 9, 1539 *s.v.* " Infamia "; also Green in *CP* 28, 301–304.

[3] Though the explanations of the gods are characteristically Stoic, Varro, like his friend Cicero, adhered to the Academy. Both had studied under Antiochus of Ascalon, who regarded himself as the restorer of the old Academy of Plato (cf. *City of God*, 19.1, 3, VI, pp. 105, 121). Antiochus and his pupils were thoroughly eclectic, and borrowed freely from the Stoics. Some of Varro's explanations, however, are more Platonic than Stoic, and thus anticipate the manner of the Neoplatonists. See Boyancé, 74–80.

INTRODUCTION

is the air (or earth) beneath; Pluto is the earth,
Vesta the hearth-fire, and so on. Those deities not
traditionally assigned to a local abode were regarded
as functions or parts of the world-soul; they attended
to special activities, for example, Apollo in divination,
Mercury in trade, Janus in beginnings, and so on.[1]
No difficulty was felt in assigning several explanations
to one god, or several gods to one sphere of activity.

This method of reconciling the ancient myths with
later rational thought was current from the time of
Theagenes of Rhegium (about 525 B.C.) until the end
of paganism. It flourished most notably among
the Stoics, and came to play a prominent part in the
defence of paganism in the fourth century. The
Neoplatonists went on from the " physical " explanations of the Stoics to their own " psychical " and
" theological " interpretations.[2] But since there had
always been complete freedom in devising and
multiplying explanations, these later refinements
could easily be accepted as part of the old system.
Thus the emperor Julian (360–363) and his friend
Sallustius, both Neoplatonists and zealous for the old
gods, made use of the myths in their effort to revive
and reform the pagan cult. To quote from Gilbert
Murray:

> The myths are all expressions of God and the
> goodness of God, but they follow the usual method
> of divine revelation, to wit, mystery and allegory.
> The myths state clearly the one tremendous fact
> that the Gods are; that is what Julian cared about

[1] 4.11, p. 45.
[2] Sallustius, *On the Gods and the World*, 4.

and the Christians denied; what they are the myths reveal only to those who have understanding.

After citing examples of Sallustius' exposition of the story of Kronos devouring his children, the judgement of Paris, and the myth of Attis and Cybele, Murray continues:

So much for the whole traditional mythology. It had been explained completely away, and made subservient to philosophy and edification, while it can still be used as a great well-spring of religious emotion.[1]

Of the later writers Augustine cites only Porphyry,[2] but besides him and Julian and Sallustius there are others, such as Iamblichus and Proclus among the Greeks, and Servius and Macrobius among the Latin writers. The indexes of these authors will guide one to a host of examples which parallel and amplify those which Augustine takes from Varro. Servius was a contemporary grammarian and teacher of Virgil, who embodies such material as would be used in a classroom to elucidate the poet. Augustine speaks with irony of the tender minds being thus initiated into the pagan mythology.[3] Macrobius' writings also have a didactic purpose: both his *Saturnalia* and his *Commentary on Scipio's Dream* are addressed to his son, as texts for his instruction. The former presents a dialogue in which men of prominence in literary and public life discourse on every sort of topic. The

[1] Murray, 168 f.   [2] 7.25, p. 467.   [3] 1.3, I, p. 19 f.

Commentary is a more connected description of the after life, as viewed by the pagans. In both works we find explanations of the gods comparable to those found in Varro.

So much for the *theologia naturalis*, so far as it is considered by Augustine in Book VII. His debate with the Neoplatonists on the subject of demons, magic, divination, astrology and purification of the soul will appear in the next volume. A comparison with what is found on these topics in other writings will show that they were equally familiar in the controversies of the time.[1]

Varro's third kind of theology, the *theologia civilis*, deals with the gods of the state. The Roman state religion was really the subject of all sixteen books of his *Antiquitates Rerum Divinarum*.[2] The other two kinds of theology are discussed in order to distinguish what the poets and philosophers have said about the gods from the actual religion which the statesmen have established. The state itself comes first, according to Varro, then its religious institutions, and this explains why, in his *Antiquities*, the twenty-five books on *res humanae* come before the sixteen on *res divinae*.[3] As a conservative, he considered the worship of the gods necessary to the welfare of the state, and was alarmed by the prevalent neglect in his day. He declares his literary efforts to rescue the gods from oblivion comparable to the act of Metellus the pontifex, who rescued the sacred things of Vesta from her burning temple, or that of Aeneas, who carried the Penates to safety,

---

[1] See Madden's index, 133–135.   [2] 7.1, p. 373, below.
[3] 6.4, p. 303.

out of the city of Troy.[1] From the disorder of the
fragments in which Varro is quoted by Augustine it
is impossible to gain a satisfactory view of the
original.[2] But it appears that in the first book
Varro made clear his intention to instruct both
citizens and priests about the Roman religion, since
it included both the official cult performed by magistrates and the private cult of the family.[3] He gave a
historical sketch of the temples and cults set up by
various kings—Romulus, Titus Tatius, Numa, Tullus
Hostilius, and the last Tarquin. As time went on
other gods were introduced of Italian origin, or
Greek, or Egyptian.[4] The pontiff Scaevola had declared that the gods of the poets were worthless,
and those of the philosophers unsuited to the state.
But Varro pointed out that the state religion had
borrowed features both from poets and from philosophers; he advised adhering more closely to the
latter.[5] Indeed, he declares that if he were founding a new city he would consecrate gods and give
them names according to the principles of nature,
but as things were, he was bound by tradition.[6]

---

[1] 6.2, p. 297. On Metellus' exploit see also 3.18, I, p. 351.
Vesta had no image, but what the sacred objects in her temple
were was a subject of ancient speculation; see Wissowa,
RK[2], 159 n. 5.

[2] Of the various attempts at reconstruction that of R.
Agahd is the most complete and satisfactory. In the fragments I cite below are passages from Tertullian and others
besides those from Augustine.

[3] Varro, *Antiquitates Rerum Divinarum*, I, frg. 31 f. Agahd
p. 155 f.

[4] *Ibid.* frg. 38–52 pp. 157–162.

[5] *Ibid.* frg. 7, 54 pp. 145, 162.

[6] *Ibid.* frg. 55 p. 163.

INTRODUCTION

All the gods are really one, and they are best worshipped without the aid of any image, as is the Jewish
custom. In fact, it was also the custom of the
Romans for the first 170 years of the city's history.[1]
After this introduction Varro continued with twelve
books which described the persons, places, times and
rites connected with Roman religion, concluding with
three books on the gods—*di certi, incerti* and *selecti*.

Enough has already been said about Augustine's
use of these books. As the reader proceeds, he will
note how frequently Augustine resumes his ridicule
of the gods of polytheism. Ridicule, in fact, was a
favourite method on each side of the controversy.
There is extant an exchange of letters between
Augustine and one Maximus, a pagan grammarian
of Madaura, who was annoyed to see Christians
doing honour to their African martyrs—Miggo,
Saname and Namphamo—in preference to Jupiter,
Juno, Minerva, Venus and Vesta. Surely Miggo
and the rest are odd names to worship! Augustine
was stung to reply at some length, mentioning various
absurdities of the Roman cult. As for something
to laugh at, what about Stercutius, the god of manure,
he asks. And there was Cluacina, goddess of the
sewer, Bald-headed Venus, Fear and Pallor, Fever
and countless others for whom the Romans had
temples and sacrifices. " But if you neglect these,"
Augustine adds, " you are neglecting Roman gods,
and thus show that you are not initiated in the
Roman rites." [2] It will be noted that later, in the

---

[1] Varro, *Antiquitates Rerum Divinarum*, I, frg. 56–59 p.
163 f.

[2] *Letter*, 17.2, p. 27 of Loeb edition.

City of God, when Augustine turns to attack the host of petty gods found in Varro, he chooses Cluacina as a suitably ridiculous figure.[1] Even if Maximus and the other pagans of the time were not worshipping her, she was a part of the Roman pantheon, and could not be repudiated. Varro was an authority who could not be challenged. Pagan sentiment was attached to the old, but the perusal of Varro was enough to make the old look absurd.

BIBLIOGRAPHY

Agahd, R. *M. Terenti Varronis Antiquitatum Rerum Divinarum Libri I XIV XV XVI*, in *Jahrbücher für classische Philologie*, Supplementband 24, 1898, 1–220, 367–381.

Angus, S. *The Sources of the First Ten Books of Augustine's City of God* (Princeton, 1906).

Battenhouse, Roy, ed. *A Companion to the Study of St. Augustine* (New York, 1954).

Boyancé, P. "Sur la Théologie de Varron," in *Revue des Études Anciennes*, 57, 1955, 57–84.

Cumont, F. *The Oriental Religions in Roman Paganism* (1911, 1956 reprint).

Deferrari, R. J. and Keeler, M. J. "St. Augustine's City of God: its Plan and Development," in *American Journal of Philology* 50, 1929, 109–137.

Fowler, W. W. *The Religious Experience of the Roman People* (London, 1911).

Gilson, E. "Foreword," in *Saint Augustine: the City of God*, translated by D. B. Zema and G. G. Walsh (New York, 1950), xi–xcviii.

[1] 4.8, p. 29, below.

INTRODUCTION

Green, W. M. "The Status of Actors at Rome," in *Classical Philology* 28, 1933, 301–304.

Huttmann, M. A. *The Establishment of Christianity and the Proscription of Paganism* (Columbia University, Studies in History, Economics and Public Law, Vol. 60: 2. New York, 1914).

Hanson, J. A. *Roman Theater-Temples* (Princeton, 1959).

Lacroix, B. "Les Adversaires Visées par Saint Augustin dans la Cité de Dieu," in *Mediaeval and Renaissance Studies* 4, 1958, 163–175.

Lindemann, H. *Die Sondergötter in der Apologetik der Civitas Dei Augustins* (München, 1930).

Madden, M. D. *The Pagan Divinities and their Worship as Depicted in the Works of Saint Augustine Exclusive of the City of God* (Washington, 1930).

Maier, F. G. *Augustin und das antike Rom* (Tübinger Beiträge zur Altertumswissenschaft 39. Stuttgart, 1955).

Mandouze, A. "Saint Augustin et la Religion Romaine," in *Recherches Augustiniennes* 1, 1958, 187–223.

Marrou, H.-I. "Civitas Dei, civitas terrena: num tertium quid?" in *Studia Patristica* 2, 1957, 342–350.

Meer, A. van der. *Saint Augustin: Pasteur d'Ames* (Colmar, 1959).

Murray, Gilbert. *Four Stages of Greek Religion* (New York, 1912).

Welldon, J. E. C. *S. Aurelii Augustini De Civitate Dei contra Paganos Libri XXII* (London, 1924).

Wissowa, G. "Echte und falsche Sondergötter in

der römischen Religion," in *Gesammelte Abhandlungen zur römischen Religions- und Stadtgeschichte*
(München, 1904), 304–326.

Wissowa, G. *Religion und Kultus der Römer*, 2. Auflage
(München, 1912).

TABLE OF ABBREVIATIONS

OCD   *The Oxford Classical Dictionary.* Oxford,
        1949.

RE   A. Pauly, G. Wissowa, and W. Kroll. *Real-
        encyclopädie der klassischen Altertumswissen-
        schaft.* Stuttgart, 1893–1956.

RK²   see Wissowa, above.

SVF   H. von Arnim. *Stoicorum Veterum Fragmenta.*
        Leipzig, 1903–24.

Other works, referred to by author's name only,
or by author's name and abbreviated title, may be
found in the bibliography above.

SAINT AUGUSTINE

THE CITY OF GOD AGAINST THE PAGANS

S. AURELII AUGUSTINI

DE CIVITATE DEI CONTRA PAGANOS

LIBER IV

I

De his, quae primo volumine disputata sunt.

DE civitate Dei dicere exorsus prius respondendum
putavi eius inimicis qui terrena gaudia consectantes
rebusque fugacibus inhiantes, quidquid in eis triste
misericordia potius admonentis Dei quam punientis
severitate patiuntur, religioni increpitant Christianae,
quae una est salubris et vera religio. Et quoniam,
cum sit in eis etiam vulgus indoctum, velut doctorum
auctoritate in odium nostrum gravius inritantur,
existimantibus imperitis ea quae suis temporibus
insolite acciderint per alia retro tempora accidere
non solere, eorumque opinionem etiam his qui eam
falsam esse noverunt, ut adverus nos iusta murmura
habere videantur, suae scientiae dissimulatione
firmantibus, de libris, quos auctores eorum ad cog-

SAINT AURELIUS AUGUSTINE

THE CITY OF GOD AGAINST THE PAGANS

BOOK IV

I

On the matters discussed in the first book.

WHEN I began to write on the City of God, I first
felt it necessary to reply to its enemies who, as they
pursue earthly joys and greedily snatch at fleeting
goods, make an outcry against the Christian religion,
which is the one sound and true religion, whenever
they suffer any disappointment in these matters.
On such occasions we must suppose that God is
mercifully warning them rather than that he is
sternly inflicting punishment. Now among our
enemies is the mass of ignorant men whose hatred
of us is stirred to greater heat by the sanction, so
they suppose, of the learned. For the ignorant are
convinced that the unusual events of their time were
not a usual occurrence in the eras that lie behind
us. And this conviction of theirs is supported even
by men who know that it is false, but pretend not to
know in order to create the impression that they have
good ground to grumble at us. I was therefore

3

noscendam praeteritorum temporum historiam memoriae mandaverunt, longe aliter esse quam putant demonstrandum fuit et simul docendum deos falsos, quos vel palam colebant vel occulte adhuc colunt, eos esse inmundissimos spiritus et malignissimos ac fallacissimos daemones, usque adeo ut aut veris aut fictis etiam, suis tamen criminibus delectentur, quae sibi celebrari per sua festa voluerunt, ut a perpetrandis damnabilibus factis humana revocari non possit infirmitas, dum ad haec imitanda velut divina praebetur auctoritas.

Haec non ex nostra coniectura probavimus, sed partim ex recenti memoria, quia et ipsi vidimus talia ac talibus numinibus exhiberi, partim ex litteris eorum qui non tamquam in contumeliam, sed tamquam in honorem deorum suorum ista conscripta posteris reliquerunt, ita ut vir doctissimus apud eos Varro et gravissimae auctoritatis, cum rerum humanarum atque divinarum dispertitos faceret libros, alios humanis, alios divinis pro sua cuiusque rei dignitate distribuens non saltem in rebus humanis, sed in rebus divinis ludos scaenicos poneret, cum utique, si tantummodo boni et honesti homines in civitate essent, nec in rebus humanis ludi scaenici esse debuissent. Quod profecto non auctoritate sua

obliged to cite evidence from the books that their
own authors left to acquaint us with the story of past
eras, thus proving that they are quite astray in their
views.   It was also my duty to show that the false
gods whom they once worshipped openly and still
worship secretly are unclean spirits, and most malign,
deceitful demons, so much so that they find amuse-
ment in crimes, which whether real or fictitious, are
in any case their own, for they have chosen to see
them solemnly presented in their honour during their
public festivals.   The result is that human weakness
cannot be restrained from perpetrating damnable
deeds, as long as supposedly divine authority is given
to the imitating of these deeds.

All this was not the fruit of my own conjecture;
I cited evidence, some of it that of recent events
that I recall, for I myself have seen such spectacles
presented in honour of such deities, and some of it
that of the writings of men who left to posterity
descriptions of these things, not as a reproach, but
for the honour of their gods.   Take Varro, for example, who in the eyes of the pagans is a most learned
man and a most weighty authority.   When he wrote
a treatise in two parts, one on human and one on
divine things, he allotted some books to human
things, the others to divine, and assigned each topic
to the level that he deemed proper to it.   He gave
theatrical shows a place not at most among human,
but among divine things, although certainly if there
had been none but good and respectable men in the
state, the theatrical shows could have had no place
even among human things.   Varro certainly did not
make these assertions arbitrarily; he was born and

fecit, sed quoniam eos Romae natus et educatus in divinis rebus invenit.

Et quoniam in fine primi libri, quae deinceps dicenda essent, breviter posuimus et ex his quaedam in duobus consequentibus diximus, expectationi legentium quae restant reddenda cognoscimus.

II

De his, quae libro secundo et tertio continentur.

Promiseramus ergo quaedam nos esse dicturos adversus eos qui Romanae rei publicae clades in religionem nostram referunt, et commemoraturos quaecumque et quantacumque occurrere potuissent vel satis esse viderentur mala quae illa civitas pertulit vel ad eius imperium provinciae pertinentes antequam eorum sacrificia prohibita fuissent; quae omnia procul dubio nobis tribuerent, si iam vel illis clareret nostra religio vel ita eos a sacris sacrilegis prohiberet.

Haec in secundo et tertio libro satis, quantum existimo, absolvimus, in secundo agentes de malis morum, quae mala vel sola vel maxima deputanda sunt, in tertio autem de his malis quae stulti sola perpeti exhorrent, corporis videlicet externarumque rerum, quae plerumque patiuntur et boni; illa vero mala non dico patienter, sed libenter habent quibus ipsi fiunt mali.

brought up in Rome, and he found the shows classified as divine service.

At the end of the first book I briefly set down the
topics which were next to be discussed, and in the
two books which followed I discussed some of these.
The remainder of my debt must now be paid, to
satisfy the expectation of my readers.

II

On the matters contained in the second and third books.

WELL, I promised that I should have something to
say in reply to those who hold our religion responsible for the disasters of the Roman state, and that I
should record the miseries which that state and the
provinces under its rule suffered before their sacrifices
were prohibited, that is, as many misfortunes as I
could recall, or as seemed enough for my purpose.
Without doubt they would attribute all these disasters to us if our religion had already been known to
them or had forbidden them their sacrilegious
sacrifices.

These matters, I think, I have adequately disposed
of in the second and third books. In the second I
dealt with moral evils, which should be regarded
either as the only evils, or as the greatest evils. In
the third I dealt with the only evils that fools dread
to suffer, namely, bodily and external ills, to which
the righteous are also commonly subject. Our foes
accept the former evils, I do not say with patience,
but with pleasure, though this kind of evil makes
them evil themselves.

Et quam pauca dixi de sola ipsa civitate atque eius imperio! nec inde omnia usque ad Caesarem Augustum. Quid si commemorare voluissem et exaggerare illa mala quae non sibi invicem homines faciunt, sicut sunt vastationes eversionesque bellantium, sed ex ipsius mundi elementis terrenis accidunt rebus (quae uno loco Apuleius breviter stringit in eo libello quem de mundo scripsit, terrena omnia dicens mutationes, conversiones et interitus habere; namque inmodicis tremoribus terrarum, ut verbis eius utar, dissiluisse humum et interceptas urbes cum populis dicit; abruptis etiam imbribus prolutas totas esse regiones; illas etiam, quae prius fuerant continentes, hospitibus atque advenis fluctibus insulatas aliasque desidia maris pedestri accessu pervias factas; ventis ac procellis eversas esse civitates; incendia de nubibus emicasse, quibus Orientis regiones conflagratae perierunt, et in Occidentis plagis scaturrigines quasdam ac proluviones easdem strages dedisse; sic ex Aetnae verticibus quondam effusis crateribus divino incendio per declivia torrentis vice flammarum flumina cucurrisse),—si haec atque huius modi quae habet historia, unde possem, colligere voluissem, quando finissem? Quae illis temporibus evenerunt, antequam Christi nomen ulla istorum vana et verae saluti perniciosa conprimeret.

---

[1] Chapter 34, page 170, 2–16, ed. Thomas. Augustine turns Apuleius' text into indirect discourse, with slight modifications. Apuleius' work is an amplified paraphrase of a pseudo-Aristotelian treatise with the same title. Apuleius was an African writer of the second century much quoted by Augus-

And how little I said about events in Rome itself, and in its Empire! I did not even tell the whole story of it as far as the time of Augustus Caesar. What a story it would be if I had wished to relate and emphasize, not those evils which men do to each other, such as the devastation and destruction wrought by men in their wars, but by those afflictions which befall the earth from the elements of the universe itself! Apuleius in one place briefly touches on these, in his treatise *On the Universe*, where he says that all things on earth have their changes, reversals and annihilations. For indeed, to use his own words, " in violent earthquakes the ground has burst open and swallowed cities with their inhabitants. Whole districts have been washed away by cloudbursts; some that had been parts of the mainland became islands by the occurrence of invading floods, while others by a recession of the sea have become accessible on foot. Cities have been overthrown by wind and storm. Fires have flashed from the clouds, by which regions of the East were consumed and perished; in the western lands there were springs and floods that wrought the same destruction. Once, for instance, craters erupted from the peaks of Aetna in a godsent conflagration, and rivers of flame ran down the slopes like a torrent."[1] If I had wanted to collect historical incidents of this sort from every possible source, when should I have finished the task? And these things happened in former times, before the name of Christ had suppressed any rites of theirs, vain and ruinous as they are to true salvation.

tine, and described by him as a " noble Platonist " (below 8, 12).

Promiseram etiam me demonstraturum, quos eorum mores et quam ob causam Deus verus ad augendum imperium adiuvare dignátus est, in cuius potestate sunt regna omnia, quamque nihil eos adiuverint hi, quos deos putant, et potius quantum decipiendo et fallendo nocuerint: unde nunc mihi video esse dicendum, et magis de incrementis imperii Romani. Nam de noxia fallacia daemonum, quos velut deos colebant, quantum malorum invexerit moribus eorum, in secundo maxime libro non pauca iam dicta sunt. Per omnes autem absolutos tres libros, ubi oportunum visum est, commendavimus, etiam in ipsis bellicis malis quantum solaciorum Deus per Christi nomen, cui tantum honoris barbari detulerunt praeter bellorum morem, bonis malisque contulerit, quo modo *qui facit solem suum oriri super bonos et malos et pluit super iustos et iniustos.*

III

An latitudo imperii, quae non nisi bellis adquiritur, in bonis sive sapientium habenda sit sive felicium.

IAM itaque videamus quale sit quod tantam latitudinem ac diuturnitatem imperii Romani illis diis audent tribuere, quos etiam per turpium ludorum obsequia et per turpium hominum ministeria se honeste coluisse contendunt.

---

[1] Above 1, 36 (vol. I, 141).   [2] Matthew 5.45.

I promised also [1] that I would show what their moral standards were, and for what reason the true God, in whose power all kingdoms are, deigned to help them extend their empire, and how far from helping them were those whom they rate as gods, and how much harm they did instead, with their trickery and deceit. So I see that I must now take up this topic, especially the extension of the Roman rule. For the pernicious deceit of the demons whom they used to worship as gods and the great harm that they did to Roman morals have been discussed at some length already, especially in the second book. Moreover in all three of the books now finished I have pointed out, as opportunity offered, how much relief amid the very disasters of war God has granted to good and evil men alike through the name of Christ, to which the barbarians have shown great honour contrary to the usages of war. In this way " he makes his sun rise on the good and the bad, and sends rain on the just and the unjust." [2]

III

Whether extent of rule, acquired only by war, should be counted among the blessings of the wise or happy.

Now therefore let us see on what ground they venture to ascribe the extent and duration of the Roman rule to those gods whom they claim to have worshipped with good grace, even when the service consisted of disgraceful shows and the employment of disgraceful men.

Quamquam vellem prius paululum inquirere quae
sit ratio, quae prudentia, cum hominum felicitatem
non possis ostendere, semper in bellicis cladibus et in
sanguine civili vel hostili, tamen humano, cum tene-
broso timore et cruenta cupiditate versantium, ut
vitrea laetitia comparetur fragiliter splendida, cui
timeatur horribilius ne repente frangatur, de imperii
latitudine ac magnitudine velle gloriari.

Hoc ut facilius diiudicetur, non vanescamus inani
ventositate iactati atque obtundamus intentionis
aciem altisonis vocabulis rerum, cum audimus populos
regna provincias; sed duos constituamus homines
(nam singulus quisque homo, ut in sermone una lit-
tera, ita quasi elementum est civitatis et regni,
quantalibet terrarum occupatione latissimi), quorum
duorum hominum unum pauperem vel potius mediocrem, alium praedivitem cogitemus; sed divitem
timoribus anxium, maeroribus tabescentem, cupiditate flagrantem, numquam securum, semper inquie-
tum, perpetuis inimicitiarum contentionibus anhe-
lantem, augentem sane his miseriis patrimonium
suum in inmensum modum atque illis augmentis
curas quoque amarissimas aggerantem; mediocrem
vero illum re familiari parva atque succincta sibi
sufficientem, carissimum suis, cum cognatis vicinis

But I should like to get a small point clear before going on. You cannot show that men are happy who live always amid the disasters of war. It matters not whether the blood shed is that of fellow-citizens or of enemies; in any case it is the blood of men. The dark shadow of fear and the lust for blood are always with them. Any joy that they know is like the glitter of brittle glass, which inspires the frightful thought that it may suddenly be shattered. How then is it rational, how can it be wise to see something to boast of in the area and greatness of an empire?

It will be easier to make up our minds about this if we let no windy nonsense sway us, if we let no grandiloquent terminology dull the sharpness of our thinking when such words as "peoples," "kingdoms," "provinces" meet our ears. Let us rather imagine two individuals, since each particular individual is to the republic or kingdom what one letter is to a whole discourse, namely the elementary particle. It does not matter how large the kingdom has become by annexation of land. Then let us suppose that one of these two men is poor, or rather of modest means, while the other is very rich. Let us suppose that the rich man is troubled by fears, pining with grief, burning with desire, never secure, always restless, panting in ceaseless struggles with his foes, though he does, to be sure, by dint of such suffering accumulate great additions to his estate even beyond measure, these additions adding also their quota of corrosive anxieties. Let the man of modest means, on the other hand, be self-sufficient on his trim and tiny property, beloved by his family, enjoying the most agreeable relations with his kindred,

13

amicis dulcissima pace gaudentem, pietate religiosum, benignum mente, sanum corpore, vita parcum, moribus castum, conscientia securum. Nescio utrum quisquam ita desipiat, ut audeat dubitare quem praeferat. Ut ergo in his duobus hominibus, ita in duabus familiis, ita in duobus populis, ita in duobus regnis regula sequitur aequitatis, qua vigilanter adhibita si nostra intentio corrigatur, facillime videbimus ubi habitet vanitas et ubi felicitas.

Quapropter si verus Deus colatur eique sacris veracibus et bonis moribus serviatur, utile est ut boni longe lateque diu regnent; neque hoc tam ipsis quam illis utile est quibus regnant. Nam quantum ad ipsos pertinet, pietas et probitas eorum, quae magna Dei dona sunt, sufficit eis ad veram felicitatem, qua et ista vita bene agatur et postea percipiatur aeterna. In hac ergo terra regnum bonorum non tam illis praestatur quam rebus humanis; malorum vero regnum magis regnantibus nocet, qui suos animos vastant scelerum maiore licentia; his autem qui eis serviendo subduntur non nocet nisi propria iniquitas. Nam iustis quidquid malorum ab iniquis dominis inrogatur, non est poena criminis, sed virtutis examen. Proinde bonus etiamsi serviat, liber est; malus autem etiamsi regnet, servus est, nec unius hominis, sed, quod est gravius, tot dominorum quot vitiorum. De quibus vitiis cum ageret

neighbours and friends, devoutly religious, kindly disposed, in good physical condition, leading a simple life, free from vice and untroubled in conscience. I don't suppose that there is anyone so foolish as to think of doubting which one he would prefer. Hence, as in the case of these two men, so in the case of two families, or two peoples, or two kingdoms, the same rule of equity applies. If we employ it with our eyes open to guide our search, we shall very easily discover where folly dwells, and where happiness.

Therefore if that true God is revered and served with true worship and good morals, it is expedient that good men should rule far and wide and long; nor is this expedient so much in their interest as in that of their subjects. For as far as they themselves are concerned, their religion and good conduct, which are great gifts of God, are enough to ensure true happiness, whereby this life may be well spent, and eternal life attained hereafter. It follows that on this earth the rule of good men is a boon conferred not so much on them as on society. On the other hand, the rule of wicked men does harm rather to those who rule, for they ravage their own souls because they are freer to commit crimes, while those who are their servants and subjects are not harmed except by their own evil-doing. For whatever evils are imposed upon the just by unjust masters are not punishment of crime, but a testing of virtue. Hence even if a good man be a slave, he is free; whereas if a wicked man rule, he is a slave—and a slave not to one man but, what is worse, to as many masters as he has vices. In speaking of these vices the

scriptura divina: *A quo enim quis,* inquit, *devictus est, huic et servus addictus est.*

IV

Quam similia sint latrociniis regna absque iustitia.

REMOTA itaque iustitia quid sunt regna nisi magna latrocinia? Quia et latrocinia quid sunt nisi parva regna? Manus et ipsa hominum est, imperio principis regitur, pacto societatis astringitur, placiti lege praeda dividitur. Hoc malum si in tantum perditorum hominum accessibus crescit ut et loca teneat, sedes constituat, civitates occupet, populos subiuget, evidentius regni nomen adsumit, quod ei iam in manifesto confert non dempta cupiditas, sed addita inpunitas. Eleganter enim et veraciter Alexandro illi Magno quidam comprehensus pirata respondit. Nam cum idem rex hominem interrogaret, quid ei videretur, ut mare haberet infestum, ille libera contumacia: Quod tibi, inquit, ut orbem terrarum; sed quia id ego exiguo navigio facio, latro vocor; quia tu magna classe, imperator.

V

De fugitivis gladiatoribus, quorum potentia similis fuerit regiae dignitati.

PROINDE omitto quaerere quales Romulus congregaverit, quoniam multum eis consultum est ut ex illa

---

[1] 2 Peter 2.19.   [2] See Introduction, pp. x–xii.
[3] Compare Cicero, *Republic,* 3.14.24.

Scripture says: " For whatever overcomes a man, to that he is enslaved." [1]

IV

Kingdoms without justice are similar to robber bands. [2]

AND so if justice is left out, what are kingdoms except great robber bands? For what are robber bands except little kingdoms? The band also is a group of men governed by the orders of a leader, bound by a social compact, and its booty is divided according to a law agreed upon. If by repeatedly adding desperate men this plague grows to the point where it holds territory and establishes a fixed seat, seizes cities and subdues peoples, then it more conspicuously assumes the name of kingdom, and this name is now openly granted to it, not for any subtraction of cupidity, but by addition of impunity. For it was an elegant and true reply that was made to Alexander the Great by a certain pirate whom he had captured. When the king asked him what he was thinking of, that he should molest the sea, he said with defiant independence: " The same as you when you molest the world! Since I do this with a little ship I am called a pirate. You do it with a great fleet and are called an emperor." [3]

V

On the revolt of the gladiators, whose power approached the grandeur of kings.

NEXT I refrain from asking what sort of men Romulus brought together, inasmuch as great care was

vita dato sibi consortio civitatis poenas debitas cogitare desisterent, quarum metus eos in maiora facinora propellebat, ut deinceps pacatiores essent rebus humanis.

Hoc dico quod ipsum Romanum imperium iam magnum multis gentibus subiugatis ceterisque terribile acerbe sensit, graviter timuit, non parvo negotio devitandae ingentis cladis oppressit, quando paucissimi gladiatores in Campania de ludo fugientes magnum exercitum compararunt, tres duces habuerunt, Italiam latissime et crudelissime vastaverunt. Dicant quis istos deus adiuverit ut ex parvo et contemptibili latrocinio pervenirent ad regnum tantis iam Romanis viribus arcibusque metuendum. An quia non diu fuerunt, ideo divinitus negabuntur adiuti? Quasi vero ipsa cuiuslibet hominis vita diuturna est. Isto ergo pacto neminem dii adiuvant ad regnandum, quoniam singuli quique cito moriuntur, nec beneficium deputandum est quod exiguo tempore in unoquoque homine ac per hoc singillatim utique in omnibus vice vaporis evanescit.

Quid enim interest eorum, qui sub Romulo deos coluerunt et olim sunt mortui, quod post eorum mortem Romanum tantum crevit imperium, cum illi apud inferos causas suas agant? utrum bonas an malas, ad rem praesentem non pertinet. Hoc

---

[1] See 3, 26 above (vol. I, 379 and note). Spartacus, with two lieutenants Crixus and Oenomaus, was in revolt 73–71 B.C.

taken in their case that, when they were given an
opportunity to escape from their previous way of life
by casting their lot with a city-state, they might cease
to dwell on the penalties that were in store for them,
might no longer be driven by such terror to greater
crimes, and so in the future be less hostile to society.

I shall, however, mention an affair by which the
Roman Empire itself, after it had become great by
the conquest of many nations and was a menace to
the rest, was sorely hurt and profoundly alarmed.
This was a revolt which the Romans suppressed,
averting major disaster only by a great effort, when
a very few gladiators escaped from their school in
Campania, gathered a large army under three generals, and ravaged Italy far and wide with the utmost
savagery.[1] Now let them tell us what god helped
those men to rise from a small and negligible robber
band to be a kingdom that the Romans had to fear,
great as their forces had become, and numerous their
citadels? Will they say that because the rebels did
not long hold out they were not helped by the gods?
As if the life of any man were long! By that reasoning the gods help no one to rule, for each individual
dies in a little while, and you must not count as a
benefit a thing that vanishes in a moment like a
puff of smoke for each individual, and so, of course,
for all men one by one.

For what does it matter to those who worshipped
the gods under Romulus and died long ago, that after
their death the Roman Empire has grown so great,
while they are pleading their cases before the judges
of the underworld? Whether their cases are good
or bad does not matter in the present argument.

autem de omnibus intellegendum est, qui per ipsum imperium (quamvis decedentibus succedentibusque mortalibus in longa spatia protendatur) paucis diebus vitae suae cursim raptimque transierunt, actuum suorum sarcinas baiulantes. Sin vero etiam ipsa brevissimi temporis beneficia deorum adiutorio tribuenda sunt, non parum adiuti sunt illi gladiatores: servilis condicionis vincla ruperunt, fugerunt, evaserunt, exercitum magnum et fortissimum collegerunt, oboedientes regum suorum consiliis et iussis multum Romanae celsitudini metuendi et aliquot Romanis imperatoribus insuperabiles multa ceperunt, potiti sunt victoriis plurimis, usi voluptatibus quibus voluerunt, quod suggessit libido fecerunt, postremo donec vincerentur, quod difficillime factum est, sublimes regnantesque vixerunt. Sed ad maiora veniamus.

VI

De cupiditate Nini regis, qui ut latius dominaretur primus intulit bella finitimis.

IUSTINUS, qui Graecam vel potius peregrinam Trogum Pompeium secutus non Latine tantum, sicut ille, verum etiam breviter scripsit historiam, opus librorum suorum sic incipit: " Principio rerum gentium nationumque imperium penes reges erat, quos ad fastigium huius maiestatis non ambitio popularis, sed spectata inter bonos moderatio provehebat.

Moreover the same must be said of all who have passed swiftly and hastily through the imperial office itself in the few days of their life, bearing the heavy burden of their own deeds. And this is true for however long a time the empire maintains its existence, as one generation of mortals dies and another takes its place. But if any benefits of even the shortest duration are to be ascribed to the help of the gods, those gladiators received no little help. They burst the bonds of their servile condition, they fled, they escaped, they collected a large and very brave army and, obedient to the advice and commands of their kings, a mighty threat to the haughty power of Rome and invincible to a number of Roman generals, they took much booty, gained many victories, enjoyed what pleasures they chose, did what their lust suggested and finally they lived exalted and enthroned until they were conquered, which was a feat of the greatest difficulty.

But let us go on to more important matters.

VI

Of the ambition of King Ninus, who was the first to make war on his neighbours to extend his dominion.

JUSTIN, who followed Pompeius Trogus in writing Greek, or rather, foreign history, not only in Latin, as Trogus did, but also in condensed form, begins his first book thus: "At the beginning of the history of tribes and nations, power was in the hands of kings, who were not raised to this summit of power by courting the people, but by the recognition that their self-

Populi nullis legibus tenebantur, fines imperii tueri magis quam proferre mos erat, intra suam cuique patriam regna finiebantur. Primus omnium Ninus rex Assyriorum veterem et quasi avitum gentibus morem nova imperii cupiditate mutavit. Hic primus intulit bella finitimis et rudes adhuc ad resistendum populos ad terminos usque Libyae perdomuit." Et paulo post: " Ninus," inquit, " magnitudinem quaesitae dominationis continua possessione firmavit. Domitis igitur proximis cum accessione virium fortior ad alios transiret et proxima quaeque victoria instrumentum sequentis esset, totius Orientis populos subegit."

Qualibet autem fide rerum vel iste vel Trogus scripserit (nam quaedam illos fuisse mentitos aliae fideliores litterae ostendunt), constat tamen et inter alios scriptores regnum Assyriorum a Nino rege fuisse longe lateque porrectum. Tam diu autem perseveravit ut Romanum nondum sit eius aetatis. Nam sicut scribunt qui chronicam historiam persecuti

---

[1] Justin was a Latin writer of the second or third century who composed an epitome of the huge world history of Pompeius Trogus, a contemporary of Livy. Like Diodorus Siculus, who wrote a similar work in Greek about the same time, Trogus derived his account of Assyrian history from Ctesias, who was a Greek physician at the Persian court until about 390 B.C. In his account Ninus, the founder of Nineveh and

control gained among good men. The people were
not ruled by any laws. It was the custom to defend
rather than to extend the boundaries, and each
monarch's rule was limited to his own native land.
Ninus, king of Assyria, was the first to give up the
ancient and ancestral custom of the nations and adopt
the novelty of a lust for empire. He was the first to
make war on his neighbours, and extended his conquests as far as the borders of Libya, over peoples
who till then were inexperienced in the art of self-
defence." And a little later he says: "Ninus rein-
forced by constant new acquisitions the mighty
dominion he had won. Consequently when he had
conquered his neighbours, he went on with increased
forces against other peoples, and since each new
victory became the means of winning the next, he
subdued all the nations of the East." [1]

Now whatever may be the reliability of the writings of Justin or Trogus (for other more trustworthy
accounts make it clear that they lied about some
things), other writers nevertheless establish the fact
that the Assyrian kingdom was extended far and
wide by Ninus. Moreover that kingdom lasted so
long that the Roman Empire has not yet reached the
same age. For according to the account of students

of Assyrian power, was married to Semiramis, who survived
him and became the founder of Babylon. A century later
Berossus wrote a history of Babylon in Greek, rejecting the
legends of Ninus as spurious. Oldfather (in the Loeb Diodorus, Introduction, p. xxvi) remarks: "It is astonishing to
observe that a writer with the opportunities which Ctesias
enjoyed should have been content to do little more than pass
on the folk tales which constitute the 'history' of the
Assyrian Empire."

sunt, mille ducentos et quadraginta annos ab anno
primo quo Ninus regnare coepit, permansit hoc regnum, donec transferretur ad Medos. Inferre autem
bella finitimis et in cetera inde procedere ac populos
sibi non molestos sola regni cupiditate conterere et
subdere, quid aliud quam grande latrocinium nomi-
nandum est?

VII

*An regna terrena inter profectus suos atque defectus
deorum iuventur vel deserantur auxilio.*

Si nullo deorum adiutorio tam magnum hoc regnum
et prolixum fuit, quare diis Romanis tribuitur
Romanum regnum locis amplum temporibusque diuturnum? Quaecumque enim causa est illa, eadem
est etiam ista. Si autem et illud deorum adiutorio
tribuendum esse contendunt, quaero quorum. Non
enim aliae gentes, quas Ninus domuit et subegit,
alios tunc colebant deos. Aut si proprios habuerunt
Assyrii, quasi peritiores fabros imperii construendi
atque servandi, numquidnam mortui sunt quando
et ipsi imperium perdiderunt, aut mercede non sibi
reddita vel alia maiore promissa ad Medos transire

---

[1] The chronology is from Jerome's translation of Eusebius'
Chronicle. Opposite the year of Abraham 1197 he writes:
" All the years of the Assyrian kingdom from the first year of
Ninus are reckoned as 1,240." Abraham was supposed to be
born in the fifty-third year of Ninus' reign (2016 B.C.). The
Assyrian Empire thus lasted from 2059–819 B.C., a period
longer than Rome's history from 753 B.C. to A.D. 414, when
Augustine was writing this passage. Although in the first
book of his *Chronicle* Eusebius quotes Berossus and others who
had rejected the legends of Ninus and Semiramis, this part of

of chronology,[1] from the first year of Ninus' reign this kingdom endured 1,240 years, until its power passed to the Medes. Now to make war on one's neighbours and from them to move on against the rest, crushing and subduing peoples who have given no offence, out of mere lust for dominion—what else can this be called except brigandage on a grand scale?

VII

Whether earthly kingdoms in their rise and fall are either helped by the gods or deserted by them.

IF this Assyrian kingdom was so vast and prolonged with no help from the gods, why is the geographical extension and temporal duration of the Roman rule ascribed to the Roman gods? For whatever is the cause of the one, the same is the cause of the other. But if they argue that Assyrian prosperity also must be ascribed to the help of the gods, I ask, of what gods? For the different nations that Ninus conquered and subdued did not at that time worship gods different from his. Or if the Assyrians had gods of their own who were better workmen, so to speak, in building and maintaining an empire, were they dead then, when the Assyrians lost their empire? Or did they prefer to go over to the Medes because their wages were not paid, or better wages were promised? And again after that,

the work was not translated by Jerome, hence presumably unknown to Augustine. So we do not know what " trustworthy accounts " Augustine had to prove that Trogus " lied about some things."

maluerunt, atque inde rursus ad Persas Cyro invitante et aliquid commodius pollicente? Quae gens non angustis Orientis finibus post Alexandri Macedonis regnum magnum locis, sed brevissimum tempore in suo regno adhuc usque perdurat.

Hoc si ita est, aut infideles dii sunt, qui suos deserunt et ad hostes transeunt (quod nec homo fecit Camillus, quando victor et expugnator adversissimae civitatis Romam, cui vicerat, sensit ingratam, quam tamen postea oblitus iniuriae, memor patriae a Gallis iterum liberavit), aut non ita fortes sunt ut deos esse fortes decet, qui possunt humanis vel consiliis vel viribus vinci; aut si, cum inter se belligerant, non dii ab hominibus, sed dii ab aliis diis forte vincuntur, qui sunt quarumque proprii civitatum, habent ergo et ipsi inter se inimicitias, quas pro sua quisque parte suscipiunt. Non itaque deos suos debuit colere civitas magis quam alios a quibus adiuvarentur sui.

Postremo quoquo modo se habeat deorum iste vel transitus vel fuga, vel migratio vel in pugna defectio, nondum illis temporibus atque in illis terrarum partibus Christi nomen fuerat praedicatum quando illa regna per ingentes bellicas clades amissa atque translata sunt. Nam si post mille ducentos et quod excurrit annos, quando regnum Assyriis ablatum est,—si iam ibi Christiana religio aliud regnum prae-

to go over to the Persians when Cyrus invited them and promised something better still? This nation, since the fall of the vastly extended but short-lived kingdom of Alexander of Macedon, has maintained its rule until the present over no small territory in the East.

Now if this is true, the gods are faithless in deserting their own people and going over to the enemy. This is a thing that even a man, namely Camillus, did not do. After he had taken in battle a most hostile city, he experienced the ingratitude of Rome, for whom he had won the victory. Yet later he forgot the wrong and, mindful only of his native land, saved Rome a second time, delivering her from the Gauls. Or else gods are not as strong as gods ought to be, if they can be defeated by human plans or strength. Or if gods fighting with each other are defeated not by man, but by other gods who are the special deities of particular states, then they have enmities among themselves, which each one takes up on behalf of his own party. It follows that the city ought not to have worshipped its own gods more than others, in order that its own gods might receive assistance from these others.

Finally, whatever the truth may be about the gods' going over to the other side, or flight, whether mere migration or desertion in battle, the name of Christ had not yet been preached in those times and in those parts of the earth when those kingdoms were lost by mighty disasters in war and passed on to others. For when the dominion was taken from the Assyrians after 1,200 years and more, if at that time the Christian religion had already been proclaiming

dicaret aeternum et deorum falsorum cultus sacrilegos inhiberet, quid aliud illius gentis vani homines
dicerent nisi regnum, quod tam diu conservatum est,
nulla alia causa nisi suis religionibus desertis et illa
recepta perire potuisse? In qua voce vanitatis,
quae poterat esse, isti adtendant speculum suum,
et similia conqueri, si ullus in eis pudor est, eru-
bescant. Quamquam Romanum imperium adflictum
est potius quam mutatum, quod et aliis ante Christi
nomen temporibus ei contigit et ab illa est adflictione
recreatum, quod nec istis temporibus desperandum
est. Quis enim de hac re novit voluntatem Dei?

VIII

*Quorum deorum praesidio putent Romani imperium suum
auctum atque servatum, cum singulis vix singularum
rerum tuitionem committendam esse crediderint.*

DEINDE quaeramus, si placet, ex tanta deorum
turba quam Romani colebant quem potissimum vel
quos deos credant illud imperium dilatasse atque
servasse. Neque enim in hoc tam praeclaro opere et
tantae plenissimo dignitatis audent aliquas partes
deae Cluacinae tribuere aut Volupiae, quae a volup-

---

[1] With this chapter Augustine begins his attack on Roman
polytheism by arguing that the various gods were so busy,
each with his own trivial business, that none of them could
have given Rome her world empire. The lists of deities, with
the functions of each, is taken from Varro's *Antiquities* (see
chapter 22, page 79 below). As a suitably ridiculous figure,
Augustine begins with Cluacina, the goddess of sewers. For

a new and everlasting kingdom, and had been suppressing the sacrilegious worship of false gods, what else would foolish men of that nation have said except that a kingdom which had been preserved for so long could not have perished for any other reason that because it had deserted its own religion and accepted Christianity? In that absurd statement, which might have been made, let the pagans see themselves in a glass, and if they have any shame left, let them blush to make similar charges now. However, the Roman Empire is only afflicted, not replaced by another. The same thing has happened to it in other eras before the name of Christ was known, and it recovered from its ordeal. This gives us ground for hope of recovery in these times, for who knows the will of God in this matter?

VIII

By the help of what gods could the Romans suppose that their empire was made to grow and was preserved, while they could hardly bring themselves to entrust a single department to a single god? [1]

Next let us inquire, if you like, which god or which gods, out of the mighty throng worshipped by the Romans, they believe did most to extend and preserve their empire. For in such a glorious achievement and in one so exalted in its importance they do not venture to assign any part to Cluacina, [the goddess of sewers (*cloacae*)], or to Volupia, who gets

a discussion of Augustine's use of Varro, see the introduction to this volume.

tate appellata est, aut Lubentinae, cui nomen est a
libidine, aut Vaticano, qui infantum vagitibus praesidet, aut Cuninae, quae cunas eorum administrat.
Quando autem possunt uno loco libri huius com-
memorari omnia nomina deorum et dearum quae illi
grandibus voluminibus vix comprehendere potuerunt
singulis rebus propria dispertientes officia numinum?
Nec agrorum munus uni alicui deo committendum
arbitrati sunt, sed rura deae Rusinae, iuga montium
deo Iugatino; collibus deam Collatinam, vallibus
Valloniam praefecerunt. Nec saltem potuerunt
unam Segetiam talem invenire cui semel segetes
commandarent, sed sata frumenta, quamdiu sub terra
essent, praepositam voluerunt habere deam Seiam;
cum vero iam essent super terram et segetem facerent, deam Segetiam; frumentis vero collectis atque
reconditis, ut tuto servarentur, deam Tutilinam
praeposuerunt.

Cui non sufficere videretur illa Segetia, quamdiu
seges ab initiis herbidis usque ad aristas aridas per-
veniret? Non tamen satis fuit hominibus deorum
multitudinem amantibus, ut anima misera daemoniorum turbae prostitueretur, unius Dei veri castum
dedignata complexum. Praefecerunt ergo Proserpinam frumentis germinantibus, geniculis nodisque
culmorum deum Nodutum, involumentis folliculorum
deam Volutinam; cum folliculi patescunt, ut spica

her name from pleasure (*voluptas*), or to Lubentina, whose name is from lust (*libido*), or to Vaticanus, who presides over the wailing (*vagitus*) of infants, or to Cunina, who administers the department of cradles (*cunae*). But how is it possible in one passage of this book to record all the names of the gods and goddesses that they were scarcely able to find room for in the huge volumes in which they divided up the services of the deities among the departments, assigning each to his own? They did not reach the conclusion that they should put some god in charge of all their land, but assigned fields to the goddess Rusina, mountain peaks to the god Jugatinus, hills to the goddess Collatina, and valleys to Vallonia. Nor could they even find a single Segetia who was worthy to be entrusted once for all with the grain in the fields (*segetes*), but as long as the seed was under ground they chose to have the goddess Seia in charge, then when it was above ground and moving toward harvest, the goddess Segetia, and when the grain was harvested and stored away, they gave the goddess Tutulina the job of guarding it safely.

Who would not suppose that this Segetia was competent to care for the crop all the way from its grassy start to the ripe and solid grain in the ear? But that was not enough for men who were so enamoured of a multitude of gods that each wretched soul became the harlot of a throng of demons because she scorned the chaste embrace of the one true God. So they put Proserpina in charge of germinating seeds, the god Nodutus in charge of the joints and knots of the stems, the goddess Volutina in charge of the sheaths of the follicles, and the goddess Patelana when the

exeat, deam Patelanam, cum segetes novis aristis
aequantur, quia veteres aequare hostire dixerunt,
deam Hostilinam; florentibus frumentis deam
Floram, lactescentibus deum Lacturnum, mature-
scentibus deam Matutam; cum runcantur, id est a
terra auferuntur, deam Runcinam. Nec omnia
commemoro, quia me piget quod illos non pudet.

Haec autem paucissima ideo dixi ut intellegeretur
nullo modo eos dicere audere ista numina imperium
constituisse auxisse conservasse Romanum, quae ita
suis quaeque adhibebantur officiis ut nihil universum
uni alicui crederetur. Quando ergo Segetia curaret
imperium, cui curam gerere simul et segetibus et
arboribus non licebat? Quando de armis Cunina
cogitaret, cuius praepositura parvulorum cunas non
permittebatur excedere? Quando Nodutus adiu-
varet in bello, qui nec ad folliculum spicae, sed tantum ad nodum geniculi pertinebat? Unum quisque
domui suae ponit ostiarium, et quia homo est, omnino
sufficit: tres deos isti posuerunt, Forculum foribus,
Cardeam cardini, Limentinum limini. Ita non
poterat Forculus simul et cardinem limenque servare.

---

[1] The goddess Mater Matuta was from the earliest times
worshipped at the Matralia of June 11. Her primary function,
it seems, was to defend women against miscarriage and to
watch over the healthy growth of children. Like other
deities of multiple functions, she is here given a place in the
catalogue of the grain-farmer's gods. See Wissowa, *Religion*

sheaths open so that the ears may emerge. When the grain stood level in the field with ears newly formed, the goddess Hostilina was in charge (for the ancients used *hostire* to mean, " make level "); when the grain was in flower, the goddess Flora; when it was milky, the god Lacturnus; when it ripened, the goddess Matuta;[1] and when the weeds were cleared (*runcantur*), that is, removed from the field, the goddess Runcina. I do not record them all, for I am bored by all this, though they are not ashamed of it.

But I wanted to show by this very small sample that they by no means venture to assert that it was these deities who founded, extended and preserved the Roman Empire. These were so occupied, each with his special duties, that no one thing as a whole was entrusted to any one of them. So how could Segetia care for the empire, when she was not allowed to take care of the grain crop and of trees at the same time? How could Cunina think of weapons, when they did not permit her charge to reach beyond the cradled babies? How could Nodutus help in war, when he was not concerned with the follicle of wheat, but only with the node on the joint? Everyone has a single doorkeeper for his house, and since he is a man, that is quite sufficient. But they put three gods there: Forculus for the doors (*fores*), Cardea for the hinges (*cardo*) and Limentinus for the threshold (*limen*). Thus Forculus was not competent to guard both the hinge and the threshold along with the door.

und Kultus der Römer[2], 110 f. and H. R. W. Smith, *Votive Religion at Caere: Prolegomena* (*Univ. of Calif. Pub. in Class. Arch.* 4.1, 1959), 85.

SAINT AUGUSTINE

IX

*An imperii Romani amplitudo et diuturnitas Iovi
fuerit adscribenda, quem summum deum cultores
ipsius opinantur.*

OMISSA igitur ista turba minutorum deorum vel
aliquantum intermissa officium maiorum deorum
debemus inquirere, quo Roma tam magna facta est
ut tam diu tot gentibus imperaret. Nimirum ergo
Iovis hoc opus est. Ipsum enim deorum omnium
dearumque regem volunt; hoc eius indicat sceptrum,
hoc in alto colle Capitolium. De isto deo quamvis a
poeta dictum convenientissime praedicant: Iovis
omnia plena. Hunc Varro credit etiam ab his coli
qui unum Deum solum sine simulacro colunt, sed
alio nomine nuncupari. Quod si ita est, cur tam
male tractatus est Romae, sicut quidem et in ceteris
gentibus, ut ei fieret simulacrum? Quod ipsi etiam
Varroni ita displicet ut, cum tantae civitatis perversa
consuetudine premeretur, nequaquam tamen dicere
et scribere dubitaret quod hi, qui populis instituerunt simulacra, et metum dempserunt et errorem
addiderunt.

IX

*Whether the extent and the duration of the Roman
Empire should have been ascribed to Jupiter,
whose worshippers consider him the greatest god.*

WE must therefore leave this throng of little gods,
or put them aside for a while, and examine the role
of the greater gods, by which Rome became so great
as to rule so long over so many nations. Well,
undoubtedly this is the work of Jupiter. For he is
the one whom they represent as king of all the gods
and goddesses; this is the meaning of his sceptre,
and of the Capitol on its high hill. Of this god they
declare that it was most aptly said, though by a poet:
"All things are full of Jupiter." [1] Varro believes
that he is worshipped even by those who worship one
God only, without an image, though he is called by
another name. If this is true, why was he so badly
treated in Rome, and also by other peoples, that an
image was made for him? This fact displeased even
Varro so much that, although he was bound by the
perverse custom of his great city, he still never
scrupled to say and write that those who had set up
images for their peoples had both subtracted rever-
ence and added error.

[1] Virgil, *Eclogues* 3.60. Virgil is here apparently translating
from the Stoic Aratus. The idea of Zeus, or Jupiter, as a universal god was an ancient commonplace. However, as
Augustine points out, the Jupiter of the state religion was an
image enshrined in the Capitol, and was required to share his
realm with Juno and the rest; hence he was inextricably
involved in the inconsistencies and absurdities of polytheism.

X

Quas opiniones secuti sint qui diversos deos diversis mundi partibus praefecerunt.

Cur illi etiam Iuno uxor adiungitur quae dicatur "soror et coniux"? Quia Iovem, inquiunt, in aethere accipimus, in aere Iunonem, et haec duo elementa coniuncta sunt, alterum superius, alterum inferius. Non est ergo ille de quo dictum est "Iovis omnia plena,"¹ si aliquam partem implet et Iuno. An uterque utrumque implet, et ambo isti coniuges et in duobus istis elementis et in singulis simul sunt? Cur ergo aether datur Iovi, aer Iunoni? Postremo ipsi duo satis essent; quid est quod mare Neptuno tribuitur, terra Plutoni? Et ne ipsi quoque sine coniugibus remanerent, additur Neptuno Salacia, Plutoni Proserpina. Nam sicut inferiorem caeli partem, id est aerem, inquiunt, Iuno tenet, ita inferiorem maris Salacia et terrae inferiorem Proserpina. Quaerunt quem ad modum sarciant fabulas, nec inveniunt. Si enim haec ita essent, tria potius elementa mundi esse, non quattuor, eorum veteres proderent, ut singula deorum coniugia dividerentur singulis elementis. Nunc vero omni modo adfirmaverunt aliud esse aetherem, aliud aerem. Aqua vero sive superior sive inferior utique aqua est; puta quia dissimilis, numquid in tantum ut aqua non sit?

---

¹ Virgil, *Aeneid* 1.47. The physical explanations which follow were a part of Varro's "natural theology," expounded most fully in Book 16 of his *Antiquities*. The same kind of theology is set forth by the Stoic disputant in Cicero's dialogue *On the Nature of the Gods*, 2.24.63 ff.

X

*What opinions were followed by those who placed
different gods in charge of different parts of the
universe.*

WHY is a wife, Juno, also joined to him to be called
his " sister and spouse "? [1] Because, they say, we
understand Jupiter to be in the aether and Juno in
the air, and these two elements are joined together,
the one above, the other beneath.   Then he is not
the one of whom it was said, "All things are full of
Jupiter," if Juno also fills some part.   Or do both of
them fill both regions, husband and wife in both of
these elements and together in each one?   Then
why is the aether given to Jupiter and the air to
Juno?   At any rate, these two should be enough—
why is it that the sea is assigned to Neptune and the
earth to Pluto?   And in order that these too should
not lack wives, Salacia is joined to Neptune and
Proserpina to Pluto.   For, they say, just as Juno
occupies the lower part of heaven, that is, the air,
so Salacia occupies the lower part of the sea and
Proserpina the lower part of the earth.   They are
looking for a way to mend their fables, but they do
not find any.   For if these things were as they say,
their ancient writers would have said that there are
three elements of the universe, not four, so that one
pair of gods could be assigned to each element.   As
it is, however, they have fully affirmed that the
aether is one thing, the air another.   But water,
whether it is above or below, is still water.   Suppose
that there is a difference, is it so great that it ceases

Et inferior terra quid aliud potest esse quam terra quantalibet diversitate distincta?

Deinde ecce iam totus in his quattuor vel tribus elementis corporeus completus est mundus. Minerva ubi erit? Quid tenebit? Quid implebit? Simul enim cum his in Capitolio constituta est, cum ista filia non sit amborum. Aut si aetheris partem superiorem Minervam tenere dicunt et hac occasione fingere poetas quod de Iovis capite nata sit, cur non ergo ipsa potius deorum regina deputatur quod sit Iove superior? An quia indignum erat praeponere patri filiam? Cur non de Iove ipso erga Saturnum iustitia ista servata est? An quia victus est? Ergo pugnarunt? Absit, inquiunt; fabularum est ista garrulitas. Ecce fabulis non credatur et de diis meliora sentiantur: cur ergo non data est patri Iovis, etsi non sublimior, aequalis certe sedes honoris? Quia Saturnus, inquiunt, temporis longitudo est. Tempus ergo colunt qui Saturnum colunt, et rex deorum Iuppiter insinuatur natus ex tempore. Quid enim indignum dicitur, cum Iuppiter et Iuno nati dicuntur ex tempore, si caelum est ille et illa terra, cum facta sint utique caelum et terra?

Nam hoc quoque in libris suis habent eorum docti

---

[1] The connection of Saturn with time (" Father Time ") is borrowed from the Greek Kronos, and in both languages is supported by a fictitious etymology. Thus Cicero says: " Saturn's Greek name is Cronos, which is the same as *chronos*, a space of time. The Latin designation ' Saturn ', on the other hand, is due to the fact that he is ' saturated ' or ' satiated ' with years " (*On the Nature of the Gods* 2.25.64). Kronos seems to be pre-Hellenic and Saturn pre-Roman, of Etruscan origin, and very early identified with Kronos. See the articles

to be water? And as for the deeper earth, what else can it be except earth, however great the diversity that marks it?

And now, lo and behold, the whole physical universe is complete with these three or four elements. Where will Minerva be? What will she occupy? What will she fill? For she has her place in the Capitol along with Jupiter and Juno, though she is not the daughter of both. Or if they say that Minerva occupies the upper part of the aether, and that on this basis the poets have invented the story that she was born from the head of Jupiter, then why isn't she rather than Juno considered the queen of the gods, since she is higher than Jupiter? Is it because it was improper to put a daughter above her father? Why was this just rule not observed in the case of Jupiter himself in his relation to Saturn? Is it because Saturn was vanquished? Then did they fight each other? " Hush," they say, " such babbling belongs only to fables." Very well, let us not believe the fables, but adopt better notions about the gods. Why, then, did they not give the father of Jupiter a place of honour at least equal to his son's, if not higher? That is because Saturn, they say, is the duration of time.[1] Therefore those who worship Saturn worship Time, and they imply that Jupiter, the king of the gods, is born from Time. For why is it improper to say that Jupiter and Juno are born of Time, if he is the sky and she the earth, since heaven and earth were certainly created?

For this notion is also found in the books of learned

on the two by Rose, in *Oxford Classical Dictionary* (hereafter referred to as OCD) on " Saturn " and " Kronos."

atque sapientes. Neque de figmentis poeticis, sed de philosophorum libris a Vergilio dictum est:

> Tum pater omnipotens fecundis imbribus aether
> Coniugis in gremium laetae descendit,

id est in gremium telluris aut terrae; quia et hic aliquas differentias volunt esse atque in ipsa terra aliud Terram, aliud Tellurem, aliud Tellumonem putant, et hos omnes deos habent suis nominibus appellatos, suis officiis distinctos, suis aris sacrisque veneratos. Eandem terram etiam matrem deum vocant, ut iam poetae tolerabiliora confingant, si secundum istorum non poeticos, sed sacrorum libros non solum Iuno, " soror et coniux, " sed etiam mater est Iovis. Eandem terram Cererem, eandem etiam Vestam volunt, cum tamen saepius Vestam non nisi ignem esse perhibeant pertinentem ad focos, sine quibus civitas esse non potest, et ideo illi virgines solere servire quod sicut ex virgine, ita nihil ex igne nascatur. Quam totam vanitatem aboleri et extingui utique ab illo oportuit, qui est natus ex virgine.

Quis enim ferat, quod, cum tantum honoris et quasi castitatis igni tribuerint, aliquando Vestam non erubescunt etiam Venerem dicere, ut vanescat in ancillis eius honorata virginitas? Si enim Vesta

---

[1] Virgil, *Georgics* 2.325. For an extended discussion of the various earth gods and goddesses, see 7.23–27 (pp. 451–473), below.

[2] Vesta is elsewhere (7.16, p. 433, below) identified with both the earth and the hearth fire; see Ovid, *Fasti* 6.267 and note

and wise pagans. It was not from poetic fiction, but from the books of the philosophers that Vergil took the statement: " Then Heaven, the Father almighty, comes down in fruitful showers into the lap of his joyful spouse," [1] that is, into the lap of Tellus, or Terra; for here again they choose to make a good many distinctions, and in the case of earth itself they think Terra is one thing, Tellus another, and Tellumo another. And they have all these gods marked by their proper names, separate in their special functions, and worshipped at altars of their own with their own rites. This same earth they also call the Mother of the gods, with the consequence that it is now the tales devised by the poets that are more respectable. It is according to their books of ritual, not of poetry, that Juno is not only sister and spouse, but also the mother of Jupiter! The same earth is Ceres, the same is also Vesta,[2] as they will have it. More often, however, they say that Vesta is only the fire connected with hearths, without which there could be no city, and that the reason why it is customary for virgins to serve her is that from fire, as from a virgin, nothing is born. It was assuredly appropriate that all this folly should be abolished and destroyed by that One who was born of a virgin.

Who, indeed, could tolerate the fact that although they have attributed so much honour and, as it were, chastity to fire, they sometimes do not blush to say that Vesta is also Venus? Thus the honour shown

in Frazer's edition. On primitive Vestal rites as belonging to the earth goddess, see Koch in Pauly-Wissowa's *Real-Encyklopädie*, 8A.2, 1738 (hereafter referred to as *RE*).

Venus est, quo modo ei rite virgines a Veneris operibus abstinendo servierunt? An Veneres duae sunt, una virgo, altera mulier? An potius tres, una virginum, quae etiam Vesta est, alia coniugatarum, alia meretricum? Cui etiam Phoenices donum dabant de prostitutione filiarum antequam eas iungerent viris. Quac illarum est matrona Vulcani? Non utique virgo, quoniam habet maritum. Absit autem ut meretrix, ne filio Iunonis et cooperario Minervae facere videamur iniuriam. Ergo haec ad coniugatas intellegitur pertinere; sed eam nolumus imitentur in eo quod fecit illa cum Marte. Rursus, inquiunt, ad fabulas redis. Quae ista iustitia est, nobis suscensere, quod talia dicimus de diis eorum, et sibi non suscensere, qui haec in theatris libentissime spectant crimina deorum suorum? Et (quod esset incredibile, nisi contestatissime probaretur) haec ipsa theatrica crimina deorum in honorem instituta sunt eorundem deorum.

XI

De multis diis, quos doctiores paganorum unum eundemque Iovem esse defendunt.

QUODLIBET igitur physicis rationibus et disputationibus adserant. Modo sit Iuppiter corporei huius

to virginity in her handmaids disappears. For if
Vesta is Venus, how have virgins rightly served her
by abstaining from the works of Venus? Or are
there two Venuses, one a virgin, the other not? Or
rather, three: one, who is also Vesta, a goddess of
virgins; another of married women; another of harlots? To the last the Phoenicians used to make a
gift of money gained from the prostitution of their
daughters before marrying them to husbands.
Which of these is the wife of Vulcan? Certainly
not the virgin, since she has a husband. Perish the
thought, moreover, that it should be the harlot, lest
we seem to wrong the son of Juno and fellow-patron
with Minerva of the crafts. Therefore it is clear
that she is the one concerned with married women,
but we don't want them to imitate her in what she
did with Mars. " Once more," they said, " you
are going back to fables." But what sort of justice
is this, to be angry with us for speaking thus about
their gods, and not be angry with themselves, when
they are delighted to see in the theatres these crimes
of their gods enacted? And it is a thing that would
be incredible if it were not proved by the best of
witnesses that these very exhibitions of crimes committed by the gods were founded in honour of those
same gods.

XI

*Of the many gods, whom the more learned affirm to
be one and the same with Jupiter.*

Accordingly, let them assert whatever they
please in their physical explanations and discussions.

mundi animus, qui universam istam molem ex quattuor vel quot eis placet elementis constructam atque compactam implet et movet, modo inde suas partes sorori et fratribus cedat; modo sit aether, ut aerem Iunonem subterfusam desuper amplectatur, modo totum simul cum aere sit ipse caelum, terram vero tamquam coniugem eandemque matrem (quia hoc in divinis turpe non est) fecundis imbribus et seminibus fetet; modo autem (ne sit necesse per cuncta discurrere) deus unus, de quo multi a poeta nobilissimo dictum putant:

> deum namque ire per omnes
> Terrasque tractusque maris caelumque profundum;

ipse in aethere sit Iuppiter, ipse in aere Iuno, ipse in mari Neptunus, in inferioribus etiam maris ipse Salacia, in terra Pluto, in terra inferiore Proserpina, in focis domesticis Vesta, in fabrorum fornace Vulcanus, in sideribus sol et luna et stellae, in divinantibus Apollo, in merce Mercurius, in Iano initiator, in Termino terminator, Saturnus in tempore, Mars et Bellona in bellis, Liber in vineis, Ceres in frumentis, Diana in silvis, Minerva in ingeniis.

Ipse sit postremo etiam in illa turba quasi plebe-

---

[1] Virgil, *Georgics*, 4.221 f.

[2] Janus and Terminus are elsewhere paired as the gods of beginnings and endings, respectively in 7.7, p. 399. Janus was invoked first in prayers; the first day of each month and the first month of the year were sacred to him; and he stands first in Varro's list of *di certi* connected with moments of man's life (6.9, p. 349), also of the *di selecti* of his latest book (7.2, p. 375). Varro elsewhere (*On the Latin Language* 6.13) speaks of the festival of Terminus (*Terminalia*) on February

Let us assume that Jupiter is now the soul of this
material world, filling and moving this entire mass
which is composed and compacted of the four elements, or as many as they like; or assume now again
that he yields parts of it to his sister and his brothers.
Now let him be the aether, that he may embrace
from above Juno, the air spread below; now let him
be the whole sky, including the air, and impregnate
with life-giving rain and seed the earth, who is called
at the same time his wife and his mother, for this is
no disgrace in divine affairs. And now—not to
speak of all his work in detail—let him be the one
god to whom many think the greatest of poets refers
when he says:

> For through all the god doth pass,
> All lands, and tracts of sea, and depths of sky.[1]

Let him be Jupiter in aether, Juno in air, Neptune in
the sea, and also Salacia in the lower parts of the
sea, Pluto in the earth, Proserpina in the lower
earth, Vesta in the household hearth, Vulcan in the
workman's forge; among heavenly bodies let him be
sun, moon and stars; let him be Apollo among
diviners, Mercury in commerce; in Janus let him be
the opener, in Terminus the closer of action;[2] let him
be Saturn in time, Mars and Bellona in war, Liber in
the vineyards, Ceres in the grain fields, Diana in the
woods and Minerva in mental endowments.

And finally, let us assume his presence also in that
throng of plebeian gods, if I may so describe them.

24 as the last day of the year according to the primitive
calendar: in this matter he is followed by Ovid (*Fasti* 2.49 f.
Cf. Altheim, *History of Roman Religion*, 175 f.).

iorum deorum; ipse praesit nomine Liberi virorum
seminibus et nomine Liberae feminarum, ipse sit
Diespater, qui partum perducat ad diem; ipse sit
dea Mena, quam praefecerunt menstruis feminarum,
ipse Lucina, quae a parturientibus invocetur; ipse
opem ferat nascentibus excipiendo eos sinu terrae
et vocetur Opis, ipse in vagitu os aperiat et vocetur
deus Vaticanus; ipse levet de terra et vocetur dea
Levana, ipse cunas tueatur et vocetur ⟨dea⟩ Cunina;
non sit alius, sed ipse in illis deabus, quae fata nascentibus canunt et vocantur Carmentes, praesit fortuitis
voceturque Fortuna; in diva Rumina mammam par-
vulo inmulgeat, quia rumam dixerunt veteres mammam, in diva Potina potionem ministret, in diva
Educa escam praebeat; de pavore infantum Paventia
nuncupetur, de spe, quae venit, Venilia, de voluptate
Volupia, de actu Agenoria; de stimulis, quibus ad
nimium actum homo inpellitur, dea Stimula nomine-
tur; Strenia dea sit strenuum faciendo, Numeria,
quae numerare doceat, Camena, quae canere; ipse
sit et deus Consus praebendo consilia et dea Sentia
sententias inspirando.

Ipse dea Iuventas, quae post praetextam excipiat

---

[1] The goddess Rumina belonged to the most ancient settlement on the Palatine. She was connected with the *ficus
Ruminalis*, a fig tree where the wolf is said to have nursed
Romulus. Wine was excluded from her sacrifices, and milk
took its place. Despite Varro's etymology (" ruma " breast)
the name is now believed to be derived from an Etruscan
family name, along with the name of Rome itself. K. Latte
(*Römische Religionsgeschichte*, 111) would describe her as the

Under the name of Liber let him preside over the
seeds of men, and as Libera over the seeds of women;
let him be Diespater to bring the offspring to the
light of day, Mena whom they put in charge of the
menstrual periods of women, Lucina to be invoked by
women in labour; let him bring help to the new-born
by receiving them in the lap of earth, under the name
of Ops; let him open their mouths to wail and be called
the god Vaticanus; let him lift them from the earth
and be called the goddess Levana, let him guard
cradles and be called Cunina. Let no other than he
be present in those goddesses who sing the destiny
of children at birth and are called Carmentes; let
him preside over chance events and be called Fortuna. As the goddess Rumina[1] let him bring milk
from the breast for the babe, because the ancients
called the breast " ruma "; as the goddess Potina
let him serve drink, as the goddess Educa let him
furnish food. From the fear (*pavor*) of infants let
him be called Paventia, from the hope that comes
(*quae venit*) Venilia, from pleasure (*voluptas*) Volupia,
from action (*agere*) Agenoria, from the goads (*stimuli*)
by which a man is goaded to excessive action let his
name be Stimula, let him be the goddess Strenia
from his making a man vigorous (*strenuus*), Numeria
from teaching to count (*numerare*), Camena from
teaching to sing (*canere*). Let him also be the god
Consus from giving counsel (*consilium*), and the goddess Sentia from inspiring opinions (*sententiae*).

Let him be the goddess Iuventas who takes over

Ortsgottheit of Rome itself; he also ascribes a similar origin to
the cult title of Jupiter Ruminus. See also Wissowa, *RK²*,
242 and Altheim, *History of Roman Religion*, 137.

iuvenalis aetatis exordia, ipse sit et Fortuna barbata,
quae adultos barba induat (quos honorare noluerunt, ut hoc qualecumque numen saltem masculum
deum vel a barba Barbatum, sicut a nodis Nodutum,
vel certe non Fortunam, sed quia barbas habet
Fortunium nominarent); ipse in Iugatino deo coniuges iungat, et cum virgini uxori zona solvitur, ipse
invocetur et dea Virginensis vocetur; ipse sit Mutunus vel Tutunus, qui est apud Graecos Priapus: si
non pudet, haec omnia quae dixi et quaecumque non
dixi (non enim omnia dicenda arbitratus sum), hi
omnes dii deaeque sit unus Iuppiter, sive sint, ut quidam volunt, omnia ista partes eius sive virtutes eius,
sicut eis videtur, quibus eum placet esse mundi
animum, quae sententia velut magnorum multumque
doctorum est.

Haec si ita sunt (quod quale sit, nondum interim
quaero), quid perderent, si unum Deum colerent
prudentiore compendio? Quid enim eius contemneretur, cum ipse coleretur? Si autem metuendum
fuit, ne praetermissae sive neglectae partes eius
irascerentur, non ergo, ut volunt, velut unius
animantis haec tota vita est, quae omnes continet
deos, quasi suas virtutes vel membra vel partes; sed
suam quaeque pars habet vitam a ceteris separatam,

---

[1] The god Mutunus Tutunus (there are variants in the
spelling of the name) had a shrine on the Velia from the earliest
times, where women garbed in the toga praetexta made
sacrifice. In the wedding rites the god was embodied in a
sacred phallus on which the bride was required to sit before
the consummation of the marriage. Before Varro's time he
was identified with the Greek Priapus, a fertility god whose
popularity had overshadowed many local gods of similar

the beginnings of youth after the toga praetexta is put aside, and also Fortuna Barbata who provides the young men with a beard. They refused to honour the men by making their deity, whatever it is, into a male god " Barbatus " from *barba*, as they have Nodutus from *nodi*. They could at least have called it " Fortunius " and not " Fortuna," since it has got whiskers. As the god Iugatinus let him unite married couples, and when the bride's girdle is loosed let him be invoked as Virginensis. Let him be Mutunus or Tutunus, who is the same as Priapus among the Greeks.[1] If they are not ashamed, let the one god Jupiter be all this that I have said and more that I haven't said, for I did not think fit to tell all. Let him be all these gods and goddesses; or, as some will have it, let all these be parts of him, or powers of his. This is the view of those who hold that he is the world soul, a view which is that of the supposedly great and learned.

If all this is true, a question I will not go into at present, what could they lose if they should, with a wiser economy, worship only the one God? What part of him would be slighted if he himself were worshipped? But if they had reason to fear that parts of him would be angry when overlooked or neglected, then it is not true, as they urge, that this whole life is that of a single living being, which contains all the gods as powers or members or parts of itself. Instead, each part evidently has its own life separate from the others, if one may be angered more than

character. See the fragments of Varro quoted by Agahd, p. 76; also Wissowa, *RK*[2], 169, and Vahlert in *RE* 16.1, 979–87.

si praeter alteram irasci altera potest, et alia placari,
alia concitari. Si autem dicitur omnes simul, id est
totum ipsum Iovem, potuisse offendi, si partes eius
non etiam singillatim minutatimque colerentur,
stulte dicitur. Nulla quippe illarum praetermittere-
tur, cum ipse unus qui haberet omnia coleretur.
Nam ut alia omittam quae sunt innumerabilia, cum
dicunt omnia sidera partes Iovis esse et omnia vivere
atque rationales animas habere, et ideo sine controversia deos esse, non vident quam multos non colant,
quam multis aedes non construant, aras non statuant,
quas tamen paucissimis siderum statuendas esse
putaverunt et singillatim sacrificandum. Si igitur
irascuntur, qui non singillatim coluntur, non metuunt
paucis placatis toto caelo irato vivere? Si autem
stellas omnes ideo colunt quia in Iove sunt quem
colunt, isto compendio possent in illo uno omnibus
supplicare (sic enim nemo irasceretur, cum in illo
uno nemo contemneretur) potius quam cultis quibusdam iusta irascendi causa illis qui praetermissi essent
multo numerosioribus praeberetur, praesertim cum
eis de superna sede fulgentibus turpi nuditate dis-
tentus praeponeretur Pripaus.

another, or if one is appeased while another is stirred up. But if it is said that all of them together, that is, the whole Jupiter, could be offended if his parts were not also worshipped singly and in detail, the statement is absurd. Surely none of those parts would be slighted if he alone were worshipped, since he contains them all. To pass over other assertions, of which there is no end, they say that all the stars are parts of Jupiter, and that all are living and have rational souls, and thus, without controversy, are gods. But they do not see how many they fail to worship, how many temples they fail to build, and how many altars they fail to set up, for they have seen fit to erect such altars and make sacrifices to very few of the stars separately. So if those who are not separately worshipped are angry, are they not afraid to live with only a few placated, and the whole sky angry? But if they are worshipping all the stars by worshipping Jupiter who contains them, by that short cut they could worship all the gods in that one act. Thus none would be angry, since in that one act none would be slighted. That would be better than by worshipping a limited number to afford a just cause for anger to the much larger number who are neglected. Above all they might well be angry to see preferred to them, as they shine from their lofty abode, Priapus distended in obscene nudity.

XII

De opinione eorum qui Deum animam mundi et
mundum corpus Dei esse putaverunt.

QUID? Illud nonne debet movere acutos homines
vel qualescumque homines (non enim ad hoc ingenii
opus est excellentia), ut deposito studio contentionis
adtendant, si mundi animus Deus est eique animo
mundus ut corpus est, ut sit unum animal constans ex
animo et corpore, atque iste Deus est sinu quodam
naturae in se ipso continens omnia, ut ex ipsius
anima, qua vivificatur tota ista moles, vitae atque
animae cunctorum viventium pro cuiusque nascendi
sorte sumantur, nihil omnino remanere quod non sit
pars Dei. Quod si ita est, quis non videat quanta
impietas et inreligiositas consequatur, ut, quod cal-
caverit quisque, partem Dei calcet, et in omni
animante occidendo pars Dei trucidetur? Nolo
omnia dicere quae possunt occurrere cogitantibus,
dici autem sine verecundia non possunt.

XIII

De his qui sola rationalia animantia partes esse unius
Dei asserunt.

SI autem sola animalia rationalia, sicut sunt homines, partes Dei esse contendunt, non video quidem,

XII

On the opinion of those who thought God the soul of the world, and the world the body of God.

I ASK then, is that not enough to set intelligent men thinking, or men of any sort whatever, since superior intelligence is not required in this case—let them but put aside their zeal for contention and give heed. Granted that God is the world soul, and that the world is the body of that soul, so that it is one living being consisting of soul and body. Granted, too, that this God contains all things in himself, in the bosom of nature, so to speak, so that from his soul, whereby all that mass is quickened, the lives and souls of all living things are drawn, each according to his lot of birth. That being so, it follows that there is nothing at all left over which is not part of God. If this is true, who can fail to see how great are the impious and irreligious consequences? Whatever any man tramples on is a part of God! And whenever any animal is slain, a part of God is slaughtered! I refuse to name all the things that may be imagined but cannot be named without offending modesty.

XIII

Of those who assert that only rational animals are parts of the one God.

BUT if they argue that only rational animals, such as men, are parts of God, I fail to see how they exclude beasts from the number of his parts, if the

si totus mundus est Deus, quo modo bestias ab eius
partibus separent; sed obluctari quid opus est? De
ipso rationali animante, id est homine, quid infelicius
credi potest, quam Dei partem vapulare, cum puer
vapulat? Iam vero partes Dei fieri lascivas, iniquas,
impias atque omnino damnabiles quis ferre possit,
nisi qui prorsus insanit? Postremo quid irascitur eis
a quibus non colitur, cum a suis partibus non colatur?

Restat ergo ut dicant omnes deos suas habere vitas,
sibi quemque vivere, nullum eorum esse partem cuiusquam, sed omnes colendos qui cognosci et coli possunt, quia tam multi sunt ut omnes non possint.
Quorum Iuppiter quia rex praesidet, ipsum credo ab
eis putari regnum constituisse vel auxisse Romanum.
Nam si hoc ipse non fecit, quem alium deum opus
tam magnum potuisse adgredi credant, cum omnes
occupati sint officiis et operibus propriis, nec alter
inruat in alterius? A rege igitur deorum regnum
hominum potuit propagari et augeri.

XIV

Augmenta regnorum Iovi incongruenter adscribi, cum,
si Victoria ut volunt dea est, ipsa huic negotio
sola sufficeret.

Hic primum quaero cur non etiam ipsum regnum
aliquis deus est? Cur enim non ita sit, si Victoria

whole world is God. But there is no need to insist on the point. To speak only of the rational animal, that is, man: what belief could be more unfortunate than the notion that part of God gets a whipping when a boy is whipped? Who but one stark mad could endure the thought that parts of God become lewd, wicked, impious and utterly damnable? And finally, why is he angry with those by whom he is not worshipped, when it is by his own parts that he is not worshipped?

Their only recourse, then, is to say that all the gods have their own lives, that each one lives for himself, that no one of them is a part of any other, but that all who can be discovered and worshipped should be worshipped, for there are so many that not all can be discovered. And since Jupiter presides over them as king, I suppose that in their view he is the god who established and extended the Roman empire. For if it was not he, what other god can they suppose to have had the strength to embark on so great a task? For they are all busy with their own duties and tasks, and no one invades the province of another. Therefore it is only by the king of the gods that a human domain could have been planted and made to grow.

XIV

The growth of kingdoms is not properly ascribed to Jupiter, since if Victory be a goddess, as they say, she alone would be competent for this business.

HERE I first inquire, why is not the Empire itself a god? Why not, if Victory is a goddess? Or what

dea est? Aut quid ipso Iove in hac causa opus est,
si Victoria faveat sitque propitia et semper eat ad
illos quos vult esse victores? Hac dea favente et
propitia, etiam Iove vacante vel aliud agente, quae
gentes non subditae remanerent? Quae regna non
cederent? An forte displicet bonis iniquissima in-
probitate pugnare et finitimos quietos nullamque
iniuriam facientes ad dilatandum regnum bello spon-
taneo provocare? Plane si ita sentiunt approbo et
laudo.

XV

An congruat bonis latius velle regnare.

VIDEANT ergo ne forte non pertineat ad viros bonos
gaudere de regni latitudine. Iniquitas enim eorum
cum quibus iusta bella gesta sunt regnum adiuvit
ut cresceret, quod utique parvum esset, si quies et
iustitia finitimorum contra se bellum geri nulla provo-
caret iniuria ac sic felicioribus rebus humanis omnia
regna parva essent concordi vicinitate laetantia et ita
essent in mundo regna plurima gentium ut sunt in
urbe domus plurimae civium. Proinde belligerare
et perdomitis gentibus dilatare regnum malis videtur

need is there for Jupiter in this matter, if Victory is favourable and propitious and always goes to those whom she chooses for the role of victors? If she were favourable and propitious, even if Jupiter were idle, or doing something else, what nations could remain unsubdued? What kingdoms would not yield? Or are good men, perchance, reluctant to wage an unfair and wicked war, and to challenge by an unprovoked attack neighbours who are peaceful and doing no wrong, all in order to extend their dominion? If that is their sentiment, I certainly give my approval and applause.

XV

Whether good men can consistently seek to extend their rule.

Now let the Romans consider the question whether it is proper for good men to find pleasure in the extent of their dominion. It was certainly the injustice of those against whom they waged just wars that helped the empire to grow, since it would undoubtedly have remained small if peaceful and honest neighbours had never by any wrongdoing given occasion for war. The history of man would have been happier and all kingdoms would be small, enjoying harmony with their neighbours. Thus there would be a great many national kingdoms in the world, just as there are a great many homes of citizens in a city. Hence waging war and extending their dominion over conquered nations is in the eyes of the wicked a gift of fortune, but in the eyes of the good

felicitas, bonis necessitas. Sed quia peius esset ut iniuriosi iustioribus dominarentur, ideo non incongrue dicitur etiam ista felicitas. Sed procul dubio felicitas maior est vicinum bonum habere concordem quam vicinum malum subiugare bellantem.

Mala vota sunt optare habere quem oderis vel quem timeas, ut possit esse quem vincas. Si ergo iusta gerendo bella, non impia, non iniqua, Romani imperium tam magnum adquirere potuerunt, numquid tamquam aliqua dea colenda est eis etiam iniquitas aliena? Multum enim ad istam latitudinem imperii eam cooperatam videmus, quae faciebat iniuriosos, ut essent cum quibusi usta bella gererentur et augeretur imperium. Cur autem et iniquitas dea non sit vel externarum gentium, si Pavor et Pallor et Febris dii Romani esse meruerunt? His igitur duabus, id est aliena iniquitate et dea Victoria, dum bellorum causas iniquitas excitat, Victoria eadem bella feliciter terminat, etiam feriato Iove crevit imperium. Quas enim hic partes Iuppiter haberet, cum ea quae possent beneficia eius putari dii habentur, dii vocantur, dii coluntur, ipsi pro suis partibus invocantur? Haberet hic autem etiam ille aliquam partem, si Regnum etiam ipse appellaretur, sicut appellatur illa Victoria. Aut si regnum munus est Iovis, cur non et victoria munus eius habeatur? Quod profecto haberetur, si non lapis in Capitolio, sed verus rex regum et dominus dominantium cognosceretur atque coleretur.

it is a necessary evil. Yet since it would be worse
for wrongdoers to rule over the just, this necessary
evil is also properly termed a fortunate event.
But without doubt it is better fortune to live in
peace with a good neighbour than to subdue a bad
neighbour in war.

He prays badly who prays for someone to hate or
fear, in order to have someone to conquer. Hence if
it was by waging just war, not unholy or unjust, that
the Romans were able to acquire so great an empire,
should they not also worship as a goddess External
Aggression? For we see that she contributed
greatly to the growth of the empire; she made others
unjust that there might be peoples with whom just
wars could be waged, and thus the empire was en-
larged. And why shouldn't Aggression be a goddess, too, at least the Aggression of foreign nations,
if Fear and Pallor and Fever won approval as Roman
gods? So it was with the help of these two, External
Aggression and the goddess Victory, that the empire
grew. Aggression provided the occasions for wars,
and Victory brought them to a happy conclusion,
even if Jupiter was keeping holiday. For what role
could Jupiter play here, when anything that might
be taken to be a favour granted by him was named a
god, worshipped as a god, and invoked on its own
account as part of him? He might also have had
some part here if he himself were called " Empire "
as she is called Victory. Or if empire is the gift of
Jupiter, why isn't victory also regarded as his gift?
That would surely be the case if men recognized and
worshipped, not a stone in the Capitol, but the true
King of kings and Lord of lords.

XVI

Quid fuerit quod Romani omnibus rebus et omnibus
motibus deos singulos deputantes aedem Quietis
extra portas esse voluerent.

MIROR autem plurimum quod, cum deos singulos
singulis rebus et paene singulis motibus adtribuerent,
vocaverunt deam Agenoriam, quae ad agendum excitaret, deam Stimulam, quae ad agendum ultra
modum stimularet, deam Murciam, quae praeter
modum non moveret ac faceret hominem, ut ait
Pomponius, murcidum, id est nimis desidiosum et
inactuosum, deam Streniam, quae faceret strenuum,
his omnibus diis et deabus publica sacra facere
susceperunt, Quietem vero appellantes, quae faceret
quietum, cum aedem haberet extra portam Collinam,
publice illam suscipere noluerunt. Utrum indicium
fuit animi inquieti, an potius ita significatum est, qui
illam turbam colere perseveraret non plane deorum,
sed daemoniorum, eum quietem habere non posse?
ad quam vocat verus medicus dicens: *Discite a me,*
quoniam mitis sum et humilis corde, et invenietis requiem
animabus vestris.

XVI

*Why it was that the Romans assigned separate gods
to every object and every activity, but put the
temple of Quies outside the gates.*

I MARVEL greatly at another fact. The Romans
assigned a special god to every object and to almost
every movement. They gave the goddess who was
to rouse men to action the name Agenoria, the goddess who was to stimulate men to abnormal activity
the name Stimula; the name Murcia to the goddess
who was not to move a man abnormally but was to
make him *murcidus*, as Pomponius says, that is, exces-
sively lazy and inactive; Strenia was the goddess
who was to make men strenuous. For all these gods
and goddesses they established a regular cult at state
expense. But when they called upon a goddess
Quies to create quietude since her temple was outside the Colline gate,[1] they refused to adopt her into
the state cult. Was this a proof of an unquiet
mind? Or did it signify rather that one who persisted
in worshipping that throng, who were clearly not
gods, but demons, could never know quiet? To
this quiet the true Physician calls us when he says:
" Learn from me, for I am gentle and lowly in heart,
and you will find rest for your souls."[2]

[1] The only other place where Quies is known to have been
worshipped was also outside the city, on the *via Labicana*
(Livy, 4.41.8). K. Latte (*Römische Religionsgeschichte*, 130)
connects Quies with Vulcanus Quietus, known from inscriptions. Vulcan was worshipped outside the walls because of
fear of fire in the city (Vitruvius, 1.7.1).
[2] Matthew 11.29.

XVII

An, si Iovis summa potestas est, etiam Victoria dea debuerit aestimari.

AN forte dicunt, quod deam Victoriam Iuppiter mittat atque illa tamquam regi deorum obtemperans ad quos iusserit veniat et in eorum parte considat? Hoc vere dicitur non de illo Iove quem deorum regem pro sua opinione confingunt, sed de illo vero rege saeculorum, quod mittat non Victoriam, quae nulla substantia est, sed angelum suum et faciat vincere quem voluerit; cuius consilium occultum esse potest, iniquum non potest.

Nam si victoria dea est, cur non deus est et triumphus, et victoriae iungitur vel maritus vel frater vel filius? Talia quippe isti de diis opinati sunt qualia, si poetae fingerent atque a nobis exagitarentur, responderent isti ridenda esse figmenta poetarum, non veris adtribuenda numinibus; et tamen se ipsi non ridebant, cum talia deliramenta non apud poetas legebant, sed in templis colebant. Iovem igitur de omnibus rogarent, ei uni tantummodo supplicarent. Non enim, quo misisset Victoriam, si dea est et sub illo rege est, posset ei audere resistere et suam potius facere voluntatem.

XVII

*If Jupiter is the supreme power, should Victory also
be regarded as a goddess?*

Do they say, perchance, that Jupiter sends the
goddess Victory, and that she obeys him as king of
the gods, and comes to those he points out, and takes
her place at their side? This might be said with
truth, not of that Jupiter whom they fashion to
match their fancy as king of the gods, but of the true
King of the ages: that he sends, not Victory (who
is no real being), but his angel, and gives victory to
the man of his choice. His design may be hidden,
but can never be unrighteous.

If Victory is a goddess, why is not Triumph also a
god, and joined to Victory either as husband or
brother or son? Such indeed were the fancies they
had about their gods; if the poets invented such
fancies and we attacked them, they would reply that
the fictions of the poets were only ridiculous stories,
not to be taken seriously of the real deities. And
yet they did not find themselves ridiculous when
they were worshipping such absurdities in the
temples, and not merely reading about them in the
poets. Therefore they ought to have prayed to
Jupiter for everything, and made supplication to him
alone. For wherever he had sent Victory, if she
was a goddess and subject to him as king, she could
not possibly venture to oppose him and act by her
own volition instead.

XVIII

*Felicitatem et Fortunam qui deas putant, qua ratione
secernunt.*

Quid, quod et Felicitas dea est? Aedem accepit,
aram meruit, sacra congrua persoluta sunt. Ipsa
ergo sola coleretur. Ubi enim ipsa esset, quid boni
non esset? Sed quid sibi vult quod et Fortuna dea
putatur et colitur? An aliud est felicitas, aliud
fortuna? Quia fortuna potest esse et mala; felicitas
autem si mala fuerit, felicitas non erit. Certe omnes
deos utriusque sexus (si et sexum habent) non nisi
bonos existimare debemus. Hoc Plato dicit, hoc
alii philosophi, hoc excellentes rei publicae popu-
lorumque rectores. Quo modo ergo dea Fortuna
aliquando bona est, aliquando mala? An forte
quando mala est, dea non est, sed in malignum
daemonem repente convertitur? Quot sunt ergo
deae istae? Profecto quotquot homines fortunati,
hoc est bonae fortunae. Nam cum sint et alii plurimi
simul, hoc est uno tempore, malae fortunae, numquid,
si ipsa esset, simul et bona esset et mala; his aliud,
illis aliud? An illa, quae dea est, semper est bona?
Ipsa est ergo Felicitas; cur adhibentur diversa no-

XVIII

How Felicitas and Fortuna are distinguished by those who think them goddesses.

WHAT of the fact that Felicitas (happiness) also is a goddess? She received a temple, she obtained an altar, and appropriate rites were performed. Then she alone ought to have been worshipped. For where she was, what good thing could be lacking? But how does it make sense that Fortuna also is regarded as a goddess and worshipped? Is happiness one thing and fortune another? Yes, we are told, fortune can be bad as well as good, while if happiness is bad, it will not be happiness. Surely we ought to regard all gods of both sexes (if they have sex, too) as never anything but good. This is what Plato says,[1] and the other philosophers, and the distinguished rulers of our state and of all nations. Then how is the goddess Fortuna sometimes good, sometimes bad? Or do you suppose, perchance, that when she is bad she is no longer a goddess, but is suddenly changed into a malignant demon? Then how many such goddesses are there? Surely there are as many as there are fortunate men, that is, men with good fortune. There are also simultaneously, that is, at the same time, very many others with bad fortune. Well, if she is the same, is she at once both good and bad, one thing for some and another for others? Or, being a goddess, is she always good? In that case, she is the same as Felicitas. Why are different names employed? But this

[1] *Republic* 2.379.

mina? Sed hoc ferendum est; solet enim et una res duobus nominibus appellari.

Quid diversae aedes, diversae arae, diversa sacra? Est causa, inquiunt, quia felicitas illa est quam boni habent praecedentibus meritis; fortuna vero quae dicitur bona sine ullo examine meritorum fortuito accidit hominibus et bonis et malis, unde etiam Fortuna nominatur. Quo modo ergo bona est, quae sine ullo iudicio venit et ad bonos et ad malos? Ut quid autem colitur, quae ita caeca est passim in quoslibet incurrens ut suos cultores plerumque praetereat et suis contemptoribus haereat? Aut si aliquid proficiunt cultores eius, ut ab illa videantur et amentur, iam merita sequitur, non fortuito venit. Ubi est definitio illa Fortunae? Ubi est quod a fortuitis etiam nomen accepit? Nihil enim prodest eam colere, si fortuna est. Si autem suos cultores discernit, ut prosit, fortuna non est. An et ipsam, quo voluerit, Iuppiter mittit? Colatur ergo ipse solus; non enim potest ei iubenti et eam quo voluerit mittenti Fortuna resistere. Aut certe istam mali colant, qui nolunt habere merita, quibus dea possit Felicitas invitari.

can be overlooked, for it is common enough to have a single thing called by two names.

Why the different temples, different altars, different rites? The reason, they say, is that happiness (*felicitas*) is what good men have earned by their good works, while the fortune that is called good happens by luck both to good men and to bad, without any scrutiny of their deeds, and is in fact called Fortuna for that reason. Then how is she really good, if she comes both to good men and bad with no consideration of justice? Moreover, why do men worship her, if she is blind, and runs into people at random, no matter who, so that she commonly passes by those who worship her and attaches herself to those who scorn her? Or if her worshippers do accomplish anything, so as to be seen and loved by her, then she is taking account of their merits, and does not come by accident. Now where is the definition of Fortuna? How is it that she has even got her name from fortuitous events? For it is no good worshipping her if she is mere luck (*fortuna*), but if she singles out her worshippers to help them, she is not mere luck, or Fortuna. Or does Jupiter send her, too, where he pleases? Then let him alone be worshipped, since Fortuna cannot oppose him when he gives orders and sends her where he pleases. Or at least, if any are to worship her, let it be bad men who refuse to possess the merit by which the favour of the goddess Felicitas might be won.

XIX

De Fortuna Muliebri.

TANTUM sane huic velut numini tribuunt, quam Fortunam vocant, ut simulacrum eius, quod a matronis dedicatum est et appellata est Fortuna muliebris, etiam locutum esse memoriae commendaverint atque dixisse non semel, sed iterum, quod eam rite matronae dedicaverint. Quod quidem si verum sit, mirari nos non oportet. Non enim malignis daemonibus etiam sic difficile est fallere, quorum artes atque versutias hinc potius isti advertere debuerunt, quod illa dea locuta est, quae fortuito accidit, non quae meritis venit. Fuit enim Fortuna loquax et muta Felicitas. Ut quid aliud nisi ut homines recte vivere non curarent conciliata sibi Fortuna, quae illos sine ullis bonis meritis faceret fortunatos? Et certe si Fortuna loquitur, non saltem muliebris, sed virilis potius loqueretur, ut non ipsae quae simulacrum dedicaverunt putarentur tantum miraculum muliebri loquacitate finxisse.

XIX

Of Fortuna Muliebris.

To be sure, they ascribe such honour to this supposed deity which they call Fortuna that they have preserved a story how her image, which was dedicated by matrons and called Fortuna Muliebris, actually spoke, and declared not once but twice that the matrons had correctly performed the dedicatory rites. If this story is indeed true, we need not be surprised. For it is not hard for malicious demons to deceive men in this way too, but they would have done better to take note of the crafty and ingenious wiles of the demons, inasmuch as it was the goddess who comes at random that spoke, not the one who comes to reward those who deserve her. For it was Fortuna who was garrulous, and Felicitas was mute. Why? Is there any other explanation than this? They designed that men should give no heed to right living, once they had gained the favour of Fortuna, for she could make them fortunate without any requirement of good conduct. And surely, if Fortuna speaks, it should at least be masculine Fortune, not feminine, in order to prevent our reaching the conclusion that the very ones who dedicated the image made up the great miracle by virute of their wagging feminine tongues.

XX

De Virtute et Fide, quas pagani templis et sacris honora-
verunt praetermittentes alia bona, quae similiter colenda
fuerunt, si recte illis divinitas tribuebatur.

VIRTUTEM quoque deam fecerunt; quae quidem
si dea esset, multis fuerat praeferenda. Et nunc
quia dea non est, sed donum Dei est, ipsa ab illo
impetretur a quo solo dari potest, et omnis falsorum
deorum turba vanescet. Sed cur et Fides dea credita
est et accepit etiam ipsa templum et altare? Quam
quisquis prudenter agnoscit, habitaculum illi se
ipsum facit. Unde autem sciunt illi quid sit fides,
cuius primum et maximum officium est ut in verum
credatur Deum? Sed cur non suffecerat Virtus?
Nonne ibi est et Fides? Quando quidem virtutem
in quattuor species distribuendam esse viderunt,
prudentiam, iustitiam, fortitudinem, temperantiam;
et quoniam et istae singulae species suas habent, in
partibus iustitiae fides est maximumque locum apud
nos habet, quicumque scimus quid sit, quod *iustus ex*
fide vivit.

Sed illos miror adpetitores multitudinis deorum,
si fides dea est, quare aliis tam multis deabus iniuriam
fecerint praetermittendo eas, quibus similiter aedes
et aras dedicare potuerunt? Cur temperantia dea
esse non meruit, cum eius nomine nonnulli Romani
principes non parvam gloriam compararint? Cur

---

[1] Habakkuk 2.4; Romans 1.17, etc.

XX

On Virtus and Fides, whom the pagans honoured with
temples and sacrifices, passing by other virtues which
should have been similarly worshipped, if divinity is
rightly ascribed to these.

THEY have also made Virtus, or Virtue, a goddess;
and if she were really a goddess she would deserve
preference over many others. As it is, since she is
not a goddess, but the gift of God, let her be sought
and won from him by whom alone she can be granted,
and the whole throng of false gods will vanish. But
why was Fides, or Faith, also believed to be a
goddess? Why did she also receive a temple and
an altar? Whoever wisely acknowledges her makes
himself her shrine where she may dwell. But how
do they know what faith is, when her first and chief
duty is to create belief in the one true God? And
why was not Virtus enough? Doesn't virtue also
include faith? They saw that virtue was to be
divided into four divisions: wisdom, justice, fortitude
and moderation. And, since each of these has its
own divisions, faith is a subdivision of justice, though
it is the sovereign virtue for us who know the meaning of the words, " The just shall live by faith." [1]

But I marvel at these men who are greedy for a
multiplicity of gods. If Fides is a goddess, why
have they slighted so many other goddesses in passing them by, when they might have dedicated similar
temples and altars to them? Why did Moderation
not win recognition as a goddess, since many Roman
leaders have gained no small glory in her name?

denique fortitudo dea non est, quae adfuit Mucio,
cum dexteram porrexit in flammas; quae adfuit
Curtio, cum se pro patria in abruptam terram praecipitem dedit; quae adfuit Decio patri et Decio filio,
cum pro exercitu se voverunt? Si tamen his omnibus vera inerat fortitudo, unde modo non agitur,
quare prudentia, quare sapientia nulla numinum
loca meruerunt? An quia in nomine generali ipsius
virtutis omnes coluntur? Sic ergo posset et unus
Deus coli, cuius partes ceteri dii putantur. Sed in
illa una virtute et fides est et pudicitia, quae tamen
extra in aedibus propriis altaria meruerunt.

XXI

Quod unum non intellegentes Deum Virtute saltem et
Felicitate debuerint esse contenti.

Has deas non veritas, sed vanitas facit; haec enim
veri Dei munera sunt, non ipsae sunt deae. Verum
tamen ubi est virtus et felicitas, quid aliud quaeritur?
Quid ei sufficit, cui virtus felicitasque non sufficit?
Omnia quippe agenda complectitur virtus, omnia
optanda felicitas. Si Iuppiter ut haec daret ideo
colebatur, quia, si bonum aliquid est latitudo regni
atque diuturnitas, ad eandem pertinet felicitatem,

---

[1] The account of Mucius is found in Livy 2.12.12; of
Curtius in 7.6.3; Decius the father in 340 B.C. in 8.9.4–8; of
Decius the son in 295 B.C. in 10.28.12–18.

Why isn't Fortitude a goddess, a virtue which was with Mucius when he held his right hand in the flames, and with Curtius when, to save his country, he threw himself headlong into the gaping earth, and with the two Decii, father and son, when they laid a curse on themselves to save the army?[1] If then all these possessed true fortitude—a matter not now under discussion,—why have Wisdom and Prudence not won a place among the deities? Is it because all are worshipped under the general name of Virtus? This proves that it would be possible to worship but one god, since the other gods are counted as parts of him. But though Virtus includes both Fides (faith) and Pudicitia (modesty), these two nevertheless were awarded altars in their own temples.

XXI

That men who did not know the one God should at least have been content with Virtus (virtue) and Felicitas (felicity).

It was not truth, but folly, that created these goddesses, for the things they name are gifts of the true God, not goddesses themselves. But where you have virtue and felicity, why look for anything else? What would satisfy a man for whom virtue and felicity are not enough? Virtue includes everything we should do, felicity everything we should wish for. If Jupiter was worshipped that he might grant these boons (for if extent and duration of rule is something good, it falls into the category of felicity), why is it

73

SAINT AUGUSTINE

cur non intellectum est dona Dei esse, non deas?
Si autem putatae sunt deae, saltem alia tanta deorum
turba non quaereretur. Consideratis enim officiis
deorum dearumque omnium, quae sicut voluerunt
pro sua opinatione finxerunt, inveniant si possunt
aliquid quod praestari ab aliquo deo possit homini
habenti virtutem, habenti felicitatem. Quid doctrinae vel a Mercurio vel a Minerva petendum esset,
cum virtus omnia secum haberet? Ars quippe ipsa
bene recteque vivendi virtus a veteribus definita est.
Unde ab eo quod Graece ἀρετή dicitur virtus nomen
artis Latinos traduxisse putaverunt. Sed si virtus
non nisi ad ingeniosum posset venire, quid opus erat
deo Catio patre, qui catos, id est acutos faceret, cum
hoc posset conferre felicitas?

Ingeniosum quippe nasci felicitatis est, unde,
etiamsi non potuit a nondum nato coli dea Felicitas,
ut hoc ei conciliata donaret, conferret hoc parentibus
eius cultoribus suis, ut eis ingeniosi filii nascerentur.
Quid opus erat parturientibus invocare Lucinam,
cum, si adesset Felicitas, non solum bene parerent,
sed etiam bonos? Quid necesse erat Opi deae com-
mendare nascentes, deo Vaticano vagientes, deae
Cuninae iacentes, deae Ruminae sugentes, deo Stati-

not seen that they are gifts bestowed by God and are not goddesses? But once they were taken to be goddesses, at any rate the rest of the huge throng of deities should not be required. For let them consider the functions of all the gods and goddesses which they have fashioned to their taste in accordance with their fancy, and discover, if they can, some other need that can be supplied by any god, when a man already has virtue and felicity. What sort of instructions would he have to seek from Mercury or Minerva, since virtue would include the whole list? Virtue was in fact defined by the ancients as the art of living rightly and well. Hence they thought that it was from virtue, called *arete* in Greek, that the Latins derived the word " art " (*ars, artis*). But if virtue can come only to one who has natural ability, what need was there of the god, Father Catius, to make men shrewd (*catos*), that is, sharp-witted, when Felicitas could confer this gift?

It is certainly a matter of felicity to be born with natural ability. Hence, although the goddess Felicitas could not be worshipped by an unborn child so as to be won over and grant this boon, she might grant the prayer of its parents if they worshipped her, namely that children with natural wit should be born to them. What need was there for women in childbirth to invoke Lucina, since with Felicitas at hand they would not only have easy labour, but also good children? Why was it necessary to commend the new-born to the goddess Ops, wailing infants to the god Vaticanus, those in the cradle to the goddess Cunina, those at the breast to the goddess Rumina, those who could stand alone to the god Statilinus,

lino stantes, deae Adeonae adeuntes, Abeonae
abeuntes; deae Menti, ut bonam haberent mentem,
deo Volumno et deae Volumnae, ut bona vellent;
diis nuptialibus, ut bene coniugarentur, diis agresti-
bus, ut fructus uberrimos caperent, et maxime ipsi
divae Fructeseae; Marti et Bellonae, ut bene bel-
ligerarent, deae Victoriae, ut vincerent; deo Honori,
ut honorarentur, deae Pecuniae, ut pecuniosi essent,
deo Aesculano et filio eius Argentino, ut haberent
aeream argenteamque pecuniam? Nam ideo patrem
Argentini Aesculanum posuerunt, quia prius aerea
pecunia in usu coepit esse, post argentea. Miror
autem, quod Argentinus non genuit Aurinum, quia
et aurea subsecuta est. Quem deum isti si haberent,
sicut Saturno Iovem, ita et patri Argentino et avo
Aesculano Aurinum praeponerent.

Quid ergo erat necesse propter haec bona vel animi
vel corporis vel externa tantam deorum turbam
colere et invocare (quos neque omnes commemoravi,
nec ipsi potuerunt omnibus bonis humanis minutatim
singillatimque digestis deos minutos et singulos
providere), cum posset magno facilique compendio
una dea Felicitas cuncta conferre, nec solum ad bona
capienda quisquam alius, sed neque ad depellenda

---

[1] The money-gods Pecunia, Aesculanus and Argentinus are
known to us only by the fragments of Varro preserved by
Augustine and Arnobius. Argentinus was presumably
created by the pontiffs when silver coinage was introduced

those who walk toward someone to the goddess
Adeona, those who walk away to Abeona? They
would commend them to the goddess Mens that they
might have a good mind, to the god Volumnus and
goddess Volumna that they might choose (*volo*) good
things, to the gods of wedlock that they might marry
well, to the gods of the field, especially the goddess
Fructesea, that they might get good crops, to Mars
and Bellona that they might fight well, to the goddess Victoria that they might be victorious, to the
god Honos that they might be honoured, to the
goddess Pecunia for pecuniary success, to the god
Aesculanus and his son Argentinus that they might
have bronze and silver money (*aes, argentum*). They
made Aesculanus the father of Argentinus because
bronze money came into use first and silver later.
But I am surprised that Argentinus didn't beget a
son Aurinus, for gold coins (*aurum*) came a little
later. And if they had had a god Aurinus, they
would have set him above his father Argentinus and
his grandfather Aesculanus, just as they put Jupiter
above Saturn.[1]

But why was it necessary to worship and invoke
such a throng of gods to gain these blessings, mental,
physical or external? I have not mentioned them
all, nor were the pagans themselves equal to the
task of dividing up all human goods into tiny and
separate bits and providing a tiny and separate god
for each. For the one goddess Felicitas could easily
confer all blessings, and that would be a short and
easy way, making it unnecessary to look for others,

in 269 B.C., but apparently such new deities were out of style
when gold coinage began in 217.

mala quaereretur? Cur enim esset invocanda propter fessos diva Fessona, propter hostes depellendos
diva Pellonia, propter aegros medicus vel Apollo vel
Aesculapius vel ambo simul, quando esset grande
periculum? Nec deus Spiniensis, ut spinas ex agris
eradicaret; nec dea Robigo, ut non accederet,
rogaretur: una Felicitate praesente et tuente vel
nulla mala exorerentur, vel facillime pellerentur.

Postremo quoniam de duabus istis deabus Virtute
et Felicitate tractamus: si felicitas virtutis est prae-
mium, non dea, sed Dei donum est; si autem dea est,
cur non dicatur et virtutem ipsa conferre, quando
quidem etiam virtutem consequi felicitas magna est?

XXII

*De scientia colendorum deorum, quam a se Varro
gloriatur conlatam esse Romanis.*

QUID est ergo, quod pro ingenti beneficio Varro
iactat praestare se civibus suis, quia non solum commemorat deos, quos coli oporteat a Romanis, verum
etiam dicit quid ad quemque pertineat? Quoniam
nihil prodest, in quit, hominis alicuius medici nomen
formamque nosse, et quod sit medicus ignorare.
Ita dicit nihil prodesse scire deum esse Aesculapium,
si nescias eum valetudini opitulari atque ita ignores
cur ei debeas supplicare. Hoc etiam alia similitu-

either to obtain blessings or to avert evils. Why need the goddess Fessona be invoked for the tired (*fessos*), the goddess Pellonia to drive back the enemy (*pellere*), or for the sick a healing god, either Apollo or Aesculapius, or both at once when the threat was serious? Nor need the god Spiniensis be asked to uproot the thorns from the fields, nor need the goddess Robigo (rust) be begged not to come near the wheat. If Felicitas alone were present and on guard, either no evils would arise, or they would easily be banished.

A final point, while we are dealing with these two goddesses Virtus and Felicitas: if felicity is the reward of virtue, it is not a goddess, but the gift of God. And if she is a goddess, why does no one assert that she confers also the gift of virtue? For the attainment of virtue is also a matter of great felicity.

XXII

On the knowledge of correct worship, which Varro boasts he had conferred on the Romans.

WHAT is the great service then that Varro boasts he conferred on his fellow-citizens in that he not only named the gods whom the Romans should include in their worship, but also reported their several provinces? " For it is no help," he says, " to know the name and look of some man who is a doctor, and not to know that he is a doctor. Just so it is of no help to know that Aesculapius is a god if you don't know that he helps in sickness, and so don't know why you should pray to him." He supports this

dine adfirmat dicens, non modo bene vivere, sed vivere omnino neminem posse, si ignoret quisnam sit faber, quis pistor, quis tector, a quo quid utensile petere possit, quem adiutorem adsumere, quem ducem, quem doctorem; eo modo nulli dubium esse asserens ita esse utilem cognitionem deorum, si sciatur quam quisque deus vim et facultatem ac potestatem cuiusque rei habeat. " Ex eo enim poterimus, inquit, scire quem cuiusque causa deum advocare atque invocare debeamus, ne faciamus, ut mimi solent, et optemus a Libero aquam, a Lymphis vinum." Magna sane utilitas. Quis non huic gratias ageret, si vera monstraret, et si unum verum Deum, a quo essent omnia bona, hominibus colendum doceret ?

XXIII

De Felicitate, quam Romani, multorum veneratores
deorum, diu non coluerunt honore divino, cum
pro omnibus sola sufficeret.

Sed (unde nunc agitur) si libri et sacra eorum vera sunt et Felicitas dea est, cur non ipsa una quae coleretur constituta est, quae posset universa conferre et compendio facere felicem ? Quis enim optat aliquid propter aliud quam ut felix fiat ? Cur denique tam sero huic tantae deae post tot Romanos

thought also by another comparison, saying that it
is not only impossible for anyone to live well, but
impossible to live at all, if he doesn't know who is a
blacksmith, a baker, a plasterer, where to go to get
something needed, or whom to employ as a helper, a
guide or a teacher. Likewise he asserts that no one
can doubt that a knowledge of the gods is useful if it
is known what strength, what skill and what power the
particular god has in the particular case. " That,"
he says, " will enable us to know which god we must
summon to help us for each purpose, so that we
may not do as the comedians in the mimes are wont
to do, and ask water from Liber, and wine from the
water nymphs." A great service, of course! But
who would not thank Varro if he had pointed out the
way of truth, and taught men to worship the one true
God, from whom all blessings come?

XXIII

*Of Felicitas, who was not worshipped with divine honours
from early times by the Romans, though they were worshippers of many gods, and though she alone would have
taken the place of all the rest.*

But to continue this point. If their books and
their rites are true, and Felicitas is a goddess, why
was not she alone adopted as a deity to be worshipped, since she could confer all blessings, and
provide a short cut to felicity? For who desires
anything for any other purpose than to attain felicity? And above all, why was it so late, after so
many leading Romans had passed on, that Lucullus

principes Lucullus aedem constituit? Cur ipse
Romulus felicem cupiens condere civitatem non huic
templum potissimum struxit nec propter aliquid diis
ceteris supplicavit, quando nihil deesset, si haec
adesset? Nam et ipse nec prius rex, nec ut putant
postea deus fieret, si hanc deam propitiam non
haberet. Ut quid ergo constituit Romanis deos
Ianum, Iovem, Martem, Picum, Faunum, Tiberinum,
Herculem et si quos alios? Ut quid Titus Tatius
addidit Saturnum, Opem, Solem, Lunam, Vulcanum,
Lucem et quoscumque alios addidit, inter quos etiam
deam Cluacinam, Felicitate neglecta? Ut quid
Numa tot deos et tot deas sine ista? An eam forte
in tanta turba videre non potuit? Hostilius certe
rex deos et ipse novos Pavorem atque Pallorem
propitiandos non introduceret, si deam istam nosset
aut coleret. Praesente quippe Felicitate omnis
pavor et pallor non propitiatus abscederet, sed pulsus
aufugeret.

Deinde quid est hoc, quod iam Romanum imperium
longe lateque crescebat, et adhuc nemo Felicitatem
colebat? An ideo grandius imperium quam felicius
fuit? Nam quo modo ibi esset vera felicitas, ubi
vera non erat pietas? Pietas est enim verax veri
Dei cultus, non cultus falsorum tot deorum quot
daemoniorum. Sed et postea iam in deorum
numerum Felicitate suscepta magna bellorum
civilium infelicitas subsecuta est. An forte iuste
est indignata Felicitas quod et tam sero et non ad
honorem, sed ad contumeliam potius invitata est,

---

[1] After 146 B.C.

set up a little temple for so great a goddess?[1] When
Romulus wanted to found a happy city, why did he
not first of all raise a temple for her, and not trouble
the other gods for anything? For nothing would
have been lacking if Felicitas had been present.
Nor would he himself have become first a king, then
later (as they think) a god, if he had not had the
favour of this goddess. With what object did he set
up as gods for the Romans Janus, Jupiter, Mars,
Picus, Faunus, Tiberinus, Hercules and all the rest?
To what end did Titus Tatius add Saturn, Ops, Sol,
Luna, Vulcan, Lux and whatever others he added,
including the goddess Cluacina, while Felicitas was
neglected? With what design did Numa add so
many gods and goddesses without including her?
Perhaps he couldn't see her for all that crowd! Hostilius would surely not have introduced the new gods
Pavor and Pallor to worship if he had known and
worshipped this goddess. If Felicitas had been
present, fear and pallor would not have walked away
appeased; they would have run away beaten.

Next, why is it that at a time when the Roman empire was growing in every direction there was still
no worship of Felicitas? Or is that why the empire
was greater in size than in happiness? For how
could true happiness exist where there was no true
piety? Piety is the true cult of the true God, not
a cult of as many false gods as there are demons.
But even afterward, when Felicitas had now been
recognized and added to the roster of gods, the great
disaster (*infelicitas*) of the civil wars followed. Perhaps Felicitas was rightly indignant that she was
invited so late, and invited not to be honoured, but

ut cum ea coleretur Priapus et Cluacina et Pavor et
Pallor et Febris et cetera non numina colendorum,
sed crimina colentium?

Ad extremum si cum turba indignissima tanta dea
colenda visa est, cur non vel inlustrius ceteris colebatur? Quis enim ferat quod neque inter deos Consentes, quos dicunt in consilium Iovis adhiberi, nec
inter deos, quos selectos vocant, Felicitas constituta
est? Templum aliquod ei fieret, quod et loci sublimitate et operis dignitate praemineret. Cur enim
non aliquid melius quam ipsi Iovi? Nam quae etiam
Iovi regnum nisi Felicitas dedit? si tamen cum regnaret felix fuit. Et potior est felicitas regno.
Nemo enim dubitat facile inveniri hominem qui se
timeat fieri regem; nullus autem invenitur, qui se
nolit esse felicem. Ipsi ergo dii si per auguria vel
quolibet modo eos posse consuli putant, de hac re
consulerentur utrum vellent Felicitati loco cedere, si
forte aliorum aedibus vel altaribus iam fuisset locus
occupatus, ubi aedes maior atque sublimior Felicitati
construeretur; etiam ipse Iuppiter cederet, ut ipsum
verticem collis Capitolini Felicitas potius obtineret.

---

[1] Varro, *On Agriculture* 1.1.4 mentions twelve *di consentes*,
whose gilded images stood in the Forum, six male and six
female. These seem to be identical with the twelve deities
worshipped in the lectisternium of 217 B.C., when six pairs
were set out in the Greek manner on six couches: Jupiter and
Juno, Neptune and Minerva, Mars and Venus, Apollo and
Diana, Vulcan and Vesta, Mercury and Ceres (Livy 22.10.9;
see Wissowa, *RK²*, 61). The *di selecti* were twenty deities,
selected from those best known in Rome, to be explained in
the Stoic manner as identical with the world soul and its parts.

to be insulted by being worshipped along with Priapus and Cluacina and Pallor and Pavor and Febris and the rest, who are not so much deifications of the worshipful as malefactions of the worshippers.

Finally, if it seemed right to worship so great a goddess along with the most unworthy throng, why was she not at least worshipped in a more distinguished manner than the others? Who could approve the fact that Felicitas did not find a place either among the *di consentes*, who are members, they say, of the council of Jupiter, or among the gods whom they call " select "? [1] Some temple should have been built for her, outstanding for its lofty site and superb structure. Indeed, why not something better than for Jupiter himself? For who except Felicitas gave royal power even to Jupiter, that is, if he had felicity when he was reigning? And felicity is better than royal power. No one doubts that it is easy to find a man afraid to be made king, but no one can be found who refuses to be happy. Accordingly, suppose the gods themselves had been consulted by augury, or by whatever means they suppose that gods can be consulted, and the question had been put whether they were willing to yield their place to Felicitas, if it so happened that the place where a greater and more lofty temple was to be erected to Felicitas had already been occupied by the temples and altars of other gods. Even Jupiter himself would have yielded, so that Felicitas, rather than he, might possess the very pinnacle of the

They are named below 7.2, p. 375; all twelve of the *di consentes* are included, along with Janus and Tellus, Sol and Luna, Saturn, Genius, Orcus and Liber.

Non enim quispiam resisteret Felicitati, nisi, quod fieri non potest, qui esse vellet infelix.

Nullo modo omnino, si consuleretur, faceret Iuppiter quod ei fecerunt tres dii, Mars, Terminus et Iuventas, qui maiori et regi suo nullo modo cedere loco voluerunt. Nam sicut habent eorum litterae, cum rex Tarquinius Capitolium fabricari vellet eumque locum qui ei dignior aptiorque videbatur, ab diis aliis cerneret praeoccupatum, non audens aliquid contra eorum facere arbitrium et credens eos tanto numini suoque principi voluntate cessuros, quia multi erant illic ubi Capitolium constitutum est, per augurium quaesivit utrum concedere locum vellent Iovi; atque ipsi inde cedere omnes voluerunt praeter illos quos commemoravi, Martem, Terminum, Iuventatem; atque ideo Capitolium ita constructum est ut etiam isti tres intus essent tam obscuris signis ut hoc vix homines doctissimi scirent.

Nullo modo igitur Felicitatem Iuppiter ipse contemneret, sicut a Termino, Marte, Iuventate contemptus est. Sed ipsi etiam, qui non cesserant Iovi, profecto cederent Felicitati, quae illis regem fecerat Iovem. Aut si non cederent, non id contemptu eius facerent, sed quod in domo Felicitatis obscuri esse mallent quam sine illa in locis propriis eminere.

Ita dea Felicitate in loco amplissimo et celsissimo constituta discerent cives unde omnis boni voti petendum esset auxilium, ac sic ipsa suadente natura

---

[1] According to Livy 1.55.4, Terminus alone refused to yield to Jupiter. Other writers mention Juventas as equally unyielding, but only here does Mars join them. The source is presumably Varro.

Capitoline hill. For no one would resist Felicitas unless he wished to be unhappy, and this is impossible.

It is quite impossible that Jupiter, if he were consulted, would do what the three gods Mars, Terminus and Juventas [1] did to him; they absolutely refused to yield their place to a greater god, and their king at that. For according to the pagan writings, when King Tarquin wished to build the Capitol, and saw that the place which seemed most worthy and apaappropriate was already occupied by other gods, he dared not do anything against their will. But he thought that they would willingly yield to so great a deity, who was also their prince, and since there were many on the site where the Capitol was built, he inquired by augury whether they were willing to yield the site to Jupiter. They were all willing to move except those I mentioned—Mars, Terminus and Juventas. For this reason the Capitol was so constructed as to leave these three within, but with the indications so well hidden that even the most learned hardly knew about it.

As I was saying, Jupiter himself would by no means have scorned Felicitas as he was scorned by Terminus, Mars and Juventas. And these gods too, who did not yield to Jupiter, would surely have yielded to Felicitas who had made Jupiter their king. Or if they had not yielded, it would not have been for disregard of her, but because they preferred to be hidden in the home of Felicitas rather than to be conspicuous in their own places without her.

Thus, if the goddess Felicitas had been established in an ample and lofty abode, the citizens would have learned whence help should be sought for every

87

aliorum deorum superflua multitudine derelicta
coleretur una Felicitas, uni supplicaretur, unius
templum frequentaretur a civibus qui felices esse
vellent, quorum esset nemo qui nollet, atque ita ipsa
a se ipsa peteretur, quae ab omnibus petebatur.
Quis enim aliquid ab aliquo deo nisi felicitatem velit
accipere vel quod ad felicitatem existimat pertinere?
Proinde si felicitas habet in potestate cum quo
homine sit (habet autem, si dea est): quae tandem
stultitia est ab aliquo eam deo petere quam possis a
se ipsa impetrare? Hanc ergo deam super deos
ceteros honorare etiam loci dignitate debuerunt.
Sicut enim apud ipsos legitur, Romani veteres nescio
quem Summanum, cui nocturna fulmina tribuebant,
coluerunt magis quam Iovem, ad quem diurna fulmina pertinerent. Sed postquam Iovi templum
insigne ac sublime constructum est, propter aedis
dignitatem sic ad eum multitudo confluxit ut vix
inveniatur qui Summani nomen, quod audire iam
non potest, se saltem legisse meminerit. Si autem
felicitas dea non est, quoniam, quod verum est,
munus est Dei, ille Deus quaeratur qui eam dare
possit, et falsorum deorum multitudo noxia relinquatur, quam stultorum hominum multitudo vana secta-

---

[1] The cult of Summanus is said to have been instituted by
Titus Tatius, the colleague of Romulus. The god seems to
be identical with Jupiter Summanus, whose terra cotta statue
on the summit of the Capitol was struck down by lightning
(perhaps at night) during the war with Pyrrhus. This led to

good purpose. So nature herself would have persuaded them to abandon the useless multitude of other gods, and direct their worship and supplications to Felicitas alone. Her temple alone would have been thronged with citizens who wanted to be happy, and none of them would have been unwilling. And so felicity, which was formerly sought from all the gods, would now be sought from Felicitas, she herself from herself. For who would wish to get anything from any god, except happiness, or what he thinks belongs to happiness? And if Felicitas has the power to choose with whom she will abide (and she has, if she is a goddess), what folly it is to ask some other god for her favour when you can obtain it from herself directly! Therefore they should have honoured this goddess above all the gods by providing her also with a worthier abode. One may read in their books how the ancient Romans worshipped one Summanus, to whom they ascribed lightning at night,[1] rather than Jupiter, to whom lightning by day belonged. But after a distinguished and lofty temple was built for Jupiter, because of the grandeur of the building the multitude turned to him, so that a man can hardly be found who remembers even reading the name of Summanus, a name that is no longer heard.

But if happiness is not a goddess, but rather a gift of God (and this is the fact of the matter), let men seek that God who is able to grant it, and let them desert the noxious multiplicity of false gods that the foolish multitude of stupid people resorts

the erection of a temple of Summanus in the Circus Maximus. See K. Latte, *Römische Religionsgeschichte*, 209.

tur, Dei dona deos sibi faciens et ipsum cuius ea dona sunt obstinatione superbae voluntatis offendens. Sic enim carere non potest infelicitate qui tamquam deam felicitatem colit et Deum datorem felicitatis relinquit, sicut carere non potest fame qui panem pictum lingit et ab homine qui verum habet non petit.

XXIV

Qua ratione defendant pagani, quod inter deos colant ipsa dona divina.

Libet autem eorum considerare rationes. Usque adeone, inquiunt, maiores nostros insipientes fuisse credendum est ut haec nescirent munera divina esse, non deos? Sed quoniam sciebant nemini talia nisi aliquo deo largiente concedi, quorum deorum nomina non inveniebant, earum rerum nominibus appellabant deos quas ab eis sentiebant dari, aliqua vocabula inde flectentes, sicut a bello Bellonam nuncupaverunt, non Bellum; sicut a cunis Cuninam, non Cunam; sicut a segetibus Segetiam, non Segetem, sicut a pomis Pomonam, non Pomum; sicut a bubus Bubonam, non Bovem; aut certe nulla vocabuli declinatione sicut res ipsae nominantur, ut Pecunia dicta est dea, quae dat pecuniam, non omnino pecunia dea ipsa putata est; ita Virtus, quae dat virtutem, Honor,

to. They make gifts of God into gods for themselves, and offend God himself, the giver of these gifts, by the stubborness of a proud self-will. Thus they cannot escape unhappiness, when they worship happiness as a goddess and desert God, the giver of happiness. Just so a man cannot escape hunger by licking a painted loaf of bread instead of asking for a real one from a man who has it.

XXIV

By what argument the pagans defend the practice of worshipping divine gifts as gods.

Now I should like to consider their arguments. Are we to believe, they say, that our ancestors were so stupid as not to know that these things are divine gifts, and not gods? But since they knew that such gifts are not granted to anyone unless some god bestows them, in any case where they did not find the names of such gods, they gave them the names of the things that they believed came from them. To some of the words they gave a twist, as when from *bellum*, war, they called the deity of war Bellona, not Bellum; the goddess of cradles Cunina, not Cuna; of crops Segetia, not Seges; of fruits Pomona, not Pomum; of oxen Bubona, not Bos. Sometimes, to be sure, there is no change in the word, and the gods have the name of the things themselves. Thus the goddess who gives money was called Pecunia, though the money itself was by no means thought a goddess. Likewise it was Virtus who gives virtue, Honos who gives honour,

qui honorem, Concordia, quae concordiam, Victoria, quae dat victoriam. Ita, inquiunt, cum Felicitas dea dicitur, non ipsa quae datur, sed numen illud adtenditur a quo felicitas datur.

XXV

De uno tantum colendo Deo, qui licet nomine
ignoretur, tamen felicitatis dator esse sentitur.

Ista nobis reddita ratione multo facilius eis quorum cor non nimis obduruit persuadebimus fortasse quod volumus. Si enim iam humana infirmitas sensit non nisi ab aliquo deo dari posse felicitatem, et hoc senserunt homines, qui tam multos colebant deos, in quibus et ipsum eorum regem Iovem, quia nomen eius, a quo daretur felicitas, ignorabant, ideo ipsius rei nomine, quam credebant ab illo dari, eum appellare voluerunt, satis ergo indicarunt nec ab ipso Iove dari posse felicitatem, quem iam colebant, sed utique ab illo, quem nomine ipsius felicitatis colendum esse censebant. Confirmo prorsus a quodam deo, quem nesciebant, eos credidisse dari felicitatem; ipse ergo quaeratur, ipse colatur, et sufficit. Repudietur strepitus innumerabilium daemoniorum; illi non sufficiat hic deus, cui non sufficit munus eius. Illi, inquam, non sufficiat ad colendum Deus dator

Concordia who gives concord and Victoria who gives victory. Thus, they say, when Felicitas is called a goddess, the word means not the felicity which is given, but the deity by whom it is given.

XXV

On the worship of the one God, who is recognized as the giver of felicity, though his name is unknown.

Thanks to this account duly rendered to us, we shall perhaps find it easier to convince those whose heart is not too much hardened, and so fulfil our purpose. For it is admitted that human weakness already judged that felicity could be conferred only by some god, and this was the judgement of men who worshipped so many gods, including Jupiter their king himself. Since they did not know the name of the one by whom happiness was given, they therefore chose to call the deity by the name of the gift. Thus they certified clearly enough that happiness could not be obtained even from Jupiter, whom they were already worshipping, but only from that power which they thought should be worshipped under the name of happiness itself (that is, Felicitas). I thus establish the fact that they believed happiness to be conferred by some god of whom they knew nothing. Therefore, let him be sought, let him be worshipped, and it is enough. Let the din of demons innumerable be expelled in disgrace. Let this God be found not enough by that man for whom his gift is not enough. Let God, the giver of happiness, I repeat, be not enough to worship, for the man

felicitatis, cui non sufficit ad accipiendum ipsa felicitas.   Cui autem sufficit (non enim habet homo quid
amplius optare debeat), serviat uni Deo datori felicitatis.   Non est ipse quem nominant Iovem.   Nam si
eum datorem felicitatis agnoscerent, non utique
alium vel aliam, a qua daretur felicitas, nomine ipsius
felicitatis inquirerent, neque ipsum Iovem cum
tantis iniuriis colendum putarent.   Iste alienarum
dicitur adulter uxorum, iste pueri pulchri inpudicus
amator et raptor.

XXVI

De ludis scaenicis, quos sibi dii celebrari a suis
cultoribus exegerunt.

SED " fingebat haec Homerus," ait Tullius, " et
humana ad deos transferebat: divina mallem ad
nos."   Merito displicuit viro gravi divinorum criminum poeta confictor.   Cur ergo ludi scaenici, ubi
haec dictitantur cantitantur actitantur, deorum
honoribus exhibentur, inter res divinas a doctissimis
conscribuntur?   Hic exclamet Cicero non contra
figmenta poetarum, sed contra instituta maiorum,
an exclamarent et illi: Quid nos fecimus!   Ipsi dii
ista suis honoribus exhibenda flagitaverunt, atrociter
imperarunt, cladem nisi fieret praenuntiarunt; quia

---

[1] *Tusculan Disputations* 1.26.65. The criticism of mythology as harmful and degrading was a commonplace of the
philosophical schools.   So in Cicero's dialogue *On the Nature
of the Gods* both the Epicurean and Stoic disputants denounce
the myths (1.42; 2.70; see the notes in Pease's edition, with
the passages in Plato and the pre-Socratics there cited).

who finds that happiness itself is not enough to receive.
But let him who finds happiness enough—for man's
prayers cannot go beyond it—let him serve the one
God, the giver of happiness. He is not the one they
call Jupiter, for if they saw in Jupiter the giver of
happiness they would not look for another god or
goddess to confer it, calling her by the name of happiness itself, Felicitas. Nor would they have supposed
that Jupiter was to be worshipped by the great insults
that they now inflict upon him. For they speak of
him as a seducer of the wives of others, and as the
shameless lover and kidnapper of a handsome boy.

XXVI

*On the theatrical shows, whose performance the gods
demanded of their worshippers.*

BUT Cicero writes:[1] " Homer invented these
stories and transferred human qualities to the gods.
I would rather he had transferred divine qualities
to us." This responsible man rightly disapproved
of a poet who made up stories about the misdeeds of
the gods. Then what about the stage performances
where these stories are told, sung and acted out again
and again? Why are they presented in honour of
the gods, and included by the most learned writers
among divine affairs? Here Cicero should protest,
not against the fictions of the poets, but against the
institutions of our ancestors. Or they in turn might
exclaim: " What did we do? It was the gods themselves who demanded that these shows should be put
on in their honour, ferociously ordered it, threatened

neglectum est aliquid, severissime vindicarunt; quia id quod neglectum fuerat factum est, placatos se esse monstrarunt.

Inter eorum commemoratur virtutes et miranda facta quod dicam. Tito Latinio rustico Romano patri familias dictum est in somnis, in senatum nuntiaret, ut ludi Romani instaurarentur, quod primo eorum die in quodam scelerato, qui populo spectante ad supplicium duci iussus est, numinibus videlicet ex ludis hilaritatem quaerentibus triste displicuisset imperium. Cum ergo ille qui somnio commonitus erat postero die iussa facere non ausus esset, secunda nocte hoc idem rursus severius imperatum est; amisit filium, quia non fecit. Tertia nocte dictum est homini quod maior ei poena, si non faceret, inmineret. Cum etiam sic non auderet, in morbum incidit acrem et horribilem. Tum vero ex amicorum sententia ad magistratus rem detulit atque in lectica allatus est in senatum expositoque somnio recepta continuo valetudine pedibus suis sanus abscessit. Tanto stupefactus miraculo senatus quadruplicata pecunia ludos censuit instaurari.

Quis non videat qui sanum sapit subditos homines malignis daemonibus, a quorum dominatione non liberat nisi gratia Dei per Iesum Christum dominum nostrum, vi compulsos esse exhibere talibus diis

---

[1] The following story is related, with variations, by Cicero, *On Divination* 1.26.55; Livy 2.36; and Valerius Maximus 1.7.4. Augustine's version seems derived from none of these, and it may be assumed that he is following his usual source, Varro.

destruction unless it was done, severely punished inattention to any detail and made it clear that they were mollified when the detail was attended to."

Among their mighty works and remarkable deeds is recorded an incident which I shall relate.[1] Titus Latinius, a Roman farmer and the head of a family, was told in a dream that he should announce to the senate that the Roman games (*ludi Romani*) were to be repeated, because on the first day of the games a certain criminal had been ordered to be led to his execution, while the people looked on. This grim order, he was to say, had displeased the deities, who evidently preferred a cheerful performance. The man who had been warned in the dream did not have the courage to obey the command on the next day. Hence on the following night the same command was repeated with more severity. Then because he did not act he lost his son. On the third night the man was warned that a greater punishment was in store if he did not obey. When even then he did not dare to speak, he fell into an acute and fearful illness. Then at last, on the advice of his friends, he reported the affair to the magistrates. He was carried into the senate on a litter, told his dream and at once recovered his health and walked away well on his own feet. Amazed by such a miracle, the senate voted to renew the games, with an appropriation of four times the money.

Who in his right mind can fail to see that men in subjection to malignant demons (from whose rule men are freed only by the grace of God through Jesus Christ our Lord) were forcibly compelled to present to gods of this sort shows which a sound

quae recto consilio poterant turpia iudicari ? In illis
certe ludis poetica numinum crimina frequentantur,
qui ludi cogentibus numinibus iussu senatus instaura-
bantur. In illis ludis corruptorem pudicitiae Iovem
turpissimi histriones cantabant agebant placebant.
Si illud fingebatur, ille irasceretur; si autem suis
criminibus etiam fictis delectabatur, quando coleretur, nisi diabolo serviretur ? Itane iste Romanum
conderet dilataret conservaret imperium, quovis
Romano cui talia displicebant homine abiectior ?
Iste daret felicitatem, qui tam infeliciter colebatur,
et nisi ita coleretur, infelicius irascebatur ?

XXVII

*De tribus generibus deorum, de quibus Scaevola
pontifex disputavit.*

RELATUM est in litteras doctissimum pontificem
Scaevolam disputasse tria genera tradita deorum:
unum a poetis, alterum a philosophis, tertium a
principibus civitatis. Primum genus nugatorium dicit
esse, quod multa de diis fingantur indigna; secundum
non congruere civitatibus, quod habeat aliqua
supervacua, aliqua etiam quae obsit populis nosse.

---

[1] Quintus Mucius Scaevola, consul 95 B.C. and pontifex
maximus, was distinguished both as jurist and orator. The
notion of these three kinds of gods was probably derived from
the Stoic Panaetius. It was adopted by Varro, from whom
Augustine is evidently quoting. See Zeller, *Philosophie der
Griechen*[3] III.I, 566 f., and J. Pepin, " La theologie tripartite

judgement might have condemned as shameful?
At any rate, in those games the misdeeds of the gods
as told by the poets are publicly celebrated, and the
games were repeated by order of the senate because
the gods compelled it. In those games the vilest
actors used to sing and act the part of Jupiter, the
corrupter of morals, and please him by doing so. If
all that was fiction, he should have been angry. But
if he was pleased with his misdeeds, even fictitious
misdeeds, how could he be worshipped except by
servants of the devil? Could the Roman empire
have been so founded, extended and preserved by
this god, who is lower than any man of Rome who was
displeased by such shows? Could he be the giver of
felicity, who was so infelicitously worshipped and was
still more infelicitously angered if he was not so
worshipped?

XXVII

On the three kinds of gods of which the pontiff Scaevola wrote.

It is recorded that the learned pontiff Scaevola [1]
maintained that three kinds of gods are handed
down to us: one by the poets, another by the philosophers and a third by statesmen. He says that the
first class is mere rubbish, because the poets invent
many disgraceful stories about the gods; the second
is not suited to city-states, because it includes some
superfluous doctrines and some also that it is harmful
for the people to know.

de Varron," in *Revue des Études Augustiniennes*, 2 (1956),
265–94.

De supervacuis non magna causa est; solet
enim et a iuris peritis dici: Superflua non nocent.
Quae sunt autem illa, quae prolata in multitudinem
nocent? " Haec," inquit, " non esse deos Herculem,
Aesculapium, Castorem, Pollucem; proditur enim
ab doctis quod homines fuerint et humana condicione
defecerint." Quid aliud? " Quod eorum qui sint
dii non habeant civitates vera simulacra, quod verus
Deus nec sexum habeat nec aetatem nec definita
corporis membra." Haec pontifex nosse populos
non vult; nam falsa esse non putat. Expedire igitur
existimat falli in religione civitates. Quod dicere
etiam in libris rerum divinarum Varro ipse non dubitat. Praeclara religio, quo confugiat liberandus infirmus, et cum veritatem qua liberetur inquirat,
credatur ei expedire quod fallitur!

Poeticum sane deorum genus cur Scaevola respuat,
eisdem litteris non tacetur: quia sic videlicet deos
deformant, ut nec bonis hominibus comparentur,
cum alium faciant furari, alium adulterare, sic item
aliquid aliter turpiter atque inepte dicere ac facere;
tres inter se deas certasse de praemio pulchritudinis,

---

[1] Justinian, *Code* 6.23.17 de testimentis: " cum superflua
non noceant."

[2] The theory that gods were in origin merely deified mortals
was expounded by Euhemerus about 300 B.C. But the cult
of heroes, some of whom were promoted to the rank of gods,
had long since prepared the way for Euhemerism. The four
named here were worshipped as gods but were generally
believed to have lived on earth as men distinguished for their
merits. Cicero in his *Laws* (2.19) prescribes that the people
are to worship as gods "those whose merits have admitted
them to heaven: Hercules, Liber, Aesculapius, Castor,
Pollux, Quirinus." The doctrine of deification for merit was

As for the superfluous doctrines there need be no great controversy, for, as the jurists are wont to say, " Superfluous things do no harm." [1] But what are the doctrines that are harmful when made known to the crowd? It is such statements as these, he says: " That Hercules, Aesculapius, Castor, and Pollux are not gods, for it is related by the learned that they were men and passed on from the mortal state." [2] And what more? " That the city-states do not have the true images of those who are really gods, because the true God has neither sex nor age nor well-defined bodily parts." It is these doctrines that the pontiff would not let the people know, for he does not think that they are false. He therefore considers mistaken religious views to be for the advantage of a city. Nor does Varro himself hesitate to say the same in his books on divine affairs. What a splendid religion for the weak to take refuge in for deliverance—a religion which includes the belief that if the refugee seeks for the truth by which he may gain freedom, it is better for him to be cheated!

As for the gods of the poets, the same work makes it clear why they were rejected by Scaevola: Because the poets so disfigure the gods that they cannot even be compared with good men. They represent one god as stealing, another committing adultery and others speaking and acting in every sort of base and absurd fashion. They say that three goddesses contended with each other for the prize of beauty,

a Stoic commonplace (Cicero, *On the Nature of the Gods*, 1.38 f.; 2.62; compare *Stoicorum Veterum Fragmenta* I, 448 and II, 1076 f.).

victas duas a Venere Troiam evertisse; Iovem ipsum
converti in bovem aut cygnum, ut cum aliqua con-
cumbat; deam homini nubere, Saturnum liberos
devorare; nihil denique posse confingi miraculorum
atque vitiorum, quod non ibi reperiatur atque ab
deorum natura longe absit.

O Scaevola pontifex maxime, ludos tolle, si potes;
praecipe populis ne tales honores diis inmortalibus
deferant ubi crimina deorum libeat mirari et quae
fieri possunt placeat imitari. Si autem tibi respon-
derit populus: Vos nobis importastis ista pontifices;
deos ipsos roga, quibus instigantibus ista iussistis ne
talia sibi iubeant exhiberi. Quae si mala sunt et
propterea nullo modo de deorum maiestate credenda,
maior est deorum iniuria, de quibus inpune finguntur.

Sed non te audiunt, daemones sunt, prava docent,
turpibus gaudent; non solum non deputant iniuriam,
si de illis ista fingantur, sed eam potius iniuriam ferre
non possunt, si per eorum sollemnia non agantur.
Iam vero si adversus eos Iovem interpelles, maxime
ob eam causam, quia eius plura crimina ludis scaenicis
actitantur. Nonne etiamsi Deum Iovem nuncupatis,
a quo regitur totus atque administratur hic mundus,

---

[1] The public games, especially the stage performances, were
a favourite target for Christian attack, on the gound that
(1) they formed a large part of the honours paid to the pagan
deities; (2) their themes were often taken from mythology;
and (3) the performances were scandalous both to pagan and
Christian morals. Theatres and temples were often combined

and that the two who were defeated by Venus overthrew Troy. They say that Jupiter himself was
changed into a bull, and again a swan, to have intercourse with some woman; and that a goddess married a man, and that Saturn devoured his children.
In short, no marvels and no vices can be imagined
that are not found there, though these are completely
opposed to the divine character.

O Scaevola, Pontifex Maximus, do away with the
games, if you can! [1] Teach the people not to offer
such honours to the immortal gods, where people take
pleasure in admiring the misdeeds of the gods and
in imitating them as far as they can. And if the
people answer you, " You pontiffs have introduced
all this among us," then ask the gods themselves, at
whose instigation you gave the orders, not to require
such shows to be exhibited in their honour. If the
deeds are wicked and therefore utterly unfit to be
ascribed to the majesty of the gods, so much greater
is the affront to the gods about whom they are invented with impunity.

But they don't hear you. They are demons who
teach depravity and rejoice in turpitude. Not only
do they count it no affront if these stories are invented about them, the fact is rather that they cannot bear the affront if the deeds are not acted out at
their festivals. Moreover, if you appeal to Jupiter
against them, that makes it worse, since his misdeeds
are the ones most frequently acted out in the
theatre! And even if you give the name Jupiter to
the God who rules and looks after this universe, are

architecturally; see John A. Hanson, *Roman Theater-Temples*
(Princeton, 1959).

eo illi fit a vobis maxima iniuria, quod eum cum istis
colendum putatis eorumque regem esse perhibetis?

XXVIII

An ad obtinendum dilatandumque regnum profuerit
Romanis cultus deorum.

NULLO igitur modo dii tales, qui talibus placantur
vel potius accusantur honoribus ut maius sit crimen
quod eis falsis oblectantur quam si de illis vera
dicerentur, Romanum imperium augere et conservare
potuissent. Hoc enim si possent, Graecis potius
donum tam grande conferrent, qui eos in huiusce
modi rebus divinis, hoc est ludis scaenicis, honorabi-
lius digniusque coluerunt, quando et a morsibus
poetarum, quibus deos dilacerari videbant, se non
subtraxerunt, dando eis licentiam male tractandi
homines quos liberet, et ipsos scaenicos non turpes
iudicaverunt, sed dignos etiam praeclaris honoribus
habuerunt.

Sicut autem potuerunt auream pecuniam habere
Romani, quamvis deum Aurinum non colerent; sic
et argenteam habere potuerunt et aeream, si nec
Argentinum nec eius patrem colerent Aesculanum,
et sic omnia quae retexere piget. Sic ergo et regnum
invito quidem Deo vero nullo modo habere possent;
diis vero istis falsis et multis ignoratis sive contemptis

you not offering the greatest affront to him by thinking that he should be worshipped along with those
gods, and in making him their king?

XXVIII

*Whether the worship of the gods helped the Romans
to obtain and extend their empire.*

IT is certainly not such gods that could have en-
larged and preserved the Roman empire—gods
placated, or rather, accused of their misdeeds, by
such honours. It is a worse charge against them
that they were pleased by false stories than it would
be if the stories were true. For if they had the power
to confer so great a gift, they would have given it to
the Greeks, who treated them with more honour and
respect in divine concerns of this sort, that is, in
stage performances. For they did not exempt
themselves from the attacks of the poets by which
they allowed gods to be ridiculed, but gave them
licence to abuse any men they wished. And they
did not condemn the actors to infamy, but regarded
them as worthy of even outstanding honours.

But just as the Romans might have had gold money
without worshipping a god Aurinus, so they could
have had silver and bronze money without worshipping Argentinus and his father Aesculanus, and so
for all the rest, which it would be irksome to repeat
in detail. So then also for their empire—they could
by no means have gained it against the will of the
true God, but if they had ignored or scorned that
multitude of false gods and recognized and worshipped

atque illo uno cognito et fide sincera ac moribus culto
et melius hic regnum haberent, quantumcumque
haberent, et post haec acciperent sempiternum, sive
hic haberent sive non haberent.

XXIX

*De falsitate auspicii, quo Romani regni fortitudo et
stabilitas visa est indicari.*

Nam illud quale est quod pulcherrimum auspicium
fuisse dixerunt, quod paulo ante commemoravi,
Martem et Terminum et Iuventatem nec Iovi regi
deorum loco cedere voluisse? Sic enim, inquiunt,
significatum est Martiam gentem, id est Romanam,
nemini locum quem teneret daturam, Romanos
quoque terminos propter deum Terminum neminem
commoturum, iuventutem etiam Romanam propter
deam Iuventatem nemini esse cessuram. Videant
ergo quo modo habeant istum regem deorum suorum
et datorem regni sui, ut eum auspicia ista pro adver-
sario ponerent, cui non cedere pulchrum esset.
Quamquam haec si vera sunt, non habent omnino
quid timeant. Non enim confessuri sunt quod dii
cesserint Christo qui Iovi cedere noluerunt; salvis
quippe imperii finibus Christo cedere potuerunt et
de sedibus locorum et maxime de corde credentium.

Sed antequam Christus venisset in carne, antequam

the one God with purity of faith and conduct, they
would have had a better kingdom here below, whatever its size, and would have received an eternal
kingdom hereafter, whether they had any kingdom
here or not.

XXIX

*On the falsity of the prediction that seemed to indicate
the strength and stability of the Roman Empire.*

Now what is the meaning of the event that I
mentioned recently, which they said was an excellent
sign, when Mars and Terminus and Juventas would
not yield their place to Jupiter the king of the gods?
It was thus signified, they say, that the people of
Mars, that is, the Roman people, would never sur-
render to anyone a place which they held; also that
no one would disturb the Roman boundaries, on
account of the god Terminus; and that the Roman
youth would yield to no one, on account of the goddess Juventas. Now let them consider how they can
regard Jupiter as king of the gods and giver of their
empire, while the sign set him down as an adversary,
to whom it was a fine thing not to yield. Yet if this
is true, they have nothing at all to fear, for they will
never admit that gods who refused to yield to Jupiter
have yielded to Christ. Well, the fact is, they were
able to yield to Christ without harming the borders
of the empire, surrendering both their places in their
sacred precincts and especially their place in the
hearts of their worshippers.

But before Christ had come in the flesh, before

denique ista scriberentur quae de libris eorum pro-
ferimus, sed tamen postea quam factum est sub rege
Tarquinio illud auspicium, aliquotiens Romanus
exercitus fusus est, hoc est versus in fugam, falsumque
ostendit auspicium quo Iuventas illa non cesserat
Iovi, et gens Martia superantibus atque inrumpenti-
bus Gallis in ipsa Urbe contrita est, et termini imperii deficientibus multis ad Hannibalem civitatibus
in angustum fuerant coartati. Ita evacuata est
pulchritudo auspiciorum, remansit contra Iovem
contumacia, non deorum, sed daemoniorum. Aliud
est enim non cessisse, aliud unde cesseras redisse.
Quamquam et postea in orientalibus partibus Hadriani voluntate mutati sunt termini imperii Romani.
Ille namque tres provincias nobiles, Armeniam,
Mesopotamiam, Assyriam, Persarum concessit imperio, ut deus ille Terminus, qui Romanos terminos
secundum istos tuebatur et per illud pulcherrimum
auspicium loco non cesserat Iovi, plus Hadrianum
regem hominum quam regem deorum timuisse videatur. Receptis quoque alio tempore provinciis memo-
ratis nostra paene memoria retrorsus Terminus
cessit, quando Iulianus deorum illorum oraculis
deditus inmoderato ausu naves iussit incendi quibus
alimonia portabatur; qua exercitus destitutus mox
etiam ipso hostili vulnere extincto in tantam est
redactus inopiam ut inde nullus evaderet undique
hostibus incursantibus militem imperatoris morte

---

[1] On his accession to the throne in 117 Hadrian gave up the
eastern provinces previously annexed by Trajan. Julian met
his death in an attack on Persia in 363.

these things that we have cited from their books
were written, yet after the sign was enacted under
King Tarquin, at a number of times the Roman army
was routed, that is, put to flight, thus proving false
the prediction from Juventas' not yielding to Jupiter.
In the city of Rome itself the people of Mars were
beaten when the Gauls won the day and burst into
the city. As for the boundaries of the empire, they
were reduced to narrow straits when many cities deserted to Hannibal. So the fine sign came to
nothing; and what remained was defiance of Jupiter,
not by gods, but by demons. For it is one thing
not to have retreated, and quite another to have
returned to the place from which you retreated. In
any case, it also happened later that the boundaries
of the Roman empire were changed in the eastern
regions by the decision of Hadrian.[1] He gave up
three noble provinces—Armenia, Mesopotamia and
Assyria—to the rule of the Persians. Thus that god
Terminus who, they say, was guardian of the Roman
boundaries and in that favourable sign had refused to
yield to Jupiter, seems to have feared Hadrian the
king of men more than the king of the gods. Although these provinces which I have mentioned were
also recovered at another time, almost within my
memory Terminus had to retreat again. It was when
Julian, devoted to the oracles of those gods, with
unbridled daring ordered the ships burnt in which
his provisions were carried. Shortly Julian himself
was killed by an enemy's hand. Deprived of food
the army was reduced to extreme want, and when
the enemy charged from all sides upon the troops,
who were confused by the death of their leader, it

turbatum, nisi placito pacis illic imperii fines con-
stituerentur, ubi hodieque persistunt, non quidem
tanto detrimento quantum concesserat Hadrianus,
sed media tamen compositione defixi. Vano igitur
augurio deus Terminus non cessit Iovi, qui cessit
Hadriani voluntati, cessit etiam Iuliani temeritati et
Ioviani necessitati. Viderunt haec intellegentiores
gravioresque Romani; sed contra consuetudinem
civitatis, quae daemonicis ritibus fuerat obligata,
parum valebant, quia et ipsi, etiamsi illa vana esse
sentiebant, naturae tamen rerum sub unius veri Dei
regimine atque imperio constitutae religiosum cultum, qui Deo debetur, exhibendum putabant,
servientes, ut ait apostolus, *creaturae potius quam crea-
tori, qui est benedictus in saecula.* Huius Dei veri erat
auxilium necessarium, a quo mitterentur sancti viri
et veraciter pii, qui pro vera religione morerentur,
ut falsae a viventibus tollerentur.

XXX

*Qualia de diis gentium etiam cultores eorum se sentire
fateantur.*

CICERO augur inridet auguria et inridet homines
corvi et corniculae vocibus vitae consilia moderantes.
Sed iste Academicus, qui omnia esse contendit in-
certa, indignus est qui habeat ullam in his rebus

---

[1] Romans 1.25.

seemed that no one would escape. But peace was made, and the boundaries of the empire were fixed where they remain today. The loss was not so great as at the time of Hadrian's withdrawal; the settlement was rather a compromise.

Vain therefore was the sign, when Terminus did not yield to Jupiter, for he later yielded to the decision of Hadrian, to the rashness of Julian and to the pressure put on Jovian. The more intelligent and responsible Romans saw all this, but they had little power to oppose the customs of a city that had been bound over to the rites of demons. Even those who knew that there was nothing in such rites, still held that the worship due to God should be offered up to nature, which has been placed under the direction and command of the one true God. Thus, as the Apostle says, they " worshipped and served the creature rather than the Creator, who is blessed forever." ¹ The aid of this true God was indispensable. He had to send holy and truly pious men to die for the true religion before false religions could be removed from among the living.

XXX

What the worshippers of the pagan gods admit that they think about them.

CICERO the augur laughs at augury. He laughs at the men who regulate the plans of their lives by the voice of the raven and the crow. But since he is an Academic, who contends that everything is uncertain, he does not deserve to be counted as an

auctoritatem. Disputat apud eum Quintus Lucilius
Balbus in secundo de deorum natura libro, et cum
ipse superstitiones ex natura rerum velut physicas et
philosophicas inserat, indignatur tamen institutioni
simulacrorum et opinionibus fabulosis ita loquens:
" Videtisne igitur ut a physicis rebus bene atque
utiliter inventis ratio sit tracta ad commenticios et
fictos deos? Quae res genuit falsas opiniones erroresque turbulentos et superstitiones paene aniles.
Et formae enim nobis deorum et aetates et vestitus
ornatusque noti sunt, genera praeterea, coniugia,
cognationes, omniaque traducta ad similitudinem
imbecillitatis humanae. Nam et perturbatis animis
inducuntur; accepimus enim deorum cupidates
aegritudines iracundias. Nec vero, ut fabulae ferunt,
dii bellis proeliisque caruerunt; nec solum, ut apud
Homerum, cum duos exercitus contrarios alii dii ex
alia parte defenderent, sed etiam (ut cum Titanis
aut cum Gigantibus) sua propria bella gesserunt.
Haec et dicuntur et creduntur stultissime et plena
sunt vanitatis summaeque levitatis." Ecce interim
quae confitentur qui defendunt deos gentium.
Deinde cum haec ad superstitionem pertinere dicat,
ad religionem vero quae ipse secundum Stoicos videtur docere: " non enim philosophi solum," inquit,
" verum etiam maiores nostri superstitionem a
religione separaverunt; nam qui totos dies precaban-

---

[1] Cicero, *On the Nature of the Gods* 2.70.

authority on these matters. He introduces as a
disputant in the second book of his work *On the
Nature of the Gods* Quintus Lucilius Balbus, and
though he introduces superstitions, deriving them
from nature and presenting them as scientific and
philosophical, he is nevertheless offended by the use
of images and at the notions of mythology. He
speaks thus: " Do you see, then, how the good and
profitable philosophy of nature is diverted to support
artificial and fictitious gods? This has led to false
opinions, to confused errors, and to superstitions
almost worthy of old women. The shapes of the
gods are known to us, along with their age, clothing, and attributes, also their genealogies, marriages, and family relationships. Everything has
been distorted into the likeness of human weakness.
For they are represented with agitated minds—we
have been told of their passionate desires, their griefs,
and their fits of anger. And in fact, as the stories
have it, the gods are not exempt from wars and
battles. Not only, as in Homer, do they intervene
to protect the two opposing armies, some gods on
one side, some on the other, but they also have special wars of their own, as with the Titans or with
the Giants. It is most foolish to tell and to believe
such stories. They are steeped in untruth and in the
utmost frivolity." [1] Pause a moment to note what
is conceded by defenders of pagan gods. Then he
asserts that such tales come under the head of superstition, while the things that he teaches according to
Stoic doctrine, it seems, belong to religion. " Not
only the philosophers," he says, " but also our ancestors separated supersition from religion. For those

tur," inquit, "et immolabant, ut sibi sui liberi superstites essent, superstitiosi sunt appellati."

Quis non intellegat eum conari, dum consuetudinem civitatis timet, religionem laudare maiorum eamque a superstitione velle seiungere, sed quo modo id possit non invenire? Si enim a maioribus illi sunt appellati superstitiosi, qui totos dies precabantur et immolabant, numquid et illi qui instituerunt (quod iste reprehendit) deorum simulacra diversa aetate et veste distincta, deorum genera coniugia cognationes? Haec utique cum tamquam superstitiosa culpantur, inplicat ista culpa maiores talium simulacrorum institutores atque cultores; inplicat et ipsum, qui, quantolibet eloquio se in libertatem nitatur evolvere, necesse habebat ista venerari; nec quod in hac disputatione disertus insonat, muttire auderet in populi contione.

Agamus itaque Christiani Domino Deo nostro gratias, non caelo et terrae, sicut iste disputat, sed ei qui fecit caelum et terram, qui has superstitiones, quas iste Balbus velut balbutiens vix reprehendit, per altissimam Christi humilitatem, per apostolorum praedicationem, per fidem martyrum pro veritate morientium et cum veritate viventium non solum in cordibus religiosis, verum etiam in aedibus superstitiosis libera suorum servitute subvertit.

---

[1] *Ibid.* 2.71 f.

who spent whole days in prayer and in making sacrifices in order that children of their own might survive them were called superstitious." [1]

Who could fail to understand that he, while showing respect for the customs of his city, was trying to praise the religion of his ancestors and wanted to disentangle it from superstition, but could find no way to do it? For if his ancestors called " superstitious " those who spent whole days in praying and sacrificing, were those also included who set up images of the gods (a thing he condemns), gods of different ages and differently dressed, with genealogies, marriages and family relationships? When he finds fault with these things as superstitious, he certainly casts aspersions on the ancestors who set up and worshipped such images. He makes himself also an accomplice, for although he tries with all his eloquence to extricate himself from their toils, he found it necessary to worship them. And the things which he, as a learned man, loudly proclaims in this treatise he would not dare to whisper in the popular assembly.

So let Christians give thanks to the Lord our God. He is not heaven, or earth, as Cicero argues, but the one who made heaven and earth. He has overthrown these superstitions, which Balbus (as if his name " Stammerer " were a true word) scarcely takes to task. He has overthrown them through the deep humility of Christ, through the preaching of the apostles and through the faith of the martyrs who died for the truth and live with Truth. He has overthrown them not only in the hearts of believers, but also in the temples of superstition, by the freely rendered service of his people.

XXXI

De opinionibus Varronis, qui reprobata persuasione
populari, licet ad notitiam veri Dei non pervenerit,
unum tamen deum colendum esse censuerit.

QUID ipse Varro, quem dolemus in rebus divinis
ludos scaenicos, quamvis non iudicio proprio, posuisee,
cum ad deos colendos multis locis velut religiosus
hortetur, nonne ita confitetur non se illa iudicio suo
sequi quae civitatem Romanam instituisse commemorat ut, si eam civitatem novam constitueret,
ex naturae potius formula deos nominaque eorum se
fuisse dedicaturum non dubitet confiteri? Sed iam
quoniam in vetere populo esset, acceptam ab antiquis
nominum et cognominum historiam tenere, ut tradita
est, debere se dicit, et ad eum finem illa scribere ac
perscrutari ut potius eos magis colere quam despicere
vulgus velit. Quibus verbis homo acutissimus satis
indicat non se aperire omnia, quae non sibi tantum
contemptui essent, sed etiam ipsi vulgo despicienda
viderentur, nisi tacerentur.

Ego ista conicere putari debui, nisi evidenter alio
loco ipse diceret de religionibus loquens multa esse
vera, quae non modo vulgo scire non sit utile, sed
etiam, tametsi falsa sunt, aliter existimare populum

XXXI

On the views of Varro, who rejected popular belief, and though he did not come to a knowledge of the true God, still thought only one god should be worshipped.

Now what are the views of Varro himself ? We regret that he put the stage shows in his " Divine Things," though that was not his own judgement. For although in many places he exhorts the people, as a religious man, to worship the gods, does he not reveal that it is not by his own judgement that he follows the institutions that the Roman state set up ? He does not hesitate to say frankly that, if he were founding that city anew, he would consecrate the gods and give them names according to the principles of nature, rather than as they are now. But as it is, since he is living in an old country, he says that he must keep the traditional account of the names and surnames, and that the object of his writing and research was to persuade people to worship rather than disregard them. By these words this first-rate mind makes it clear enough that he is not being frank on all points, points that were not only matters of contempt to himself, but that would also appear despicable even to the common people unless the subject was kept quiet.

This must have seemed merely my own conjecture, if he did not in another place, speaking of religious ceremonies, himself say plainly that there are many truths that it is best for the common people not to know, and what is more, many mistaken views are held which it is better for the people to take as true.

expediat, et ideo Graecos teletas ac mysteria taci-
turnitate parietibusque clausisse. Hic certe totum
consilium prodidit velut sapientium per quos civitates
et populi regerentur. Hac tamen fallacia miris
modis maligni daemones delectantur, qui et decep-
tores et deceptos pariter possident, a quorum dominatione non liberat nisi gratia Dei per Iesum Christum dominum nostrum.

Dicit etiam idem auctor acutissimus atque doctissimus quod hi soli ei videantur animadvertisse quid
esset Deus qui crediderunt eum esse animam motu
ac ratione mundum gubernantem, ac per hoc, etsi
nondum tenebat quod veritas habet (Deus enim verus
non anima, sed animae quoque est effector et conditor), tamen si contra praeiudicia consuetudinis liber
esse posset, unum deum colendum fateretur atque
suaderet, motu ac ratione mundum gubernantem, ut
ea cum illo de hac re quaestio remaneret, quod eum
diceret esse animam, non potius et animae creatorem.

Dicit etiam antiquos Romanos plus annos centum
et septuaginta deos sine simulacro coluisse. " Quod
si adhuc," inquit, " mansisset, castius dii observaren-
tur." Cui sententiae suae testem adhibet inter

---

[1] According to Varro's chronology, Rome was founded in
753 B.C. A date 170 years later would fall in the reign of
Tarquinius Priscus, the king who vowed the erection of the
temple to Jupiter on the Capitol, and summoned an artist
from Etruria to fashion the clay statue of the god (Livy
1.38.7; Pliny, *Natural History* 35.157; Wissowa, *RK*²,

This explains why the Greeks held their initiations and mysteries behind closed doors under pledge of secrecy. Here he undoubtedly discloses the whole strategy of the supposedly wise men by whom the cities and nations were to be ruled. But each deceit contributes marvellously to the joy of the malicious demons. The demons possess deceivers and deceived alike, and from their despotic control there is no escape except by the grace of God through Jesus Christ our Lord.

The same highly intelligent and learned writer says that in his opinion the only ones who have discovered what God really is are those who have adopted the view that he is the soul which governs the world by a movement that accords with reason. Hence, although he did not yet hold the exact truth (for the true God is not a soul, but the Maker and builder of soul as well), still, if he could have spoken freely against the prejudice of custom, he would have acknowledged, and taught others, that one god should be the object of our worship, who governs the world by a movement that accords with reason. Then on this point the only question left for discussion would be his statement that God is soul, rather than the Maker of soul.

He also says that for more than one hundred and seventy years the ancient Romans worshipped the gods without an image.[1] "If this usage had continued to our own day," he says, "our worship of the gods would be more devout." And in support of his opinion he adduces, among other things, the

38f.; see also L. R. Taylor in *Classical Studies in Honor of John C. Rolfe*, 305–314).

cetera etiam gentem Iudaeam; nec dubitat eum
locum ita concludere ut dicat qui primi simulacra
deorum populis posuerunt eos civitatibus suis et
metum dempsisse et errorem addidisse, prudenter
existimans deos facile posse in simulacrorum stoliditate contemni. Quod vero non ait " errorem tradiderunt," sed " addiderunt," iam utique fuisse etiam
sine simulacris vult intellegi errorem. Quapropter
cum solos dicit animadvertisse quid esset Deus qui
eum crederent animam mundum gubernantem,
castiusque existimat sine simulacris observari religionem, quis non videat quantum propinquaverit
veritati? Si enim aliquid contra vetustatem tanti
posset erroris, profecto et unum Deum, a quo mundum crederet gubernari, et sine simulacro colendum
esse censeret; atque in tam proximo inventus facile
fortasse de animae mutabilitate commoneretur ut
naturam potius incommutabilem, quae ipsam quoque
animam condidisset, Deum verum esse sentiret.

Haec cum ita sint, quaecumque tales viri in suis
litteris multorum deorum ludibria posuerunt, confiteri
ea potius occulta Dei voluntate compulsi sunt quam
persuadere conati. Si qua igitur a nobis inde testi-
monia proferuntur, ad eos redarguendos proferuntur
qui nolunt advertere de quanta et quam maligna
daemonum potestate nos liberet singulare sacrificium
tam sancti sanguinis fusi et donum spiritus impertiti.

testimony of the Jewish race. And he ends with
the forthright statement that those who first set up
images of the gods for the people diminished rever-
ence in their cities as they added to error, for he
wisely judged that gods in the shape of senseless
images might easily inspire contempt. And when
he says, not " handed down error," but " added to
error," he certainly wants it understood that there
had been error even without the images. Hence
when he says that only those who believe God to be
the soul which governs the world have discovered
that he really is, and when he thinks that worship is
more devout without images, who can fail to see how
near he comes to the truth? If he had had the
strength to resist so ancient an error, assuredly he
would have held that one God should be worshipped,
by whom the world is governed, and worshipped without an image. And being found so near the truth,
he might perhaps have yielded easily to correction
in regard to the mutability of the soul, so that he
would perceive that the true God is rather an un-
changing being, who also created the soul itself.

In view of all this we conclude that whenever
such men have included in their writings jests at the
expense of the many gods, they did so under compulsion of the hidden will of God to confess the truth,
rather than because of any intention to convince the
people. It follows that whatever testimonies we
bring forward from this source are intended to refute
those who will not see how great and how malign is
the demonic power from which we are freed by the
unique sacrifice of such holy blood shed for us, and
by the gift of the Spirit imparted to us.

XXXII

Ob quam speciem utilitatis principes gentium apud
subiectos sibi populos falsas religiones voluerunt
permanere.

DICIT etiam de generationibus deorum magis ad
poetas quam ad physicos fuisse populos inclinatos,
et ideo et sexum et generationes deorum maiores
suos, id est veteres credidisse Romanos et eorum
constituisse coniugia. Quod utique non aliam ob
causam factum videtur, nisi quia hominum velut
prudentium et sapientium negotium fuit populum in
religionibus fallere et in eo ipso non solum colere,
sed imitari etiam daemones, quibus maxima est fal-
lendi cupiditas. Sicut enim daemones nisi eos quos
fallendo deceperint possidere non possunt, sic et
homines principes, non sane iusti, sed daemonum
similes, ea quae vana esse noverant religionis nomine
populis tamquam vera suadebant, hoc modo eos civili
societati velut aptius alligantes, quo similiter subditos possiderent. Quis autem infirmus et indoctus
evaderet simul fallaces et principes civitatis et daemones?

XXXII

For what supposed advantage the rulers of the nations preferred false religions to continue among the peoples subject to them.

VARRO also states that the people were more inclined to follow the poets than the philosophers with regard to the genealogies of the gods, and hence his ancestors (that is, the early Romans) believed in the sex and parentage of the gods, and included marriages among them in their system. It certainly appears that this was done for no other reason except that men who posed as prudent and wise made it their business to deceive the people in matters of religion. In this they not only worship, but also imitate the demons, whose greatest desire is to deceive. For just as demons can only possess those whom they have treacherously deceived, so also the rulers—certainly not honest men, but men like the demons—taught the people as true in matters of religion what they knew to be false. In this way they bound them with tighter chains, as it were, to the civil society, in order that they might possess men similarly enthralled. Now what weak and untaught person could at the same time escape the deception of the rulers and that of the demons?

XXXIII

Quod iudicio et potestate Dei veri omnium regum
atque regnorum ordinata sint tempora.

DEUS igitur ille felicitatis auctor et dator, quia
solus est verus Deus, ipse dat regna terrena et bonis
et malis, neque hoc temere et quasi fortuito, quia
Deus est, non fortuna, sed pro rerum ordine ac
temporum occulto nobis, notissimo sibi; cui tamen
ordini temporum non subditus servit, sed eum ipse
tamquam dominus regit moderatorque disponit;
felicitatem vero non dat nisi bonis. Hanc enim
possunt et non habere et habere servientes, possunt
et non habere et habere regnantes; quae tamen
plena in ea vita erit ubi nemo iam serviet. Et ideo
regna terrena et bonis ab illo dantur et malis ne eius
cultores adhuc in provectu animi parvuli haec ab eo
munera quasi magnum aliquid concupiscant.

Et hoc est sacramentum veteris testamenti, ubi
occultum erat novum, quod illic promissa et dona
terrena sunt, intelligentibus et tunc spiritalibus,
quamvis nondum in manifestatione praedicantibus,
et quae illis temporalibus rebus significaretur aeter-
nitas, et in quibus Dei donis esset vera felicitas.

XXXIII

*By the counsel and power of the true God the times
of all kings and kingdoms have been ordained.*

God, therefore, the author and giver of happiness,
because he is the only true God, himself gives earthly
kingdoms to the good and the bad. This is not done
rashly or at random, for he is God, not Fortuna, the
goddess of luck. He does this in accordance with an
order of things and of times which is hidden from us
but very well known to him. Yet he is not in subjection, to be a slave to this order, but he rules it as
Lord, and dispenses it as Master. But as for happiness, he gives it only to the good. Those who are
servants may gain it or fail to gain it, just as those
who are rulers may gain it or fail to gain it, but it
will be complete only in that life where no one will
any longer be a servant. And so earthly kingdoms
are granted by him both to the good and to the evil,
in order that his worshippers, who are still as little
children in the growth of their minds, may not covet
these gifts from him as if they were something great.

And this is the mystery of the Old Testament, in
which the New was hidden. There the promised
gifts are earthly blessings, but even then spiritual
men understood, though they did not yet plainly
declare, both the eternity which was signified by
those temporal things, and the gifts of God in which
true happiness resides.

SAINT AUGUSTINE

XXXIV

De regno Iudaeorum, quod ab uno et vero Deo
institutum atque servatum est, donec in vera
religione manserunt.

ITAQUE ut cognosceretur etiam illa terrena bona,
quibus solis inhiant qui meliora cogitare non possunt,
in ipsius unius Dei esse posita potestate, non in
multorum falsorum, quos colendos Romani antea
crediderunt, populum suum in Aegypto de paucissimis multiplicavit et inde signis mirabilibus liberavit.
Nec Lucinam mulieres illae invocaverunt, quando
earum partus, ut miris modis multiplicarentur et
gens illa incredibiliter cresceret, ab Aegyptiorum
persequentium et infantes omnes necare volentium
manibus ipse servavit. Sine dea Rumina suxerunt,
sine Cunina in cunis fuerunt, sine Educa et Potina
escam potumque sumpserunt, sine tot diis puerilibus
educati sunt, sine diis coniugalibus coniugati, sine
cultu Priapi coniugibus mixti; sine invocatione
Neptuni mare transeuntibus divisum patuit et sequentes eorum inimicos fluctibus in se redeuntibus
obruit. Nec consecraverunt aliquam deam Man-
niam, quando de caelo manna sumpserunt; nec
quando sitientibus aquam percussa petra profudit,
Nymphas Lymphasque coluerunt. Sine insanis sacris Martis et Bellonae bella gesserunt, et sine victoria

XXXIV

*On the kingdom of the Jews, which was set up by the
one true God, and preserved as long as they
remained firm in the true religion.*

ACCORDINGLY in order to teach the lesson that even
those earthly goods—the only objects greedily sought
by those who can imagine nothing better—rest in
the power of the one God himself, not in that of the
many false gods whom the Romans formerly believed
they should worship, he multiplied his people in
Egypt, beginning with a very few, and freed them
from Egypt by miraculous signs. Nor did those
women call upon Lucina when the Egyptian perse-
cutors had made a decision to slay all their babies.
To save their new-born children and ensure the
marvellous multiplication and unbelievable increase
of the race, God himself intervened. They were fed
at the breast without Rumina, were in cradles without Cunina, took food and drink without Educa and
Potina, were brought up without any of the gods of
childhood, married without the gods of marriage and
had intercourse without worshipping Priapus. With
no invocation of Neptune the sea was divided and
gave passage as they crossed, then overwhelmed their
pursuing foes when the waves returned to their place.
Nor did they consecrate any goddess Mannia when
they lived on the manna from heaven; when the
rock was struck and poured forth water for the thirsty
they did not worship the Nymphs and the Lymphs.
Without the mad rites of Mars and Bellona they
waged wars. While they did not conquer without

quidem non vicerunt, non eam tamen deam, sed Dei sui munus habuerunt. Sine Segetia segetes sine Bubona boves, mella sine Mellona poma sine Pomona, et prorsus omnia, pro quibus tantae falsorum deorum turbae Romani supplicandum putarunt, ab uno vero Deo multo felicius acceperunt.

Et si non in eum peccassent, impia curiositate tamquam magicis artibus seducti ad alienos deos et ad idola defluendo, et postremo Christum occidendo, in eodem regno etsi non spatiosiore, tamen feliciore mansissent. Et nunc quod per omnes fere terras gentesque dispersi sunt, illius unius veri Dei providentia est, ut, quod deorum falsorum usquequaque simulacra arae, luci templa evertuntur et sacrificia prohibentur, de codicibus eorum probetur quem ad modum hoc fuerit tanto ante prophetatum; ne forte, cum legeretur in nostris, a nobis putaretur esse confictum.

Iam quod sequitur in volumine sequenti videndum est, et hic dandus huius prolixitati modus.

victory, yet they regarded victory not as a goddess, but as the gift of their God. Their crops that they had without Segetia, their oxen without Bubona, honey without Mellona, fruits without Pomona, in short, absolutely all the blessings for which the Romans thought they must pray to the vast throng of false gods, these they received much more happily from the one true God.

And if they had not sinned against him, led astray by unholy curiosity as by some magic arts, falling away to worship idols and finally murdering the Christ, they would have remained in the same kingdom, and if it did not grow in size, it would have grown in happiness. As for their present dispersion through almost all the lands and peoples, it is by the providence of the true God, to the end that when the images, altars, groves and temples of the false gods are everywhere overthrown, and the sacrifices forbidden, it may be demonstrated by the Jewish scriptures how this was prophesied long ago. Thus the possibility is avoided that, if read only in our books, the prophecy might be taken for our invention.

Now for more on this subject my readers must turn to the next book, for a limit must be set to the undue length of this one.

BOOK V

LIBER V

PRAEFATIO

Quoniam constat omnium rerum optandarum plenitudinem esse felicitatem, quae non est dea, sed donum Dei, et ideo nullum deum colendum esse ab hominibus, nisi qui potest eos facere felices (unde si illa dea esset, sola colenda merito diceretur), iam consequenter videamus, qua causa Deus, qui potest et illa bona dare quae habere possunt etiam non boni ac per hoc etiam non felices, Romanum imperium tam magnum tamque diuturnum esse voluerit. Quia enim hoc deorum falsorum illa quam colebant multitudo non fecit, et multa iam diximus et ubi visum fuerit opportunum esse dicemus.

I

Causam Romani imperii omniumque regnorum nec fortuitam esse nec in stellarum positione consistere.

Causa ergo magnitudinis imperii Romani nec fortuita est nec fatalis secundum eorum sententiam sive opinionem qui ea dicunt esse fortuita quae vel nullas

BOOK V

PREFACE

It is evident that happiness is the sum total of all desirable things. It is not a goddess, but the gift of God. And no god should be worshipped by men except him who is able to make them happy, hence if happiness, or Felicitas, were a goddess, it could be affirmed that she alone might properly be worshipped. Now therefore let us see for what reason God willed that the Roman empire should be so great and so lasting—God who can also grant such goods as even those men who are evil, and hence unhappy, can possess. For we have already argued at length that the great number of false gods which they used to worship did not do this, and we shall argue further when it seems proper.

I

The existence of the Roman empire and of all kingdoms is not a matter of chance nor of the position of the stars.

The cause, then, of the greatness of the Roman empire is neither chance nor fate, as these words are employed whether by the judgement, or by mere opinion of those who say that things happen by chance

causas habent vel non ex aliquo rationabili ordine
venientes, et ea fatalia quae praeter Dei et hominum
voluntatem cuiusdam ordinis necessitate contingunt.
Prorsus divina providentia regna constituuntur humana. Quae si propterea quisquam fato tribuit,
quia ipsam Dei voluntatem vel potestatem fati
nomine appellat, sententiam teneat, linguam corrigat.
Cur enim non hoc primum dicit, quod postea dicturus
est, cum ab illo quisquam quaesierit quid dixerit
fatum? Nam id homines quando audiunt, usitata
loquendi consuetudine non intellegunt nisi vim
positionis siderum, qualis est quando quis nascitur
sive concipitur; quod aliqui alienant a Dei voluntate,
aliqui ex illa etiam hoc pendere confirmant.

Sed illi, qui sine Dei voluntate decernere opinantur
sidera quid agamus vel quid bonorum habeamus
malorumve patiamur, ab auribus omnium repellendi
sunt, non solum eorum qui veram religionem tenent
sed et qui deorum qualiumcumque, licet falsorum,
volunt esse cultores. Haec enim opinio quid agit
aliud, nisi ut nullus omnino colatur aut rogetur deus?
Contra quos modo nobis disputatio non est instituta,
sed contra hos qui pro defensione eorum quos deos
putant Christianae religioni adversantur.

Illi vero qui positionem stellarum quodam modo
decernentium qualis quisque sit et quid ei proveniat

---

[1] Astrology, or divination from observing heavenly bodies,
was practised from early times in Babylonia, and became
popular in the Greek-speaking world from the time of Alexander. A blend of science and religion, it came to exercise,
as Cumont says (*Oriental Religions in Roman Paganism*, 162),

when they have no causes, or no cause derived
from a rational pattern, and that things happen by
fate when they happen not by the will of God or of
men, but by the compulsion of a certain pattern.
Without any doubt, it is by divine providence that
human kingdoms are set up. If any one ascribes
them to " fate " because he uses that term for the
will or power of God, let him maintain his conviction
but correct his language. Why does he not say at the
start what he will say later when someone asks him
what he means by " fate " ? For when men hear
this word, ordinary usage leads them to think of
nothing but the influence of the position of the stars
at the moment when a child is born, or conceived.
Some make this independent of the will of God,
while others maintain that it depends upon his will.[1]

Those, however, who believe that the stars, apart
from the will of God, determine what we do, what
goods we have, or what evils we suffer, must be
thrown out of court, not only by adherents of the
true religion, but also by those who choose to worship
gods of any sort, false gods though they be. For
what is the effect of this belief except to persuade
men not to worship or pray to any god at all ? Our
present argument is not directed against the supporters of this view, but against those who, in defence
of those beings that they think are gods, make war
on the Christian religion.

But as for those who make the position of the stars
depend upon the will of God, while the stars somehow

absolute authority in the Roman empire. Augustine himself
had once believed in it and studied it. Later he was much
occupied with the task of refuting it (*Confessions* 4.3.4; 7.6.8).

boni quidve mali accidat ex Dei voluntate suspendunt, si easdem stellas putant habere hanc potestatem traditam sibi a summa illius potestate ut volentes ista decernant, magnam caelo faciunt iniuriam, in cuius velut clarissimo senatu ac splendidissima curia opinantur scelera facienda decerni, qualia si aliqua terrena civitas decrevisset, genere humano decernente fuerat evertenda. Quale deinde iudicium de hominum factis Deo relinquitur, quibus caelestis necessitas adhibetur, cum dominus ille sit et siderum et hominum? Aut si non dicunt stellas, accepta quidem potestate a summo Deo, arbitrio suo ista decernere, sed in talibus necessitatibus ingerendis illius omnino iussa complere, itane de ipso Deo sentiendum est quod indignissimum visum est de stellarum voluntate sentire?

Quod si dicuntur stellae significare potius ista quam facere, ut quasi locutio quaedam sit illa positio praedicens futura, non agens (non enim mediocriter doctorum hominum fuit ista sententia), non quidem ita solent loqui mathematici, ut verbi gratia dicant: " Mars ita positus homicidam significat," sed: " homicidam facit"; verumtamen ut concedamus non eos ut debent loqui et a philosophis accipere oportere sermonis regulam ad ea praenuntianda quae in siderum positione reperire se putant, quid fit quod nihil umquam dicere potuerunt cur in vita gemino-

decree what sort of man each shall be, what good shall come his way, and what evil shall befall him, they do a great wrong to heaven if they hold that the sovereign power of God has handed over to the aforesaid stars the power of making these decrees of their own choice. For they suppose that it is resolved in heaven, as in some exalted senate met in its refulgent senate-house, that crimes are to be committed, such crimes that if any earthly state had decreed them, all mankind would properly have decreed its destruction. Moreover, how is any room left for God to pass judgement on the deeds of men, if they are subject to astrological forces, and God is Lord both of stars and men? Or they may say that the stars have received their power from the supreme God, and do not make their decrees of their own will, but simply obey his commands in imposing compulsion upon men. Are we then to adopt a view of God himself that it seemed highly improper to adopt in regard to the will of the stars?

But sometimes it may be said that the stars portend, but do not cause those deeds, so that their position, which foretells the future, is a kind of communication, not an active force. This view has been held by men of no ordinary learning. But the astrologers are not in the habit of saying, for instance: " Mars in this position portends a murderer," but " makes a murderer." However, let us grant that they do not use the proper terms, and that they ought to take from the philosophers the correct way of stating the facts that they think they find noted in the position of the stars. How is it that they have never been able to explain why there is such diversity

rum, in actionibus, in eventis, in professionibus, artibus, honoribus ceterisque rebus ad humanam vitam
pertinentibus atque in ipsa morte sit plerumque tanta
diversitas ut similiores eis sint, quantum ad haec
adtinet, multi extranei quam ipsi inter se gemini
perexiguo temporis intervallo in nascendo separati,
in conceptu autem per unum concubitum uno etiam
momento seminati?

II

De geminorum simili dissimilique valetudine.

CICERO dicit Hippocratem, nobilissimum medicum,
scriptum reliquisse quosdam fratres, cum simul
aegrotare coepissent et eorum morbus eodem tempore ingravesceret, eodem levaretur, geminos suspi-
catum; quos Posidonius Stoicus, multum astrologiae
deditus, eadem constitutione astrorum natos eademque conceptos solebat asserere. Ita quod medicus
pertinere credebat ad simillimam temperiem valetu-

---

[1] The account of this incident is not found in the extant
works of Cicero, but may have been in his *De Fato,* which is
imperfectly preserved. The incident of the next chapter may
also be from the same source, as is maintained by S. Angus,
The Sources of the First Ten Books of Augustine's City of God,
21 f.

[2] Cumont (*Oriental Religions,* 164) says of Posidonius:
" The scholar whose authority contributed most to the final
acceptance of sidereal divination was a Syrian philosopher of
encyclopedic knowledge, Posidonius of Apamea, the teacher of
Cicero." Posidonius studied at Athens under the Stoic
Panaetius before 109 B.C., travelled widely, and settled in
Rhodes to become the most renowned Stoic teacher of his age.

in the life of twins: in their actions, their fortunes, their professions, their trades, their honours and in all the other things pertaining to human life and even in their death? It commonly happens that in these respects the twins resemble many strangers more than they resemble each other. And yet in birth they were separated by a very brief interval of time, and in conception they were begotten at one moment, by one act of intercourse.

II

Similarity and dissimilarity in the health of twins.

CICERO says that Hippocrates, the renowned physician, has left a record of two brothers who fell sick together.[1] Their disease grew worse at the same time, then better, hence he suspected that they were twins. Posidonius the Stoic,[2] who was much interested in astrology, used to assert that this happened because they were born, and were conceived, under the same constellation. Thus what the physician thought was due to a similar physical constitution,

Like the earlier Stoics he was a defender of divination and he wrote five books on the subject. Cicero says that all the Stoics except Panaetius accepted astrology, thus confirming what is here said of Posidonius. See Cicero, *De divinatione*, 1.6 and 2.87, pp. 229, 471 in the Loeb edition. Stoics and astrologers had similar views on fate, the unity of the world, and the " sympathy " between its parts. The doctrine of sympathy is supposed to have been given a scientific basis by Posidonius' discovery, on a visit to the Atlantic at Cadiz, of the connection between the tides and the phases of the moon. The fragments of Posidonius are meagre, with very little on astrology except what is said here.

dinis, hoc philosophus astrologus ad vim constitu-
tionemque siderum quae fuerat quo tempore concepti
natique sunt. In hac causa multo est acceptabilior
et de proximo credibilior coniectura medicinalis,
quoniam parentes ut erant corpore adfecti, dum con-
cumberent, ita primordia conceptorum adfici potuerunt ut consecutis ex materno corpore prioribus
incrementis paris valetudinis nascerentur; deinde in
una domo esidem alimentis nutriti, ubi aerem et loci
positionem et vim aquarum plurimum valere ad
corpus vel bene vel male accipiendum medicina testatur, eisdem etiam exercitationibus adsuefacti tam
similia corpora gererent ut etiam ad aegrotandum
uno tempore eisdemque causis similiter moverentur.
Constitutionem vero caeli ac siderum quae fuit
quando concepti sive nati sunt, velle trahere ad istam
aegrotandi parilitatem, cum tam multa diversissimi
generis diversissimorum effectuum et eventorum
eodem tempore in unius regionis terra eidem caelo
subdita potuerint concipi et nasci, nescio cuius sit
insolentiae.

Nos autem novimus geminos non solum actus et
peregrinationes habere diversas, verum etiam dispares aegritudines perpeti. De qua re facillimam,
quantum mihi videtur, rationem redderet Hippocrates, diversis alimentis et exercitationibus, quae
non de corporis temperatione, sed de animi voluntate
veniunt, dissimiles eis accidere potuisse valetudines.

the philosopher-astrologer ascribed to the influence and position of the stars at the time when they were conceived and born. In this case the conclusion of the doctor is much more acceptable, and obviously more credible. For the bodily condition of the parents at the time of copulation could affect the germ cells of the children conceived, so that after the first period of growth in the mother's body they would be born with the same constitution. Thereafter they were nourished on the same food and lived in one home, and in such a case medical science declares that the weather, climate and water supply have much to do with the good or bad predisposition of the body. Accustomed also to the same kinds of exercise, the twins were physically so similar that the same causes sufficed even to bring about the same diseases at the same time. But arbitrarily to drag in the position of the sky and the stars at the time of conception or birth in order to explain the simultaneous sickness, when so many individuals of different races, whose activities and fortunes differed so widely, could have been conceived and born at the same time in one quarter of the earth under one aspect of the celestial sphere, this is a strange piece of arrogance.

Moreover, we have known twins who not only had different occupations and travelled to different places, but also suffered different kinds of sickness. A very easy explanation of this fact, it seems to me, would be given by Hippocrates. He would say that because of differences of food and exercise (matters depending not on bodily constitution, but on the mind's free choice) they might very well experience

Porro autem Posidonius vel quilibet fatalium siderum
assertor mirum si potest hic invenire quid dicat, si
nolit imperitorum mentibus in eis quas nesciunt
rebus inludere. Quod enim conantur efficere de
intervallo exiguo temporis, quod inter se gemini
dum nascerentur habuerunt, propter caeli particulam
ubi ponitur horae notatio quem horoscopum vocant,
aut non tantum valet quanta invenitur in geminorum voluntatibus actibus moribus casibusque
diversitas, aut plus etiam valet quam est geminorum
vel humilitas generis eadem vel nobilitas, cuius
maximam diversitatem non nisi in hora qua quisque
nascitur ponunt. Ac per hoc si tam celeriter alter
post alterum nascitur ut eadem pars horoscopi
maneat, paria cuncta quaero quae in nullis possunt
geminis inveniri; si autem sequentis tarditas horoscopum mutat, parentes diversos quaero, quos gemini
habere non possunt.

III

*De argumento, quod ex rota figuli Nigidius mathe-
maticus adsumpsit in quaestione geminorum.*

Frustra itaque adfertur nobile illud commentum
de figuli rota quod respondisse ferunt Nigidium hac

---

[1] Publius Nigidius Figulus was a friend and adviser of
Cicero who became praetor in 58 B.C. After the defeat of the
senatorial party in the war with Caesar he lived in exile until
his death in 45. He was famous chiefly for his learning, in
which he was rated second only to Varro. He revived the
Pythagorean school of philosophy, combining it with Etruscan
and Oriental beliefs, including astrology. See Kroll in *RE*, 17,
200–212. Kroll rejects the explanation here given for the

different states of health. But if we ask Posidonius or any other advocate of the fatal influence of
the stars, I should be surprised if he could find anything to say, unless he should choose to dazzle the
minds of the ignorant in matters of which they know
nothing, by some illusion. They try to make a point
of the small interval of time that separates the birth
of twins, because of the minute division of the sky
where the notation of the hour is placed which they
call a " horoscope." But either this is too small to
explain the diversity in will, acts, character and good
or bad luck of twins, or else it is too great to allow
for the identity of low or high estate in the case of
twins. For they account for the greatest differences
of this sort solely by considering the hour of birth.
Hence, if one twin is born so soon after the other that
the horoscope remains the same for each, I demand
that everything in their lives should be the same—
but such twins can never be found. But if the delayed delivery of the second child changes the horoscope, I demand that they should have different
parents, which twins cannot have.

III

*Of the argument to meet the problem of twins that
Nigidius the astrologer derived from the
potter's wheel.*[1]

It is therefore a futile argument that is offered in
the well-known story of the potter's wheel. Nigi-

surname Figulus. The story is preserved only by Augustine,
who found it, perhaps, in Cicero.

quaestione turbatum, unde et Figulus appellatus est.
Dum enim rotam figuli vi quanta potuit intorsisset,
currente illa bis numero de atramento tamquam uno
eius loco summa celeritate percussit; deinde inventa
sunt signa quae fixerat, desistente motu, non parvo
intervallo in rotae illius extremitate distantia.
" Sic," inquit, " in tanta rapacitate caeli, etiamsi
alter post alterum tanta celeritate nascatur quanta
rotam bis ipse percussi, in caeli spatio plurimum est.
Hinc sunt," inquit, " quaecumque dissimillima perhibentur in moribus casibusque geminorum."

Hoc figmentum fragilius est quam vasa quae illa
rotatione finguntur. Nam si tam multum in caelo
interest quod constellationibus conprehendi non
potest ut alteri geminorum hereditas obveniat, alteri
non obveniat, cur audent ceteris qui gemini non
sunt, cum inspexerint eorum constellationes, talia
pronuntiare quae ad illud secretum pertinent quod
nemo potest conprehendere et momentis adnotare
nascentium? Si autem propterea talia dicunt in
aliorum genituris, quia haec ad productiora spatia
temporum pertinent; momenta vero illa partium
minutarum quae inter se gemini possunt habere
nascentes rebus minimis tribuuntur de qualibus
mathematici non solent consuli (quis enim consulat
quando sedeat, quando deambulet, quando vel quid
prandeat?), numquid ista dicimus quando in moribus

dius, it is said, when vexed by this question of twins, used the argument in reply, and from it derived his surname of Figulus, or "Potter." He whirled a potter's wheel with all the force he could, and while it was turning he quickly touched it twice with black ink, supposedly in one place. Then, when the motion stopped, the marks he had made were found to be some distance apart on the edge of the wheel. "Thus," he says, "given the velocity of the heavenly sphere, even if the second twin were born as quickly after the first as I made my second mark when I touched the wheel, in the broad expanse of heaven it makes a very great difference. Hence arise all the differences that are reported to occur in the character and fortunes of twins."

The product of his fiction is more fragile than the fictile vases that are fashioned on that rotating wheel. For if a difference in heaven which cannot be measured in the constellations is so important that an inheritance falls to one of the twins and not to the other, how do they dare to deliver to others who are not twins, after observing the position of their stars, statements that depend on a secret that no one can comprehend and set down for the moment of birth? But they may say that such statements are possible in dealing with the horoscopes of those who are not twins because they are based on longer intervals of time, whereas the effects of such minute intervals as may separate the birth of twins affect very small matters about which astrologers are not usually consulted. For who would consult them about when to sit down, when to take a walk, when to eat, or what to eat? But is it really the same thing when we

operibus casibusque geminorum plurima plurimum-
que diversa monstramus?

IV

De Esau et Iacob geminis multum inter se morum
et actionum qualitate disparibus.

Nati sunt duo gemini antiqua patrum memoria (ut
de insignibus loquar) sic alter post alterum ut posterior plantam prioris teneret. Tanta in eorum vita
fuerunt moribusque diversa, tanta in actibus dis-
parilitas, tanta in parentum amore dissimilitudo ut
etiam inimicos eos inter se faceret ipsa distantia.
Numquid hoc dicitur quia uno ambulante alius sede-
bat, et alio dormiente alius vigilabat, et alio loquente
tacebat alius; quae pertinent ad illas minutias quae
non possunt ab eis conprehendi qui constitutionem
siderum qua quisque nascitur scribunt, unde mathematici consulantur? Unus duxit mercennariam servitutem, alius non servivit; unus a matre diligebatur,
alius non diligebatur; unus honorem qui magnus
apud eos habebatur amisit, alter indeptus est.
Quid de uxoribus, quid de filiis, quid de rebus, quanta
diversitas! Si ergo haec ad illas pertinent minutias
temporum quae inter se habent gemini et constellationibus non adscribuntur, quare aliorum constellationibus inspectis ista dicuntur? Si autem ideo di-

---

[1] Genesis 25.26.

point out that there are very many very great differences in the characters, activities and destinies of twins?

IV

Of the twins Esau and Jacob, who were very different in character and actions.

To mention a notable case, according to the ancient record of our fathers twin brothers were born so close together that the second was grasping the heel of the first.[1] So great was the diversity in their lives and characters, so great the contrast in their behaviour, so great the unlikeness in the love shown them by their parents, that the difference in itself made them enemies of each other. Does this imply that while one was walking the other would be seated, or that one would be sleeping while the other was awake, or one speaking while the other was silent? Such things belong to the minute details that cannot be grasped by those who record the position of the stars under which each man is born, in order that astrologers may be consulted about them. One of the twins was a hired servant, the other was not; one was loved by his mother, the other was not; one lost the birthright, which people then held in great esteem, and the other obtained it. And what shall I say of their wives, their children and their property? How great was the difference! If these things depend on the brief interval between the birth of twins and are not recorded in horoscopes, why do they mention the same sort of thing when examining the horoscopes of others? But if they

cuntur, quia non ad minuta inconprehensibilia, sed ad temporum spatia pertinent quae observari notarique possunt, quid hic agit rota illa figuli nisi ut homines luteum cor habentes in gyrum mittantur ne mathematicorum vaniloquia convincantur?

V

Quibus modis convincantur mathematici vanam scientiam profiteri.

QUID idem ipsi quorum morbum, quod eodem tempore gravior leviorque apparebat amborum, medicinaliter inspiciens Hippocrates geminos suspicatus est, nonne satis istos redarguunt qui volunt sideribus dare quod de corporum simili temperatione veniebat? Cur enim similiter eodemque tempore, non alter prior, alter posterior aegrotabant sicut nati fuerant, quia utique simul nasci ambo non poterant? Aut si nihil momenti adtulit ut diversis temporibus aegrotarent quod diversis temporibus nati sunt, quare tempus in nascendo diversum ad aliarum rerum diversitates valere contendunt? Cur potuerunt diversis temporibus peregrinari, diversis temporibus ducere uxores, diversis temporibus filios procreare et multa alia propterea quia diversis temporibus nati sunt, et non potuerunt eadem causa diversis etiam temporibus aegrotare? Si enim dispar nascendi mora mutavit horoscopum et disparilitatem intulit ceteris rebus, cur illud in aegritudinibus mansit quod habebat in

mention them because they belong, not to moments too brief to be caught, but to periods of time that can be observed and recorded, then what is the purpose of that potter's wheel? Is it that men with hearts of clay may be set spinning, to ensure that the astrologers shall not be convicted of talking nonsense?

V

How the astrologers are convicted of professing a false science.

Now what of those two whose sickness was observed to grow worse, then better, at the same time, a medical observation from which Hippocrates suspected that they were twins? Does not this case sufficiently refute those who would ascribe to the stars what really came from a similar bodily constitution? For why should they grow ill in the same way at the same time, and not first one, then the other, according to the order of their birth, since of course they could not both be born at once? If their being born at different times did not result in sickness at different times, why do they contend that the different time of birth is the cause of difference in other matters? How is it that they could travel at different times, marry, beget children and do much besides at different times, all because they were born at different times, but could not for the same reason grow ill at different times? For if the brief delay in time of birth changed the horoscope and caused a difference in everything else, why did the sameness which resulted from being conceived at one time persist

temporis aequalitate conceptus? Aut si fata valetudinis in conceptu sunt, aliarum vero rerum in ortu
esse dicuntur, non deberent inspectis natalium constellationibus de valetudine aliquid dicere, quando
eis inspicienda conceptionalis hora non datur. Si
autem ideo praenuntiant aegritudines non inspecto
conceptionis horoscopo quia indicant eas momenta
nascentium, quo modo dicerent cuilibet eorum geminorum ex nativitatis hora quando aegrotaturus esset,
cum et alter, qui non habebat eandem horam nativitatis, necesse haberet pariter aegrotare?

Deinde quaero: si tanta distantia est temporis in
nativitate geminorum ut per hanc oporteat eis constellationes fieri diversas propter diversum horoscopum et ob hoc diversos omnes cardines ubi tanta
vis ponitur ut hinc etiam diversa sint fata, unde hoc
accidere potuit, cum eorum conceptus diversum tempus habere non possit? Aut si duorum uno momento
temporis conceptorum potuerunt esse ad nascendum
fata disparia, cur non et duorum uno momento temporis natorum possint esse ad vivendum atque morien-
dum fata disparia? Nam si unum momentum, quo
ambo concepti sunt, non impedivit ut alter prior,
alter posterior nasceretur, cur, uno momento si duo
nascantur, impedit aliquid ut alter prior, alter pos-

---

[1] The four cardinal points (*cardines*) were determined for
a given moment and for a given point of observation: the
ortus or *horoscopus* at the eastern horizon, the *occasus* in the
west, the *medium caelum* overhead, and the *imum caelum* under

only so far as periods of illness were concerned? Or if matters of health depend on the moment of conception, while other matters are said to depend on that of birth, they ought not to make a statement about health based on inspection of the horoscope of birth as they do, for the hour of conception is not given them for inspection. But if they foretell periods of illness without inspecting the horoscope of conception, saying that they are indicated by the moment of birth, how could they tell either of the twins, by considering his hour of birth, when he was going to be sick, seeing that the other also, who did not have the same hour of birth, of necessity had to be sick at the same time?

Now, another question. They say that there is such difference in the time of birth of twins that as a result the aspect of the planets becomes different for them, the horoscopes are different, and hence also all the cardinal points,[1] to which is ascribed such power as to determine differences of destiny. But how could this happen, when it was impossible for them to have different moments of conception? Or if two persons conceived at the same instant of time could have different destinies governing their birth, why could not two born at the same instant also have different destinies governing life and death? The single instant in which both were conceived did not prevent one being born earlier, the other later. Why, then, if two are born at one moment, does anything prevent one dying earlier, the other later? If

foot; a moment later all four would change their positions among the fixed stars. See Manilius, *Astronomicon* 2, 808–55, and Housman's introduction (vol. II², 1937, pp. xxvi–xxviii).

terior moriatur? Si conceptio momenti unius diversos casus in utero geminos habere permittit, cur
nativitas momenti unius non etiam quoslibet duos in
terra diversos casus habere permittat, ac sic omnis
huius artis vel potius vanitatis commenta tollantur?
Quid est hoc, cur uno tempore, momento uno, sub
una eademque caeli positione concepti diversa habent
fata quae illos perducant ad diversarum horarum
nativitatem, et uno momento temporis sub una
eademque caeli positione de duabus matribus duo
pariter nati diversa fata habere non possint, quae
illos perducant ad diversam vivendi vel moriendi
necessitatem?

An concepti nondum habent fata, quae nisi nascantur habere non poterunt? Quid est ergo quod
dicunt, si hora conceptionalis inveniatur, multa ab
istis dici posse divinius? Unde etiam illud a nonnullis praedicatur, quod quidam sapiens horam elegit
qua cum uxore concumberet unde filium mirabilem
gigneret. Unde postremo et hoc est, quod de illis
pariter aegrotantibus geminis Posidonius magnus
astrologus idemque philosophus respondebat, ideo
fieri quod eodem tempore fuissent nati eodemque
concepti. Nam utique propter hoc addebat concep-
tionem, ne diceretur ei non ad liquidum eodem
tempore potuisse nasci, quos constabat omnino
eodem tempore fuisse conceptos; ut hoc, quod similiter simulque aegrotabant, non daret de proximo

conception at the same instant still allows twins to have different fortunes in the womb, why does birth at the same instant not allow any two persons on earth to have different fortunes? And that would sweep away all the lies of this science, or rather, of this folly. Why is it that persons conceived at one time, in a single moment, under one and the same aspect of the heavens, have different destinies, which bring them to birth at different hours, and yet two persons similarly born at the same instant under one and the same aspect of the heavens from two mothers cannot have different destinies which conduct them to different fates of life and death?

Or do they not yet have destinies when conceived? Will they not be able to have them unless they are born? Then what do they mean by saying that if the hour of conception could be discovered, they could make statements with better divination? Thus some give currency to the well-known story about the wise man who selected the hour to lie with his wife, in order that he might thereby beget an extraordinary son. And finally, from this same notion comes the reply that Posidonius, the great astrologer and also philosopher, made about the twins who fell ill together. He said that this happened because they were born and were conceived at the same time. Assuredly he included conception in his statement lest someone should point out that it was not clear that they could have been born at the same instant,—though it was quite certain that they had been conceived at the same instant,—in order that he might ascribe their suffering similar ailments at the same time, not to the obvious cause of similar

pari corporis temperamento, sed eandem quoque
valetudinis parilitatem sidereis nexibus alligaret.
Si igitur in conceptu tanta vis est ad aequalitatem
fatorum, non debuerunt nascendo eadem fata mutari.
Aut si propterea mutantur fata geminorum quia
temporibus diversis nascuntur, cur non potius intellegamus iam fuisse mutata ut diversis temporibus
nascerentur? Itane non mutat fata nativitatis
voluntas viventium cum mutet fata conceptionis ordo
nascentium?

VI

De geminis disparis sexus.

Quamquam et in ipsis geminorum conceptibus, ubi
certe amborum eadem momenta sunt temporum,
unde fit ut sub eadem constellatione fatali alter
concipiatur masculus, altera femina? Novimus geminos diversi sexus, ambo adhuc vivunt, ambo aetate
adhuc vigent; quorum cum sint inter se similes corporum species quantum in diverso sexu potest,
instituto tamen et proposito vitae ita sunt dispares
ut praeter actus, quos necesse est a virilibus distare
femineos (quod ille in officio comitis militat et a sua
domo paene semper peregrinatur, illa de solo patrio
et de rure proprio non recedit), insuper (quod est

---

[1] The count of Africa was a military commander, entrusted
with the defence of Africa. His duties, however, were not
limited to military affairs: imperial legislation was often
addressed to him, he might be active in suppressing paganism
(see *City of God* 18.54, LCL Vol. 6, 91), or one of his officials
might arrest a tenant involved in trouble with the proprietor

bodily constitution, but might also make the similarity of their health dependent on the influence of the stars. Then if conception has such power to cause equality of destinies, these destinies should not have been altered by birth. Or, if the destinies of twins are changed because they are born at different times, why should we not rather take it that they were already changed to permit them to be born at different times? Is it possible that the will of living persons does not change the destinies fixed at birth, while the order of birth does change the destinies fixed at conception?

VI

On twins of opposite sex.

But in the case of the conception of twins, where both are certainly conceived at the same moment, how does it happen that under the same fatal position of the stars one is conceived a male, the other a female? I know twins of different sex, both of whom are still living, and still of an age to be active. Although their physical appearance is similar, as far as it can be in opposite sexes, they are nevertheless entirely unlike in plan and purpose of life. In their occupations, of course, there must be a difference between the man's and the woman's. He serves on the staff of a count [1] and is almost always away from his home, while she does not leave her native soil or her own country residence. Besides this there is

(Augustine, *Letter* 115). The verb *militare* is used of civil service as well as military service.

incredibilius, si astralia fata credantur; non autem
mirum, si voluntates hominum et Dei munera cogi-
tentur) ille coniugatus, illa virgo sacra est; ille
numerosam prolem genuit, illa nec nupsit. At enim
plurimum vis horoscopi valet. Hoc quam nihil sit,
iam satis disserui. Sed qualecumque sit, in ortu
valere dicunt; numquid et in conceptu? Ubi et
unum concubitum esse manifestum est, et tanta naturae vis est ut, cum conceperit femina, deinde alterum
concipere omnino non possit; unde necesse est
eadem esse in geminis momenta conceptus. An
forte quia diverso horoscopo nati sunt, aut ille in
masculum, dum nascerentur, aut illa in feminam
commutata est?

Cum igitur non usquequaque absurde dici posset
ad solas corporum differentias adflatus quosdam
valere sidereos, sicut in solaribus accessibus et deces-
sibus videmus etiam ipsius anni tempora variari et
lunaribus incrementis atque detrimentis augeri et
minui quaedam genera rerum, sicut echinos et con-
chas et mirabiles aestus oceani, non autem et animi
voluntates positionibus siderum subdi, nunc isti, cum
etiam nostros actus inde religare conantur, admonent
ut quaeramus unde ne in ipsis quidem corporibus
eis possit ratio ista constare. Quid enim tam ad
corpus perinens quam corporis sexus? Et tamen
sub eadem positione siderum diversi sexus gemini

something more incredible, if you believe in destinies
fixed by the stars, but not strange if you consider
the free will of man and the gifts of God. He is
married, while she is a consecrated virgin; he has
begotten a number of children, while she has never
even married. But still (they say), the power of the
horoscope is very great! I have already shown well
enough how truly it is nothing. But whatever be
the truth about it, they say that it is effective at the
time of birth. Is it also effective at the time of
conception? Here it is clear that there is but one
act of intercourse, and such is the force of nature
that when a woman has conceived, she is entirely
unable thereafter to conceive another. Hence the
conception of twins must come at the same moment.
Perhaps they will say that because they are born
with different horoscopes, either he was changed
into a male, or she into a female, while they were
being born.

It is not entirely absurd to say, with reference only
to physical differences, that there are certain sidereal
influences. We see that the seasons of the year
change with the approach and the receding of the
sun. And with the waxing and waning of the moon
we see certain kinds of things grow and shrink, such
as sea-urchins and oysters, and the marvellous tides
of the ocean. But the choices of the will are not
subject to the positions of the stars. Accordingly
when the astrologers try to make our actions depend
on them, it is a warning to us to ask why their reasoning can go wrong even in physical matters. For
what is more a part of the body than sex? And yet
under the same position of the stars twins of unlike

concipi potuerunt. Unde quid insipientius dici aut credi potest quam siderum positionem, quae ad horam conceptionis eadem ambobus fuit, facere non potuisse ut, cum quo habebat eandem constellationem, sexum diversum a fratre non haberet; et positionem siderum, quae fuit ad horam nascentium, facere potuisse ut ab eo tam multum virginali sanctitate distaret?

VII

De electione diei, quo uxor ducitur quove in agro
aliquid plantatur aut seritur.

IAM illud quis ferat, quod in eligendis diebus nova quaedam suis actibus fata moliuntur? Non erat videlicet ille ita natus ut haberet admirabilem filium, sed ita potius ut contemptibilem gigneret, et ideo vir doctus elegit horam qua misceretur uxori. Fecit ergo fatum quod non habebat, et ex ipsius factor coepit esse fatale quod in eius nativitate non fuerat. O stultitiam singularem! Eligitur dies ut ducatur uxor; credo propterea quia potest in diem non bonum, nisi eligatur, incurri et infeliciter duci. Ubi est ergo quod nascenti iam sidera decreverunt? An potest homo quod ei iam constitutum est diei electione mutare, et quod ipse in eligendo die constituerit non poterit ab alia potestate mutari?

Deinde si soli homines, non autem omnia quae

sex can be conceived. Hence what could be more
stupid to say or believe than that the position of the
stars, identical for both at the hour of conception,
could not prevent the sister from having a different
sex from her brother with whom she shared the same
constellation, while believing that the position of the
stars at the hour of birth could cause her to differ so
widely from him in her life of holy virginity?

VII

*On the choice of a day for marriage, or for planting
or sowing in the field.*

Now who could tolerate the assumption that in
choosing lucky days people manufacture new destinies by their own acts? The man I mentioned, for
instance, was not destined by birth to have an extraordinary son, but rather to beget one of no importance. And so, being a wise man, he chose the hour
to lie with his wife. Thus he created a destiny that
he did not have before, and as a result of his act a
thing became fated that was not included in his
nativity. What unparalleled foolishness! A day is
chosen to marry a wife. I suppose the reason is that
unless the day is properly selected an unlucky day
might be hit upon and the marriage be unlucky.
Then where is the destiny of the stars already decreed
when the man was born? Can a man by the choice
of a day change the destiny already decreed for him?
And then cannot another power change the destiny
that he has established by selecting the day?

Again if it is only men who are under the influence

sub caelo sunt, constellationibus subiacent, cur aliter
eligunt dies accommodatos ponendis vitibus vel
arboribus vel segetibus, alios dies pecoribus vel
domandis vel admittendis maribus, quibus equarum
vel boum fetentur armenta, et cetera huius modi?
Si autem propterea valent ad has res dies electi
quia terrenis omnibus corporibus sive animantibus
secundum diversitates temporalium momentorum
siderum positio dominatur, considerent quam innumerabilia sub uno temporis puncto vel nascantur
vel oriantur vel inchoentur, et tam diversos exitus
habeant ut istas observationes cuivis puero ridendas
esse persuadeant. Quis enim est tam excors ut
audeat dicere omnes arbores, omnes herbas, omnes
bestias serpentes aves pisces vermiculos momenta
nascendi singillatim habere diversa? Solent tamen
homines ad temptandam peritiam mathematicorum
adferre ad eos constellationes mutorum animalium
quorum ortus propter hanc explorationem domi
suae diligenter observant, eosque mathematicos
praeferunt ceteris, qui constellationibus inspectis
dicunt non esse hominem natum, sed pecus. Audent
etiam dicere quale pecus, utrum aptum lanitio, an
vectationi, an aratro, an custodiae domus. Nam et
ad canina fata temptantur et cum magnis admiran-
tium clamoribus ista respondent.

Sic desipiunt homines ut existiment, cum homo
nascitur, ceteros rerum ortus ita inhiberi ut cum illo
sub eadem caeli plaga nec musca nascatur. Nam si
hanc admiserint, procedit ratiocinatio quae gradatim

of the stars, and not everything that lies under heaven, why do they choose certain days as suited to planting vines and trees and grain, and other days for the taming of animals or for letting in the males that are to make herds of mares and cows fertile, and similarly for other matters? But if selected days are important for these matters because the position of the stars, as it varies from moment to moment, has dominion over all earthly bodies and living things, then let them consider what a countless number of things are born, or start, or begin to be at one point of time, and still have such different ends as to convince any child that these observations are absurd. For who is so witless as to make bold to say that all trees, herbs, beasts, serpents, birds, fish and worms have each a different moment of birth? Still, men sometimes do bring to the astrologers to test their skill the horoscopes of dumb animals whose birth they carefully observe at home with a view to this consultation. And they prefer to the rest those astrologers who, after studying the horoscopes, declare that it is not a man, but an animal, that has been born. They even venture to say what sort of animal it is, whether suited for shearing, for riding, for ploughing, or for guarding the house. For they are even tested by inquiry about the destinies of dogs, and their replies are greeted with great shouts of approval.

Men are so foolish as to think that when a man is born, the birth of all other creatures is delayed so that not even a fly is born simultaneously under the same region of the sky. For if they admit this fly, logic will go on, and step by step small increases in

accessibus modicis eos a muscis ad camelos elephan-
tosque perducat. Nec illud volunt advertere, quod
electo ad seminandum agrum die tam multa grana in
terram simul veniunt, simul germinant, exorta segete
simul herbescunt pubescunt flavescunt, et tamen
inde spicas ceteris coaevas atque, ut ita dixerim,
congerminales alias robigo interimit, alias aves
depopulantur, alias homines avellunt. Quo modo
istis alias constellationes fuisse dicturi sunt, quas
tam diversos exitus habere conspiciunt? An eos
paenitebit his rebus dies eligere easque ad caeleste
negabunt pertinere decretum, et solos sideribus sub-
dent homines, quibus solis in terra Deus dedit liberas
voluntates?

His omnibus consideratis non inmerito creditur,
cum astrologi mirabiliter multa vera respondent,
occulto instinctu fieri spirituum non bonorum,
quorum cura est has falsas et noxias opiniones de
astralibus fatis inserere humanis mentibus atque
firmare, non horoscopi notati et inspecti aliqua arte,
quae nulla est.

VIII

De his, qui non astrorum positionem, sed conexionem
causarum ex Dei voluntate pendentem fati nomine
appellant.

Qui vero non astrorum constitutionem, sicuti est
cum quidque concipitur vel nascitur vel inchoatur,

size will lead them to admit the camel and the elephant. Nor are they willing to notice this point: when a day has been selected to sow wheat in the field, many seeds fall on the ground together, germinate together, and as the crop comes up from the ground they become green blades, mature and turn yellow. Yet of this crop some stalks of wheat, that entered the earth and germinated with the others, are destroyed by rust, others devoured by birds and others plucked by men. How can they say that these were governed by any different pattern of stars, although they clearly have such different ends? Or will they change their minds about choosing days for these things, and say that they are not subject to the decree of heaven? Will they make men alone subject to the stars—men, the only creatures on earth to whom God has granted free wills?

Considering all this, the belief is justified that when astrologers miraculously give true replies, as they often do, this is due to the furtive prompting of evil spirits, whose aim is to plant in the minds of men these harmful beliefs about the control of destiny by the stars, and to confirm them. It is not due to any art of observing and studying the horoscope, for no such art exists.

VIII

Of those who give the name " Fate," not to the position of the stars, but to the system of causes that is linked to the will of God.

THERE are some who use the word fate, not of the position of the stars as it is at the time of conception

sed omnium conexionem seriemque causarum, qua
fit omne quod fit, fati nomine appellant, non multum
cum eis de verbi controversia laborandum atque
certandum est, quando quidem ipsum causarum
ordinem et quandam conexionem Dei summi tribuunt
voluntati et potestati, qui optime et veracissime creditur et cuncta scire antequam fiant et nihil inordi-
natum relinquere; a quo sunt omnes potestates,
quamvis ab illo non sint omnium voluntates. Ipsam
itaque praecipue Dei summi voluntatem, cuius
potestas insuperabiliter per cuncta porrigitur, eos
appellare fatum sic probatur. Annaei Senecae sunt,
nisi fallor, hi versus:

> Duc, summe pater altique dominator poli,
> Quocumque placuit, nulla parendi mora est.
> Adsum impiger: fac nolle, comitabor gemens
> Malusque patiar, facere quod licuit bono.
> Ducunt volentem fata, nolentem trahunt.

Nempe evidentissime hoc ultimo versu ea fata appel-
lavit, quam supra dixerat summi patris voluntatem;
cui paratum se oboedire dicit, ut volens ducatur, ne
nolens trahatur; quoniam scilicet

> Ducunt volentem fata, nolentem trahunt.

---

[1] Seneca, *Epistle* 107, gives the verses as a translation from
Cleanthes.

or birth or beginning of a thing, but to the connection and sequence of all the causes whereby everything happens that happens. No great effort need be expended in debate with them on a verbal difference, inasmuch as they ascribe this order and chain, as it were, of causes to the will and power of the supreme God. Most excellently and truly do they believe that he knows all things before they come to pass, and leaves nothing disorderly. All powers are derived from him, though the wills of all men are not ruled by him. Thus it is above all simply the will of the supreme God, whose power reaches out with invincible might through the whole universe, that they call fate. This is shown by the following words (the verses, I think, are by Annaeus Seneca): [1]

Lead, O thou Father supreme, of lofty heaven the ruler,
Whithersoever thou wilt, and without delay will I hearken.
Here I am, eager; but should I refuse, then with groans shall I follow;
Vilely shall I endure what I might have performed as a good man.
Led is the willing soul by the Fates; they drag the unwilling.

It is quite evident that in this last verse he gives the name of fate to what he had referred to above as the will of the supreme Father. He says that he is ready to obey him, to be led willingly and not dragged unwillingly, for be it noted,

Led is the willing soul by the Fates; they drag the unwilling.

Illi quoque versus Homerici huic sententiae suffragantur quos Cicero in Latinum vertit:

Tales sunt hominum mentes, quali pater ipse
Iuppiter auctiferas lustravit lumine terras.

Nec in hac quaestione auctoritatem haberet poetica sententia; sed quoniam Stoicos dicit vim fati asserentes istos ex Homero versus solere usurpare, non de illius poetae, sed de istorum philosophorum opinione tractatur, cum per istos versus, quos disputationi adhibent quam de fato habent, quid sentiant esse fatum apertissime declaratur, quoniam Iovem appellant, quem summum deum putant, a quo conexionem dicunt pendere fatorum.

IX

*De praescientia Dei et libera hominis voluntate contra
Ciceronis definitionem.*

Hos Cicero ita redarguere nititur ut non existimet aliquid se adversus eos valere nisi auferat divinationem. Quam sic conatur auferre ut neget esse scientiam futurorum, eamque omnibus viribus nullam esse omnino contendat, vel in homine vel in deo, nullamque rerum praedictionem. Ita et Dei praescientiam negat et omnem prophetiam luce clariorem

---

[1] A free translation by Cicero from *Odyssey* 18.136–7, preserved only here, and generally taken to be a fragment of *De Fato*.

This opinion is also supported by the verses of
Homer that Cicero has translated into Latin: [1]

Such are the hearts of men as the brightness of day,
    that the Father,
Even Jove himself, has dispersed over growth-teem-
    ing ploughlands.

On this problem a poet's opinion would have no
weight, but Cicero says that the Stoics are accustomed
to quote these verses from Homer when asserting the
power of fate.   So the discussion is not concerned
with the opinion of Homer, but with that of these
philosophers.   These verses, which they employ in
the discussion, bring us a clear statement of their
view of the nature of fate.   They call it Jupiter, who
in their belief is the supreme god, and from him, they
say, the interconnected links of destiny depend.

IX

*On the foreknowledge of God and the free will of
man, against Cicero's definition of them.*

CICERO, in undertaking to refute the Stoics, considers himself helpless against them unless he can do
away with divination.   This he attempts to do by
denying that there is any knowledge of the future.
He argues with might and main that there is no such
foreknowledge, either in man or in God, and that
there is no way of predicting events.   By this course
he both denies the foreknowledge of God and essays
to overthrow all prophecy, using futile arguments
even when the truth of prophecy is clearer than

conatur evertere vanis argumentationibus et oppo-
nendo sibi quaedam oracula quac facile possunt
refelli; quae tamen nec ipsa convincit. In his
autem mathematicorum coniecturis refutandis eius
regnat oratio, quia vere tales sunt ut se ipsae destru-
ant et refellant.

Multo sunt autem tolerabiliores qui vel siderea fata
constituunt quam iste qui tollit praescientiam futurorum. Nam et confiteri esse Deum et negare praescium futurorum apertissima insania est. Quod et
ipse cum videret, etiam illud temptavit quod scriptum est: *Dixit insipiens in corde suo: Non est Deus;*
sed non ex sua persona. Vidit enim quam esset
invidiosum et molestum, ideoque Cottam fecit
disputantem de hac re adversus Stoicos in libris de
deorum natura et pro Lucilio Balbo, cui Stoicorum
partes defendendas dedit, maluit ferre sententiam
quam pro Cotta, qui nullam divinam naturam esse
contendit. In libris vero de divinatione ex se ipso
apertissime oppugnat praescientiam futurorum. Hoc
autem totum facere videtur ne fatum esse consentiat
et perdat liberam voluntatem. Putat enim con-
cessa scientia futurorum ita esse consequens fatum
ut negari omnino non possit.

Sed quoquo modo se habeant tortuosissimae con-
certationes et disputationes philosophorum, nos ut

---

[1] *On the Nature of the Gods,* 3.95.

daylight. He sets up as targets for criticism certain oracles that can easily be refuted, but does not prove his case, even against them. However, when it comes to disposing of the guesswork of the astrologers, his speech wins the day, for their statements are really such that they destroy and refute each other.

But we can much better put up with those who maintain even that destiny lies in the stars than with the man who strikes out all foreknowledge of the future. For it is a conspicuous act of madness both to agree that God exists and to deny his foreknowledge of the future. Since Cicero too was aware of this, he even hazarded the statement referred to in Scripture: " The fool hath said in his heart, There is no God," but this not in his own person, for he saw how unpopular and offensive it would be. That was his reason for putting the argument against the Stoics on this point into the mouth of Cotta, in his work *On the Nature of the Gods*. He also chose rather to deliver his verdict for Lucilius Balbus, to whom he assigned the defence of the Stoics, rather than for Cotta, who argued that there is no divine being.[1] But in the work *On Divination* he speaks in his own person and openly attacks belief in the foreknowledge of the future. The whole argument seems designed to avoid admitting the existence of fate and thereby sacrificing free will. For he thinks that if he grants that future events can be foreseen, then he will find it quite impossible to deny the existence of fate as a corollary.

But whatever may be the course of the involved debates and disputes of the philosophers, we Christians

confitemur summum et verum Deum, ita voluntatem summamque potestatem ac praescientiam eius confitemur; nec timemus ne ideo non voluntate faciamus quod voluntate facimus quia id nos facturos ille praescivit, cuius praescientia falli non potest; quod Cicero timuit, ut oppugnaret praescientiam, et Stoici, ut non omnia necessitate fieri dicerent, quamvis omnia fato fieri contenderent.

Quid est ergo, quod Cicero timuit in praescientia futurorum, ut eam labefactare disputatione detestabili niteretur? Videlicet quia, si praescita sunt omnia futura, hoc ordine venient, quo ventura esse praescita sunt; et si hoc ordine venient, certus est ordo rerum praescienti Deo; et si certus est ordo rerum, certus est ordo causarum; non enim fieri aliquid potest, quod non aliqua efficiens causa praecesserit; si autem certus est ordo causarum quo fit omne quod fit, fato, inquit, fiunt omnia quae fiunt. Quod si ita est, nihil est in nostra potestate nullumque est arbitrium voluntatis; quod si concedimus, inquit, omnis humana vita subvertitur, frustra leges dantur, frustra obiurgationes laudes, vituperationes exhortationes adhibentur, neque ulla iustitia bonis praemia et malis supplicia constituta sunt. Haec ergo ne consequantur indigna et absurda et perniciosa rebus humanis, non vult esse praescientiam

---

[1] *De fato*, 40.

not only declare our belief in the existence of the supreme and true God, but also declare that he has a will, supreme power and foreknowledge. Nor do we fear that our acts of free will will not be acts of free will if it is granted that he whose foreknowledge cannot be mistaken foreknows that we will so act. Cicero had this fear and so rejected foreknowledge. The Stoics had it, and so they said that not everything happens by necessity, although they maintained that everything is brought about by fate.

What is it, then, that Cicero found so dangerous in the belief in foreknowledge of the future, that he strove to undermine it by his outrageous attack? Evidently the argument that, if all future events are foreknown, they will take place in the order in which their occurrence was foreknown, and if they are to take place in this order, then the order is determined for a foreknowing God. If the order of events is determined, the order of causes is determined, for nothing can happen that is not preceded by some efficient cause. But if there is a determined order of causes by which everything that happens happens, then all things that happen happen by fate. If this is the case, there is nothing really in our power, and the will really has no free choice. And if we grant this, says Cicero,[1] the whole basis of human life is overthrown: it is in vain that laws are made, that men employ reprimands and praise, denunciation and exhortation, and there is no justice in a system of rewards for the good and punishment for the bad. So in order to escape these consequences, so disgraceful and absurd and pernicious for humanity, Cicero chooses to reject foreknowledge of the future. He

futurorum; atque in has angustias coartat animum religiosum ut unum eligat e duobus, aut esse aliquid in nostra voluntate, aut esse praescientiam futurorum, quoniam utrumque arbitratur esse non posse, sed si alterum confirmabitur, alterum tolli; si elegerimus praescientiam futurorum, tolli voluntatis arbitrium; si elegerimus voluntatis arbitrium, tolli praescientiam futurorum. Ipse itaque ut vir magnus et doctus et vitae humanae plurimum ac peritissime consulens ex his duobus elegit liberum voluntatis arbitrium; quod ut confirmaretur, negavit praescientiam futurorum atque ita, dum vult facere liberos, fecit sacrilegos.

Religiosus autem animus utrumque eligit, utrumque confitetur et fide pietatis utrumque confirmat. Quo modo? inquit; nam si est praescientia futurorum, sequentur illa omnia, quae conexa sunt, donec eo perveniatur ut nihil sit in nostra voluntate. Porro si est aliquid in nostra voluntate, eisdem recursis gradibus eo pervenitur ut non sit praescientia futurorum. Nam per illa omnia sic recurritur: si est voluntatis arbitrium, non omnia fato fiunt; si non omnia fato fiunt, non est omnium certus ordo causarum; si certus causarum ordo non est, nec rerum certus est ordo praescienti Deo, quae fieri non possunt nisi praecedentibus et efficientibus causis; si rerum ordo praescienti Deo certus non est, non omnia sic veniunt ut ea ventura praescivit; porro si

reduces a god-fearing soul to the dilemma of choosing one of two alternatives: either there is something governed by our will, or there is foreknowledge of the future. He thinks that it is impossible for both to exist at once, and that any support of one proposition is a denial of the other. If we choose foreknowledge of the future, freedom of the will is destroyed, and if we choose freedom of the will, foreknowledge of the future is excluded. And so, being a great and learned man, much concerned and thoroughly informed about human welfare, of these alternatives he chose free will, and in order to uphold it he denied foreknowledge of the future. Thus in his desire to make men free he made them irreligious.

But the God-fearing mind chooses both freedom and foreknowledge. It accepts both and supports both with religious loyalty. How so? asks Cicero. For if there is foreknowledge of the future, the whole series of consequences must follow, until the conclusion is reached that nothing is in our power. And again, if there is anything in our power, by reversing the steps of the argument we reach the conclusion that there is no foreknowledge of the future. All the steps are retraced in this way: If freedom of the will exists, all things do not come to pass by fate; if all things do not come to pass by fate, there is no fixed order for all causes; if there is no fixed order of causes, neither is there an order of things fixed for a foreknowing God, for things cannot happen except as their efficient causes come first. If there is no order of things fixed for a foreknowing God, then things do not all come to pass as he knew beforehand that they would come, and if all things do not come

non omnia sic veniunt ut ab illo ventura praescita sunt, non est, inquit, in Deo praescientia omnium futurorum.

Nos adversus istos sacrilegos ausus atque impios et Deum dicimus omnia scire antequam fiant, et voluntate nos facere quidquid a nobis non nisi volentibus fieri sentimus et novimus. Omnia vero fato fieri non dicimus, immo nulla fieri fato dicimus; quoniam fati nomen ubi solet a loquentibus poni, id est in constitutione siderum cum quisque conceptus aut natus est, quoniam res ipsa inaniter asseritur, nihil valere monstramus. Ordinem autem causarum, ubi voluntas Dei plurimum potest, neque negamus neque fati vocabulo nuncupamus, nisi forte ut fatum a fando dictum intellegamus, id est a loquendo; non enim abnuere possumus esse scriptum in litteris sanctis: *Semel locutus est Deus, duo haec audivi, quoniam potestas Dei est, et tibi, Domine, misericordia, qui reddis unicuique secundum opera eius.* Quod enim dictum est: *Semel locutus est,* intellegitur " inmobiliter," hoc est incommutabiliter, " est locutus," sicut novit incommutabiliter omnia quae futura sunt et quae ipse facturus est. Hac itaque ratione possemus a fando fatum appellare, nisi hoc nomen iam in alia re soleret intellegi quo corda hominum nolumus inclinari. Non est autem consequens ut, si Deo certus est omnium ordo causarum, ideo nihil sit in

---

[1] This etymology is today accepted as correct.
[2] Psalm 62.11–12.

to pass as he knew beforehand, then, Cicero says, the foreknowledge of all things does not exist in God's mind.

As against these rash assertions, blasphemous and irreligious as they are, we Christians declare both that God knows all things before they happen, and that it is by our own free will that we act, whenever we feel and know that a thing is done by us of our own volition. But we do not say that all things come to pass by fate. No indeed, we say that nothing comes to pass by fate. For the word fate is commonly used of the position of the stars at the moment of conception or birth, and we have shown that the word means nothing, but is the frivolous assertion of an unreality. Moreover, as for the order of causes in which the will of God is all powerful, we neither deny it nor do we call it by the name " fate," unless perchance fate be understood as derived from *fari*, that is, from speaking.[1] For we cannot deny that it is written in the Scriptures : " Once God has spoken ; twice have I heard this, that power belongs to God, and that to thee, O Lord, belongs mercy, for thou dost requite each man according to his work." [2] The words " Once God has spoken " mean " God has spoken immoveably," that is, unchangeably, even as he knows unchangeably all things that will come to pass and all things that he himself will do. With this explanation we might use the word fate as derived from *fari*, " to speak," if the word were not already commonly understood in another sense, to which we would not have the minds of men directed. Moreover, even if there is in God's mind a definite pattern of causation, it does not follow that

nostrae voluntatis arbitrio. Et ipsae quippe nostrae
voluntates in causarum ordine sunt qui certus est
Deo eiusque praescientia continetur, quoniam et
humanae voluntates humanorum operum causae
sunt; atque ita, qui omnes rerum causas praescivit
profecto in eis causis etiam nostras voluntates ignorare non potuit, quas nostrorum operum causas
esse praescivit.

Nam et illud quod idem Cicero concedit, nihil fieri
si causa efficiens non praecedat, satis est ad eum in
hac quaestione redarguendum. Quid enim eum
adiuvat, quod dicit nihil quidem fieri sine causa, sed
non omnem causam esse fatalem, quia est causa
fortuita, est naturalis, est voluntaria? Sufficit quia
omne quod fit non nisi causa praecedente fieri confitetur. Nos enim eas causas quae dicuntur fortuitae,
unde etiam fortuna nomen accepit, non esse dicimus
nullas sed latentes, easque tribuimus vel Dei veri vel
quorumlibet spirituum voluntati, ipsasque naturales
nequaquam ab illius voluntate seiungimus qui est
auctor omnis conditorque naturae. Iam vero causae
voluntariae aut Dei sunt aut angelorum aut hominum
aut quorumque animalium, si tamen voluntates
appellandae sunt animarum rationis expertium motus
illi quibus aliqua faciunt secundum naturam suam
cum quid vel adpetunt vel evitant. Angelorum
autem voluntates dico seu bonorum, quos angelos
Dei dicimus, seu malorum, quos angelos diaboli vel

nothing is left to the free choice of our will. For
in fact, our wills also are included in the pattern of
causation certainly known to God and embraced in
his foreknowledge. For the wills of men are among
the causes of the deeds of men, and so he who foresaw the causes of all things cannot have been ignorant
of our wills among those causes, since he foresaw that
these wills are the causes of our deeds.

Moreover, even the concession that Cicero makes,
that nothing happens unless preceded by an efficient
cause, is enough to refute him in this debate. He
says that nothing happens without a cause, but that
not every cause is a matter of fate, since there is
also a fortuitous cause, a natural cause and a voluntary cause. But how does this help him? It is
enough when he admits that everything that happens
happens only by virtue of a preceding cause. As for
those causes which he calls fortuitous (the word fortune is derived from the same root), we do not say
that they are nonexistent, but that they are hidden,
and we ascribe them to the will of the true God, or
to the will of spirits of any sort you please. We by
no means disconnect even the natural causes from
the will of him who is the Author and Creator of all
nature. Finally the voluntary causes belong either
to God's will or to that of angels or men or animals,
if indeed we may speak of wills in reference to those
movements of irrational animals in which they act
according to their nature when moving to get or to
escape something. When I speak of the wills of
angels, I include both good angels, whom we call
angels of God, and wicked angels, whom we call
angels of the devil or also demons. So too we

etiam daemones appellamus—sic et hominum, et bonorum scilicet et malorum.

Ac per hoc colligitur non esse causas efficientes omnium quae fiunt nisi voluntarias, illius naturae scilicet quae spiritus vitae est. Nam et aer iste seu ventus dicitur spiritus; sed quoniam corpus est, non est spiritus vitae. Spiritus ergo vitae, qui vivificat omnia creatorque est omnis corporis et omnis creati spiritus, ipse est Deus, spiritus utique non creatus. In eius voluntate summa potestas est, quae creatorum spirituum bonas voluntates adiuvat, malas iudicat, omnes ordinat et quibusdam tribuit potestates, quibusdam non tribuit. Sicut enim omnium naturarum creator est, ita omnium potestatum dator, non voluntatum. Malae quippe voluntates ab illo non sunt, quoniam contra naturam sunt, quae ab illo est. Corpora igitur magis subiacent voluntatibus, quaedam nostris, id est omnium animantium mortalium et magis hominum quam bestiarum; quaedam vero angelorum; sed omnia maxime Dei voluntati subdita sunt, cui etiam voluntates omnes subiciuntur, quia non habent potestatem nisi quam ille concedit. Causa itaque rerum, quae facit nec fit, Deus est; aliae vero causae et faciunt et fiunt, sicut sunt omnes creati spiritus, maxime rationales. Corporales autem causae, quae magis fiunt quam faciunt, non sunt inter causas efficientes adnumerandae, quoniam hoc possunt quod ex ipsis faciunt spirituum voluntates.

Quo modo igitur ordo causarum, qui praescienti

include in wills of men both those of good and of bad men.

We draw from this the conclusion that the only efficient causes of all things that come to pass are voluntary causes, derived, of course, from that Being who is the breath (*spiritus*) of life. To be sure, this air or wind around us is also called " breath," but since it is a material thing, it is not the breath of life. The breath of life, accordingly, which gives life to all things and is creator of every body and of every created spirit, is God himself, the absolutely un-created spirit. In his will lies the supreme power that strengthens the good wills of created spirits, judges the evil wills, and subjects them all to his divine order. To some he grants powers, to others he does not; for just as he is the creator of all beings, so he is the giver of all powers, but not of all wills. Bad wills of course do not come from him, since they are contrary to the strand of our nature that does come from him. Bodies, in turn, are rather subject to wills, some to our wills (that is, wills of all living, mortal creatures, and they are more subject to the wills of men than they are to those of beasts), some to the wills of angels, but all are subject to him, for they have no power except what he has granted. Hence God is the first cause, which causes and is not caused. Other causes, among them created spirits, especially rational spirits, both cause and are caused. But material causes, which are more passive than active, are not to be counted among efficient causes, for their only power is to do what the wills of im-material beings do with them.

How, then, can the order of causes that is fixed in

certus est Deo, id efficit, ut nihil sit in nostra voluntate, cum in ipso causarum ordine magnum habeant
locum nostrae voluntates? Contendat ergo Cicero
cum eis qui hunc causarum ordinem dicunt esse
fatalem vel potius ipsum fati nomine appellant, quod
nos abhorremus praecipue propter vocabulum, quod
non in re vera consuevit intellegi. Quod vero negat
ordinem omnium causarum esse certissimum et Dei
praescientiae notissimum, plus eum quam Stoici
detestamur. Aut enim esse Deum negat, quod
quidem inducta alterius persona in libris de deorum
natura facere molitus est; aut si esse confitetur
Deum, quem negat praescium futurorum, etiam sic
nihil dicit aliud quam quod ille *dixit insipiens in corde
suo: Non est Deus.* Qui enim non est praescius omnium futurorum, non est utique Deus. Quapropter
et voluntates nostrae tantum valent quantum Deus
eas valere voluit atque praescivit; et ideo quidquid
valent, certissime valent, et quod facturae sunt, ipsae
omnino facturae sunt, quia valituras atque facturas
ille praescivit, cuius praescientia falli non potest.
Quapropter si mihi fati nomen alicui rei adhibendum
placeret, magis dicerem fatum esse infirmioris poten-
tioris voluntatem, qui eum habet in potestate, quam
illo causarum ordine, quem non usitato, sed suo more
Stoici fatum appellant, arbitrium nostrae voluntatis
auferri.

God's foreknowledge deprive us of all use of our will, when our wills play an important part in the order of causes itself? So let Cicero argue the case with those who say that this order of causes is determined by fate, or rather, call the order itself fate. We refuse to do this, because the word is commonly used to refer to a false notion. As for Cicero's denial that the order of all causes is perfectly defined and perfectly visible to the foreknowledge of God, that is an abomination to us, even more than to the Stoics. Either he is denying the existence of God, as he essayed to do in the speech that he gave to a disputant in the dialogue *On the Nature of the Gods*, or if he agrees that God exists, but denies his knowledge of the future, even so it amounts to nothing more than what " the fool has said in his heart, There is no God." [1] For one who does not know all future things is surely not God. Hence our acts of will also have just so much power as God chose to give them and also foresaw. Therefore, whatever power they have, they have it most assuredly. They themselves will in any case do what they are going to do, because he whose foreknowledge cannot be mistaken foresaw that they would have the power to do it, and that they would do it. Hence if I saw fit to apply the word fate to anything, I would rather say that the fate of the weaker is the will of the stronger, who has the other in his power, than to admit that the order of causes which the Stoics call fate (in their own, but not the common usage of the word) does away with our free will.

[1] Psalm 14.1.

X

An voluntatibus hominum aliqua dominetur necessitas.

UNDE nec illa necessitas formidanda est, quam for-
midando Stoici laboraverunt causas rerum ita
distinguere, ut quasdam subtraherent necessitati,
quasdam subderent, atque in his, quas esse sub
necessitate noluerunt, posuerunt etiam nostras
voluntates, ne videlicet non essent liberae, si sub-
derentur necessitati. Si enim necessitas nostra illa
dicenda est, quae non est in nostra potestate, sed
etiamsi nolimus efficit quod potest, sicut est necessitas mortis, manifestum est voluntates nostras,
quibus recte vel perperam vivitur, sub tali necessitate
non esse. Multa enim facimus, quae si nollemus,
non utique faceremus. Quo primitus pertinet ipsum
velle; nam si volumus, est, si nolumus, non est; non
enim vellemus, si nollemus.

Si autem illa definitur esse necessitas secundum
quam dicimus necesse esse ut ita sit aliquid vel ita
fiat, nescio cur eam timeamus ne nobis libertatem
auferat voluntatis. Neque enim et vitam Dei et
praescientiam Dei sub necessitate ponimus, si dicamus necesse esse Deum semper vivere et cuncta
praescire; sicut nec potestas eius minuitur, cum
dicitur mori fallique non posse. Sic enim hoc non
potest, ut potius, si posset, minoris esset utique
potestatis. Recte quippe omnipotens dicitur, qui
tamen mori et falli non potest. Dicitur enim omni-

X

Whether Necessity reigns over the wills of men.

HENCE we need not fear that necessity which the Stoics feared so much that they took pains to discriminate among causes by exempting some from the decree of necessity while leaving others subject to it. Under the heading of causes that they would not leave in the realm of necessity they put our acts of will, obviously thinking that they would not be free if they were made subject to necessity. If the term necessity should be used of what is not in our power, but accomplishes its end even against our will, for example, the necessity of death, it is clear that our wills, by which we live rightly or wrongly, are not under such necessity. For we do many things that we certainly should not do if we were unwilling. To this class of things belongs first of all the will itself. If we will, the will exists; if not, it does not. For we should not will if we were unwilling.

But if the term necessity is used in the sense that it is necessary for something to be as it is, or happen as it does, I do not know why we should fear that it may destroy our freedom of will. In fact, we do not make the life of God, or the foreknowledge of God, subject to necessity if we say that it is necessary for God to live forever and to foreknow all things. Likewise his power is not lessened when we say that he cannot die, or be mistaken. In saying this we understand that he would rather have less power if he could die or be mistaken. Of course he is rightly called omnipotent, although he cannot die or be

potens faciendo quod vult, non patiendo quod non vult; quod ei si accideret, nequaquam esset omnipotens. Unde propterea quaedam non potest quia omnipotens est. Sic etiam cum dicimus necesse esse, ut, cum volumus, libero velimus arbitrio: et verum procul dubio dicimus, et non ideo ipsum liberum arbitrium necessitati subicimus, quae adimit libertatem.

Sunt igitur nostrae voluntates et ipsae faciunt quidquid volendo facimus, quod non fieret si nollemus. Quidquid autem aliorum hominum voluntate nolens quisque patitur, etiam sic voluntas valet, etsi non illius, tamen hominis voluntas; sed potestas Dei, (Nam si voluntas tantum esset nec posset quod vellet, potentiore voluntate impediretur; nec sic tamen voluntas nisi voluntas esset, nec alterius, sed eius esset qui vellet, etsi non posset implere quod vellet.) Unde quidquid praeter suam voluntatem patitur homo, non debet tribuere humanis vel angelicis vel cuiusquam creati spiritus voluntatibus, sed eius potius qui dat potestatem volentibus.

Non ergo propterea nihil est in nostra voluntate quia Deus praescivit quid futurum esset in nostra voluntate. Non enim qui hoc praescivit nihil praescivit. Porro si ille qui praescivit quid futurum esset in nostra voluntate non utique nihil sed aliquid praescivit, profecto et illo praesciente est aliquid in nostra voluntate. Quocirca nullo modo cogimur aut

deceived, for he is omnipotent in that he does what he wills and does not suffer to be done what he does not will; otherwise he would certainly not be omnipotent. Hence it is because he is omnipotent that there are certain things he cannot do. The case is similar when we say that it is necessary, when we exercise will, to do so of our own free will. This that we say is undoubtedly true, yet we do not thereby put our free will under the necessity that takes away liberty.

Our wills, therefore, exist, and they do whatever it is that we do with a will, which would not be done if we were unwilling. Furthermore, when anyone suffers something against his will because of the will of other men, even so will is in control. Though it is not his own will, it is still a man's will, but its power is from God. If it were only a man's will, without the power to accomplish its will, the thing that held it fettered would be some more powerful will. Yet the will would still be a will, not another's, but the will of him who had a will, even if he could not carry it out. Hence what a man suffers against his will should be ascribed, not to the wills of men or angels or any created spirit, but rather to the will of him who bestows the power to realize the wish.

It is not true, then, that there is no reality in our will just because God foresaw what would be in our will. For when he foresaw this, he foresaw something. Further, he who foresaw what would be in our will certainly foresaw something real, not a mere nothing. Hence assuredly there is something in our will, even though God has foreknowledge of it. Therefore we are in no way compelled either to abolish free will

retenta praescientia Dei tollere voluntatis arbitrium
aut retento voluntatis arbitrio Deum (quod nefas est)
negare praescium futurorum; sed utrumque amplec-
timur, utrumque fideliter et veraciter confitemur,
illud ut bene credamus, hoc ut bene vivamus. Male
autem vivitur si de Deo non bene creditur. Unde
absit a nobis eius negare praescientiam, ut libere
velimus, quo adiuvante sumus liberi vel erimus.
Proinde non frustra sunt leges obiurgationes exhortationes laudes et vituperationes, quia et ipsas futuras
esse praescivit, et valent plurimum, quantum eas
valituras esse praescivit, et preces valent ad ea impetranda quae se precantibus concessurum esse
praescivit, et iuste praemia bonis factis et peccatis
supplicia constituta sunt. Neque enim ideo non
peccat homo, quia Deus illum peccaturum esse praescivit; immo ideo non dubitatur ipsum peccare cum
peccat quia ille cuius praescientia falli non potest
non fatum, non fortunam, non aliquid aliud, sed
ipsum peccaturum esse praescivit. Qui si nolit,
utique non peccat; sed si peccare noluerit, etiam hoc
ille praescivit.

XI

De universali providentia Dei, cuius legibus omnia
continentur.

Deus itaque summus et verus cum Verbo suo et
Spiritu sancto, quae tria unum sunt, Deus unus

---

[1] Some manuscripts omit *non*: "does not in fact sin."

when we keep the foreknowledge of God, or blasphemously to deny that God foreknows the future because we keep free will. Instead we embrace both truths; with faith and trust we assert both. The former is required for correct belief, the latter for right living. And there is no right living if there is no correct belief in God. Far be it then, from us, in order to enjoy free will, to deny the foreknowledge of him by whose assistance alone we are free, or shall ever be free. Consequently laws, reprimands, exhortations, praise and denunciation are not useless, for God knew that they would be used, and they are most effective as far as he foreknew that they would be. Prayers too are effective for obtaining those things which he foreknew he would grant to those who pray. And it accords with justice that rewards are provided for good deeds and punishments for sins. For man does not in fact fail to [1] sin because God foresaw that he would sin. Nay, it is precisely because of foreknowledge that there is no doubt that man himself sins when he sins. For he whose foreknowledge cannot be mistaken foresaw that neither fate, nor fortune, nor anything else but the man himself would sin. If he chooses not to sin, he certainly does not sin, and this choice not to sin was also foreseen by God.

XI

Of the universal providence of God, by whose laws all things are ruled.

THE supreme and true God with his Word and Holy Spirit, which three are one, is the one almighty

omnipotens, creator et factor omnis animae atque
omnis corporis, cuius sunt participatione felices
quicumque sunt veritate non vanitate felices, qui
fecit hominem rationale animal ex anima et corpore,
qui eum peccantem nec inpunitum esse permisit nec
sine misericordia dereliquit; qui bonis et malis
essentiam etiam cum lapidibus, vitam seminalem
etiam cum arboribus, vitam sensualem etiam cum
pecoribus, vitam intellectualem cum solis angelis
dedit; a quo est omnis modus omnis species omnis
ordo; a quo est mensura numerus pondus; a quo
est quidquid naturaliter est, cuiuscumque generis est,
cuiuslibet aestimationis est; a quo sunt semina for-
marum formae seminum motus seminum atque for-
marum; qui dedit et carni originem pulchritudinem
valetudinem, propagationis fecunditatem membrorum dispositionem salutem concordiae; qui et
animae inrationali dedit memoriam sensum adpeti-
tum, rationali autem insuper mentem intellegentiam
voluntatem; qui non solum caelum et terram, nec
solum angelum et hominem, sed nec exigui et con-
temptibilis animantis viscera nec avis pinnulam, nec
herbae flosculum nec arboris folium sine suarum
partium convenientia et quadam veluti pace dereliquit, nullo modo est credendus regna hominum
eorumque dominationes et servitutes a suae provi-
dentiae legibus alienas esse voluisse.

God, the creator and maker of every soul and every body. It is by participation in him that happiness is found by all who are happy in verity and not in vanity. He made man a rational animal, combining soul and body. When man sinned, God did not permit him to go unpunished, nor yet did he abandon him without mercy. To the good and to the evil he gave being, possessed also by stones; germinative life, possessed also by trees; conscious life, possessed also by animals; and intellectual life, possessed also by angels alone. From him comes all limit, all form, all order; from him comes measure, number and weight; from him comes whatever exists in nature, whatever its kind and whatever its worth; from him come seeds of forms and forms of seeds and movements in seeds and forms. He gave also to flesh a source, beauty, health, fruitfulness in propagation, arrangement of limbs and the saving grace of harmony. To the irrational soul also he gave memory, sensation and appetite; to the rational soul he gave in addition mind, intelligence and will. Neither heaven nor earth, neither angel nor man, not even the inner organs of a tiny and despised animal, not the pinfeather of a bird nor the tiny flower in the meadow nor the leaf on the tree did God leave unprovided with a suitable harmony of parts, a peace, so to speak, between its members. It is impossible to suppose that he would have excluded from the laws of his providence the kingdoms of men and their dominations and servitudes.

XII

*Quibus moribus antiqui Romani meruerint ut Deus
verus, quamvis non eum colerent, eorum augeret
imperium.*

PROINDE videamus quos Romanorum mores et
quam ob causam Deus verus ad augendum imperium
adiuvare dignatus est, in cuius potestate sunt etiam
regna terrena. Quod ut absolutius disserere possemus, ad hoc pertinentem et superiorem librum con-
scripsimus, quod in hac re potestas nulla sit eorum
deorum quos etiam rebus nugatoriis colendos putarunt, et praesentis voluminis partes superiores, quas
huc usque perduximus, de fati quaestione tollenda,
ne quisquam cui iam persuasum esset non illorum
deorum cultu Romanum imperium propagatum atque
servatum, nescio cui fato potius id tribueret quam
Dei summi potentissimae voluntati.

Veteres igitur primique Romani, quantum eorum
docet et commendat historia, quamvis ut aliae gentes
excepta una populi Hebraeorum deos falsos colerent
et non Deo victimas sed daemoniis immolarent, tamen
" laudis avidi, pecuniae liberales erant, gloriam
ingentem, divitias honestas volebant "; hanc arden-
tissime dilexerunt, propter hanc vivere voluerunt,
pro hac emori non dubitaverunt; ceteras cupiditates
huius unius ingenti cupiditate presserunt. Ipsam

---

[1] Sallust, *Catiline* 7.6.

XII

*By what virtues the ancient Romans gained the favour
of the true God, so that he increased their empire
although they did not worship him.*

NEXT let us consider the virtues of the Romans,
and why the true God, in whose power are earthly
kingdoms too, deigned to help them to enlarge their
empire. I had in view the fuller discussion of this
subject when I composed the preceding book also
with reference to it. In that book I demonstrated
that their gods have no power to grant empire, gods
which the Romans thought fit to worship for their
help even in trifling matters. The preceding portion
of the present book, up to this point, is also relevant,
for its intent is to dispose of the problem of fate. I
would not have anyone, after I had convinced him
that the Roman empire was not extended and preserved because the gods were worshipped, go on to
ascribe Roman success to fate of some sort or other,
rather than to the overruling will of God most high.

Although the ancient Romans of the earliest times
worshipped false gods—as did all other races except
one, the Hebrew race,—and sacrificed victims not to
God, but to demons, nevertheless, as their history
declares with approval, " they were eager for praise,
generous with money, and sought unbounded glory,
and riches honourably gained." [1] This glory they
most ardently loved. For its sake they chose to
live and for its sake they did not hesitate to die.
They suppressed all other desires in their boundless
desire for this one thing. In short, since they

denique patriam suam, quoniam servire videbatur
inglorium, dominari vero atque imperare gloriosum,
prius omni studio liberam, deinde dominam esse
concupiverunt. Hinc est quod regalem dominationem non ferentes " annua imperia binosque im-
peratores sibi fecerunt, qui consules appellati sunt a
consulendo, non reges aut domini a regnando atque
dominando "; cum et reges utique a regendo dicti
melius videantur, ut regnum a regibus, reges autem,
ut dictum est, a regendo; sed fastus regius non disciplina putata est regentis vel benivolentia consulentis,
sed superbia dominantis.

Expulso itaque rege Tarquinio et consulibus institutis secutum est, quod idem auctor in Romanorum
laudibus posuit, quod " civitas incredibile memoratu
est adepta libertate quantum brevi creverit; tanta
cupido gloriae incesserat." Ista ergo laudis aviditas
et cupido gloriae multa illa miranda fecit, laudabilia
scilicet atque gloriosa secundum hominum existima-
tionem.

Laudat idem Sallustius temporibus suis magnos et
praeclaros viros, Marcum Catonem et Gaium Caesarem, dicens quod diu illa res publica non habuit
quemquam virtute magnum, sed sua memoria fuisse
illos duos ingenti virtute, diversis moribus. In laudibus autem Caesaris posuit quod sibi magnum im-

---

[1] Sallust, *Catiline* 6.7. Sallust has the first part of this
sentence. The whole is printed as a doubtful fragment of
Cicero, *Republic* 2.31.53.
[2] *Ibid.* 7.3.

held it shameful for their native land to be in servitude, and glorious for it to rule and command, their first passion to which they devoted all their energy was to maintain their independence; the second was to win dominion. Hence it was that they could not endure the rule of kings. " They made the term of command annual, and selected two commanders [1] who were called consuls from taking counsel, not kings or masters from reigning or having mastery." But it would surely seem better to derive kings from the verb which means to rule (*reges a regendo*). As kingdom is derived from king, so (I repeat) is king from the word for ruling. But royal state was regarded not as the mark of a proper ruler, nor that of a benevolent adviser, but rather as the arrogance of a tyrant.

When Tarquin had consequently been expelled and the consuls had been established, there followed a time which Sallust, the writer I have quoted, sets down to the credit of the Romans. He says: " After the state gained its liberty, it is incredible to relate how great it grew in a short time, so strong was the passion for glory that had arisen." [2] So it was this eagerness for praise and passion for glory that performed so many marvellous deeds, which were no doubt praiseworthy and glorious as men judge things.

The same Sallust praises as great and distinguished men of his time Marcus Cato and Gaius Caesar. He says that for a long time the republic had had no men of outstanding merit, but that in his own time these two men had appeared, who were alike in their personal distinction but unlike in character. He sets it down to the credit of Caesar that he set his

perium, exercitum, bellum novum exoptabat, ubi
virtus enitescere posset. Ita fiebat in votis virorum
virtute magnorum ut excitaret in bellum miseras
gentes et flagello agitaret Bellona sanguineo, ut esset
ubi virtus eorum enitesceret. Hoc illa profecto
laudis aviditas et gloriae cupido faciebat. Amore
itaque primitus libertatis, post etiam dominationis
et cupiditate laudis et gloriae multa magna fecerunt.
Reddit eis utriusque rei testimonium etiam poeta
insignis illorum; inde quippe ait:

Nec non Tarquinium eiectum Porsenna iubebat
Accipere ingentique urbem obsidione premebat;
Aeneadae in ferrum pro libertate ruebant.

Tunc itaque magnum illis fuit aut fortiter ⟨e⟩mori
aut liberos vivere.

Sed cum esset adepta libertas, tanta cupido gloriae
incesserat ut parum esset sola libertas nisi et domi-
natio quaereretur, dum pro magno habetur quod
velut loquente Iove idem poeta dicit:

Quin aspera Iuno,
Quae mare nunc terrasque metu caelumque fatigat,
Consilia in melius referet mecumque fovebit

---

[1] Virgil, *Aeneid* 8.646–8. The reference just above to
Bellona and her bloody scourge is an echo of a passage in the
same book of the *Aeneid* (8.703).

heart on an important command, an army and a new war in which he might win distinction by his valour. Thus it came to be the dearest wish with men eminent for virtue that Bellona should arouse unhappy nations to war and inflict her bloody scourge upon them in order that they personally might find occasion to give lustre to their valour. Such, forsooth, was the result of that famous eagerness for praise and passion for glory. In this way their love of liberty at first, and later their love of dominion as well, as well as their passion for praise and glory, led to many great deeds. Their famous poet bears witness to both when he says:

And when Porsena ordered that Tarquin, the king they had banished,
Be restored to his throne, and was holding the city besieged,
Then did the sons of Aeneas seize arms in defence of their freedom.[1]

So great a thing was it then in their eyes either to die bravely or to live as free men.

But once they had freedom, so great was the passion for glory which arose that liberty seemed too little by itself unless they were also seeking dominion over others. And men set great store by the achievements which our poet puts into the mouth of Jupiter as a promise:

Even the envious Juno
Who now vexes the sea and the lands and the sky with her terror,
Shall for the better change her intent, and with me be protectress

Romanos rerum dominos gentemque togatam.
Sic placitum.   Veniet lustris labentibus aetas,
Cum domus Assaraci Phthiam clarasque Mycenas
Servitio premet ac victis dominabitur Argis.

Quae quidem Vergilius Iovem inducens tamquam futura praedicentem ipse iam facta recolebat cernebatque praesentia; verum propterea commemorare illa volui ut ostenderem dominationem post libertatem sic habuisse Romanos ut in eorum magnis laudibus poneretur.   Hinc est et illud eiusdem poetae quod, cum artibus aliarum gentium eas ipsas proprias Romanorum artes regnandi atque imperandi et subiugandi ac debellandi populos anteponeret, ait:

Excudent alii spirantia mollius aera,
Cedo equidem, vivos ducent de marmore vultus,
Orabunt causas melius caelique meatus
Describent radio et surgentia sidera dicent:
Tu regere imperio populos, Romane, memento

---

[1] Virgil, *Aeneid* 1.279–85.

Unto the toga-clad race, the Romans, the masters of
all things.
Thus 'tis decreed.   For an age shall come as the years
glide onward
When Assaracus' house shall enslave the land of
Achilles,
Famous Mycenae to servitude bring, and be lord
over Argos.[1]

When Virgil represents Jupiter as predicting all this
as if the events were in the future, the poet was
really reviewing past history and looking at things
as they were in his own present. But my reason
for quoting these words is to show that the Romans
had such regard for dominion, after liberty, that they
put it high in their scale of noble achievements.
The same thought is again expressed in the famous
passage of the same poet where, above the arts
of the other nations, he gives first place to the
peculiarly Roman art of reigning and command-
ing and subjugating and beating down nations in
war:

Others with tenderer touch shall beat out the bronze
to be lifelike.
That I must grant, for faces that live shall they draw
from the marble,
Cases at law with more eloquence plead, and the
pathways of heaven
Trace with the compass, predict as they rise both the
stars and the planets.
Thy task, O Roman, remember: to rule by thy
sceptre the nations.

(Hae tibi erunt artes) pacique inponere mores,
Parcere subiectis et debellare superbos.

Has artes illi tanto peritius exercebant, quanto minus
se voluptatibus dabant et enervationi animi et corporis in concupiscendis et augendis divitiis et per illas
moribus corrumpendis, rapiendo miseris civibus,
largiendo scaenicis turpibus.

Unde qui tales iam morum labe superabant atque
abundabant, quando scribebat ista Sallustius cane-
batque Vergilius, non illis artibus ad honores et
gloriam, sed dolis atque fallaciis ambiebant. Unde
idem dicit: " Sed primo magis ambitio quam avaritia
animos hominum exercebat, quod tamen vitium
propius virtutem erat. Nam gloriam honorem imperium bonus et ignavus aeque sibi exoptant; sed
ille," inquit, " vera via nititur, huic quia bonae artes
desunt, dolis atque fallaciis contendit." Hae sunt
illae bonae artes, per virtutem scilicet, non per falla-
cem ambitionem ad honorem et gloriam et imperium
pervenire; quae tamen bonus et ignavus aeque sibi
exoptant; sed ille, id est bonus, vera via nititur.
Via virtus est, qua nititur tamquam ad possessionis
finem, id est ad gloriam honorem imperium.

Hoc insitum habuisse Romanos etiam deorum apud
illos aedes indicant quas coniunctissimas constituerunt, Virtutis et Honoris, pro diis habentes quae

---

[1] Virgil, *Aeneid* 6.847–53.
[2] Sallust, *Catiline* 11.1–2.

Here are the arts to be thine, all the folkways of
  peace to establish,
Sparing the foe that is fallen, and beat down the
  proud who would fight thee.[1]

The Romans practised these arts with the more
perfection, the less they devoted themselves to
pleasure, the less they weakened mind and body by
the love and pursuit of wealth, for wealth under-
mined morals and led to the plundering of poor citizens, while bounty was lavished on vile actors.

Hence when Sallust wrote his prose and Virgil his
verses, men had outstripped their famous ancestors
in moral decline and in affluence: they no longer
employed those ancient arts in their competition for
honours and glory, but plotted with treachery and
deceit. Thus the same writer states: " At first,
instead of avarice, it was ambition that stirred the
minds of men, a vice that comes close to being a
virtue. Glory, honour and power are sought by
hero and coward alike; but the former climbs by the
honest path, while the latter, because he has no good
arts, resorts to plots and trickery for weapons."[2]
He means obviously by good arts the using of virtuous means to arrive at honour, glory and power,
and not to employ deceitful cunning. The hero and
the coward alike desire these things, but the former,
that is, the hero, climbs by the honest path. The
path is virtue, by which he climbs to the prize he
would possess, that is, glory, honour and power.

That this ideal was ingrained in the Romans is
shown also by the temples of two gods that they set
up in closest proximity, those of Honos and Virtus,

dantur a Deo. Unde intellegi potest quem finem volebant esse virtutis et quo eam referebant qui boni erant, ad honorem scilicet; nam mali nec habebant eam, quamvis honorem habere cuperent, quem malis artibus conabantur adipisci, id est dolis atque fallaciis.

Melius laudatus est Cato. De illo quippe ait: " Quo minus petebat gloriam, eo illum magis sequebatur." Quando quidem gloria est, cuius illi cupiditate flagrabant, iudicium hominum bene de hominibus opinantium; et ideo melior est virtus, quae humano testimonio contenta non est nisi conscientiae suae. Unde dicit apostolus: *Nam gloria nostra haec est: testimonium conscientiae nostrae;* et alio loco: *Opus autem suum probet unusquisque, et tunc in semet ipso tantum gloriam habebit et non in altero.* Gloriam ergo et honorem et imperium, quae sibi exoptabant et quo bonis artibus pervenire nitebantur boni, non debet sequi virtus, sed ipsa virtutem. Neque enim est vera virtus nisi quae ad eum finem tendit ubi est bonum hominis quo melius non est. Unde et honores, quos petivit Cato, petere non debuit, sed eos civitas ob eius virtutem non petenti dare.

Sed cum illa memoria duo Romani essent virtute magni, Caesar et Cato, longe virtus Catonis veritati videtur propinquior fuisse quam Caesaris. Proinde

---

[1] Sallust, *Catiline* 54.6.   [2] 2 Corinthians 1.12.
[3] Galatians 6.4.

since they took as gods the gifts of God. This gives us a clue to the goal of virtue that they chose, and the standard by which the good among them gave judgement, namely honour. For the bad among them had no virtue, although they desired to have honour, and tried to gain it by bad arts, that is, by fraud and deceit.

Cato fares better in the tribute paid to him, for of him it is said: " The less he sought for glory, the more it attached itself to him." [1] For the glory that the Romans burned to possess, be it noted, is the favourable judgement of men who think well of other men. And so virtue is a better thing, since it is not content with the testimony of men, except that of its own conscience. Hence the Apostle says: " For our glory is this, the testimony of our conscience." [2] And in another passage: " But let each one test his own work and then he will have glory in himself alone, and not in his neighbour." [3] Therefore glory and honour and power, which the Romans desired above all, the goal to which their good men climbed by good arts, should not bring virtue in its train, but they should follow virtue. For there is no true virtue except that which aims at the goal where the good of man is found, the good that has no better. Hence Cato ought not even to have sought the honours that he sought; rather, the state should have granted them to reward his virtue without his seeking them.

But though at that time there were two great characters among the Romans, Caesar and Cato, the virtue of Cato seems to have been far nearer to true virtue than that of Caesar. Now let us observe the

qualis esset illo tempore civitas et antea qualis fuisset,
videamus in ipsa sententia Catonis: " Nolite," inquit, " existimare maiores nostros armis rem publicam ex parva magnam fecisse. Si ita esset, multo
pulcherrimam eam nos haberemus. Quippe socio-
rum atque civium, praeterea armorum et equorum
maior copia nobis quam illis est. Sed alia fuere
quae illos magnos fecerunt, quae nobis nulla sunt:
domi industria, foris iustum imperium, animus in
consulendo liber, neque delicto neque libidini ob-
noxius. Pro his nos habemus luxuriam atque avari-
tiam, publice egestatem, privatim opulentiam;
laudamus divitias, sequimur inertiam; inter bonos
et malos discrimen nullum; omnia virtutis praemia
ambitio possidet. Neque mirum: ubi vos separatim
sibi quisque consilium capitis, ubi domi voluptatibus
hic pecuniae aut gratiae servitis, eo fit ut impetus
fiat in vacuam rem publicam."

Qui audit haec Catonis verba sive Sallustii putat
quales laudantur Romani veteres, omnes eos tales
tunc fuisse vel plures. Non ita est; alioquin vera
non essent quae ipse item scribit, ea quae commemoravi in secundo libro huius operis, ubi dicit
iniurias validiorum et ob eas discessionem plebis a
patribus aliasque dissensiones domi fuisse iam inde a
principio, neque amplius aequo et modesto iure
actum quam expulsis regibus, quamdiu metus a
Tarquinio fuit, donec bellum grave, quod propter

---

[1] Sallust, *Catiline* 52.19–23.
[2] *City of God* 2.18 (Vol. I, 203).

moral condition of the state at that time, and what it had been before, in Cato's own verdict. " Do not suppose," he says, " that our ancestors made the state great from its small beginnings by the use of arms. If that were so, we should have a much fairer state than in their time, for we have a greater number of allies and citizens than they had, also more arms and horses. No, it was other things that made them great, which we lack: hard work at home, a just rule abroad, and in counsel a free spirit, incapable of crime or of yielding to lust. Instead of these we have luxury and greed. The state is impoverished while private citizens are rich. We praise riches, but follow the path of idleness. We make no distinction between the good citizens and the bad. All the rewards of virtue are appropriated by ambition. And no wonder, when each of you takes thought for himself alone, when you are slaves to pleasure at home and to money and influence here in the Senate. The result is that any stroke that comes falls on a state without defences." [1]

One who hears these words of Cato (or rather, of Sallust) supposes that all the Romans of early times, or the greater part, were like the ones he praises. That is not the case. If it were, the statements of Sallust that I quoted in the second book of this work [2] would not be true, where he says that the injuries done by the powerful and the resulting secession of the plebs from the patricians and other civil dissensions existed already in the beginning. After the kings were expelled, men acted with justice and moderation only so long as there was fear of Tarquin, that is, until the end of the serious war with Etruria

ipsum cum Etruria susceptum fuerat, finiretur;
postea vero servili imperio patres exercuisse plebem,
regio more verberasse, agro pepulisse et ceteris ex-
pertibus solos egisse in imperio; quarum discordi-
arum, dum illi dominari vellent, illi servire nollent,
finem fuisse bello Punico secundo, quia rursus gravis
metus coepit urguere atque ab illis perturbationibus
alia maiore cura cohibere animos inquietos et ad
concordiam revocare civilem.

Sed per quosdam paucos, qui pro suo modo boni
erant, magna administrabantur atque illis toleratis
ac temperatis malis paucorum bonorum providentia
res illa crescebat; sicut idem historicus dicit multa
sibi legenti et audienti, quae populus Romanus domi
militiaeque, mari atque terra praeclara facinora
fecerit, libuisse adtendere quae res maxime tanta
negotia sustinuisset; quoniam sciebat saepenumero
parva manu cum magnis legionibus hostium conten-
disse Romanos, cognoverat parvis copiis bella gesta
cum opulentis regibus; sibique multa agitanti constare dixit paucorum civium egregiam virtutem cuncta patravisse, eoque factum ut divitias paupertas,
multitudinem paucitas superaret. "Sed postquam
luxu atque desidia," inquit, "civitas corrupta est,
rursus res publica magnitudine sui imperatorum atque
magistratuum vitia sustentabat."

Paucorum igitur virtus ad gloriam honorem

---

[1] Sallust, *Catiline* 53.2–5.

that the Romans engaged in on his account. After that, however, the patricians treated the plebeians as if they were slaves, scourged them tyrannically, drove them from their land and exercised power alone, excluding all others. The one class were bent on being masters, the other refused to be slaves, and the end of these dissensions came only with the Second Punic War. For then once more they felt the pressure of a great terror; a new and greater anxiety restrained their restless spirits from those disturbances and recalled them to domestic harmony.

Yet important affairs were managed by a few, who were good citizens according to their own standards. When those evils were endured or mitigated the state grew because of the foresight of a few good men. The same historian says that, as he read or heard of the many famous deeds that the Roman people performed at home and on the battle field, on sea and on land, he liked to ponder what the main thing was that carried through such great affairs. For he knew that time and again a small band of Romans had done battle with great armies of the enemy, and that wars had been waged with small resources against wealthy kings. He said that after long reflection he came to the conclusion that it was the unusual character of a few citizens that had accomplished everything, and this it was that enabled poverty to overcome wealth, and the few to defeat the many. " But," he adds, " after the state was corrupted by luxury and idleness, the republic in its turn by its very size supplied the means for the vices of its generals and magistrates."[1]

There were only a few, then, whose character was

imperium vera via, id est ipsa virtute, nitentium etiam a Catone laudata est. Hinc erat domi industria quam commemoravit Cato, ut aerarium esset opulentum, tenues res privatae. Unde corruptis moribus vitium e contrario posuit, publice egestatem, privatim opulentiam.

XIII

De amore laudis, qui, cum sit vitium, ob hoc virtus putatur quia per ipsum vitia maiora cohibentur.

QUAM ob rem cum diu fuissent regna Orientis inlustria, voluit Deus et Occidentale fieri, quod tempore esset posterius, sed imperii latitudine et magnitudine inlustrius, idque talibus potissimum concessit hominibus ad domanda gravia mala multarum gentium, qui causa honoris laudis et gloriae consuluerunt patriae, in qua ipsam gloriam requirebant, salutemque eius saluti suae praeponere non dubitaverunt, pro isto uno vitio, id est amore laudis, pecuniae cupiditatem et multa alia vitia conprimentes. Nam sanius videt qui et amorem laudis vitium esse cognoscit, quod nec poetam fugit Horatium, qui ait:

Laudis amore tumes? Sunt certa piacula, quae te
Ter pure lecto poterunt recreare libello.

---

[1] *Epistles* 1.1.36–7.

praised even by Cato, men who climbed to glory, honour and power by the true path, that is, by virtue alone. That was the source of the hard work at home that Cato mentioned, which aimed to have a full treasury but keep private wealth small. Hence in the opposite case, when morals had degenerated, he sets it down as a vice that the state was poor and private citizens rich.

XIII

On the love of praise: though a vice, it is regarded as a virtue because it checks the greater vices.

HENCE when splendid empires had long been known in the East, God willed that an empire of the West should arise, later in time, but more splendid for its extent and greatness. To overcome the grievous vices of many nations he granted supremacy to men who for the sake of honour, praise and glory served the country in which they were seeking their own glory, and did not hesitate to prefer her safety to their own. Thus for one vice, that is, love of praise, they overcame the love of money and many other vices. For that man has a saner view who recognizes that even the love of praise is a vice. This truth did not escape the poet Horace, for he says:

Do you swell with the love of praise? There are certain purgations,
Which can restore you to health, if, clean, you thrice read the booklet.[1]

Idemque in carmine lyrico ad reprimendam dominandi libidinem ita cecinit:

> Latius regnes avidum domando
> Spiritum, quam si Libyam remotis
> Gadibus iungas et uterque Poenus
> Serviat uni.

Verum tamen qui libidines turpiores fide pietatis im-
petrato Spiritu sancto et amore intellegibilis pulchritudinis non refrenant, melius saltem cupiditate
humanae laudis et gloriae non quidem iam sancti,
sed minus turpes sunt. Etiam Tullius hinc dissimu-
lare non potuit in eisdem libris quos de re publica
scripsit, ubi loquitur de instituendo principe civitatis,
quem dicit alendum esse gloria, et consequenter commemorat maiores suos multa mira atque praeclara
gloriae cupiditate fecisse. Huic igitur vitio non
solum non resistebant, verum etiam id excitandum
et accendendum esse censebant, putantes hoc utile
esse rei publicae. Quamquam nec in ipsis philo-
sophiae libris Tullius ab hac peste dissimulet, ubi
eam luce clarius confitetur. Cum enim de studiis
talibus loqueretur, quae utique sectanda sunt fine
veri boni, non ventositate laudis humanae, hanc
intulit universalem generalemque sententiam: " Honos alit artes, omnesque accenduntur ad studia
gloria iacentque ea semper quae apud quosque improbantur."

---

[1] *Odes* 2.2.9–12.   [2] Cicero, *Republic* 5.7.9.
[3] Cicero, *Tusculan Disputations* 1.2.4.

And likewise in lyric verse, to curb the lust for power
he sang:

> Wider will be your realm if you can conquer
> Greed in heart, than if to distant Gades
> Libya you should join, and the two Punic peoples
> Give to one master.[1]

However, men who do not obtain the gift of the Holy
Spirit and bridle their baser passions by pious faith
and by love of intelligible beauty, at any rate live
better because of their desire for human praise and
glory. While these men are not saints, to be sure,
they are less vile. Cicero also could not disguise
this fact. For in the books which he wrote *On the
Commonwealth*, when he spoke about training the
leader of the state, he says that he should be nur-
tured on glory.[2] Following this up, he records the
fact that his own ancestors had done many marvellous and famous deeds because of their passion for
glory. This proves that they not only failed to resist
this vice, but even judged it a thing to be aroused
and kindled, because they believed it to be advan-
tageous to the state. Moreover, not even in his
philosophical works did Cicero shrink from this pesti-
lential notion, for he declares allegiance to it in them
as plain as day. When speaking about such pursuits
as should in any case be taken up with the true good
in mind as their goal, not the windy praise of men,
he brought in this universal and general maxim:
" Honour fosters the arts. All men are fired to
endeavour by glory; and there can never be high
achievement in matters that are held in low esteem
by a particular people."[3]

XIV

De resecando amore laudis humanae, quoniam
iustorum gloria omnis in Deo sit.

Huic igitur cupiditati melius resistitur sine dubitatione quam ceditur. Tanto enim quisque est Deo
similior quanto et ab hac inmunditia mundior.
Quae in hac vita etsi non funditus eradicatur ex
corde, quia etiam bene proficientes animos temptare
non cessat, saltem cupiditas gloriae superetur dilectione iustitiae ut, si alicubi iacent quae apud quosque
improbantur, si bona, si recta sunt, etiam ipse amor
humanae laudis erubescat et cedat amori veritatis.
Tam enim est hoc vitium inimicum piae fidei, si
maior in corde sit cupiditas gloriae quam Dei timor
vel amor ut Dominus diceret: *Quo modo potestis*
credere gloriam ab invicem expectantes et gloriam quae a
solo Deo est non quaerentes? Item de quibusdam, qui
in eum crediderant et verebantur palam confiteri,
ait evangelista: *Dilexerunt gloriam hominum magis*
quam Dei.

Quod sancti apostoli non fecerunt; qui cum in his
locis praedicarent Christi nomen ubi non solum
improbabatur (sicut ille ait: Iacentque ea semper,
quae apud quosque improbantur), verum etiam sum-
mae detestationis habebatur, tenentes quod audi-

---

[1] John 5.44.   [2] John 12.43.

XIV

*On cutting back the desire for human praise, since all
the glory of the righteous is in God.*

WITHOUT doubt, therefore, it is better to resist
this passion for praise than to yield to it, for each
man resembles God the more, the more he is un-
stained by this impurity too.   Perhaps in this life it
cannot be completely eradicated from the heart, for
it does not cease to tempt even such minds as are
making good progress.   But at least the passion for
glory should be surpassed by the love of righteousness.
So if in some place no advance is made in matters
that are held in low esteem by the people, if such
matters are good and right, then love for the praise
of men should itself blush, and yield to the love of
the truth.   This vice is so great a foe of pious faith,
if the passion for glory is stronger in the heart than
the fear or love of God, that the Lord said: " How
can you believe, when you expect to receive glory
from one another, and do not seek the glory that
comes from the only God ? " [1]   Likewise concerning
certain ones who had believed on him and feared to
confess it openly the evangelist says: " They loved
the glory that is of men more than the glory that is
of God." [2]

The holy apostles did not do this.   They preached
the name of Christ, not only in places where it was
held in low esteem, just as Cicero says: " There is
no high achievement in matters that are held in low
esteem by a particular people," but even where it
was held in extreme abhorrence.   They remembered

erant a bono magistro eodemque medico mentium: *Si quis me negaverit coram hominibus, negabo eum coram patre meo, qui in caelis est,* vel *coram angelis Dei,* inter maledicta et opprobria, inter gravissimas persecutiones crudelesque poenas non sunt deterriti a praedicatione salutis humanae tanto fremitu offensionis humanae. Et quod eos divina facientes atque dicentes divineque viventes debellatis quodam modo cordibus duris atque introducta pace iustitiae ingens in ecclesia Christi gloria consecuta est, non in ea tamquam in suae virtutis fine quieverunt, sed eam quoque ipsam ad Dei gloriam referentes, cuius gratia tales erant, isto quoque fomite eos, quibus consulebant, ad amorem illius a quo et ipsi tales fierent accendebant. Namque ne propter humanam gloriam boni essent, docuerat eos magister illorum dicens: *Cavete facere iustitiam vestram coram hominibus, ut videamini ab eis; alioquin mercedem non habebitis apud patrem vestrum, qui in caelis est.* Sed rursus ne hoc perverse intellegentes hominibus placere metuerent minusque prodessent latendo quod boni sunt, demonstrans quo fine innotescere deberent: *Luceant,* inquit, *opera vestra coram hominibus, ut videant bona facta vestra et glorificent patrem vestrum, qui in caelis est.* Non ergo *ut videamini ab eis,* id est hac intentione, ut eos ad vos converti velitis, quia non per vos

---

[1] Matthew 10.33; Luke 12.9.
[2] Matthew 6.1.
[3] Matthew 5.16.

the words of the good teacher who is also the
healer of men's hearts: " Whoever denies me before
men, I will deny him before my father who is in
heaven " (or " before the angels of God ").[1] Amid
curses and reviling, amid bitter persecutions and cruel
tortures, they were not deterred from preaching
man's salvation, in spite of all the raging of man's
hatred. By their godly deeds and words and godly
manner of life they subdued the hard hearts of men
in a sort of war and filled them with the peace of
righteousness, thereby winning great glory in the
church of Christ. But they did not rest in that glory
as if it were the goal of their virtuous endeavour.
Instead, they ascribed that very glory also to the
glory of God, by whose grace they were such as they
were. And with that tinder they set fire to those
whom they taught, so that they also burned with the
love of him who had made them too such as they
were. For their master had taught them not to be
good for the sake of human glory, when he said:
" Beware of practising your piety before men to be
seen by them; for then you will have no reward from
your father who is in heaven." [2] But again, lest they
should take this in the wrong sense and be afraid to
please men and so, concealing their goodness, should
be of less help to others, he showed them with what
object they ought to attract attention: " Let your
works so shine before men that they may see your
good deeds and glorify your father who is in heaven." [3] Your purpose, therefore, is not to be seen
of men, that is, a desire that they should turn and
notice you, for of yourselves you are nothing.
Rather, it is that they may glorify your father who

aliquid estis; sed *ut glorificent patrem vestrum, qui in caelis est,* ad quem conversi fiant quod estis.

Hos secuti sunt martyres, qui Scaevolas et Curtios et Decios non sibi inferendo poenas, sed inlatas ferendo et virtute vera, quoniam vera pietate, et innumerabili multitudine superarunt. Sed cum illi essent in civitate terrena, quibus propositus erat omnium pro illa officiorum finis incolumitas eius et regnum non in caelo, sed in terra, non in vita aeterna, sed in decessione morientium et successione morituRorum, quid aliud amarent quam gloriam, qua volebant etiam post mortem tamquam vivere in ore laudantium?

XV

De mercede temporali, quam Deus reddidit bonis moribus Romanorum.

QUIBUS ergo non erat daturus Deus vitam aeternam cum sanctis angelis suis in sua civitate caelesti, ad cuius societatem pietas vera perducit, quae non exhibet servitutem religionis, quam λατρείαν Graeci vocant, nisi uni vero Deo, si neque hanc eis terrenam gloriam excellentissimi imperii concederet, non redderetur merces bonis artibus eorum, id est virtutibus, quibus ad tantam gloriam pervenire nitebantur. De talibus enim, qui propter hoc boni aliquid facere

is in heaven, and that they may turn to him and become what you are.

These apostles were followed by martyrs who surpassed men like Scaevola, Curtius and the Decii both in true courage, because they had true religion, and in their vast number. Their tortures were not self-inflicted, but they bore tortures that were inflicted by others. Those Roman heroes were citizens of an earthly city, and the goal of all their loyal service to it was its security and a kingdom not in heaven but on earth. Since there was no eternal life for them, but merely the passing away of the dying, who were succeeded by others soon to die, what else were they to love apart from glory, whereby they chose to find even after death a sort of life on the lips of those who sang their praises?

XV

On the temporal reward that God gave to the Romans in return for their good morals.

IT was not God's purpose to grant these men eternal life with the angels in his heavenly city. Only true piety leads to membership in that society, piety which offers only to the one true God the religious service which the Greeks call *latreia*. If he were not to grant them even this earthly glory of pre-eminent rule, he would not be granting a proper reward for their good arts, that is, the virtues by which they pursued the hard road that brought them at last to such glory. For it is such men, men who give the appearance of doing something good

videntur ut glorificentur ab hominibus, etiam Dominus ait: *Amen dico vobis, perceperunt mercedem suam.*
Sic et isti privatas res suas pro re communi, hoc est
re publica, et pro eius aerario contempserunt, avaritiae restiterunt, consuluerunt patriae consilio libero,
neque delicto secundum suas leges neque libidini
obnoxii; his omnibus artibus tamquam vera via nisi
sunt ad honores imperium gloriam; honorati sunt in
omnibus fere gentibus, imperii sui leges inposuerunt
multis gentibus, hodieque litteris et historia gloriosi
sunt paene in omnibus gentibus. Non est quod de
summi et veri Dei iustitia conquerantur; *perceperunt
mercedem suam.*

XVI

*De mercede sanctorum civium civitatis aeternae, quibus
utilia sunt Romanorum exempla virtutum.*

MERCES autem sanctorum longe alia est etiam hic
opprobria sustinentium pro veritate Dei, quae
mundi huius dilectoribus odiosa est. Illa civitas
sempiterna est; ibi nullus oritur, quia nullus moritur;
ibi est vera et plena felicitas, non dea, sed donum
Dei; inde fidei pignus accepimus, quamdiu peregrinantes eius pulchritudini suspiramus; ibi non
oritur sol super bonos et malos, sed sol iustitiae solos

---

[1] Matthew 6.2.

in order to gain human glory, of whom the Lord himself says: "Truly I say unto you, they have received their reward."[1] It was the same with the great Romans. They disregarded private wealth for the sake of the commonwealth, that is, for the republic and for its treasury. They stood firm against avarice, gave advice to their country with an unshackled mind and were not guilty of any crime against its laws, nor of any unlawful desire. By all these arts, as by a proper path, they strove to reach honour, power and glory. They were honoured among almost all nations; they imposed the laws of their empire upon many nations, and today they enjoy the glory conferred by literature and historical writing among almost all nations. They have no ground of complaint against the justice of the supreme and true God. "They have received their reward."

XVI

On the reward of the holy citizens of the eternal city and how the examples of virtue among the Romans may be of use to them.

VERY different is the reward of the saints, who even here endure reproaches for the truth of God, truth hateful to those who love this world. That city is eternal; there no one is born, because no one dies. True and perfect happiness (*felicitas*) is found there, and this is no goddess, but a gift of God. We have received from it the pledge of our faith, to be with us on our journey while still we aspire to its beauty. There the sun does not rise on the good and the evil,

protegit bonos; ibi non erit magna industria ditare publicum aerarium privatis rebus angustis, ubi thensaurus communis est veritatis. Proinde non solum ut talis merces talibus hominibus redderetur Romanum imperium ad humanam gloriam dilatatum est; verum etiam ut cives aeternae illius civitatis, quamdiu hic peregrinantur, diligenter et sobrie illa intueantur exempla et videant quanta dilectio debeatur supernae patriae propter vitam aeternam, si tantum a suis civibus terrena dilecta est propter hominum gloriam.

XVII

*Quo fructu Romani bella gesserint et quantum his
quos vicere contulerint.*

QUANTUM enim pertinet ad hanc vitam mortalium, quae paucis diebus ducitur et finitur, quid interest sub cuius imperio vivat homo moriturus, si illi qui imperant ad impia et iniqua non cogant? Aut vero aliquid nocuerunt Romani gentibus, quibus subiugatis inposuerunt leges suas, nisi quia id factum est ingenti strage bellorum? Quod si concorditer fieret, id ipsum fieret meliore successu; sed nulla esset gloria triumphantium. Neque enim et Romani non vivebant sub legibus suis, quas ceteris inponebant.

but the Sun of righteousness protects only the good.
There will be no devotion to hard work there, to
enrich the public treasury while private property is
scanty, for the treasury of truth is there a common
property. Furthermore, the Roman empire was
expanded to be glorious among men, not merely to
pay such men such recompense as they deserved. It
was also intended for the benefit of the citizens of the
eternal city while they are pilgrims here. Let them
give careful and sober attention to those examples,
and see how much love is due to the heavenly city
for the sake of eternal life, if the earthly city was so
much loved by its citizens for its gift of human glory.

XVII

*For what profit the Romans waged wars, and how
much they conferred on those whom they
conquered.*

As far as this mortal life is concerned, which is
passed and ended in a few days, what difference does
it make for a man who is soon to die, under what
ruler he lives, if only the rulers do not force him to
commit unholy and unjust deeds? Did the Romans
really do any harm to the conquered nations that they
brought under their laws, apart from the vast slaughter of the wars by which this was accomplished?
Suppose the same result were obtained by agreement, that would be a better success, but there would
be no glory for generals in triumphs. For the
Romans too were not exempt from living under their
own laws, the same laws that they imposed on others.

Hoc si fieret sine Marte et Bellona, ut nec Victoria
locum haberet, nemine vincente ubi nemo pugnaverat, nonne Romanis et ceteris gentibus una esset
eademque condicio? Praesertim si mox fieret,
quod postea gratissime atque humanissime factum
est, ut omnes ad Romanum imperium pertinentes
societatem acciperent civitatis et Romani cives essent,
ac sic esset omnium quod erat ante paucorum;
tantum quod plebs illa, quae suos agros non haberet,
de publico viveret; qui pastus eius per bonos ad-
ministratores rei publicae gratius a concordibus
praestaretur quam victis extorqueretur.

Nam quid intersit ad incolumitatem bonosque
mores, ipsas certe hominum dignitates, quod alii
vicerunt, alii victi sunt, omnino non video, praeter
illum gloriae humanae inanissimum fastum, in quo
perceperunt mercedem suam qui eius ingenti cupi-
dine arserunt et ardentia bella gesserunt. Numquid
enim illorum agri tributa non solvunt? Numquid
eis licet discere, quod aliis non licet? Numquid
non multi senatores sunt in aliis terris qui Romam
ne facie quidem norunt? Tolle iactantiam, et omnes
homines quid sunt nisi homines? Quod si perversitas
saeculi admitteret ut honoratiores essent quique
meliores, nec sic pro magno haberi debuit honor
humanus, quia nullius est ponderis fumus.

Suppose this came to pass without Mars and Bellona, so that Victory too had no place, with no one to conquer when no one had fought. Then would not the Romans and the other nations be in one and the same condition? This would be particularly true if the welcome and humane step had been taken at once that was taken later, of granting partnership in the state to all who were subjects of the empire, so that they were Roman citizens. Thus the privilege that formerly belonged to but few would have belonged to all, except that the Roman populace, having no land of their own, would have continued to live at public expense. Under good public administrators this feeding of the people would have been more cheerfully provided by agreement than by extortion from the conquered.

As far as security and morality are concerned, those true values of human life, I am quite unable to see what difference it makes that some men are victors and others vanquished, except for the utterly empty pride in human glory. In that pride those men received their reward, burning with intense desire for glory and spreading the flames of war. Do not Roman lands pay tribute? Have Romans permission to learn anything that is forbidden to others? Are there not many senators in other lands, who do not know Rome even by sight? Take away their boasting, and what are all men? Nothing but men. And if the perversity of the world permitted honours to be distributed according to merit, even so honour in the eyes of men ought not to have been considered of great importance, for it is a smoke that has no weight.

Sed utamur etiam in his rebus beneficio Domini
Dei nostri; consideremus quanta contempserint,
quae pertulerint, quas cupiditates subegerint pro
humana gloria qui eam tamquam mercedem talium
virtutum accipere meruerunt, et valeat nobis etiam
hoc ad opprimendam superbiam ut, cum illa civitas,
in qua nobis regnare promissum est, tantum ab hac
distet quantum distat caelum a terra, a temporali
laetitia vita aeterna, ab inanibus laudibus solida
gloria, a societate mortalium societas angelorum, a
lumine solis et lunae lumen eius qui solem fecit et
lunam, nihil sibi magnum fecisse videantur tantae
patriae cives, si pro illa adipiscenda fecerint boni
operis aliquid vel mala aliqua sustinuerint, cum illi
pro hac terrena iam adepta tanta fecerint, tanta per-
pessi sint, praesertim quia remissio peccatorum, quae
cives ad aeternam colligit patriam, habet aliquid cui
per umbram quandam simile fuit asylum illud Romu-
leum, quo multitudinem, qua illa civitas conderetur,
quorumlibet delictorum congregavit inpunitas.

But let us even in this matter make use of the profitable lesson that the Lord our God provides. Let us consider what great things those Romans disregarded, what they endured, what passions they subdued, all to get glory in the eyes of men. And so they earned the right to receive it as a reward for such virtues. And let this new thought be strong enough to hold down our pride. Let us reflect that the city in which we Christians have the promise of reigning is as far removed from this Rome as heaven is from earth, eternal life from temporal joys, solid glory from hollow praise, the company of angels from that of mortals, and the light of him who made sun and moon from the light of sun and moon; that accordingly we citizens of such a state should not look upon ourselves as having done any great thing if we have accomplished some good works to attain it, or endured some evils, seeing that the Romans did such deeds and suffered such evils for the earthly home that they possessed already. And the remission of sins that gathers citizens for the eternal city has something in it of the famous asylum of Romulus, which was a sort of shadow cast ahead. For there the multitude which was to found the city was brought together by a promised amnesty for all and sundry crimes.

SAINT AUGUSTINE

XVIII

Quam alieni a iactantia esse debeant Christiani, si aliquid fecerint pro dilectione patriae aeternae, cum tanta Romani gesserint pro humana gloria et civitate terrena.

QUID ergo magnum est pro illa aeterna caelestique patria cuncta saeculi huius quamlibet iucunda blandimenta contemnere, si pro hac temporali atque terrena filios Brutus potuit et occidere, quod illa facere neminem cogit? Sed certe difficilius est filios interimere quam quod pro ista faciendum est, ea quae filiis congreganda videbantur atque servanda vel donare pauperibus vel, si existat temptatio quae id pro fide atque iustitia fieri compellat, amittere. Felices enim vel nos vel filios nostros non divitiae terrenae faciunt aut nobis viventibus amittendae aut nobis mortuis a quibus nescimus vel forte a quibus nolumus possidendae; sed Deus felices facit, qui est mentium vera opulentia. Bruto autem, quia filios occidit, infelicitatis perhibet testimonium etiam poeta laudator. Ait enim:

Natosque pater nova bella moventes
Ad poenam pulchra pro libertate vocabit
Infelix utcumque ferent ea facta minores.

XVIII

How far from boasting Christians should be, if they have done anything for love of their eternal country, seeing that the Romans did such deeds for glory among men, and for an earthly city.

How, then, is it any great thing to despise all the allurements of this world, however sweet they be, for the sake of that eternal and heavenly country, if Brutus was able even to kill his sons for this temporal and earthly country? That is a thing that the heavenly country compels no one to do. Surely it is harder to kill sons than to do what the heavenly country requires, that is, either to give to the poor the wealth that it had been thought right to accumulate and preserve for those sons, or, if a trial should come that requires it for the sake of righteousness, to abandon it. For neither we nor our children are made happy by earthly riches, since they are bound either to be lost while we are living or to be acquired after our death by persons unknown and perhaps unwelcome. It is God that makes us happy, and he is the true wealth of our souls. As for Brutus, because he killed his sons, even the poet who praises him bears witness to his unhappiness; for he says

And when of new wars his sons are the authors,
Then for fair liberty's sake shall their sire to dire
    punishment call them,
Sire unblest, no matter how great be his praise
    through the ages.

Sed versu sequenti consolatus est infelicem:

Vincit amor patriae laudumque inmensa cupido.

Haec sunt duo illa, libertas et cupiditas laudis humanae, quae ad facta compulit miranda Romanos. Si
ergo pro libertate moriturorum et cupiditate laudum
quae a mortalibus expetuntur, occidi filii a patre
potuerunt, quid magnum est, si pro vera libertate,
quae nos ab iniquitatis et mortis et diaboli dominatu
liberos facit, nec cupiditate humanarum laudum, sed
caritate liberandorum hominum, non a Tarquinio
rege, sed a daemonibus et daemonum principe, non
filii occiduntur, sed Christi pauperes inter filios com-
putantur?

Si alius etiam Romanus princeps, cognomine Torquatus, filium, non quia contra patriam, sed etiam
pro patria, tamen quia contra imperium suum, id
est contra quod imperaverat pater imperator, ab
hoste provocatus iuvenali ardore pugnaverat, licet
vicisset, occidit, ne plus mali esset in exemplo imperii
contempti quam boni in gloria hostis occisi: ut quid
se iactent qui pro inmortalis patriae legibus omnia
quae multo minus quam filii diliguntur, bona terrena
contemnunt?

Si Furius Camillus etiam ingratam patriam, a
cuius cervicibus acerrimorum hostium Veientium
iugum depulerat damnatusque ab aemulis fuerat, a

---

[1] Virgil, *Aeneid* 6.820–23.

But in the following verse the poet has consoled the unhappy man:

Love of his country prevails, and unbounded passion
    for glory.[1]

These are the two motives that spurred the Romans on to perform miracles of valour, namely, love of freedom and desire for praise. To gain freedom for men who were destined to die, and to gratify a passion for the praise that is won from mortal men, a father could kill his sons. Then what is so great in what we Christians do? We seek true freedom, which makes men free from the tyranny of sin and death and the devil. Our motive is not a passion for the praise of men, but a love that would set men free, not from King Tarquin, but from demons and the prince of demons. We do not kill our sons, but reckon Christ's poor among our sons.

There was also another Roman leader, named Torquatus, who slew his son. He had not fought against his country, but for his country, and yet in violation of the order that his father, as general, had given. When challenged by the enemy he fought with youthful ardour, and though he was victor, he was put to death, lest there should be more harm in the example of insubordination than good in the glorious slaughter of the enemy. Then why should Christians boast if, in obedience to the laws of their immortal country, they despise all earthly goods, which they love much less than sons?

After Furius Camillus had cast from the necks of his countrymen the yoke of those bitter foes, the men of Veii, he was condemned and banished by his

Gallis iterum liberavit, quia non habebat potiorem ubi posset vivere gloriosius, cur extollatur, velut grande aliquid fecerit, qui forte in ecclesia ab inimicis carnalibus gravissimam exhonorationis passus iniuriam non se ad eius hostes haereticos transtulit aut aliquam contra illam ipse haeresem condidit, sed eam potius quantum valuit ab haereticorum perniciosissima pravitate defendit, cum alia non sit, non ubi vivatur in hominum gloria, sed ubi vita adquiratur aeterna?

Si Mucius, ut cum Porsenna rege pax fieret, qui gravissimo bello Romanos premebat, quia Porsennam ipsum occidere non potuit et pro eo alterum deceptus occidit, in ardentem aram ante eius oculos dexteram extendit, dicens multos se tales qualem illum videret in eius exitium coniurasse, cuius ille fortitudinem et coniurationem talium perhorrescens sine ulla dubitatione se ab illo bello facta pace compescuit, quis regno caelorum inputaturus est merita sua, si pro illo non unam manum neque hoc sibi ultro faciens, sed persequente aliquo patiens totum flammis corpus inpenderit?

Si Curtius armatus equo concito in abruptum hiatum terrae se praecipitem dedit, deorum suorum oraculis serviens, quoniam iusserant ut illuc id quod

---

[1] See p. 195 above.

rivals. But though his country was thus ungrateful, when she was attacked by the Gauls, he freed her a second time, since he had no other country in which he could live with more honour. Then why is a man extolled as if he had done something great when he is deprived of his office and suffers grievous wrong from carnal enemies in the church, but does not go over to its enemies, the heretics, or himself found some heresy to oppose the church, but instead defends it with all his power against the deadly depravity of the heretics? It is not for lack of another place where he may live with glory in men's eyes that he does it, but for lack of another place where he may gain eternal life.

It was Mucius' aim to force King Porsenna to make peace with the Romans, at a time when he was pressing them hard in war. Since he was unable to kill Porsenna himself, and killed another instead by mistake, he stretched out his right hand and put it in the fire that was burning on an altar before the king's eyes, saying that there were many men like himself who had sworn to destroy him. The king, terrified by his fortitude and by the revelation of a joint oath taken by such men, took no time to deliberate, but at once withdrew from the war and made peace.[1] Then who will reckon up his services to the kingdom of heaven, even if for its sake he sacrifices, not a hand, and that of his own volition, but his whole body, which, at the demand of a persecutor, he gives over to the flames?

Curtius, fully armed, spurred on his horse and plunged headlong into a sheer chasm in the earth, in obedience to the oracles of his gods. They had

Romani haberent optimum mitteretur, nec aliud in-
tellegere potuerunt quam viris armisque se excellere,
unde videlicet oportebat ut deorum iussis in illum
interitum vir praecipitaretur armatus, quid se magnum pro aeterna patria fecisse dicturus est qui aliquem fidei suae passus inimicum non se ultro in talem
mortem mittens, sed ab illo missus obierit; quando
quidem a Domino suo eodemque rege patriae suae
certius oraculum accepit: *Nolite timere eos, qui corpus
occidunt, animam autem non possunt occidere?*

Si se occidendos certis verbis quodam modo con-
secrantes Decii devoverunt, ut illis cadentibus et
iram deorum sanguine suo placantibus Romanus
liberaretur exercitus, nullo modo superbient sancti
martyres, tamquam dignum aliquid pro illius patriae
participatione fecerint ubi aeterna est et vera felicitas,
si usque ad sui sanguinis effusionem non solum suos
fratres, pro quibus fundebatur, verum et ipsos
inimicos, a quibus fundebatur, sicut eis praeceptum
est, diligentes caritatis fide et fidei caritate certa-
runt.

Si Marcus Pulvillus dedicans aedem Iovis, Iunonis,
Minervae falso sibi ab invidis morte filii nuntiata, ut
illo nuntio perturbatus abscederet atque ita dedica-
tionis gloriam collega eius consequeretur, ita con-

---

[1] Matthew 10.28.

given orders that the Romans should throw into that chasm the best thing that they had, and they could find no other meaning for the oracle but this. It was in men and in arms that they excelled; hence it was clearly required by the gods' command that a man in armour should be hurled headlong to perish so. Then what great deed will anyone say he has done for his eternal country when he encounters some enemy of his faith and suffers such a death, not dispatching himself to such a death voluntarily, but dispatched by his foe? For from his Lord, who is also king of his country, he has received a surer oracle: " Do not fear those who kill the body but cannot kill the soul." [1]

The Decii devoted themselves to death, consecrating themselves by a fixed form of ritual words, ensuring that when they fell, and placated the wrath of the gods with their blood, the Roman army should be freed from danger. If Romans could do this, then by no means will the holy martyrs be proud, as if they had done a thing worthy to earn them a share in that country where happiness is eternal and true, though they fought the good fight even to the shedding of their blood, loving not only the brethren for whom it was shed, but also the enemies by whom it was shed, even as the Lord commanded, with the faith of charity and the charity of faith.

When Marcus Pulvillus was dedicating the temple of Jupiter, Juno and Minerva, envious men brought him a false report of the death of his son, hoping that he would be disturbed by the news and withdraw, leaving his colleague to obtain the glory of the dedication. But he thought so little of it that he

tempsit ut eum etiam proici insepultum iuberet (sic
in eius corde orbitatis dolorem gloriae cupiditas
vicerat), quid magnum se pro evangelii sancti praedicatione, qua cives supernae patriae de diversis
liberantur et colliguntur erroribus, fecisse dicturus
est, cui Dominus de sepultura patris sui sollicito ait:
Sequere me et sine mortuos sepelire mortuos suos?

Si M. Regulus, ne crudelissimos hostes iurando
falleret, ad eos ab ipsa Roma reversus est, quoniam,
sicut Romanis eum tenere volentibus respondisse
fertur, postea quam Afris servierat, dignitatem illic
honesti civis habere non posset, eumque Carthagini-
enses, quoniam contra eos in Romano senatu egerat,
gravissimis suppliciis necaverunt, qui cruciatus non
sunt pro fide illius patriae contemnendi ad cuius
beatitudinem fides ipsa perducit? Aut *quid retri-
buetur Domino pro omnibus quae retribuit,* si pro
fide quae illi debetur talia fuerit homo passus qualia
pro fide quam perniciosissimis inimicis debebat passus
est Regulus?

Quo modo se audebit extollere de voluntaria paupertate Christianus, ut in huius vitae peregrinatione
expeditior ambulet viam, quae perducit ad patriam
ubi verae divitiae Deus ipse est, cum audiat vel legat
L. Valerium, qui in suo defunctus est consulatu,

---

even ordered the body to be cast out unburied—so far had the passion for glory in his heart outweighed the grief for his loss.[1] Then how will that man say that he has done anything great for the preaching of the gospel, by which citizens of the heavenly country are freed from their various errors and gathered together, to whom the Lord said, when he was worried about the burial of his father: " Follow me, and leave the dead to bury their own dead." [2]

Marcus Regulus, in order not to break the oath that he had sworn to his cruel foes, returned to them from Rome itself. When the Romans wished to detain him he is said to have answered that after being a slave to Africans he could not have the rank of an honoured citizen at home. Since in the Roman senate he had opposed accepting the Carthaginian offer, they put him to death with the most frightful torments.[3] Then what tortures are there that should not be disregarded, while we keep faith with that country to whose blessedness faith itself leads? Or " what shall be rendered to the Lord for all that he has rendered? " [4] if to keep the faith which is owed Him a man shall suffer such things as Regulus suffered to keep faith with his most deadly foes?

How will a Christian dare to exalt himself because of his voluntary poverty, undertaken in order to walk with lighter load in his pilgrimage of this life, following the path that leads to the country where God himself is the true riches? How will he dare, when he hears or reads that Lucius Valerius, who

from a variety of sources. The account here seems to resemble Eutropius' *Breviarium* 2.24.

[4] Psalms 116.12.

usque adeo fuisse pauperem ut nummis a populo
conlatis eius sepultura curaretur? audiat vel legat
Quintium Cincinnatum, cum quattuor iugera pos-
sideret et ea suis manibus coleret, ab aratro esse
adductum ut dictator fieret, maior utique honore
quam consul, victisque hostibus ingentem gloriam
consecutum in eadem paupertate mansisse?

Aut quid se magnum fecisse praedicabit qui nullo
praemio mundi huius fuerit ab aeternae illius patriae
societate seductus, cum Fabricium didicerit tantis
muneribus Pyrrhi, regis Epirotarum, promissa etiam
quarta parte regni a Romana civitate non potuisse
develli ibique in sua paupertate privatum manere
maluisse? Nam illud quod rem publicam, id est rem
populi, rem patriae, rem communem, cum haberent
opulentissimam atque ditissimam, sic ipsi in suis
domibus pauperes erant ut quidam eorum, qui iam
bis consul fuisset, ex illo senatu hominum pauperum
pelleretur notatione censoria, quod decem pondo
argenti in vasis habere compertus est; ita idem ipsi
pauperes erant, quorum triumphis publicum ditaba-
tur aerarium. Nonne omnes Christiani, qui excel-
lentiore proposito divitias suas communes faciunt
secundum id quod scriptum est in actibus apostolorum ut distribuatur unicuique sicut cuique opus est,

---

[1] Eutropius, *Breviarium* 1.11.4. Livy 2.16.7 says that
Valerius died in the year after his consulship.

[2] Again Augustine's words seem closest to Eutropius
(*Breviarium* 1.17); compare Livy 3.26 f.

[3] Eutropius, *Breviarium* 2.12.

died while holding the office of consul, was so poor
that money was collected from the people to pay the
expense of his burial? [1] Or when he hears or reads
the story of Quintius Cincinnatus, who owned four
acres and was cultivating them with his own hands
when he was taken from the plough in order to be
dictator, greater in honour surely than a consul, and
that after defeating the foe and attaining great
glory he settled down again to the same poverty? [2]

Or how will anyone proclaim that he has done
something great in refusing to be lured, by any reward that this world offers, to desert his allegiance
to that eternal country, when he learns the story of
Fabricius? In spite of the lavish bribes of Pyrrhus,
king of Epirus, including even the offer of a fourth of
his kingdom, Fabricius refused to be torn from the
Roman state, but preferred to continue in his poverty,
an ordinary private citizen.[3] For although the state
or republic (that is, the people's estate, the country's
estate, the common estate, or commonwealth) was
very rich and wealthy, the people who owned it
were in their houses so poor that one of them who
had been consul twice was expelled from that senate
of poor men by the action of the censors, who crossed
off his name because he was found to possess silver
vessels of ten pounds' weight.[4] Such was the poverty
of the very men by whose triumphs the public treasury was enriched. There are Christians who put
their wealth into a common fund with a more noble
purpose. They follow the example recorded in the
Acts of the Apostles, whereby distribution is made

[4] The senator was P. Cornelius Rufinus, whose expulsion is
related by several writers.

et nemo dicat aliquid proprium, sed sint illis omnia communia, intellegunt se nulla ob hoc ventilari oportere iactantia, id faciendo pro obtinenda societate angelorum, cum paene tale aliquid illi fecerint pro conservanda gloria Romanorum?

Haec et alia, si qua huius modi reperiuntur in litteris eorum, quando sic innotescerent, quando tanta fama praedicarentur, nisi Romanum imperium longe lateque porrectum magnificis successibus augeretur? Proinde per illud imperium tam latum tamque diuturnum virorumque tantorum virtutibus praeclarum atque gloriosum et illorum intentioni merces quam quaerebant est reddita, et nobis proposita necessariae commonitionis exempla ut, si virtutes quarum istae utcumque sunt similes, quas isti pro civitatis terrenae gloria tenuerunt, pro Dei gloriosissima civitate non tenuerimus, pudore pungamur; si tenuerimus, superbia non extollamur; quoniam, sicut dicit apostolus, *indignae sunt passiones huius temporis ad futuram gloriam, quae revelabitur in nobis.* Ad humanam vero gloriam praesentisque temporis satis digna vita aestimabatur illorum.

Unde etiam Iudaei, qui Christum occiderunt, revelante testamento novo quod in vetere velatum fuit, ut non pro terrenis et temporalibus beneficiis quae divina providentia permixte bonis malisque

---

[1] Acts 2.44; 4.43–45.   [2] Romans 8.18.

to each man according to his need, and no one calls anything his own, but they have all things common.[1] Do not these all understand that they should not for this cause puff themselves up and put on airs? They do this to obtain a place in the company of the angels, while those others did something very like it to preserve the glory of the Romans.

How would these deeds have become known, and others of the same kind that are found recorded in their books, how would they have gained such renown, if the Roman empire had not spread far and wide, as mighty victories made it greater and greater? Yes, it was through that empire, so far reaching in time and in space, so famous and glorious for the deeds of its heroes, that these men received the reward that they sought for their efforts, and that we have before us such models to remind us of our duty. If in serving the glorious city of God we do not cling to the virtues that they clung to in serving the glory of the earthly city, let us be pricked to our hearts with shame. If we do hold them fast, let us not be exalted with pride. For, as the Apostle says: "The sufferings of this present time are not worthy to be compared with the glory that is to be revealed in us."[2] But to obtain the glory of men in this present age the life of those Romans was deemed worthy enough.

Hence it was that the Jews also, who put Christ to death, were most justly added to the Roman endowment of glory. The New Testament reveals what was hidden in the Old, that the one true God should be worshipped, not for earthly and temporal benefits such as the providence of God grants to the

concedit, sed pro aeterna vita muneribusque perpetuis et ipsius supernae civitatis societate colatur
Deus unus et verus, rectissime istorum gloriae donati
sunt, ut hi qui qualibuscumque virtutibus terrenam
gloriam quaesiverunt et adquisiverunt vincerent eos
qui magnis vitiis datorem verae gloriae et civitatis
aeternae occiderunt atque respuerunt.

XIX

Quo inter se differant cupiditas gloriae et cupiditas dominationis.

INTEREST sane inter cupiditatem humanae gloriae
et cupiditatem dominationis. Nam licet proclive sit
ut qui humana gloria nimium delectatur etiam dominari ardenter affectet, tamen qui veram licet humanarum laudum gloriam concupiscunt, dant operam
bene iudicantibus non displicere. Sunt enim multa
in moribus bona de quibus multi bene iudicant, quamvis ea multi non habeant; per ea bona morum nituntur ad gloriam et imperium vel dominationem, de
quibus ait Sallustius: " Sed ille vera via nititur."
Quisquis autem sine cupiditate gloriae, qua veretur
homo bene iudicantibus displicere, dominari atque
imperare desiderat, etiam per apertissima scelera
quaerit plerumque obtinere quod diligit. Proinde
qui gloriam concupiscit, aut vera via nititur aut certe
" dolis atque fallaciis contendit," volens bonus
videri esse, quod non est.

---

[1] See p. 199 above.

good and bad alike, but for eternal life and everlasting rewards and for a place in the company of that heavenly city. So it was abundantly just that those who sought and gained earthly glory by their virtues, such as they were, should conquer those who most wickedly slew and rejected the giver of true glory and of the eternal city.

XIX

How desire for glory and desire for domination differ.

THERE is, indeed, a difference between a desire for human glory and desire for rule. Although it is an easy step for one who finds excessive delight in human glory to conceive also an ardent eagerness to rule, still those who covet true glory, though it be the praise of men, take pains not to give offence to good judges. There are many good traits of character of which there are many good judges, even though but few possess them. It is by means of these good traits that men climb to glory and power and rule, and of such a man Sallust says: " But he climbs by the true path." On the other hand, whenever anyone desires to rule and command without the desire for glory that will deter him from offending good judges, he commonly seeks to obtain the thing that he loves even by the most unconcealed deeds of crime. It follows that anyone who covets glory either strives " by the true path," or at least " pushes ahead by treachery and deceit," wishing to appear good though he is not.[1]

Et ideo virtutes habenti magna virtus est contemnere gloriam, quia contemptus eius in conspectu Dei est, iudicio autem non aperitur humano. Quidquid enim fecerit ad oculos hominum quo gloriae contemptor appareat, ad maiorem laudem, hoc est ad maiorem gloriam, facere si credatur, non est unde se suspicantium sensibus aliter esse quam suspicantur ostendat. Sed qui contemnit iudicia laudantium, contemnit etiam suspicantium temeritatem, quorum tamen, si vere bonus est, non contemnit salutem, quoniam tantae iustitiae est qui de spiritu Dei virtutes habet ut etiam ipsos diligat inimicos, et ita diligat ut suos osores vel detractores velit correctos habere consortes non in terrena patria, sed superna; in laudatoribus autem suis, quamvis parvipendat quod eum laudant, non tamen parvipendit quod amant, nec eos vult fallere laudantes ne decipiat diligentes; ideoque instat ardenter ut potius ille laudetur a quo habet homo quidquid in eo iure laudatur.

Qui autem gloriae contemptor dominationis est avidus, bestias superat sive crudelitatis vitiis sive luxuriae. Tales quidam Romani fuerunt. Non enim cura existimationis amissa dominationis cupiditate caruerunt. Multos tales fuisse prodit historia; sed huius vitii summitatem et quasi arcem quandam

Thus for the virtuous man it is a great virtue to disregard glory, for his disregard of it comes under the
eye of God, but is not disclosed to the judgement of
men. For if anyone does anything before the eyes
of men in order to appear to disregard glory, if they
think that he does this to gain greater praise (that
is, greater glory), there is no way for him to demon-
strate to the senses of those who suspect his motives
that he is really not what they think. Yet he who
disregards the opinion of those who praise, will disregard also the hasty conclusion of those who suspect
his motives. If he is truly good, however, he does
not disregard their salvation. For so great is the
righteousness of him whose virtues are the gift of the
spirit of God, that he loves even his enemies, and
loves them in such a way that he wishes to convert
those who hate or belittle him and make them fellow-
citizens with him, now set right, not of an earthly
country, but a heavenly. When, however, he has to
do with those who praise him, though he makes little
of their praising him, he does not make little of their
loving him. He would not have them mistaken in
their praise because he would not disappoint them
in their affection for him. Consequently he earnestly
entreats them to give praise rather to Him from whom
man receives whatever he has that is rightly praised.

But he who disregards glory and yet is eager for
rule outstrips wild beasts in vicious cruelty or in
luxurious living. There have been Romans of this
type, who, though they had lost interest in their
reputation, still were not free from lust for domination. History publishes the names of many such
men, but it was the emperor Nero who first mounted

Nero Caesar primus obtinuit, cuius fuit tanta luxuries ut nihil ab eo putaretur virile metuendum; tanta crudelitas ut nihil molle habere crederetur, si nesciretur. Etiam talibus tamen dominandi potestas non datur nisi summi Dei providentia, quando res humanas iudicat talibus dominis dignas. Aperta de hac re vox divina est loquente Dei sapientia: *Per me reges regnant et tyranni per me tenent terram.* Sed ne tyranni non pessimi atque improbi reges, sed vetere nomine fortes dicti existimentur (unde ait Vergilius:

Pars mihi pacis erit dextram tetigisse tyranni),

apertissime alio loco de Deo dictum est: *Quia regnare facit hominem hypocritam propter perversitatem populi.*

Quam ob rem, quamvis ut potui satis exposuerim, qua causa Deus unus verus et iustus Romanos secundum quandam formam terrenae civitatis bonos adiuverit ad tanti imperii gloriam consequendam, potest tamen et alia causa esse latentior propter diversa merita generis humani, Deo magis nota quam nobis, dum illud constet inter omnes veraciter pios, neminem sine vera pietate, id est veri Dei vero cultu, veram posse habere virtutem, nec eam veram esse quando gloriae servit humanae; eos tamen qui cives

---

[1] Proverbs 8.15.
[2] *Aeneid* 7.266
[3] Job 34.30.

to the summit and citadel, so to speak, of this vice.
So far did he go in his luxury that it might seem need-
less to fear any manly act from him, yet so cruel was
he that, except for knowing him, we might suppose
that he was exempt from weakness. And yet the
power to dominate is granted even to such men only
by the providence of the supreme God, when he
deems mankind worthy of such masters. The voice
of God puts the matter clearly in a passage where
the wisdom of God is the speaker: " By me kings
reign, and by me tyrants hold the earth." [1] It
might be supposed that the word tyrant here does
not refer to bad and unjust kings, but, according to
an old usage, to strong men. It is by this usage that
Vergil says:

Token of peace it shall be, to have touched the right
hand of the tyrant.[2]

But to avoid this misunderstanding, another passage
plainly says of God: " That he causes a hypocrite
to rule because of the perversity of the people." [3]

Thus I have sufficiently explained, as best I could,
the reason why the one true and just God gave his
aid to the Romans that they might win the glory of
so great an empire, for they were good men by the
particular standard of the earthly city. There may,
however, be another cause as well, less apparent, based
on the varied merits of mankind, better known to God
than to us. Only let there be agreement among all who
are truly religious that no one can have true virtue
without true religion, that is, without true worship of
the true God, and that there is no true virtue where
virtue is subordinated to human glory. However, those

non sint civitatis aeternae quae in sacris litteris nostris dicitur civitas Dei utiliores esse terrenae civitati quando habent virtutem vel ipsam quam si nec ipsam.

Illi autem qui vera pietate praediti bene vivunt, si habent scientiam regendi populos, nihil est felicius rebus humanis quam si Deo miserante habeant potestatem. Tales autem homines virtutes suas, quantascumque in hac vita possunt habere, non tribuunt nisi gratiae Dei quod eas volentibus credentibus petentibus dederit, simulque intellegunt quantum sibi desit ad perfectionem iustitiae, qualis est in illorum sanctorum angelorum societate, cui se nituntur aptare. Quantumlibet autem laudetur atque praedicetur virtus quae sine vera pietate servit hominum gloriae, nequaquam sanctorum exiguis initiis comparanda est, quorum spes posita est in gratia et misericordia veri Dei.

XX

Tam turpiter servire virtutes humanae gloriae quam corporis voluptati.

SOLENT philosophi qui finem boni humani in ipsa virtute constituunt ad ingerendum pudorem quibusdam philosophis, qui virtutes quidem probant, sed

who are not citizens of the eternal city (in our sacred books it is called the City of God) are more useful to the earthly city when they have their own kind of virtue than if they did not have even that.

But if those who are endowed with true religion and live good lives know the art of ruling the nations, there is no greater blessing for mankind than for them, by the mercy of God, to have the power. Such men, whether the virtues that they have in this life be great or small, ascribe them only to the grace of God, because he has granted virtue to them according to their good will, their faith and their prayers. At the same time they understand how far they fall short of perfection in righteousness, such as exists in the company of the holy angels, for which they strive to fit themselves. However much we praise and proclaim the sort of virtue that, in the absence of true religion, is subordinate to human glory, it cannot even be compared with the first faint steps of the saints who have put their hope in the grace and mercy of the true God.

XX

For the virtues to be the slaves of human glory is as shameful as for them to be the slaves of bodily pleasure.

THERE are certain philosophers who approve of the virtues, but judge them as means toward the end of bodily pleasure. This, they think, should be sought for its own sake, and the former for the sake of the latter. But other philosophers, who regard virtue

eas voluptatis corporalis fine metiuntur et illam per
se ipsam putant adpetendam, istas propter ipsam,
tabulam quandam verbis pingere, ubi voluptas in
sella regali quasi delicata quaedam regina considat,
eique virtutes famulae subiciantur, observantes eius
nutum ut faciant quod illa imperaverit, quae pruden-
tiae iubeat ut vigilanter inquirat quo modo voluptas
regnet et salva sit; iustitiae iubeat ut praestet beneficia quae potest ad comparandas amicitias corporalibus commodis necessarias, nulli faciat iniuriam, ne
offensis legibus voluptas vivere secura non possit;
fortitudini iubeat ut, si dolor corpori acciderit qui
non compellat in mortem, teneat dominam suam, id
est voluptatem, fortiter in animi cogitatione ut per
pristinarum deliciarum suarum recordationem mitiget
praesentis doloris aculeos; temperantiae iubeat ut
tantum capiat alimentorum et si qua delectant, ne per
inmoderationem noxium aliquid valetudinem turbet
et voluptas, quam etiam in corporis sanitate Epicurei
maximam ponunt, graviter offendatur. Ita virtutes
cum tota suae gloria dignitatis tamquam imperiosae
cuidam et inhonestae mulierculae servient voluptati.
Nihil hac pictura dicunt esse ignominiosius et de-
formius et quod minus ferre bonorum possit aspectus;
et verum dicunt.

Sed non existimo satis debiti decoris esse picturam,
si etiam talis fingatur, ubi virtutes humanae gloriae

---

[1] The satirical description of Queen Pleasure with the
Virtues as her handmaids is taken from Cicero, *De Finibus*

itself as the highest good of man, in order to make
the former ashamed, are accustomed to paint a certain picture in words.[1] They depict Pleasure as
sitting on a royal throne, like some dainty queen,
with the virtues serving as handmaids, watching for
her nod, so as to do whatever she orders. She orders
Prudence to inquire carefully how Pleasure may
reign and be safe. She orders Justice to bestow
such benefits as she can, in order to gain the friend-
ships necessary for physical satisfaction, and to wrong
no one, lest, if laws are broken, Pleasure be not able
to live untroubled. If there should be some bodily
pain that does not drive the victim to suicide, she
orders Fortitude to keep her mistress (that is,
Pleasure) steadfastly in view, and to soften the pangs
of present pain by the recollection of former delights.
She orders Temperance to take just so much food,
even if some kinds are tempting, for fear that some
harmful result of excess should interfere with health,
and Pleasure—which the Epicureans think is also
very largely a matter of physical health—should be
seriously hindered. Thus the virtues, with all their
glory and honour, will be the slaves of Pleasure, as
of some domineering and vulgar woman. They say
that there is nothing more disgraceful and perverted
than this picture, nothing that the eyes of good
men are less able to endure; and they speak the
truth.

But if another picture also were painted, where the
virtues are in the service of human glory, I do not
think that it would have the beauty that it should.

2.21.69, who, in turn, was translating from the Stoic Cleanthes
(compare Arnim, *Stoicorum Veterum Fragmenta* I, 125 f.).

serviunt. Licet enim ipsa gloria delicata mulier
non sit, inflata est et multum inanitatis habet. Unde
non ei digne servit soliditas quaedam firmitasque
virtutum, ut nihil provideat providentia, nihil dis-
tribuat iustitia, nihil toleret fortitudo, nihil temperantia moderetur, nisi unde placeatur hominibus
et ventosae gloriae serviatur.

Nec illi se ab ista foeditate defenderint qui, cum
aliena spernant iudicia velut gloriae contemptores,
sibi sapientes videntur et sibi placent. Nam eorum
virtus, si tamen ulla est, alio modo quodam humanae
subditur laudi; neque enim ipse qui sibi placet
homo non est. Qui autem vera pietate in Deum,
quem diligit, credit et sperat, plus intendit in ea in
quibus sibi displicet quam in ea, si qua in illo sunt,
quae non tam ipsi quam veritati placent; neque id
tribuit unde iam potest placere nisi eius misericordiae
cui metuit displicere; de his sanatis gratias agens,
de illis sanandis preces fundens.

XXI

Romanum regnum a Deo vero esse dispositum, a quo
est omnis potestas et cuius providentia reguntur
universa.

QUAE cum ita sint, non tribuamus dandi regni atque
imperii potestatem nisi Deo vero, qui dat felicitatem

of his death, to be sure, was much less harsh than
that of Pompey the Great,[1] who worshipped the so-
called gods of the Romans. For Cato, to whom Pompey bequeathed the legacy, as it were, of the civil
war, was not able to avenge his death, but Gratian
(though pious souls require no such consolation) was
avenged by Theodosius, whom he had made his
associate in the royal power, although he had a little
brother; for Gratian was more bent on getting a
reliable partner than on getting overmuch power.

XXVI

On the faith and piety of the emperor Theodosius.

For this reason Theodosius not only showed
Gratian due loyalty while he lived, but also after his
death. For Maximus had slain Gratian, and drove
his little brother Valentinian from his realm. Then
Theodosius, like a good Christian, received him as a
ward into his part of the empire, and guarded him
with paternal affection. Since he was destitute of all
resources, Theodosius could have removed him with
no effort if he had been fired more by desire to
extend his rule than by yearning to do good. But he
chose rather to receive him, maintaining his imperial
dignity and solacing him with his kindness and
favour. Then, although success had made Maximus
a formidable foe, and Theodosius was hard pressed
by anxious cares, he did not go astray into wicked
and forbidden superstitions, but instead sent to John,

Uticensis. For other names here found, see the index in
Volume VII.

Aegypti heremo constitutum, quem Dei servum prophetandi spiritu praeditum fama crebrescente didicerat, misit atque ab eo nuntium victoriae certissimum accepit.

Mox tyranni Maximi extinctor Valentinianum puerum imperii sui partibus, unde fugatus fuerat, cum misericordissima veneratione restituit, eoque sive per insidias sive quo alio pacto vel casu proxime extincto alium tyrannum Eugenium, qui in illius imperatoris locum non legitime fuerat subrogatus, accepto rursus prophetico responso fide certus oppressit, contra cuius robustissimum exercitum magis orando quam feriendo pugnavit. Milites nobis qui aderant rettulerunt extorta sibi esse de manibus quaecumque iaculabantur, cum a Theodosii partibus in adversarios vehemens ventus iret et non solum quaecumque in eos iaciebantur concitatissime raperet, verum etiam ipsorum tela in eorum corpora retorqueret. Unde et poeta Claudianus, quamvis a Christi nomine alienus, in eius tamen laudibus dixit:

O nimium dilecte Deo, cui militat aether,
Et coniurati veniunt ad classica venti!

Victor autem sicut crediderat et praedixerat, Iovis simulacra, quae adversus eum fuerant nescio quibus

---

[1] Valentinian was strangled in 392, presumably by Arbogast, a Frank whom Theodosius had made commander in Gaul. Not venturing to claim the throne for himself, Arbogast named Eugenius as emperor, a rhetorician who favoured the pagan party in Rome. Theodosius refused to accept the new usurpers, allied as they were with the pagans. His victory at the Frigidus river, near Aquileia, in 394, marks the end of

a hermit established in the desert of Egypt. He had learned from repeated acclaim that this servant of God was endowed with the spirit of prophecy, and from him he received a most reliable assurance of victory.

Soon he destroyed the tyrant Maximus, and restored the boy Valentinian with the greatest kindness and respect to that part of his empire from which he had been driven. When Valentinian perished soon after, whether by treachery or by accident or by some other means, another tyrant, Eugenius, was illegally substituted in his place.[1] Again he obtained a prophetic reply and, made sure by faith, he crushed the tyrant. It was more by prayer than by sword that he fought against this powerful army. Soldiers who were present have told me that the darts they were hurling were torn from their hands by a strong wind that blew against the enemy from the direction of Theodosius. It not only greatly accelerated all the missiles hurled against them, but also turned their own darts backward to pierce their own bodies. Hence even the poet Claudian, though a stranger to the name of Christ, nevertheless speaks in praise of Theodosius:

O prince, beloved of God, for whom heaven is
  fighting the battle,
Even the winds come, sworn to obey, at the call
  of the trumpet![2]

Being now victor, as he had believed and foretold, he overthrew the statues of Jupiter which had

armed resistance against the religious policy of the Christian emperors.

[2] Claudian, *On the Third Consulship of Honorius,* 96–98.

ritibus velut consecrata et in Alpibus constituta, deposuit, eorumque fulmina, quod aurea fuissent, iocantibus (quod illa laetitia permittebat) cursoribus et se ab eis fulminari velle dicentibus hilariter benigneque donavit. Inimicorum suorum filios, quos, non ipsius iussu, belli abstulerat impetus, etiam nondum Christianos ad ecclesiam confugientes, Christianos hac occasione fieri voluit et Christiana caritate dilexit, nec privavit rebus et auxit honoribus. In neminem post victoriam privatas inimicitias valere permisit. Bella civilia non sicut Cinna et Marius et Sulla et alii tales nec finita finire voluerunt, sed magis doluit exorta quam cuiquam nocere voluit terminata.

Inter haec omnia ex ipso initio imperii sui non quievit iustissimis et misericordissimis legibus adversus impios laboranti ecclesiae subvenire, quam Valens haereticus favens Arrianis vehementer adflixerat; cuius ecclesiae se membrum esse magis quam in terris regnare gaudebat. Simulacra gentilium ubique evertenda praecepit, satis intellegens nec terrena munera in daemoniorum, sed in Dei veri esse posita potestate.

Quid autem fuit eius religiosa humilitate mirabilius, quando in Thessalonicensium gravissimum scelus, cui iam episcopis intercedentibus promiserat

---

[1] In 390 a mob in Thessalonica murdered the governor of the city. Despite the appeal of Ambrose, Theodosius resolved to make an example of the city, and his troops slaughtered at least 7,000 victims. Ambrose refused to admit Theodosius to communion until he should do penance (see *Cambridge Medieval History* I, 244 f.).

been consecrated by some kind of ritual to accomplish his defeat and had been set up in the Alps. When his couriers, in the happy licence of victory, were jesting about the golden thunderbolts of these statues, saying that they would like to be struck by such bolts, Theodosius presented the bolts to them with jovial condescension. When his enemies met their end, not by his order, but by the fury of war, their children took refuge in a church, although they were not yet Christians. Taking advantage of this, he asked them to become Christians and treated them with Christian charity, not confiscating their property, but adding to their honours. After the victory he allowed no one to suffer because of personal enmities. He was not like Cinna, Marius, Sulla and other such men in the civil wars, who refused to end the wars that were ended. Instead of wishing the end of war to bring harm to any one he rather regretted that the war had ever begun.

Meanwhile, from the beginning of his reign he did not cease to help the church by just and merciful laws, in her struggle with the foes of religion. Valens the heretic had favoured the Arians and grievously afflicted the church, but Theodosius rejoiced more in being a member of it than in being the ruler of the world. He ordered that the statues of the pagans should everywhere be overthrown, knowing full well that not even earthly favours are in the power of demons to bestow, but in the power of the true God.

Moreover, what sight was more marvellous than the pious humility of Theodosius after he had punished the aggravated crime of the Thessalonians?[1] On the intercession of the bishops he had

indulgentiam, tumultu quorundam qui ei cohaerebant, vindicare compulsus est et ecclesiastica cohercitus disciplina sic egit paenitentiam ut imperatoriam celsitudinem pro illo populus orans magis fleret videndo prostratam quam peccando timeret iratam?

Haec ille secum et si qua similia, quae commemorare longum est, bona opera tulit ex isto temporali vapore cuiuslibet culminis et sublimitatis humanae; quorum operum merces est aeterna felicitas, cuius dator est Deus solis veraciter piis. Cetera vero vitae huius vel fastigia vel subsidia, sicut ipsum mundum lucem auras, terras aquas fructus ipsiusque hominis animam corpus, sensus mentem vitam, bonis malisque largitur; in quibus est etiam quaelibet imperii magnitudo, quam pro temporum gubernatione dispensat.

Proinde iam etiam illis respondendum esse video qui manifestissimis documentis quibus ostenditur quod ad ista temporalia quae sola stulti habere concupiscunt nihil deorum falsorum numerositas prosit confutati atque convicti conantur asserere non propter vitae praesentis utilitatem, sed propter eam quae post mortem futura est colendos deos. Nam istis qui propter amicitias mundi huius volunt vana colere et non se permitti puerilibus sensibus con-

promised indulgence for their offence, when the loud
complaint of certain members of his court drove him
to take vengeance on the people. Then, curbed by
the discipline of the Church, he did penance so
humbly that the throng, as they prayed for him,
wept with more emotion to see the imperial majesty
thus prostrate than they had felt in fear of that
majesty, when it was angered by their wrongdoing.

These deeds and others like them, which it would
take too long to relate, are the good works that
Theodosius carried with him from this temporal life,
a life that is no more than a vapour, no matter how
lofty the elevation at which any person lives. The
reward of these works is eternal happiness, which God
grants only to those of the true religion. All other
things of this life, whether lofty heights or mere
support, God bestows on both good and evil. These
include the world itself, the light, the air, the lands,
the seas, the harvests, the soul and body of man himself, sensation, mind and life. Among these things
is also the gift of empire, large or small, which God
dispenses according to his plan for the ages.

Thus it is shown by the clearest proofs that to gain
these temporal goods, which are the only goods that
fools aspire to possess, the multiplicity of false gods
is of no help at all. There are those who, when convicted of error by these proofs, seek to maintain that
the gods should be worshipped, not for any advantage
in the present life, but for the sake of that life which
is to come after death. The time has now come to
give them an answer. As for those who, for the loves
of this world, wish to worship vanities and complain
that they are not left to their childish whims, I believe

queruntur his quinque libris satis arbitror esse
responsum. Quorum tres priores cum edidissem et
in multorum manibus esse coepissent, audivi quosdam
nescio quam adversus eos responsionem scribendo
praeparare. Deinde ad me perlatum est quod iam
scripserint, sed tempus quaerant quo sine periculo
possint edere. Quos admoneo, non optent quod eis
non expedit. Facile est enim cuiquam videri
respondisse, qui tacere noluerit. Aut quid est
loquacius vanitate? Quae non ideo potest quod
veritas quia, si voluerit, etiam plus potest clamare
quam veritas.

Sed considerent omnia diligenter, et si forte sine
studio partium iudicantes talia esse perspexerint,
quae potius exagitari quam convelli possint garruli-
tate inpudentissima et quasi satyrica vel mimica
levitate, cohibeant suas nugas et potius a prudentibus
emendari quam laudari ab inpudentibus eligant.
Nam si non ad libertatem vera dicendi, sed ad
licentiam maledicendi tempus expectant, absit ut eis
eveniat quod ait Tullius de quodam, qui peccandi
licentia felix appellabatur: O miserum, cui peccare
licebat! Unde quisquis est, qui maledicendi licentia
felicem se putat, multo erit felicior, si hoc illi omnino

---

[1] From this passage it appears that Augustine first published three books of the *City of God*; this must have been
before September of 413, the date of the execution of Marcel-
linus, to whom the work was dedicated (vol. I, pp. 11, 147).
In *Letter* 169, written presumably late in 415, Augustine
mentions books four and five among the works written in that
year. Since the time of the Benedictine edition of 1679
(*Patrologia Latina* 32, 471, 475) this dating of the letter has
been generally accepted (see Goldbacher in *CSEL* 58, 44;
Zarb, *Chronologia Operum S. Augustini*, 63–6). McCracken

that my first five books are an adequate reply. When I had published the first three books and they had come into the hands of many, I heard that certain men were preparing some sort of written reply to them.[1] Then I was told that they had already written the reply but were looking for a time when they could publish it without risk to themselves. I advise these men not to wish for what is not to their advantage. It is easy for anyone who chooses not to remain silent, to think that he has answered my arguments. What is more talkative than folly? The fact that it can, if it chooses, shout louder than truth, does not prove that it has the power of truth.

But let them consider the case carefully and judge the matter, if they can, without partisan zeal. Then they may see that there are arguments that can be more easily shaken than uprooted by shameless garrulity and a frivolity like that of lampooners and clowns. So let them keep their folly in check and choose rather to be corrected by the prudent than to be praised by the shameless. If they are waiting for a future time, not of freedom to speak the truth, but of licence to revile, I hope that they may not be like the man of whom Cicero speaks. He was called happy because of the licence he enjoyed in wrong-doing, but Cicero says: "O wretched man, who had licence to do wrong!"[2] So whoever thinks himself happy in enjoying licence to revile will be much happier if he is altogether forbidden to speak. He

(vol. I, p. lxxix) expressed doubt about the dating in 415, but offers no alternative.

[2] An uncertain fragment from Cicero; compare *Tusculan Disputations* 5.19.55.

non liceat, cum possit deposita inanitate iactantiae etiam isto tempore tamquam studio consulendi quidquid voluerit contradicere et, quantum possunt, ab eis quos consulit amica disputatione honeste graviter libere quod oportet audire.

can put aside empty boasting and even at this time adopt the part of a questioner and raise all the objections he likes, and from those whom he consults he can hear what he needs to hear in a friendly discussion where they will give answer to the best of their ability and in an honourable, serious and candid manner.

BOOK VI

LIBER VI

PRAEFATIO

Quinque superioribus libris satis mihi adversus eos videor disputasse qui multos deos et falsos, quos esse inutilia simulacra vel inmundos spiritus et perniciosa daemonia vel certe creaturas, non creatorem veritas Christiana convincit, propter vitae huius mortalis rerumque terrenarum utilitatem eo ritu ac servitute quae Graece λατρεία dicitur et uni vero Deo debetur, venerandos et colendos putant. Et nimiae quidem stultitiae vel pertinaciae nec istos quinque nec ullos alios quanticumque numeri libros satis esse posse quis nesciat? quando ea putatur gloria vanitatis, nullis cedere viribus veritatis, in perniciem utique eius cui vitium tam inmane dominatur. Nam et contra omnem curantis industriam non malo medici, sed aegroti insanabilis morbus invictus est. Hi vero, qui ea quae legunt vel sine ulla vel non cum magna ac nimia veteris erroris obstinatione intellecta et considerata perpendunt, facilius nos isto numero terminatorum quinque voluminum plus quam quaestionis ipsius necessitas postulabat quam minus disseruisse iudicabunt, totamque invidiam quam

BOOK VI

PREFACE

In the five preceding books I believe that I have argued at sufficient length against those who think that the many false gods should be honoured and worshipped with the ritual and service called *latria* by the Greeks, in order to ensure enjoyment of mortal life and worldly goods. Such *latria* is due to the true God alone. For Christian truth demonstrates that pagan gods are either useless images or unclean spirits and pernicious demons, or at best only created beings and not the Creator. And who can be unaware that neither these five books nor any number, however great, can satisfy the demands of their excessive stupidity and stubbornness? For folly finds a cause for boasting in refusing to yield to the force of truth, though the result is fatal to the slave of so gross a fault. When an incurable disease resists all the efforts of a physician, it is not the doctor, but the patient who suffers. There are some, however, who understand what they read and thoughtfully weigh the arguments without any of the stubbornness of ingrained error, or without too much stubbornness. Their verdict will be that in these five books I have rather exceeded the minimum required by the argument than come short of it. As for all the hatred which the uninstructed would stir

Christianae religioni de huius vitae cladibus terrena-
rumque contritione ac mutatione rerum imperiti
facere conantur, non solum dissimulantibus, sed
contra suam conscientiam etiam faventibus doctis,
quos impietas vesana possedit, omnino esse inanem
rectae cogitationis atque rationis plenamque levissi-
mae temeritatis et perniciosissimae animositatis
dubitare non poterunt.

I

*De his qui dicunt deos a se non propter praesentem
vitam coli, sed propter aeternam.*

Nunc ergo quoniam deinceps, ut promissus ordo
expetit, etiam hi refellendi et docendi sunt qui non
propter istam vitam, sed propter illam quae post
mortem futura est, deos gentium, quos Christiana
religio destruit, colendos esse contendunt, placet a
veridico oraculo sancti psalmi sumere exordium dis-
putationis meae: *Beatus, cuius est Dominus Deus spes
ipsius et non respexit in vanitates et insanias mendaces.*
Verum tamen in omnibus vanitatibus insaniisque
mendacibus longe tolerabilius philosophi audiendi
sunt quibus displicuerunt istae opiniones erroresque
populorum, qui populi constituerunt simulacra
numinibus multaque de his quos deos inmortales
vocant, falsa atque indigna sive finxerunt sive ficta
crediderunt et credita eorum cultui sacrorumque

---

[1] Psalms 40.4.

up against the Christian religion by pointing to the calamities of this life and its grinding tribulations and reversals—while learned men, possessed by a mad impiety, not only fail to acknowledge the facts but support the attack in violation of their own consciences—these honest people will be unable to doubt that such hatred is quite devoid of honest reflection and sound logic, but is full of frivolous, reckless, deadly animosity.

I

Of those who say that the gods are not worshipped for the sake of the present life, but for eternal life.

Now in the next place, as the plan that I have announced requires, I must also refute and instruct those who maintain that the gods of the heathen, whom the Christian religion overthrows, deserve to be worshipped not for the sake of our present life, but to gain the life which is to come after death, I choose as a text for my discussion the true and inspired statement of the holy Psalm: "Blessed is the man whose hope is the Lord God, and who does not heed vanities and false delusions." [1] Nevertheless, among all the vanities and false delusions, we are bound to listen with far less impatience to those philosophers who set themselves against the opinions and errors of the nations—nations that set up statues for their deities, and either invented many false and unworthy stories about those whom they called immortal gods, or at least put faith in such false tales, and combined such faith with the worship and sacred rites of their

ritibus miscuerunt. Cum his hominibus, qui, etsi
non libere praedicando, saltem utcumque in disputationibus mussitando, talia se inprobare testati
sunt, non usque adeo inconvenienter quaestio ista
tractatur: utrum non unum Deum, qui fecit omnem
spiritalem corporalemque creaturam, propter vitam
quae post mortem futura est, coli oporteat, sed multos
deos, quos ab illo uno factos et sublimiter conlocatos
quidam eorundem philosophorum ceteris excellen-
tiores nobilioresque senserunt.

Ceterum quis ferat dici atque contendi deos illos
quorum in quarto libro quosdam commemoravi,
quibus rerum exiguarum singulis singula distri-
buuntur officia, vitam aeternam cuique praestare?
An vero peritissimi illi et acutissimi viri, qui se pro
magno beneficio conscripta docuisse gloriantur ut
sciretur quare cuique deo supplicandum esset, quid
a quoque esset petendum, ne absurditate turpissima,
qualis ioculariter in mimo fieri solet, peteretur a
Libero aqua, a Lymphis vinum, auctores erunt
cuipiam hominum diis inmortalibus supplicanti ut,
cum a Lymphis petierit vinum eique responderint:
Nos aquam habemus, hoc a Libero pete, possit recte
dicere: Si vinum non habetis, saltem date mihi vitam
aeternam? Quid hac absurditate monstrosius?
Nonne illae cachinnantes (solent enim esse ad risum

---

[1] According to Plato, *Timaeus* 40, the fixed stars, as well as
sun, moon, planets and earth, were gods, but the stars have
the highest place.

gods. These philosophers did not freely proclaim
their views, but did in one way or another, at least in
the quiet of their debates, bear witness to their
rejection of such views. With these men it is not so
very inappropriate to discuss the question whether,
in order to gain the life which is to come after death,
we should worship, not the one God who made every
spiritual and corporeal creature, but the many gods
who—as some of the same philosophers, and these
more excellent than the rest, have believed—were
created by the one God and raised by him to their
place on high.[1]

But as for those gods, some of whom I mentioned
in the fourth book, to each of whom his own petty
function is assigned, who could give a patient hearing
to the claim that they offer eternal life to anyone?
Will this really be upheld by those most acute and
learned men who boast of the great service that they
have rendered in writing books of instruction to in-
form men why each god should be worshipped, and
what is the favour to be sought from each one?
Their purpose is that men may avoid such shameful
absurdity as is a common jest in the mimes, when
someone asks Liber for water or a water nymph for
wine. Well, suppose that a man who worships the
immortal gods does ask the nymphs for wine, and
they tell him, " No, we have only water. Ask Liber
for wine." Will these authorities advise him that he
may rightly say, " If you have no wine, at least give
me eternal life "? What could be more monstrous
than such absurdity? Won't the nymphs burst out
laughing at him, since they are always ready to laugh
—assuming that they do not like demons try to

285

faciles), si non adfectent fallere ut daemones, supplici respondebunt: O homo, putasne in potestate nos habere vitam, quas audis non habere vel vitem?

Inpudentissimae igitur stultitiae est vitam aeternam a talibus diis petere vel sperare qui vitae huius aerumnosissimae atque brevissimae et si qua ad eam pertinent adminiculandam atque fulciendam ita singulas particulas tueri asseruntur ut, si id quod sub alterius tutela ac potestate est petatur ab altero, tam sit inconveniens et absurdum ut mimicae scurrilitati videatur esse simillimum. Quod cum fit ab scientibus mimis, digne ridentur in theatro; cum vero a nescientibus stultis, dignius inridentur in mundo. Cui ergo deo vel deae propter quid supplicaretur, quantum ad illos deos adtinet quos instituerunt civitates, a doctis sollerter inventum memoriaeque mandatum est; quid a Libero, verbi gratia, quid a Lymphis, quid a Vulcano ac sic a ceteris, quos partim commemoravi in quarto libro, partim praetereundos putavi. Porro si a Cerere vinum a Libero panem, a Vulcano aquam a Lymphis ignem petere erroris est, quanto maioris deliramenti esse intellegi debet, si cuiquam istorum pro vita supplicetur aeterna!

Quam ob rem si, cum de regno terreno quaereremus, quosnam illud deos vel deas hominibus credendum esset posse conferre, discussis omnibus longe alienum a veritate monstratum est a quoquam istorum multorum numinum atque falsorum saltem regna terrena existimare constitui, nonne insanissimae impietatis est, si aeterna vita, quae terrenis

deceive him—and answer the suppliant, " O man, do you think we have it in our power to give life (*vitam*), when you have been told that we can't even give wine (*vitem*) ? "

It is therefore a matter of shameless folly to ask or expect eternal life from such gods, who are said to have charge each one of a tiny bit of this brief and troubled life, and of the things which prop and sustain it. So if anyone asks of one god a thing that is under the guardianship and power of another, the request is so inappropriate and absurd that it is exactly like a jest from the mimes. When such jests are intentionally made by actors, they properly get a laugh in the theatre; when unintentionally made by fools, they even more properly provoke the laughter of the world. That is why learned men have ingeniously discovered and committed to writing the name of the god or goddess who should be invoked for each item, as far as the gods of the state religion are concerned. Liber is included, for example, and the nymphs and Vulcan and the rest. Part of these I mentioned in the fourth book, but thought fit to omit the rest. Well, if it is a mistake to ask wine from Ceres, bread from Liber, water from Vulcan and fire from the nymphs, how much sillier must we hold the act of praying to any of these gods for eternal life to be!

When we were inquiring with reference to earthly rule, which gods or goddesses must be supposed capable of conferring it on men, after a full discussion it was shown that it is a far cry from the truth to suppose that even earthly kingdoms are established by any of those many false gods. Then is it not the most mad impiety to believe that eternal life, which

omnibus regnis sine ulla dubitatione vel comparatione
praeferenda est, ab istorum quoquam dari cuiquam
posse credatur? Neque enim propterea dii tales vel
terrenum regnum dare non posse visi sunt quia illi
magni et excelsi sunt, hoc quiddam parvum et
abiectum, quod non dignarentur in tanta sublimitate
curare; sed quantumlibet consideratione fragilitatis
humanae caducos apices terreni regni merito quisque
contemnat, illi dii tales apparuerunt ut indignissimi
viderentur quibus danda atque servanda deberent
vel ista committi. Ac per hoc, si (ut superiora
proximis duobus libris pertractata docuerunt) nullus
deus ex illa turba vel quasi plebeiorum vel quasi
procerum deorum idoneus est regna mortalia mortalibus dare, quanto minus potest inmortales ex
mortalibus facere!

Huc accedit quia, si iam cum illis agimus qui non
propter istam, sed propter vitam quae post mortem
futura est esistimant colendos deos, iam nec propter
illa saltem quae deorum talium potestati tamquam
dispertita et propria non ratione veritatis, sed vanitatis opinione tribuuntur, omnino colendi sunt, sicut
credunt hi qui cultum eorum vitae huius mortalis
utilitatibus necessarium esse contendunt; contra
quos iam quinque praecedentibus voluminibus satis,
quantum potui, disputavi. Quae cum ita sint, si
eorum qui colerent deam Iuventatem aetas ipsa
floreret insignius, contemptores autem eius vel intra
annos occumberent iuventutis, vel in ea tamquam

is without a doubt incomparably preferable to all
earthly kingdoms, is at the disposal of any of them?
And such gods were thought unable to grant even
earthly rule, not because they were great and exalted,
while the gift was small and base, so that in their
sublimity they would not deign to bother with it, but
for another reason. Granted that when we con-
template the frailty of human life, anyone may well
despise the tottering summits of earthly power, yet
these gods have shown themselves quite unworthy to
have the granting and preserving even of these
things entrusted to their hands. Therefore if, as the
argument of the last two books has shown, no god out
of that throng of what one may call plebeian gods, or
noble gods either, is fit to grant mortal kingdoms to
mortals, how much less can any god make immortal
beings out of mortals!

A further observation may be added. If we are
now dealing with men who think that the gods
should be worshipped not for the sake of this life, but
to gain that which is to come after death, it is clear
now that such gods should not be worshipped at all,
even to gain the things that are singled out and
assigned to their power, not by any consideration of
truth, but by idle fancy. This is the belief of those
who argue that their worship is necessary for the
interests of this mortal life, but I have already
refuted them sufficiently, to the best of my ability, in
the five preceding books. Suppose it to be true that
those who worship the goddess Juventas are mark-
edly superior in the bloom of youth, while those who
slight her either die prematurely in youth, or lose
their vigour while still young, as in a sluggish old age.

senili torpore frigescerent; si malas cultorum suorum
speciosius et festivius Fortuna barbata vestiret, a
quibus autem sperneretur glabros aut male barbatos
videremus, etiam sic rectissime diceremus huc usque
istas deas singulas posse, suis officiis quodam modo
limitatas, ac per hoc nec a Iuventate oportere peti
vitam aeternam, quae non daret barbam, nec a
Fortuna barbata boni aliquid post hanc vitam esse
sperandum, cuius in hac vita potestas nulla esset, ut
eandem saltem aetatem quae barba induitur ipsa
praestaret.

Nunc vero cum earum cultus nec propter ista ipsa
quae putant eis subdita sit necessarius, quia et multi
colentes Iuventatem deam minime in illa aetate
viguerunt, et multi non eam colentes gaudent robore
iuventutis, itemque multi Fortunae barbatae supplices
ad nullam vel deformem barbam pervenire potuerunt,
et si qui eam pro barba impetranda venerantur, a
barbatis eius contemptoribus inridentur, itane desipit
cor humanum ut, quorum deorum cultum propter ista
ipsa temporalia et cito praetereuntia munera, quibus
singulis singuli praeesse perhibentur, inanem ludi-
briosumque cognoscit, propter vitam aeternam
credat esse fructuosum? Hanc dare illos posse nec
hi dicere ausi sunt qui eis, ut ab insipientibus populis
colerentur, ista opera temporalia, quoniam nimis

BOOK VI. 1

And suppose it is true that Fortuna Barbata clothes the cheeks of her worshippers with a fairer and smarter beard, while we observe that those who slight her are beardless, or bearded with unfortunate results. Even so we should be absolutely right if we declared that the power of each of those goddesses reaches thus far and no further; each is by some means restricted to her own sphere of duty. It follows that it is a mistake to pray to Juventas for eternal life, a goddess unable to grant a beard, and wrong to expect any good after this life from Fortuna Barbata, a goddess who has no power to bestow even life for the period when the beard is worn.

The truth is, however, that there is no need to worship these goddesses even to obtain the very things that are held to be under their care. Many worshippers of Juventas have been anything but vigorous in their youth. and many who do not worship her still rejoice in youthful strength. So too, many suppliants of Fortuna Barbata have been unable to get a beard, or any but an ugly one, and those who revere her in order to obtain a beard are ridiculed by bearded men who despise her. Is any human mind so witless as to believe that the worship of such gods will be rewarded by eternal life, when he knows that their worship is unavailing and a mockery even when it merely seeks to gain the temporal and transitory favours that particular gods are severally reported to have in their keeping? To assert that they can grant eternal life was a claim too bold even for the men who divided up the temporal duties and assigned them to the gods piecemeal in order to ensure them a place in the worship of ignorant people. There

multos putarunt, ne quisquam eorum sederet otiosus, minutatim divisa tribuerunt.

II

Quid Varronem de diis gentium sensisse credendum sit, quorum talia et genera et sacra detexit, ut reverentius cum eis ageret, si de illis omnino reticeret.

Quis Marco Varrone curiosius ista quaesivit? Quis invenit doctius? quis consideravit adtentius? Quis distinxit acutius? Quis diligentius pleniusque conscripsit? Qui tametsi minus est suavis eloquio, doctrina tamen atque sententiis ita refertus est ut in omni eruditione, quam nos saecularem, illi autem liberalem vocant, studiosum rerum tantum iste doceat, quantum studiosum verborum Cicero delectat, Denique et ipse Tullius huic tale testimonium perhibet ut in libris Academicis dicat eam quae ibi versatur disputationem se habuisse cum Marco Varrone, " homine," inquit, " omnium facile acutissimo et sine ulla dubitatione doctissimo." Non ait " eloquentissimo " vel " facundissimo," quoniam re vera in hac facultate multum impar est; sed " omnium," inquit, " facile acutissimo," et in eis libris, id est Academicis, ubi cuncta dubitanda esse contendit, addidit " sine ulla dubitatione doctissimo." Profecto de hac re sic erat certus ut auferret dubitationem quam solet in

---

[1] A fragment preserved only here.

were too many gods for the jobs, they thought, but by slicing the work thin they left none unemployed.

II

What we must suppose was Varro's view of the gods, whose nature and rites he disclosed in such a way that it would have been more reverent to have kept altogether silent about them.

WHO has investigated these questions more carefully than Marcus Varro? Who has been more scholarly in his research? Who has given closer attention to the subject? Who has made sharper distinctions? Who has written a more careful and complete survey of the matter? Although he is not so pleasant in his style, his writings are so packed with information and maxims that in the whole range of studies which we call " secular " and the pagans call " liberal " he imparts as much instruction to the student of history as Cicero imparts delight to the student of oratory. Besides, Tullius himself goes so far in praising him as to say in his *Academica* that the discussion there reported was carried on with Marcus Varro, " Of all men," he says, " easily the most acute and without doubt the most learned." [1] He does not say " most eloquent " or " most fluent ", for indeed in that department he is much inferior. But he did say, " of all men easily the most acute," and adds— this is in the *Academica*, in books where he argues that everything is doubtful—" without doubt the most learned." Indeed, he was so certain of this point that he dismissed the doubt that he usually musters

omnibus adhibere, tamquam de hoc uno etiam pro
Academicorum dubitatione disputaturus se Academi-
cum fuisset oblitus. In primo autem libro cum
eiusdem Varronis litteraria opera praedicaret:
" Nos," inquit, " in nostra urbe peregrinantes
errantesque tamquam hospites tui libri quasi domum
reduxerunt, ut possemus aliquando qui et ubi esse-
mus agnoscere. Tu aetatem patriae, tu descriptiones
temporum, tu sacrorum iura, tu sacerdotum, tu
domesticam, tu publicam disciplinam, tu sedem
regionum locorum, tu omnium divinarum humana-
rumque rerum nomina genera, officia causas ape-
ruisti."

Iste igitur vir tam insignis excellentisque peritiae
et, quod de illo etiam Terentianus elegantissimo
versiculo breviter ait:

Vir doctissimus undecumque Varro,

qui tam multa legit ut aliquid ei scribere vacuisse
miremur; tam multa scripsit quam multa vix quemquam legere potuisse credamus, iste, inquam, vir
tantus ingenio tantusque doctrina, si rerum velut
divinarum de quibus scripsit oppugnator esset atque
destructor easque non ad religionem, sed ad superstitionem diceret pertinere, nescio utrum tam multa
in eis ridenda contemnenda detestanda conscriberet.
Cum vero deos eosdem ita coluerit colendosque
censuerit ut in eo ipso opere litterarum suarum dicat
se timere ne pereant, non incursu hostili, sed civium

---

[1] *Academica* 1.3.9.
[2] Terentianus Maurus, *De Metris* 2846.

on every disputed point, as if in this one matter
he had forgotten that he was an Academic, even
when he was about to argue in defence of Academic
scepticism. And in the first book he commends the
literary efforts of this same Varro in these words:
" When we were like foreigners in our own city, and
like strangers gone astray, your books led us back to
our home, as it were; at last we could know who we
were and where we were. You it is who have disclosed the age of our country, the periods of its history,
the laws of its religion and its priesthoods, the rules of
private and public life, the topography of its regions
and places, the names, classifications, functions and
origins of all divine and human institutions." [1]

This man, then, was a remarkable and outstanding
expert, and, as Terentianus puts it briefly in an
elegant line of verse:

" A man of the highest learning, start where you
will, this Varro." [2]

He read so much that we marvel that he found any
time to write; he wrote so much that we scarce believe
that anyone ever found time to read it all. If this
man, I say, of such ability and learning, had intended
to attack and destroy the so-called divine things of
which he writes, and had said that they belong not
to religion, but to superstition, I wonder whether he
would have included in his work so many things that
are worthy of ridicule, of scorn or of detestation. But
in fact he worshipped the gods and considered their
worship so necessary that he says in this very work
that he was alarmed for fear they would perish, not
by an enemy's invasion, but by the neglect of his

neglegentia, de qua illos velut ruina liberari a se dicit
et in memoria bonorum per eius modi libros recondi
atque servari utiliore cura quam Metellus de incendio
sacra Vestalia et Aeneas de Troiano excidio penates
liberasse praedicatur; et tamen ea legenda saeculis
prodit, quae a sapientibus et insipientibus merito
abicienda et veritati religionis inimicissima iudi-
centur, quid existimare debemus nisi hominem
acerrimum ac peritissimum, non tamen sancto
Spiritu liberum, oppressum fuisse suae civitatis
consuetudine ac legibus, et tamen ea quibus move-
batur sub specie commendandae religionis tacere
noluisse?

III

*Quae sit partitio Varronis librorum suorum, quos de
antiquitatibus rerum humanarum divinarumque
composuit.*

QUADRAGINTA et unum libros scripsit antiquitatum;
hos in res humanas divinasque divisit, rebus humanis
viginti quinque, divinis sedecim tribuit, istam secutus
in ea partitione rationem ut rerum humanarum
libros senos quattuor partibus daret. Intendit enim
qui agant, ubi agant, quando agant, quid agant. In
sex itaque primis de hominibus scripsit, in secundis
sex de locis, sex tertios de temporibus, sex quartos
eosdemque postremos de rebus absolvit. Quater
autem seni viginti et quattuor fiunt. Sed unum

---

[1] Metellus was pontifex maximus in 241 B.C. For his rescue
of sacred objects, see above 3.18 (vol. 1, 351).

fellow citizens.   He says that in rescuing them from
this downfall, and in storing and preserving them in
the memory of good citizens by writing such books,
he is performing a service more essential than the
much renowned deeds of Metellus, who rescued the
holy appurtenances of Vesta from the fire,[1] and of
Aeneas, who saved the Penates from the fall of Troy.
Yet Varro gives the world things to read that wise
men and fools alike might justly condemn as worthless and incompatible with true religion.   What are
we to think of this, except that a man of the greatest
acumen and learning, though not emancipated by the
Holy Spirit, was under pressure from the customs and
laws of his city, yet under the show of commending
religion chose not to veil in silence his strong feelings
about things that troubled him?

III

*The plan of Varro's books, which he wrote " On the
Antiquities of Human and Divine Things."*

VARRO wrote forty-one books of " Antiquities "
which he divided into " Human Things " and
" Divine Things," assigning twenty-five books to the
former and sixteen to the latter.   " Human Things "
he divided into four parts of six books each, taking up
in turn the persons who act, the places, the times and
the actions.   That is, in the first six books he writes
about men, in the next six about places, in the next six
about times, and finishes the work in the last six by
writing about things.   Four times six are twenty-
four, but at the head of these books he placed a single

singularem, qui communiter prius de omnibus loqueretur, in capite posuit. In divinis identidem rebus
eadem ab illo divisionis forma servata est, quantum
adtinet ad ea quae diis exhibenda sunt. Exhibentur
enim ab hominibus in locis et temporibus sacra.
Haec quattuor, quae dixi, libris complexus est ternis:
nam tres priores de hominibus scripsit, sequentes
de locis, tertios de temporibus, quartos de sacris,
etiam hic, qui exhibeant, ubi exhibeant, quando exhibeant, quid exhibeant, subtilissima distinctione
commendans.

Sed quia oportebat dicere et maxime id expecta-
batur quibus exhibeant, de ipsis quoque diis tres conscripsit extremos, ut quinquies terni quindecim
fierent. Sunt autem omnes, ut diximus, sedecim,
quia et istorum exordio unum singularem, qui prius
de omnibus loqueretur, apposuit. Quo absoluto
consequenter ex illa quinquepertita distributione
tres praecedentes, qui ad homines pertinent, ita
subdivisit ut primus sit de pontificibus, secundus de
auguribus, tertius de quindecimviris sacrorum;
secundos tres ad loca pertinentes ita ut in uno eorum
de sacellis, altero de sacris aedibus diceret, tertio de
locis religiosis; tres porro, qui istos sequuntur et ad
tempora pertinent, id est ad dies festos, ita ut unum
eorum faceret de feriis, alterum de ludis circensibus,
de scaenicis tertium; quartorum trium ad sacra

---

[1] The word *feriae* (*fesìae*) was originally identical in meaning
with *dies festus*, " a holiday, a day dedicated to the gods," and
hence *nefas*, on which no profane business could be done.

298

book to discuss in a general way all the matters that follow. Again in the treatment of " Divine Things " the same plan is followed, as far as it is applicable to the rites performed for the gods. For men, in certain places, at certain times, perform certain sacred rites. These four topics which I have named, Varro discussed in three books each. In the first three he writes about men, in the next about places, in the third about times, and in the fourth about sacred rites, thus presenting the reader in this case also with a very neat distinction between those who perform, where and when they perform, and what they perform.

But since it was necessary to state for whom these rites were performed, which is what his readers would especially look for, he also wrote a final set of three books about the gods themselves. Five times three make fifteen, but these books, as we have said, total sixteen, for here, too, he added a single book as an introduction, to provide a preliminary discussion of the whole subject. After this introduction he went on to subdivide the five divisions that I have named. Of the first three books on men, the first book is on the pontiffs, the second on augurs, and the third on the quindecimvirs. Of the second three on places, he writes in one of them on shrines, in another on sacred temples, and in a third on religious places. The three books that follow " On Times," that is, on festivals, include one book on holidays,[1] another on the games of the circus, and a third on theatrical performances. Of the fourth trio on sacred rites he

Later *dies festi* came to include the days of circus and theatrical performances, which were not *nefas*.

pertinentium uni dedit consecrationes, alteri sacra
privata, ultimo publica. Hanc velut pompam obse-
quiorum in tribus qui restant dii ipsi sequuntur
extremi, quibus iste universus cultus inpensus est:
in primo dii certi, in secundo incerti, in tertio cunctorum novissimo dii praecipui atque selecti.

IV

*Quod ex disputatione Varronis apud cultores deorum
antiquiores res humanae quam divinae reperiantur.*

IN hac tota serie pulcherrimae ac subtilissimae dis-
tributionis et distinctionis vitam aeternam frustra
quaeri et sperari inpudentissime vel optari, ex his
quae iam diximus et quae deinceps dicenda sunt,
cuivis hominum qui corde obstinato sibi non fuerit
inimicus, facillime apparet. Vel hominum enim sunt
ista instituta vel daemonum, non quales vocant illi
daemones bonos, sed, ut loquar apertius, inmun-
dorum spirituum et sine controversia malignorum,
qui noxias opiniones, quibus anima humana magis
magisque vanescat et incommutabili aeternaeque
veritati coaptari atque inhaerere non possit, invi-
dentia mirabili et occulte inserunt cogitationibus
impiorum et aperte aliquando ingerunt sensibus et
qua possunt fallaci adtestatione confirmant. Iste

assigned one book to consecrations, one to private
rites, and the last to public rites. This parade, as it
were, of obsequious rites is concluded by the gods
themselves, to whom this whole system of worship is
devoted. They are described in the three books
which remain: in the first the " certain gods "; in
the second the " uncertain gods "; and in the third
and last of all the " principal and select gods."

IV

*From Varro's account it appears that among the pagans
" human things " are older than " divine things."*

IN this whole succession of topics, so beautifully and
neatly divided and distinguished, one looks in vain
for the way to eternal life; it is a shameless piece of
folly to hope or desire to find it there. To any man
who has not by obstinacy of mind become his own
enemy this fact is clearly evident from what I have
already said and from what I have yet to say. For
these institutions are either the work of men or of
demons. Nor are these demons of the kind the
pagans call good. To speak more clearly, they are
unclean spirits, unquestionably malignant, who with
astounding malice secretly implant in the minds of
unbelievers harmful opinions, in order that the human
soul may grow more and more frivolous and so be unable to grasp and cleave to the unchangeable,
eternal truth. They also work openly, presenting
these deadly beliefs at times to the senses and
confirming them by such deceitful evidence as they
have power to produce. Varro himself says that the

ipse Varro propterea se prius de rebus humanis, de
divinis autem postea scripsisse testatur quod prius
extiterint civitates, deinde ab eis haec instituta sint.
Vera autem religio non a terrena aliqua civitate
instituta est, sed plane caelestem ipsa instituit
civitatem. Eam vero inspirat et docet verus Deus,
dator vitae aeternae, veris cultoribus suis.

Varronis igitur confitentis ideo se prius de rebus
humanis scripsisse, postea de divinis, quia divinae
istae ab hominibus institutae sunt, haec ratio est:
" Sicut prior est," inquit, " pictor quam tabula
picta, prior faber quam aedificium, ita priores sunt
civitates quam ea quae a civitatibus instituta sunt."
Dicit autem prius se scripturum fuisse de diis, postea
de hominibus, si de omni natura deorum scriberet,
quasi hic de aliqua scribat et non de omni, aut vero
etiam aliqua, licet non omnis, deorum natura non
prior debeat esse quam hominum. Quid quod in
illis tribus novissimis libris deos certos et incertos et
selectos diligenter explicans nullam deorum naturam
praetermittere videtur ? Quid est ergo, quod ait :
" Si de omni natura deorum et hominum scriberemus,
prius divina absolvissemus, quam humana adtigisse-
mus ? " Aut enim de omni natura deorum scribit,
aut de aliqua, aut omnino de nulla. Si de omni,
praeponenda est utique rebus humanis ; si de aliqua,
cur non etiam ipsa res praecedat humanas ? An

reason why he wrote first about human things and
later about divine things was that states came into
existence first, and that these institutions were
established by the states. But true religion was not
instituted by any earthly city-state, but was itself
clearly the founder of a heavenly city, a city truly
inspired and instructed by the true God, who gives
eternal life to his true worshippers.

Now when Varro confesses that his reason for writing first about human things and later about divine
things was that the latter were instituted by men, he
gives this explanation: " Just as the painter exists
before the picture, and the builder before the building, so the city-states precede the institutions that
are set up by them." Yet he says that he would
have written first about the gods and then about men
if he had been writing about the divine nature as a
whole. The implication is that he deals with part of
their nature, and not the whole, and that a good part
of the divine being, though not the whole, should not
be given precedence over human beings. And what
of the fact that in the last three books, when carefully
explaining the " certain " and " uncertain " and
" select " gods, he seems to omit no part of the
divine nature? Then why does he say, " If we were
writing about the whole nature of gods and of men,
we should have dealt with divine matters before
touching on human matters"? For either he is
writing about the whole nature of the gods, or about
some part, or about no part at all. If he is writing
about the whole, it should by all means be placed
before human things; and if he is writing only about a
part, why does not that part also not take precedence

indigna est praeferri etiam universae naturae
hominum pars aliqua deorum?

Quod si multum est, ut aliqua pars divina prae-
ponatur universis rebus humanis, saltem digna est vel
Romanis. Rerum quippe humanarum libros, non
quantum ad orbem terrarum, sed quantum ad solam
Roman pertinet, scripsit, quos tamen rerum divinarum libris se dixit scribendi ordine merito praetu-
lisse, sicut pictorem tabulae pictae, sicut fabrum
aedificio, apertissime confitens quod etiam istae res
divinae, sicut pictura, sicut structura, ab hominibus
institutae sint. Restat ut de nulla deorum natura
scripsisse intellegatur, neque hoc aperte dicere
voluisse, sed intellegentibus reliquisse. Ubi enim
dicitur "non omnis," usitate quidem intellegitur
aliqua; sed potest intellegi et "nulla," quoniam
quae nulla est nec omnis nec aliqua est. Nam, ut
ipse dicit, si omnis esset natura deorum de qua
scriberet, scribendi ordine rebus humanis praeponenda esset; ut autem et ipso tacente veritas
clamat, praeponenda esset certe rebus Romanis,
etiamsi non omnis, sed saltem aliqua esset. Recte
autem postponitur; ergo nulla est.

Non itaque rebus divinis anteferre voluit res
humanas, sed rebus veris noluit anteferre res falsas.

over human things? Or is there some part of the
gods that is unworthy to be preferred to the entirety
of mankind?

If this is too much, for some part of the divine to be
preferred to all human affairs, at least some part is
surely worthy to be put ahead of Roman affairs. For
in the books on human affairs he dealt not with the
whole world, but with Rome alone, and yet he said
that he had properly put these books ahead of the
divine in his plan of composition, just as the painter
comes before the painting and the builder before the
building. Thus he openly avows that this edifice of
religion, like the picture and the building, was fabri-
cated by men. So only the third hypothesis remains,
that he was not writing about any existing gods at
all, and that he did not wish to state this openly, but
left it to be discerned by the intelligent. For when
he says that he was not writing about the whole,
according to common usage the reader supposes that
he was writing about some part. But he can also be
understood to mean no part, for that is neither the
whole nor any part. For, as he himself says, if it were
the whole divine nature about which he was writing,
then in the order of composition he should have put it
before human affairs. And even if he said nothing,
the truth itself cries out that this should in any case
have been put before Roman affairs, for even if it was
not the whole, it was at least a part of the divine.
But he is right to put it last, and consequently he
writes of what is not divine at all.

It follows, not that Varro chose to give human
affairs precedence over divine, but that he did not
choose to give precedence to fiction over truth. For

In his enim quae scripsit de rebus humanis, secutus
est historiam rerum gestarum; quae autem de his
quas divinas vocat, quid nisi opiniones rerum
vanarum? Hoc est nimirum quod voluit subtili
significatione monstrare, non solum scribens de his
posterius quam de illis, sed etiam rationem reddens
cur id fecerit. Quam si tacuisset, aliter hoc factum
eius ab aliis fortasse defenderetur. In ea vero ipsa
ratione quam reddidit, nec aliis quicquam reliquit
pro arbitrio suspicari et satis probavit homines se
praeposuisse institutis hominum, non naturam
hominum naturae deorum. Ita se libros rerum
divinarum non de veritate quae pertinet ad naturam,
sed de falsitate quae pertinet ad errorem scripsisse
confessus est. Quod apertius alibi posuit, sicut in
quarto libro commemoravi, ex naturae formula se
scripturum fuisse, si novam ipse conderet civitatem;
quia vero iam veterem invenerat, non se potuisse nisi
eius consuetudinem sequi.

V

De tribus generibus theologiae secundum Varronem, id
est uno fabuloso, altero naturali tertioque civili.

DEINDE illud quale est quod tria genera theologiae
dicit esse, id est rationis quae de diis explicatur,
eorumque unum mythicon appellari, alterum physi-

---

[1] 4.31, p. 117 above.

in what he wrote of human affairs he followed the record of historical events, but when he writes about matters that he calls " divine," what does he include except speculations about unrealities? This is no doubt what he wanted to convey by a subtle indication, not only by putting these after human affairs in his book, but also by giving his reason for doing so. If he had not stated his reason, various people might perhaps have defended his procedure on various grounds, but by actually giving the reason as he did he left others no occasion to guess at what he meant. He gives proof enough that he had put men before the institutions of men, not the truth about men before the truth about the gods. Thus he admits that when he wrote his books on the divine, his subject was not a truth that pertains to the real world, but a fiction that belongs to the realm of error. And this he stated even more clearly elsewhere, as I have recounted in the fourth book.[1] For he says that if he were himself founding a new city, he would have written in accordance with the rule of nature, but since he found himself a citizen of an ancient city he could do nothing except follow its traditions.

V

Of the three kinds of theology according to Varro: first the mythical, second the natural, and third the civil.

NEXT, what is the significance of his saying that there are three kinds of theology, that is, of the account that is given of the gods? Of these one is called mythical, another physical, and the third, civil.

con, tertium civile ? Latine si usus admitteret, genus
quod primum posuit fabulare appellaremus; sed
fabulosum dicamus; a fabulis enim mythicon dictum
est, quoniam μῦθος Graece fabula dicitur. Secundum autem ut naturale dicatur, iam et consuetudo
locutionis admittit. Tertium etiam ipse Latine
enuntiavit, quod civile appellatur. Deinde ait:
" Mythicon appellant, quo maxime utuntur poetae;
physicon, quo philosophi; civile, quo populi. Primum," inquit, " quod dixi, in eo sunt multa contra
dignitatem et naturam inmortalium ficta. In hoc
enim est ut deus alius ex capite, alius ex femore sit,
alius ex guttis sanguinis natus; in hoc ut dii furati
sint, ut adulterarint, ut servierint homini; denique in
hoc omnia diis adtribuuntur quae non modo in
hominem, sed etiam quae in contemptissimum hominem cadere possunt." Hic certe ubi potuit, ubi
ausus est, ubi inpunitum putavit, quanta mendacissi-
mis fabulis naturae deorum fieret iniuria, sine caligine
ullius ambiguitatis expressit. Loquebatur enim non
de naturali theologia, non de civili, sed de fabulosa,
quam libere a se putavit esse culpandam.

Videamus quid de altera dicat. " Secundum genus
est," inquit, " quod demonstravi, de quo multos
libros philosophi reliquerunt; in quibus est dii qui
sint, ubi, quod genus, quale est; a quodam tempore

If Latin usage allowed, we should call the kind that he placed first " fabular." But let us call it " fabulous," for the term " mythical " is derived from fables, since in Greek a·fable is called *mythos*. The second kind may be called " natural," as common usage already approves. To the third kind Varro himself gives a Latin name, that of " civil." Then he continues: " They call the theology that is used chiefly by poets ' mythical,' that used by philosophers ' physical,' and that used by city-states ' civil.' The first kind that I named," Varro says next, " has much fiction that is inconsistent with the dignity and true nature of immortal beings. In such fiction, for instance, we are told how one god sprang from the head, another from the thigh, another from drops of blood; and again how gods have been thieves, adulterers or slaves of a man. In short, in this theology everything is ascribed to the gods that can befall a man, even the very lowest of men." Here, at least, where he could, where he dared, where he thought he could speak with impunity, he pointed out without any obscurity or ambiguity what injustice is done to the true nature of the gods by such utterly mendacious fables. For he was speaking not of natural theology, or of civil, but of the mythical, which he thought deserved his frank denunciation.

Now let us see what he says of the second kind of theology. " The second kind of theology that I have pointed out," he says, " is the subject of many books that philosophers have bequeathed to us, in which they set forth what gods there are, where they are, what their origin is and what their nature, that is, whether they were born at a certain time or have

an a sempiterno fuerint dii; ex igni sint, ut credit Heraclitus, an ex numeris, ut Pythagoras, an ex atomis, ut ait Epicurus. Sic alia, quae facilius intra parietes in schola quam extra in foro ferre possunt aures." Nihil in hoc genere culpavit, quod physicon vocant et ad philosophos pertinet, tantum quod eorum inter se controversias commemoravit, per quos facta est dissidentium multitudo sectarum. Removit tamen hoc genus a foro, id est a populis; scholis vero et parietibus clausit. Illud autem primum mendacissimum atque turpissimum a civitatibus non removit. O religiosas aures populares atque in his etiam Romanas! Quod de diis inmortalibus philosophi disputant, ferre non possunt; quod vero poetae canunt et histriones agunt, quae contra dignitatem ac naturam inmortalium ficta sunt, quia non modo in hominem, sed etiam in contemptissimum hominem cadere possunt, non solum ferunt, sed etiam libenter audiunt. Neque id tantum, sed diis quoque ipsis haec placere et per haec eos placandos esse decernunt.

Dixerit aliquis: Haec duo genera mythicon et physicon, id est fabulosum atque naturale, discernamus ab hoc civili de quo nunc agitur, unde illa et ipse discrevit, iamque ipsum civile videamus qualiter explicet. Video quidem cur debeat discerni fabulo-

always existed, whether they are of fire as Heraclitus believes, or of numbers as Pythagoras thinks, or of atoms as Epicurus says. And there are many other such points, which our ears can endure to hear better within the walls of a school than outside in the market-place." He found nothing to censure in this theology, which they call physical and which appertains to philosophers. He merely mentions their controversies with each other, which have resulted in a multitude of quarrelling sects. However, he banished this kind of religion from the forum, that is, from the people, and locked it up inside the walls of the schools. But he did not banish that first kind of theology from the cities, though it was utterly false and vile. O how sensitive are the pious ears of the peoples, among them the Roman people! They are unable to tolerate the disputes of the philosophers about the immortal gods, but as for the tales chanted by the poets and enacted by players on the stage, that is, fictitious tales inconsistent with the dignity and true nature of immortal beings, because they relate tales appropriate only for a man, even the very lowest of men,—these they not merely tolerate, but even gladly give ear to them. And not only so, but they have decided that such stories are pleasing to the gods themselves, and that they are to be employed as a means of propitiation.

Perhaps someone will say, " Let us separate the two kinds of religion, the mythical and the physical, which we call the fabulous and the natural, from the civil religion which we are now discussing, just as Varro himself separated them, and let us see how he expounds the civil religion." I can see very well why

sum: quia falsum, quia turpe, quia indignum est.
Naturale autem a civili velle discernere quid est aliud
quam etiam ipsum civile fateri esse mendosum? Si
enim illud naturale est, quid habet reprehensionis ut
excludatur? Si autem hoc quod civile dicitur
naturale non est, quid habet meriti ut admittatur?
Haec nempe illa causa est quare prius scripserit de
rebus humanis, posterius de divinis, quoniam in
divinis rebus non naturam, sed hominum instituta
secutus est.

Intueamur sane et civilem theologian. " Tertium
genus est," inquit, " quod in urbibus cives, maxime
sacerdotes, nosse atque administrare debent. In
quo est, quos deos publice colere, quae sacra et
sacrificia quemque par sit." Adhuc quod sequitur
adtendamus. " Prima, inquit, theologia maxime
accommodata est ad theatrum, secunda ad mundum,
tertia ad urbem." Quis non videat, cui palmam
dederit? Utique secundae, quam supra dixit esse
philosophorum. Hanc enim pertinere testatur ad
mundum, quo isti nihil esse excellentius opinantur in
rebus. Duas vero illas theologias, primam et
tertiam, theatri scilicet atque urbis, distinxit an
iunxit? Videmus enim non continuo quod est urbis
pertinere posse et ad mundum, quamvis urbes esse
videamus in mundo; fieri enim potest ut in urbe

---

[1] The text here translated is from Migne's *Patrologia*. The
manuscipts are confused, and the passage is marked with a
crux in the Teubner edition.

he ought to discriminate against the mythical theology, for the reason that it is false, vile and unworthy of the gods. But deliberately to separate the natural from the civil, what else is that but to confess that the civil theology is a sham? For if the other theology is natural, what is found wrong with it that it should be excluded? And if the theology called civil is not natural, what is its qualification for admission? In fact, this is the reason why he wrote first about human affairs and later about divine, namely that in describing the divine he was not following what exists in nature, but rather the institutions of men.

But in any case let us scrutinize the civil theology too. "The third kind," he says, "is that which citizens in the states, and especially the priests, have an obligation to learn and carry out. It tells us what gods are to be worshipped by the state and what rites and sacrifices individuals should perform." [1] Let us note also his further comment: "The first theology," he says, "is chiefly suited to the theatre, the second to the universe, the third to the city." Who does not see to which he awards the palm? Surely it is the second, which he had already said was the province of philosophers. This, he testifies, relates to the universe, and philosophers hold the view that nothing exists that is superior to the universe. But what of the other two theologies, the first and the third, the theatrical and the civil? Has he made a difference between them or combined them into one? We can see that what belongs to the city does not necessarily belong to the universe, although we see that cities are in the universe. For

secundum falsas opiniones ea colantur et ea credantur
quorum in mundo vel extra mundum natura sit
nusquam. Theatrum vero ubi est nisi in urbe?
Quis theatrum instituit nisi civitas? Propter quid
instituit nisi propter ludos scaenicos? Ubi sunt ludi
scaenici nisi in rebus divinis, de quibus hi libri tanta
sollertia conscribuntur?

VI

De theologia mythica, id est fabulosa, et de civili
contra Varronem.

O MARCE Varro, cum sis homo omnium acutissimus
et sine ulla dubitatione doctissimus, sed tamen homo,
non Deus, nec spiritu Dei ad videnda et adnuntianda
divina in veritatem libertatemque subvectus, cernis
quidem quam sint res divinae ab humanis nugis atque
mendaciis dirimendae; sed vitiosissimas populorum
opiniones et consuetudines in superstitionibus publicis vereris offendere, quas ab deorum natura abhorrere vel talium quales in huius mundi elementis
humani animi suspicatur infirmitas, et sentis ipse,
cum eas usquequaque consideras, et omnis vestra
litteratura circumsonat. Quid hic agit humanum
quamvis excellentissimum ingenium? Quid tibi
humana licet multiplex ingensque doctrina in his
angustiis suffragatur? Naturales deos colere cupis,

it can happen that in the city false opinions lead to the worship of such things and the belief in such things as exist nowhere, neither in the universe nor outside it. But where is there a theatre, if not in the city? Who established the theatre, if not the city-state? For what purpose was it established, if not for the stage plays? And where do the stage plays belong, if not among the divine things, which Varro in his treatise describes with such skill?

VI

Of the mythical, or fabulous theology, and the civil theology: a critique of Varro.

O Marcus Varro, since you are the most acute of all men and beyond doubt the most learned—though still a man and not a god, and not lifted up by the spirit of God into truth and freedom to see and declare divine things—you do perceive how necessary it is to separate things divine from the frivolities and lies of men. But you are afraid to oppose the beliefs and customs of the people, altogether vicious as they are, where superstition appears in public rites. These superstitions clash with the true nature of the gods, even such gods as the weakness of the human mind supposes it finds in the elements of this world. You see this yourself whenever you reflect upon the matter, and all your literature has echoes of the same view. Of what avail is a man's ingenuity here, even the most outstanding? In such straits what support do you find in man's learning, however varied and profound it be? You desire to worship the gods of

civiles cogeris. Invenisti alios fabulosos, in quos
liberius quod sentis evomas, unde et istos civiles
velis nolisve perfundas. Dicis quippe fabulosos
accommodatos esse ad theatrum, naturales ad mundum, civiles ad urbem, cum mundus opus sit divinum,
urbes vero et theatra opera sint hominum, nec alii
dii rideantur in theatris quam qui adorantur in templis, nec aliis ludos exhibeatis quam quibus victimas
immolatis. Quanto liberius subtiliusque ista divi-
deres dicens alios esse deos naturales, alios ab
hominibus institutos, sed de institutis aliud habere
litteras poetarum, aliud sacerdotum, utrasque tamen
ita esse inter se amicas consortio falsitatis ut gratae
sint utraeque daemonibus quibus doctrina inimica est
veritatis!

Sequestrata igitur paululum theologia quam
naturalem vocant, de qua postea disserendum est,
placetne tandem vitam aeternam peti aut sperari ab
diis poeticis theatricis, ludicris scaenicis? Absit;
immo avertat Deus verus tam inmanem sacrile-
gamque dementiam. Quid? Ab eis diis quibus
haec placent et quos haec placant, cum eorum illic
crimina frequententur, vita aeterna poscenda est?
Nemo, ut arbitror, usque ad tantum praecipitium
furiosissimae impietatis insanit. Nec fabulosa igitur
nec civili theologia sempiternam quisquam adipiscitur

nature, but you are forced to worship those of the
state. You have discovered other mythical gods,
against whom you may blurt out more freely what
you think, and thereby, whether you intend it or not,
also cast aspersions on the gods of the state. For you
say that the mythical gods are made for the theatre,
the natural gods for the universe, and the civil for the
city. But the universe is a divine creation, while
cities and theatres are the creations of man; and the
gods ridiculed in the theatres are none other than
those who are worshipped in the temples, and those
for whom you present the shows are none other than
those to whom you sacrifice victims. How much
more honest and accurate would your analysis be if
you had said that some gods exist in nature while
others are set up by men, and that of those so set up
the poets give one description and the priests
another, while both are so bound together in a
friendly society of deceivers that both are pleasing
to the demons, to whom the teaching of the truth is
hateful!

Leaving aside then for later discussion the theology
that they call natural, does anyone really propose to
ask or expect eternal life from the gods of the poets
and the theatres, of the farces and the other plays?
God forbid! Rather, may the true God avert from
us such monstrous and sacrilegious madness! What!
Are we to claim eternal life from gods who are
pleased and placated by such shows when their
crimes are celebrated there? No one, I think, is so
insane as to throw himself into such an abyss of
the wildest blasphemy. It follows then that no one
obtains eternal life either by way of mythical or civil

vitam. Illa enim de diis turpia fingendo seminat,
haec favendo metit; illa mendacia spargit, haec
colligit; illa res divinas falsis criminibus insectatur,
haec eorum criminum ludos in divinis rebus amplecti-
tur; illa de diis nefanda figmenta hominum carminibus personat, haec ea deorum ipsorum festivitatibus
consecrat; facinora et flagitia numinum illa cantat,
haec amat; illa prodit aut fingit, haec autem aut
adtestatur veris aut oblectatur et falsis. Ambae
turpes ambaeque damnabiles; sed illa, quae theatrica
est, publicam turpitudinem profitetur; ista, quae
urbana est, illius turpitudine ornatur. Hincine vita
aeterna sperabitur, unde ista brevis temporalisque
polluitur? An vero vitam polluit consortium nefario-
rum hominum, si se inserant affectionibus et assen-
sionibus nostris, et vitam non polluit societas
daemonum qui coluntur criminibus suis? Si veris,
quam mali! Si falsis, quam male!

Haec cum dicimus, videri fortasse cuipiam nimis
harum rerum ignaro potest ea sola de diis talibus
maiestati indigna divinae et ridicula detestabilia
celebrari, quae poeticis cantantur carminibus et ludis
scaenicis actitantur; sacra vero illa, quae non histriones, sed sacerdotes agunt, ab omni esse dedecore

theology. The former plants the seed by inventing
vile stories about the gods, and the latter reaps the
harvest by giving its approval; the one sows false-
hoods, the other garners them; the one charges
divinity with fictitious crimes, the other includes
among religious rites the shows that portray the
crimes; the one makes those unspeakable stories of
the gods resound in the songs of men, the other
sanctifies them as part of the festivals of the gods;
the one sings of the crimes and shameful deeds of the
deities while the other is enamoured of them; the
one reports or invents these deeds while the other
either bears witness to their truth or enjoys them
even though they are fictitious. Both are vile and
both are damnable, but one, that of the theatre,
makes public profession of its indecency, while the
other, that of the city, makes that indecency its own
adornment. Are we to look for eternal life from a
source that stains with its pollution our short temporal
life? If our life is in fact polluted when we associate
with wicked men who worm their way into our
affection and admiration, surely it must be polluted
when we associate with demons who are worshipped
by the enactment of their crimes. If the crimes are
really so, how evil the demons! If they are fiction,
how evil the worship!

On hearing my statement the thought might occur
to someone who is ill informed about these matters
that only those stories of such gods as are the subjects
of the poets' songs and are acted out on the stage,
depict things unworthy of the divine majesty, being
ridiculous or detestable, while the deeds enacted by
priests, not by actors, are purged of all shame and

purgata et aliena. Hoc si ita esset, numquam
theatricas turpitudines in eorum honorem quisquam
celebrandas esse censeret, numquam eas ipsi dii
praeciperent sibimet exhiberi. Sed ideo nihil pudet
ad obsequium deorum talia gerere in theatris quia
similia geruntur in templis.

Denique cum memoratus auctor civilem theologian
a fabulosa et naturali tertiam quandam sui generis
distinguere conaretur, magis eam ex utraque tem-
peratam quam ab utraque separatam intellegi voluit.
Ait enim ea, quae scribunt poetae, minus esse quam
ut populi sequi debeant; quae autem philosophi, plus
quam ut ea vulgum scrutari expediat. " Quae sic
abhorrent," inquit, " ut tamen ex utroque genere ad
civiles rationes adsumpta sint non pauca. Quare
quae erunt communia, una cum propriis civilibus
scribemus; e quibus maior societas debet esse nobis
cum philosophis quam cum poetis." Non ergo nulla
cum poetis. Et tamen alio loco dicit de generationibus deorum magis ad poetas quam ad physicos
fuisse populos inclinatos. Hic enim dixit quid fieri
debeat, ibi quid fiat. Physicos dixit utilitatis causa
scripsisse, poetas delectationis. Ac per hoc ea
quae a poetis conscripta populi sequi non debent,

---

¹ The text at this point is that of Hoffmann in the Vienna
Corpus. The Teubner text follows the manuscripts: " quae
erunt communia cum propriis, una cum civilibus scribemus."
Most editors have found this unintelligible; for *propriis* the
Benedictines substitute *poetis,* Dombart *populis.*

clean. If this were so, no one would ever have
proposed that the shameful acts depicted in the
theatre should be included in shows given in their
honour, and the gods themselves would never have
required their exhibition. But the reason why men
are not ashamed to perform such deeds in the theatres
in obedience to the gods, is because performances in
the temples are of the same sort.

Finally, when our renowned author was trying to
distinguish the civil theology from the mythical and
the natural, as being a third and special kind, he
wished it to be understood that it is rather a com-
bination of the other two kinds, and not one separate
from both. For he says that the writings of the
poets are too low to serve as a guide for the people,
while the writings of the philosophers are too high for
them to investigate safely. " These disagree with
each other," he says, " but still not so much as to
prevent the adoption of many items from each source
in the civil theology. Hence we shall describe what
it has in common with each of the others, along with
the special features of the civil theology,[1] but we
must keep company with the philosophers more than
with the poets." Then it does have something in
common with the poets. But in another passage he
says of the genealogies of the gods that the people
are more inclined to follow the poets than the physical philosophers. In one passage he says what ought
to be done, in the other what is actually done. He
says that the natural philosophers wrote in order to
benefit the people, and the poets to please them.
Hence the tales of the poets that the people ought
not to follow must be the crimes of the gods, which

crimina sunt deorum, quae tamen delectant et
populos et deos. Delectationis enim causa, sicut
dicit, scribunt poetae, non utilitatis; ea tamen
scribunt, quae dii expetant, populi exhibeant.

VII

*De fabulosae et civilis theologiae similitudine atque
concordia.*

Revocatur igitur ad theologian civilem theologia
fabulosa theatrica scaenica, indignitatis et turpitudinis plena, et haec tota, quae merito culpanda et
respuenda iudicatur, pars huius est, quae colenda et
observanda censetur; non sane pars incongrua, sicut
ostendere institui, et quae ab universo corpore aliena
importune illi conexa atque suspensa sit, sed omnino
consona et tamquam eiusdem corporis membrum
convenientissime copulata. Quid enim aliud ostendunt illa simulacra formae aetates sexus habitus
deorum? Numquid barbatum Iovem, imberbem
Mercurium poetae habent, pontifices non habent?
Numquid Priapo mimi, non etiam sacerdotes enormia
pudenda fecerunt? An aliter stat adorandus in locis
sacris quam procedit ridendus in theatris? Num
Saturnus senex, Apollo ephebus ita personae sunt

nevertheless give pleasure both to the people and to the gods. For, as he says, the poets write to please, not to benefit. Moreover, they write tales for the gods to exact and for the people to perform in their honour.

VII

On the similarity and agreement of the mythical and civil theology.

THUS we see that the mythical theology, the theology of the theatre and the stage, with all its vulgarity and foulness, harks back to the civil theology. The whole of the mythical theology, which is properly judged on its merits to be worthy of denunciation and scorn, is a subdivision of the other which is accepted as worthy of honour and observance. As I have made it a point to show, it is certainly not an incongruous part, foreign to the body as a whole, unsuitably joined and fastened to it. No, it fits perfectly and is joined with the utmost propriety, like a limb of the same body. For how are the statues any different, as they display the figures of the gods with their age, sex and dress? The poets have a bearded Jupiter and a beardless Mercury; don't the pontiffs have the same? Have not the priests as well as the mimes represented Priapus with an enormous phallus? Does his cult statue, set up to be worshipped in sacred grounds, look any different from the figure that comes on to be laughed at in the theatre? The aged Saturn and the youthful Apollo are represented by actors on the stage. Does that mean that they are not so represented by

323

histrionum, ut non sint statuae delubrorum? Cur
Forculus, qui foribus praeest, et Limentinus, qui
limini, dii sunt masculi, atque inter hos Cardea
femina est, quae cardinem servat? Nonne ista in
rerum divinarum libris reperiuntur, quae graves
poetae suis carminibus indigna duxerunt? Numquid
Diana theatrica portat arma et urbana simpliciter
virgo est? Numquid scaenicus Apollo citharista est
et ab hac arte Delphicus vacat?

Sed haec honestiora sunt in comparatione tur-
piorum. Quid de ipso Iove senserunt, qui eius nutri-
cem in Capitolio posuerunt? Nonne adtestati sunt
Euhemero, qui omnes tales deos non fabulosa gar-
rulitate, sed historica diligentia homines fuisse
mortalesque conscripsit? Epulones etiam deos,
parasitos Iovis, ad eius mensam qui constituerunt,
quid aliud quam mimica sacra esse voluerunt? Nam
parasitos Iovis ad convivium eius adhibitos si mimus
dixisset, utique risum quaesisse videretur. Varro
dixit! non cum inrideret deos, sed cum commendaret
hoc dixit; divinarum, non humanarum rerum libri
hoc eum scripsisse testantur, nec ubi ludos scaenicos
exponebat, sed ubi Capitolina iura pandebat. Deni-

---

¹ Amalthea was the nurse of the infant Jupiter. Whether
she was a goat, or a nymph who owned the goat, is disputed.
Both versions of the myth are illustrated in ancient altar
reliefs and paintings. See Daremberg-Saglio, *Dictionnaire* I,
220.

² On Euhemerus, see note on page 100, above.

³ The *epulones* were a college of priests to whom the pontiffs
in 196 B.C. assigned the management of the *epulum*, or banquet
of Jupiter, at the annual festivals. The word is also rarely
used of men who enjoy banquets. In one inscription it is an
epithet of Jupiter, in another an epithet of Mercury. Here,

statues in the shrines? Why are Forculus, who presides at the door, and Limentinus at the threshold, male gods, while between them Cardea, who guards the hinge, is female? Are not these matters found in the books " On Divine Things," matters that serious poets have judged unworthy of poetic treatment? Diana of the theatre comes on with her weapons; is Diana of the city a simple, unarmed maid? Apollo on the stage is a performer on the lyre; does the god of Delphi lack such skill?

But these matters are comparatively respectable in view of viler things to come. What idea of Jupiter did those men have who put a nymph as his nurse in the Capitol?[1] Did they not give evidence in support of Euhemerus who wrote, not as a garrulous story-teller, but as a careful historian, that all such gods had once been men, and subject to death?[2] Men have also given the " feasting gods " a place at the table of Jupiter as his parasites.[3] What else did they intend except that the sacred rites should agree with the mimes? If a mime had said that they were parasites of Jupiter invited to dine with him, he would obviously seem to have been trying to get a laugh. But Varro said it, and said it not in a context of mockery, but of favourable comment on the gods. This statement is found in his books " On Divine Things," not in the ones " On Human Things," and it is not in the part where he was describing stage plays, but where he was revealing the ritual of the Capitoline temple. Finally he is forced by such

apparently, all the gods are included who shared Jupiter's *lectisternium* (see note on p. 84, above; compare also *Thesaurus* V, 703 on *epulo*; Wissowa, *RK²*, 120).

que talibus vincitur et fatetur, sicut forma humana
deos fecerunt, ita eos delectari humanis voluptatibus
credidisse.

Non enim et maligni spiritus suo negotio defuerunt
ut has noxias opiniones humanarum mentium ludi-
ficatione firmarent. Unde etiam illud est quod
Herculis aedituus otiosus atque feriatus lusit tesseris
secum utraque manu alternante, in una constituens
Herculem, in altera se ipsum, sub ea condicione ut, si
ipse vicisset, de stipe templi sibi cenam pararet
amicamque conduceret; si autem victoria Herculis
fieret, hoc idem de pecunia sua voluptati Herculis
exhiberet; deinde cum a se ipso tamquam ab
Hercule victus esset, debitam cenam et nobilissimam
meretricem Larentinam deo Herculi dedit. At illa
cum dormisset in templo, vidit in somnis Herculem
sibi esse commixtum sibique dixisse quod inde dis-
cedens, cui primum iuveni obvia fieret, apud illum
esset inventura mercedem quam sibi credere deberet
ab Hercule persolutam. Ac sic abeunti cum primus
iuvenis ditissimus Tarutius occurrisset eamque
dilectam secum diutius habuisset, illa herede defunctus est. Quae amplissimam adepta pecuniam
ne divinae mercedi videretur ingrata, quod acceptissi-
mum putavit esse numinibus, populum Romanum

---

[1] Acca Larentia (or Larenta, or Larentina) was a goddess
whose festival, the Larentalia (or Larentinalia) fell on December 23, when the pontiffs brought a sacrifice to her altar in the
Velabrum (Cicero, *Epistle to Brutus*, 1.15.8). Varro, Plutarch

evidence to confess that, just as men made gods in
human form, so they also believed that the gods
enjoyed the same pleasures as men.

Nor, in fact, did the evil spirits fail to do their
work of confirming these harmful notions by tricks
that delude men's minds. An example of this is
found in the following story. A custodian of the
temple of Hercules, when at leisure and unoccupied,
was playing dice with himself, his right hand against
his left. One hand was for Hercules, the other for
himself, the terms being that if he should win he
would use the temple funds to buy a dinner and hire
a mistress for himself, while if he lost to Hercules he
would provide as much from his own funds for the
pleasure of Hercules. Then when he was beaten by
himself, by the hand representing Hercules, he gave
the god the dinner that was due, along with the
famous courtesan Larentina.[1] So when she had
fallen asleep in the temple, she dreamed that Hercules lay with her and told her that when she left the
place she would get her pay from the first young man
she met, and should count it as paid to her by
Hercules. As she took her leave on these terms, the
first one to meet her was the very rich youth Tarutius.
He fell in love with her, and after living with her for
some time he died and left his property to her. Thus
she gained an ample fortune, and in order not to seem
ungrateful for the god's reward, she did what she
thought would be most pleasing to the gods, and

and Macrobius speak of the site as the grave of Acca, so that
Wissowa (*RK*[2], 233 f.) places her among the spirits of the lower
world. Latte, however, argues that Cicero's words exclude
this possibility (*Römische Religionsgeschichte*, 92).

etiam ipsa scripsit heredem, atque illa non comparente inventum est testamentum; quibus meritis eam ferunt etiam honores meruisse divinos.

Haec si poetae fingerent, si mimi agerent, ad fabulosam theologian dicerentur procul dubio pertinere et a civilis theologiae dignitate separanda iudicarentur. Cum vero haec dedecora non poetarum, sed populorum; non mimorum, sed sacrorum; non theatrorum, sed templorum; id est non fabulosae, sed civilis theologiae, a tanto doctore produntur, non frustra histriones ludicris artibus fingunt deorum quae tanta est turpitudinem, sed plane frustra sacerdotes velut sacris ritibus conantur fingere deorum quae nulla est honestatem.

Sacra sunt Iunonis, et haec in eius dilecta insula Samo celebrabantur, ubi nuptum data est Iovi; sacra sunt Cereris ubi a Plutone rapta Proserpina quaeritur; sacra sunt Veneris ubi amatus eius Adon aprino dente extinctus iuvenis formosissimus plangitur; sacra sunt Matris deum ubi Attis pulcher adulescens ab ea dilectus et muliebri zelo abscisus etiam hominum abscisorum, quos Gallos vocant, infelicitate deploratur. Haec cum deformiora sint omni scaenica foeditate, quid est quod fabulosa de

---

[1] Attis was a Phrygian shepherd boy, beloved by the Mother of the gods, but he deserted her for a nymph. In jealous rage

named the Roman people as her heir. When she disappeared, her will was found, and they say that for such services she even won divine honours.

If the poets were to invent tales like this and the mimes to act them out, they would undoubtedly be assigned to the mythical theology and thus banished from the high estate of the civil theology. But our great scholar publishes these scandals, not as poetic inventions, but as public dogma; not as part of the mimes, but as part of the sacred rites; not as belonging to the theatres, but to the temples—in short, not to the mythical, but to the civil theology. The actors do not fail by their comic art to portray the infamy of the gods, great as that is, but the priests certainly fail when in their so-called sacred rites they attempt to fashion a respectable character for their gods, a character which does not exist.

There are rites of Juno, formerly celebrated on her beloved island of Samos, where she was given as a bride to Jupiter. There are rites of Ceres where Proserpina is sought, after she has been carried off by Pluto. There are rites of Venus where her lover, the handsome youth Adonis, is mourned as slain by the tusk of a boar. There are rites of the Mother of the gods where the fair youth Attis, beloved by her and castrated because of a woman's jealousy, is bewailed by unhappy castrated men who are called Galli.[1] Since these rites are more shameful than all the filth of the stage, why is it that they make such efforts to

she destroyed the nymph, driving Attis mad, so that he castrated himself. He thus set an example for those who were afterward to become her priests. See Ovid, *Fasti* 4.223–244, Catullus 73 and Rose, *Handbook of Greek Mythology*, 170.

diis figmenta poetarum ad theatrum videlicet pertinentia velut secernere nituntur a civili theologia,
quam pertinere ad urbem volunt, quasi ab honestis
et dignis indigna et turpia? Itaque potius est unde
gratiae debeantur histrionibus, qui oculis hominum
pepercerunt nec omnia spectaculis nudaverunt quae
sacrarum aedium parietibus occuluntur.

Quid de sacris eorum boni sentiendum est, quae
tenebris operiuntur, cum tam sint detestabilia quae
proferuntur in lucem? Et certe quid in occulto
agant per abscisos et molles, ipsi viderint; eosdem
tamen homines infeliciter ac turpiter enervatos
atque corruptos occultare minime potuerunt. Persuadeant cui possunt se aliquid sanctum per tales
agere homines, quos inter sua sancta numerari atque
versari negare non possunt. Nescimus quid agant,
sed scimus per quales agant. Novimus autem quae
agantur in scaena, quo numquam vel in choro
meretricum abscisus aut mollis intravit; et tamen
etiam ipsa turpes et infames agunt; neque enim ab
honestis agi debuerunt. Quae sunt ergo illa sacra
quibus agendis tales elegit sanctitas quales nec
thymelica in se admisit obscenitas?

---

[1] The stage performances of the Floralia were noted for their
unrestrained character. Instead of the regular actresses
(*mimae*), harlots (*meretrices*) were substituted, who would
disrobe themselves at the demand of the audience (Wissowa,
RE 6, 2751). The festival became popular in the provinces as
well as in Rome (Latte, *Römische Religionsgeschichte*, 73).

separate the fictions of the poets, which of course belong to the theatre, from the civil theology which they say belongs to the city, as if they were separating unworthy and base things from things honourable and worthy? Consequently we have reason rather to thank the actors who have spared men's eyes, and have not laid bare in public shows everything that is screened by the walls of the temples.

What good can we think of the rites that are shrouded in darkness, when the things that are brought out to the light are so detestable? To be sure, the rites that are secretly performed by castrated and effeminate men are their own affair; they were, however, quite unable to keep these same men out of sight, men unhappily and shamefully unmanned and depraved. Let them persuade whoever they can that some holy act is performed by the ministry of such men, since they cannot deny that these men are counted as holy and occupied with their holy rites. We do not know what they do, but we do know the men that they use to do it. Moreover, we know what happens on the stage, where no eunuch or effeminate man has ever come on, even as one of a chorus of harlots.[1] And still the plays too are enacted by base and infamous men, for in fact they could not have been presented by men of good standing. What sort of sacred rites, then, are those, for whose performance their holy purity has chosen such men as not even the obscenity of the stage has admitted to its company?

Augustine implies that a similar custom was followed in Carthage in connection with the worship of the Virgo Caelestis (Vol. I, 251 f.).

SAINT AUGUSTINE

VIII

De interpretationibus naturalium rationum quas doctores pagani pro diis suis conantur ostendere.

At enim habent ista physiologicas quasdam, sicut aiunt, id est naturalium rationum interpretationes. Quasi vero nos in hac disputatione physiologian quaerimus et non theologian, id est rationem non naturae, sed Dei. Quamvis enim qui verus Deus est non opinione, sed natura Deus sit, non tamen omnis natura deus est, quia et hominis et pecoris, et arboris et lapidis utique natura est, quorum nihil est deus. Si autem interpretationis huius, quando agitur de sacris Matris deum, caput est certe quod Mater deum terra est, quid ultra quaerimus, quid cetera perscrutamur? Quid evidentius suffragatur eis qui dicunt omnes istos deos homines fuisse? Sic enim sunt terrigenae, sic eis mater est terra. In vera autem theologia opus Dei est terra, non mater. Verum tamen quoquo modo sacra eius interpretentur et referant ad rerum naturam, viros muliebria pati non est secundum naturam, sed contra naturam.

Hic morbus, hoc crimen, hoc dedecus habet inter illa sacra professionem, quod in vitiosis hominum moribus vix habet inter tormenta confessionem. Deinde si ista sacra, quae scaenicis turpitudinibus convincuntur esse foediora, hinc excusantur atque

---

[1] The Galli, or eunuch priests of Cybele, had a bad reputation. Augustine repeatedly mentions his recollection of their behaviour in Carthage (2.4, Vol. I, 155; 7.26, pp. 467–471, below). For a citation of witnesses, including Juvenal and a fourth-century scholiast on Juvenal, see Cumont in *RE* 7.1, 676.

VIII

*On the explanations that learned pagans offer in defence
of their gods as symbols of natural phenomena.*

BUT these obscenities, it is replied, have certain
scientific interpretations, that is, interpretations
as symbols of natural phenomena. As if in this
discussion we were doing scientific research, not
aiming at a theology, that is, an explanation, not of
nature, but of God! For although the true God is
God by nature and not by man's opinion, still not
every natural being is a god. For assuredly there is
a nature of man and of beast and of tree and stone,
and none of these is a god. If, however, when the
rites of the Mother of the gods are under consideration, the basic thought is that the Mother of the gods
is the earth, why do we inquire further? Why
investigate all the rest? What gives clearer support
to the view of those who say that all their gods were
once human beings? In this view they are earth-
born, and their mother is the earth. But according
to true theology the earth is God's handiwork, and
not his mother. And in any case, however they
interpret her rites as symbols referring to nature, it
is not according to nature, but against nature for men
to play the part of women sexually.[1]

And yet this malady, this crime, this indecency, of
which even men of depraved character can hardly be
compelled under torture to make confession, is a
part of their sacred rites of which they freely make
profession. Moreover, if these rites, which are
demonstrably filthier than the indecencies of the

333

purgantur, quod habent interpretationes suas quibus
ostendantur rerum significare naturam, cur non
etiam poetica similiter excusentur atque purgentur?
Multi enim et ipsa ad eundem modum interpretati
sunt, usque adeo ut quod ab eis inmanissimum et
infandissimum dicitur, Saturnum suos filios devorasse,
ita nonnulli interpretentur quod longinquitas temporis, quae Saturni nomine significatur, quidquid
gignit ipsa consumat, vel, sicut idem opinatur Varro,
quod pertineat Saturnus ad semina, quae in terram,
de qua oriuntur, iterum recidunt. Itemque alii
alio modo et similiter cetera.

Et tamen theologia fabulosa dicitur et cum omnibus huiusce modi interpretationibus suis repre-
henditur abicitur inprobatur, nec solum a naturali,
quae philosophorum est, verum etiam ab ista civili,
de qua agimus, quae ad urbes populosque asseritur
pertinere, eo quod de diis indigna confinxerit, merito
repudianda discernitur, eo nimirum consilio ut,
quoniam acutissimi homines atque doctissimi, a
quibus ista conscripta sunt, ambas inprobandas
intellegebant, et illam scilicet fabulosam et istam
civilem, illam vero audebant inprobare, hanc non
audebant; illam culpandam proposuerunt, hanc eius
similem comparandam exposuerunt,—non ut haec
prae illa tenenda eligeretur, sed ut cum illa respuenda

---

[1] Varro elsewhere says that the name of Saturn is derived
from sowing (*On the Latin Language* 5.64: " ab satu est dictus
Saturnus.") The derivation from *satus* is now generally

stage, are excused and justified by explanations that
make them symbols of natural phenomena, why are
not the stories of the poets also excused and justified
in the same way? For many have explained these,
too, after the same manner. Some of them have
gone so far as to explain the most monstrous and
unspeakable story that they tell, how Saturn devoured his sons, by saying that the long stretch of
time denoted by the name Saturn [1] swallows up all
that it begets. Or else, as the same Varro believes,
the name Saturn is connected with the seeds that
fall back once more into the earth from which they
spring. Others give other explanations here, and
similar variety is found elsewhere.

Yet this theology is called mythical, and is denounced, rejected and condemned, even when combined with all the interpretations of this kind. It is
distinguished not only from the natural theology of
the philosophers, but also from the civil theology
that we are discussing, which is said to belong to
cities and peoples; and it is marked as worthy of
rejection on the ground that it invented unworthy
stories about the gods. The very brilliant and
learned men who dealt with the subject were well
aware that both theologies, the mythical and the
civil, ought to have been condemned, but they dared
not condemn the latter, though they did the former.
So they proposed the one as a target for criticism, and
exposed the other, which was very similar to it, for
comparison. It was not their purpose to get the
second adopted and retained in preference to the

regarded as impossible, and the name is supposed to be of
Etruscan origin (see Rose in *OCD*, 797, also note p. 38 above).

intellegeretur, atque ita sine periculo eorum qui
civilem theologian reprehendere metuebant, utraque
contempta ea quam naturalem vocant apud meliores
animos inveniret locum. Nam et civilis et fabulosa
ambae fabulosae sunt ambaeque civiles; ambas
inveniet fabulosas qui vanitates et obscenitates
ambarum prudenter inspexerit; ambas civiles qui
scaenicos ludos pertinentes ad fabulosam in deorum
civilium festivitatibus et in urbium divinis rebus
adverterit.

Quo modo igitur vitae aeternae dandae potestas
cuiquam deorum istorum tribuitur, quos sua simulacra
et sacra convincunt diis fabulosis apertissime repro-
batis esse simillimos formis aetatibus, sexu habitu,
coniugiis generationibus ritibus, in quibus omnibus
aut homines fuisse intelleguntur et pro uniuscuiusque
vita vel morte sacra eis et sollemnia constituta, hunc
errorem insinuantibus firmantibusque daemonibus,
aut certe ex qualibet occasione inmundissimi spiritus
fallendis humanis mentibus inrepsisse?

IX

De officiis singulorum deorum.

QUID? Ipsa numinum officia tam viliter minutatimque concisa, propter quod eis dicunt pro

former, but to let men see that it should be rejected along with the former. Thus when these two were regarded with scorn, and that without risk to authors who were afraid to criticize the civil theology, they hoped that the theology which they call natural would find a place of welcome among the better minds. For the civil and the mythical theologies are both of them mythical and both civil. Both will be found mythical by one who thoughtfully examines the follies and indecencies of both. Both will be found civil by one who takes note that the stage plays of the mythical theology are included in the festivals of the civic deities and in the catalogue of " Divine Things " of the cities.

Then how can the power to bestow eternal life be ascribed to any of those gods, when their images and rites show that they closely resemble the openly rejected gods of fable? They are the same in appearance, age, sex, dress, marriage partners, lineage and rites. In all this it appears that they were once men, and that sacred rites and ceremonies were severally instituted to honour the life or death of each, while demons implanted and confirmed the mistaken belief in their divinity. Or else the gods are themselves unclean spirits who seized every opportunity to slip into the minds of men in order to deceive them.

IX

On the functions of the individual gods.

AND what of those functions of the deities, parcelled out in such petty and minute assignments, a thing

uniuscuiusque proprio munere supplicari oportere,
unde non quidem omnia, sed multa iam diximus,
nonne scurrilitati mimicae quam divinae consonant
dignitati? Si duas quisquam nutrices adhiberet
infanti, quarum una nihil nisi escam, altera nihil nisi
potum daret, sicut isti ad hoc duas adhibuerunt deas,
Educam et Potinam, nempe desipere et aliquid
mimo simile in sua domo agere videretur.   Liberum
a liberamento appellatum volunt, quod mares in
coeundo per eius beneficium emissis seminibus
liberentur; hoc idem in feminis agere Liberam,
quam etiam Venerem putant, quod et ipsam perhibeant semina emittere; et ob haec Libero eandem
virilem corporis partem in templo poni, femineam
Liberae. Ad haec addunt mulieres adtributas
Libero et vinum propter libidinem concitandam.
Sic Bacchanalia summa celebrabantur insania; ubi
Varro ipse confitetur a Bacchantibus talia fieri non
potuisse nisi mente commota.   Haec tamen postea
displicuerunt senatui saniori, et ea iussit auferri.
Saltem hic tandem forsitan senserunt quid inmundi

---

[1] Liber and Libera were deities of fertility widely worshipped
in Italy, and honoured in the Roman Liberalia (see 7. 21, p. 444
below for the cult at crossroads and in Lavinium).   In the
early republic their cult was Hellenized and subordinated to
that of Demeter-Ceres; Liber was identified with Dionysus-
Bacchus and Libera with Kore-Persephone. But their
originally independent character was recognized by the pontifical books that were used by Varro.   Learned etymology was

that is responsible for their rule that each must be invoked for his own special kind of service? I have already said a great deal on this subject, but not everything. Isn't this better suited to the buffoonery of the mimes than to the dignity of the gods? If anyone employed two nurses for a child, of whom one gave nothing but food to him, and the other nothing but drink, as the pagans employed for this purpose two goddesses, Educa and Potina, he would certainly seem to be playing the fool, and acting out something like a farce in his house. They say that the god Liber gets his name from liberating because it is through his favour that males in intercourse are liberated from, or relieved of, the semen which they emit. For women they say that the same service is performed by Libera, whom they also identify with Venus; for they think that the woman also emits seed. Hence in the temple of Liber they dedicate to the god the male sexual organs, and in the temple of Libera the corresponding female organs.[1] In addition they assign women attendants to Liber, as well as wine to arouse the sexual appetite. It was thus that the Bacchanalia were once celebrated with the wildest frenzy, and there, as Varro himself admits, deeds were done by the Bacchantes that were possible only when the mind was deranged. The Senate thereafter, with a mind more sane, was displeased with these rites, and ordered them to be abolished.[2] In this case perhaps they at last came to see what

added, as well as an alternative identification with Venus-Aphrodite. Augustine returns to the topic frequently.

[2] Livy 39.8.18 describes the Bacchic cult in Italy and its suppression by the Senate in 186 B.C. Cf. *C.I.L.* I, 581.

spiritus, dum pro diis habentur, in hominum mentibus possint. Haec certe non fierent in theatris; ludunt quippe ibi, non furiunt; quamvis deos habere qui etiam ludis talibus delectentur simile sit furoris.

Quale autem illud est quod, cum religiosum a superstitioso ea distinctione discernat ut a superstitioso dicat timeri deos, a religioso autem tantum vereri ut parentes, non ut hostes timeri, atque omnes ita bonos dicat ut facilius sit eos nocentibus parcere quam laedere quemquam innocentem, tamen mulieri fetae post partum tres deos custodes commemorat adhiberi, ne Silvanus deus per noctem ingrediatur et vexet, eorumque custodum significandorum causa tres homines noctu circuire limina domus et primo limen securi ferire, postea pilo, tertio deverrere scopis, ut his datis culturae signis deus Silvanus prohibeatur intrare, quod neque arbores caeduntur ac putantur sine ferro, neque far conficitur sine pilo, neque fruges coacervantur sine scopis; ab his autem tribus rebus tres nuncupatos deos, Intercidonam a securis intercisione, Pilumnum a pilo, Deverram ab scopis, quibus diis custodibus contra vim dei Silvani feta conservaretur. Ita contra dei nocentis saevitiam non valeret custodia bonorum, nisi plures essent adversus

effect unclean spirits have on the minds of men, when they are regarded as gods. Such things certainly could not happen in the theatres, for there they act plays, and do not go mad, although to have gods who also find pleasure in such plays comes close to madness.

Moreover, what can be said of the following statements from Varro? He makes a distinction between religious and superstitious, saying that a superstitious man fears the gods, whereas a religious man does not fear them as if they were enemies, but reveres them as if they were parents. He also says that they are all so kind that they more readily spare the guilty than harm the innocent. He mentions, however, three gods who are employed to guard a woman after childbirth, lest the god Silvanus come in by night and trouble her. To represent the three guardian gods, three men go about the thresholds of the house at night and strike the threshold first with an axe, next with a pestle, and in the third place sweep it with a broom. These symbols of agriculture prevent Silvanus from entering—for trees are not cut down or pruned without iron tools, nor is grain ground without a pestle, nor is the harvested grain collected in a heap without a broom. From these operations three gods get their names: Intercidona from cutting down (*intercisio*) with an axe, Pilumnus from the pestle, Deverra from the broom. These gods were the guardians by whom the new mother was to be preserved from attack by the god Silvanus. Thus we see that the protection of good gods was ineffective against the fury of a harmful god unless there were several of them against one, and

unum eique aspero horrendo inculto, utpote silvestri,
signis culturae tamquam contrariis repugnarent.
Itane ista est innocentia deorum, ista concordia?
Haecine sunt numina salubria urbium, magis ridenda
quam ludibria theatrorum?

Cum mas et femina coniunguntur, adhibetur deus
Iugatinus; sit hoc ferendum. Sed domum est
ducenda quae nubit; adhibetur et deus Domiducus;
ut in domo sit, adhibetur deus Domitius; ut maneat
cum viro, additur dea Manturna. Quid ultra quaeritur? Parcatur humanae verecundiae; peragat
cetera concupiscentia carnis et sanguinis procurato
secreto pudoris. Quid impletur cubiculum turba
numinum, quando et paranymphi inde discedunt?
Et ad hoc impletur, non ut eorum praesentia cogitata
maior sit cura pudicitiae, sed ut feminae sexu
infirmae, novitate pavidae illis cooperantibus sine
ulla difficultate virginitas auferatur. Adest enim dea
Virginensis et deus pater Subigus, et dea mater
Prema et dea Pertunda, et Venus et Priapus. Quid
est hoc? Si omnino laborantem in illo opere virum
ab diis adiuvari oportebat, non sufficeret aliquis unus
aut aliqua una? Numquid Venus sola parum esset,
quae ab hoc etiam dicitur nuncupata, quod sine vi
femina virgo esse non desinat? Si est ulla frons in
hominibus, quae non est in numinibus, nonne, cum

unless they fought to repel the fierce, horrid, un-
cultivated god, forest-dweller that he was, with the
symbols of agriculture, conceived as his natural
enemies. Is this an example of the innocence of
the gods and of their unity? Are these the deities
that are needed to keep cities safe—gods more comic
than the very clowns on the stage?

When male and female are joined the god Iugatinus is summoned—that can be tolerated as proper.
But the bride must be led home, so the god Domiducus is also employed; to keep her at home, the
god Domitius; to see that she stays with her husband
the goddess Manturna is enlisted. What more is
needed? Have some pity on human modesty; allow
the cravings of flesh and blood to finish the job when
they have arranged for a decent privacy. Why pack
the bed-chamber with a throng of deities, when even
the wedding attendants withdraw? The object of
such packing is not to increase concern for modesty
by their imagined presence, but rather to insure that
the bride, though weak as a woman and frightened as
a novice, may, if they lend assistance, lose her
virginity without any difficulty. The goddess
Virginensis is there, the father-god Subigus, the
mother-goddess Prema, the goddess Pertunda, and
Venus and Priapus. What does all this mean? If
the man had to be helped at all costs while working
at the task before him, wouldn't some one god or
goddess be enough? Would Venus alone be unequal
to the occasion? She is said to derive her name
Venus from the fact that without violence a woman
does not cease to be a virgin. If there is any
modesty among men, though there be none among

343

credunt coniugati tot deos utriusque sexus esse
praesentes et huic operi instantes, ita pudore
adficiuntur, ut et ille minus moveatur et illa plus
reluctetur? Et certe si adest Virginensis dea ut
virgini zona solvatur, si adest deus Subigus ut viro
subigatur, si adest dea Prema ut subacta ne se
commoveat conprimatur, dea Pertunda ibi quid facit?
Erubescat, eat foras; agat aliquid et maritus.
Valde inhonestum est ut quod vocatur illa impleat
quisquam nisi ille. Sed forte ideo toleratur quia dea
dicitur esse, non deus. Nam si masculus crederetur
et Pertundus vocaretur, maius contra eum pro uxoris
pudicitia posceret maritus auxilium quam feta contra
Silvanum. Sed quid hoc dicam, cum ibi sit et
Priapus nimius [1] masculus, super cuius inmanissimum et turpissimum fascinum sedere nova nupta
iubebatur, more honestissimo et religiosissimo mat-
ronarum?

Eant adhuc et theologian civilem a theologia fabulosa, urbes a theatris, templa ab scaenis, sacra
pontificum a carminibus poetarum, velut res honestas
a turpibus, veraces a fallacibus, graves a levibus,

---

[1] The Louvain editors of 1576 substituted *nimis* for *nimius*.
All subsequent editors follow the manuscripts, despite the
rather harsh collocation of the two adjectives.

---

[1] Priapus is to be identified with the Roman Mutunus
Tutunus (see 4.11, p. 48, note). The nuptial rite here

the gods, when a bridal pair believe that so many
gods of both sexes are present and intent on the
operation, are they not so affected with shame that he
will lose his ardour and she increase her resistance?
And surely if the goddess Virginensis is there to
undo the virgin's girdle, the god Subigus to subject
her to her husband, the goddess Prema to keep her
down when subjected so that she will not stir, then
what job does the goddess Pertunda have here?   Let
her blush and go outside; let the husband also have
something to do!   It is surely disgraceful for any but
a husband to do the act that is her name.   But perhaps she is tolerated because she is called goddess,
not god; for if she were supposed to be masculine
and so called Pertundus, the husband to defend his
wife's chastity would require more help against him
than the new mother against Silvanus.   But what am
I saying?   Priapus[1] is also there, and he is only too
masculine.   On his huge and ugly phallus the new
bride was once ordered to sit, according to the very
respectable and highly religious custom of the
matrons.

Let them still go on, and try to make the distinction
with whatever subtlety they can between the civil
and the mythical theology—that is, between cities
and theatres, between temples and stages, between
the rites of the pontiffs and the songs of the poets—
as if they were separating the decent from the indecent, truth from falsehood, serious from frivolous,

referred to is mentioned again in 7.24, p. 464 f., and also in
Lactantius, *Institutes* 1.20.36: " Tutinus, in cuius sinu pu-
dendo nubentes praesident, ut illarum pudicitiam prior deus
delibasse videatur."

serias a ludicris, adpetendas a respuendis, qua possunt quasi conentur subtilitate discernere. Intellegimus quid agant; illam theatricam et fabulosam theologian ab ista civili pendere noverunt et ei de carminibus poetarum tamquam de speculo resultare, et ideo ista exposita, quam damnare non audent, illam eius imaginem liberius arguunt et reprehendunt ut, qui agnoscunt quid velint et hanc ipsam faciem cuius illa imago est detestentur; quam tamen dii ipsi tamquam in eodem speculo se intuentes ita diligunt ut qui qualesque sint in utraque melius videantur. Unde etiam cultores suos terribilibus imperiis compulerunt ut inmunditiam theologiae fabulosae sibi dicarent, in suis sollemnitatibus ponerent, in rebus divinis haberent, atque ita et se ipsos inmundissimos spiritus manifestius esse docuerunt, et huius urbanae theologiae velut electae et probatae illam theatricam abiectam atque reprobatam membrum partemque fecerunt ut, cum sit universa turpis et fallax atque in se contineat commenticios deos, una pars eius sit in litteris sacerdotum, altera in carminibus poetarum. Utrum habeat et alias partes, alia quaestio est. Nunc propter divisionem Varronis et urbanam et theatricam theologian ad unam civilem pertinere satis, ut opinor, ostendi. Unde, quia sunt ambae similis turpitudinis absurditatis,

grave from gay, and things that men should seek from those that they should reject. We are aware of their purpose. They recognize that the mythical theology of the theatres derives from the civil theology and is reflected like an image of it in the mirror provided by the songs of the poets. So after expounding the theology that they dare not condemn they go on to refute and censure its image with less restraint. Thus those who detect their purpose will also detest the real face of which the other is an image. The gods themselves, however, seeing their own faces, so to speak, in the same mirror, are so much in love with the image that their identity and character stand out clearer if we keep in view both the original and the image. This has moved them to force their worshippers by dire threats to dedicate to them the indecencies of the mythical theology, to give these a place in their solemn festivals, and to include them in the class of " Divine Things." [1] Furthermore, in doing this they have revealed more clearly that they are unclean spirits, and this theology of the theatre, though worthless and condemned, they have made an organic part of the civil theology, which passes as superior and approved. Thus their theology as a whole is base and deceiving and filled with imaginary gods, one part of it being found in the writings of the priests and the other in the songs of the poets. Whether it has other parts as well is another question. I am now following Varro's division and have given sufficient proof, I think, that his theology of the city and that of the theatre both belong to the one civil theology. Hence, since both are equally foul,

---

[1] See 4.26, p. 95, above.

indignitatis falsitatis, absit a veris religiosis ut sive
ab hac sive ab illa vita speretur aeterna.

Denique et ipse Varro commemorare et enumerare
deos coepit a conceptione hominis, quorum numerum
est exorsus a Iano, eamque seriem perduxit usque ad
decrepiti hominis mortem, et deos ad ipsum hominem pertinentes clausit ad Neniam deam, quae in
funeribus senum cantatur; deinde coepit deos alios
ostendere qui pertinerent non ad ipsum hominem,
sed ad ea quae sunt hominis, sicuti est victus atque
vestitus et quaecumque alia huic vitae sunt necessaria, ostendens in omnibus quod sit cuiusque munus
et propter quid cuique debeat supplicari; in qua
universa diligentia nullos demonstravit vel nominavit
deos a quibus vita aeterna poscenda sit, propter
quam unam proprie nos Christiani sumus.

Quis ergo usque adeo tardus sit ut non intellegat
istum hominem civilem theologian tam diligenter
exponendo et aperiendo eamque illi fabulosae,
indignae atque probrosae, similem demonstrando
atque ipsam fabulosam partem esse huius satis
evidenter docendo non nisi illi naturali, quam dicit

---

[1] From the analysis of Varro's sixteen books on religious
Antiquities given by Augustine 6.3, p. 297 f., above, and the
statement about the *di incerti* made in 7.17, p. 435, it appears
that the *di certi* of Book 14 were those deities about whose
special function Varro had reliable information. From this
passage it is clear that the *di certi* were arranged in classified
groups, the first of them being the special deities connected

absurd, vile and false, far be it from any who are truly religious to expect eternal life from either the one or the other.

Finally, it is Varro himself who recalls the names of the gods and lists them in order, beginning with the conception of a man. The list begins with Janus and goes on to the death of the aged man, bringing the list of deities who are concerned with the man himself to an end with the goddess Nenia, who is invoked in song at the funerals of old men. Then he begins another series of gods who are not attached to the man himself, but to the things which concern a man, such as food and clothing and any other necessities of this life. In every case he makes clear the function of each god and the end for which each should be invoked. But in all this diligent inquiry he has never pointed out or named any gods whom we should ask for eternal life, which is our one special reason for being Christians.[1]

Who, then, could be so slow-witted as not to understand Varro's purpose? He carefully explained and revealed the nature of the civil theology, showing that it was similar to the mythical, which is unworthy and shameful, and clearly teaching that the mythical is a part of the civil. Hence it was only for the natural theology, which he says belonged to the

with the successive moments of a human life. The fragments of Varro, scattered in such disarray by Augustine and others, have been systematically arranged by R. Agahd, *M. Terentii Varronis Antiquitatum Rerum Divinarum Libri I, XIV, XV, XVI*, in *Jahrbücher für classische Philologie*, Supplementband XXIV (1898), hereafter cited as " Agahd." See also R. Peter, " Indigitamenta " in Roscher, *Lexikon der griechischen und römischen Mythologie* 2.1 (1890), pp. 143–6.

ad philosophos pertinere, in animis hominum moliri locum, ea subtilitate ut fabulosam reprehendat, civilem vero reprehendere quidem non audeat, sed prodendo reprehensibilem ostendat, atque ita utraque iudicio recte intellegentium reprobata sola naturalis remaneat eligenda? De qua suo loco in adiutorio Dei veri diligentius disserendum est.

X

De libertate Senecae, qui vehementius civilem
theologian reprehendit quam Varro fabulosam.

LIBERTAS sane quae huic defuit ne istam urbanam theologian theatricae simillimam aperte sicut illam reprehendere auderet, Annaeo Senecae, quem nonnullis indiciis invenimus apostolorum nostrorum claruisse temporibus, non quidem ex toto, verum ex aliqua parte non defuit. Adfuit enim scribenti, viventi defuit. Nam in eo libro quem contra super-stitiones condidit, multo copiosius atque vehementius reprehendit ipse civilem istam et urbanam theo-logian quam Varro theatricam atque fabulosam. Cum enim de simulacris ageret: " Sacros," inquit, " inmortales, inviolabiles in materia vilissima atque inmobili dedicant, habitus illis hominum ferarumque

---

[1] The Stoic philosopher Seneca in his sharp criticism of Roman superstitition furnished material for the Christian apologists Tertullian, Lactantius and Augustine. G. Boissier (*La Religion Romaine d'Auguste aux Antonins* II, 85) objects to the " air de triomphe " with which these writers quote Seneca while ignoring the fact that his Stoic pantheism was equally hostile to all positive religions and external cult. The

philosophers, that he was preparing a place in the minds of men. He is subtle enough to censure the mythical theology, though he does not dare to censure the civil, but by publishing the facts he shows that it is worthy of censure. Thus when both had been rejected by the judgement of intelligent people, there would be left no alternative to the natural theology. This subject I reserve for thorough discussion in its proper place, with the help of God.

X

On the frankness of Seneca, who condemns the civil theology more sharply than Varro condemns the mythical.

THE freedom that Varro lacked, so that he did not dare to criticize openly the theology of the city, as he did that of the theatre, in spite of their similarity, was not lacking to Annaeus Seneca,[1] or at least not entirely lacking. Seneca, we learn by several indications, was flourishing in the time of our apostles. His freedom appears in his writing, but not in his life. For in the book that he compiled against superstitions he makes a much fuller and sharper attack on the civil theology of the city than Varro does on the mythical theology of the theatre. Thus, speaking of the images of the gods, he says: " To beings who are sacred, immortal and inviolable they consecrate images of the cheapest inert material. They give them the shapes of men or beasts or fishes;

quotations in this chapter and the next are from a lost treatise *On Superstition.*

et piscium, quidam vero mixto sexu, diversis corporibus induunt; numina vocant quae, si spiritu accepto subito occurrerent, monstra haberentur." Deinde aliquanto post, cum theologian naturalem praedicans quorundam philosophorum sententias digessisset, opposuit sibi quaestionem et ait: " Hoc loco dicit aliquis: Credam ego caelum et terram deos esse et supra lunam alios, infra alios? Ego feram aut Platonem aut Peripateticum Stratonem, quorum alter fecit deum sine corpore, alter sine animo? " Et ad hoc respondens: " Quid ergo tandem," inquit, " veriora tibi videntur Titi Tatii aut Romuli aut Tulli Hostilii somnia? Cluacinam Tatius dedicavit deam, Picum Tiberinumque Romulus, Hostilius Pavorem atque Pallorem taeterrimos hominum affectus, quorum alter mentis territae motus est, alter corporis ne morbus quidem, sed color. Haec numina potius credes et caelo recipies? "

De ipsis vero ritibus crudeliter turpibus quam libere scripsit! " Ille," inquit, "viriles sibi partes amputat, ille lacertos secat. Ubi iratos deos timent qui sic propitios merentur? Dii autem nullo debent coli genere, si hoc volunt. Tantus est perturbatae mentis et sedibus suis pulsae furor ut sic dii placentur quem ad modum ne quidem homines saeviunt taeterrimi et in fabulas traditae crudelitatis.

some, in fact, make them double creatures of both sexes combined or unlike bodies united. They are called divinities, but if they were suddenly brought to life and encountered, they would be regarded as monsters." Then, a little later, when he was commending the natural theology and had stated the views of certain philosophers, he puts a question to himself: " At this point some one says, ' Am I to believe that heaven and earth are gods ? That some gods are above the moon and others below ? Am I to tolerate either Plato or the Peripatetic Strabo, one of whom says that God has no body, the other that he has no soul ? ' " And in reply he continues: " What then, pray ? Do the dreams of Titus Tatius or Romulus or Tullius Hostilius seem to you nearer the truth ? Tatius made a goddess of Cluacina, Romulus made gods of Picus and Tiberinus, while Hostilius consecrated Pavor and Pallor, the basest affections of men. One of these is mental, the emotion of a frightened mind, the other is physical, not even a disease, but only a colour. Will you prefer to believe that these are deities, and admit them to heaven ? "

And notice how freely he wrote about rites that are cruel and base: " One man," he says, " cuts off his virile parts, and another slashes his arms. What can they fear from the wrath of the gods, when they use such means to win their favour ? Moreover, gods deserve no worship of any kind if they want this kind. So great is the frenzy of a disordered and unsettled mind that means are used to placate the gods that have never been employed even by the most horrible men whose cruelty is recorded in myth and legend.

Tyranni laceraverunt aliquorum membra, neminem
sua lacerare iusserunt. In regiae libidinis voluptatem castrati sunt quidam; sed nemo sibi, ne vir esset,
iubente domino manus adtulit. Se ipsi in templis
contrucidant, vulneribus suis ac sanguine supplicant.
Si cui intueri vacet, quae faciunt quaeque patiuntur,
inveniet tam indecora honestis, tam indigna liberis,
tam dissimilia sanis, ut nemo fuerit dubitaturus furere
eos, si cum paucioribus furerent; nunc sanitatis
patrocinium est insanientium turba."

Iam illa quae in ipso Capitolio fieri solere commemorat et intrepide omnino coarguit, quis credat
nisi ab inridentibus aut furentibus fieri? Nam cum
in sacris Aegyptiis Osirim lugeri perditum, mox
autem inventum magno esse gaudio derisisset, cum
perditio eius inventioque fingatur, dolor tamen ille
atque laetitia ab eis qui nihil perdiderunt nihilque
invenerunt, veraciter exprimatur: "Huic tamen,"
inquit, "furori certum tempus est. Tolerabile est
semel anno insanire. In Capitolium perveni, pudebit
publicatae dementiae, quod sibi vanus furor adtribuit
officii. Alius nomina deo subicit, alius horas Iovi

---

[1] This passage is a reminder that Roman temples served not
only for the ceremonies of the state religion, but also as places
of private devotion. Scipio Africanus is said to have visited
the Capitol daily before sunrise to consult Jupiter about the
business of the day—whether from superstition or from
political shrewdness was not clear to Livy (Livy 26.19.4–6;
Aulus Gellius 6.1.6; W. W. Fowler, *Religious Experience of
the Roman People*, 240). In Seneca's description of worship
in the Capitol, L. Friedländer (*Roman Life and Manners* III,

Tyrants have mutilated the limbs of some of their
victims, but have ordered no one to mutilate his own
limbs. Some have been castrated to serve the lust of
a king, but no one has unmanned himself with his
own hands at a master's order. They slash themselves in temples and make supplication with their
own bleeding wounds. If anyone has leisure to view
what they do and what they suffer, he will find
practices so indecent for honourable men, so unworthy of free men, so unlike those of sane men, that
if their number were fewer no one would have any
doubt that they were demented. As it is, the only
support for a plea of sanity is found in the number of
the mad throng."

He goes on next to relate the deeds which are
customary performances in the very Capitol and
completely demolishes them with absolute fearless-
ness. Who could believe that they were performed
unless by mockers or madmen? In the Egyptian
rites the loss of Osiris is first bewailed, then shortly
his restoration is celebrated with joy. Though
both his loss and restoration are fictitious, yet the
grief and joy of men who have lost nothing and found
nothing is expressed as if it were real. After scoffing
at these rites Seneca remarks: "There is, however, a
period fixed for this madness. It is permissible to be
mad once in the year. But go to the Capitol,[1] and
you will be ashamed of the folly there disclosed, and
of the duties which a deluded madness has assigned
itself. One servant informs Jupiter of the names of
his worshippers, another announces the hours; one is

169) finds some antiquated ritual and some childish superstition.

nuntiat; alius lutor est, alius unctor, qui vano motu
bracchiorum imitatur unguentem. Sunt quae
Iunoni ac Minervae capillos disponant (longe a
templo, non tantum a simulacro stantes digitos
movent ornantium modo), sunt quae speculum
teneant; sunt qui ad vadimonia sua deos advocent,
sunt qui libellos offerant et illos causam suam
doceant. Doctus archimimus, senex iam decrepitus,
cotidie in Capitolio mimum agebat, quasi dii libenter
spectarent quem illi homines desierant. Omne illic
artificum genus operatum diis inmortalibus desidet."
Et paulo post: " Hi tamen," inquit, " etiamsi
supervacuum usum, non turpem nec infamem deo
promittunt. Sedent quaedam in Capitolio, quae se
a Iove amari putant; ne Iunonis quidem, si credere
poetis velis, iracundissimae respectu terrentur."

Hanc libertatem Varro non habuit; tantum modo
poeticam theologian reprehendere ausus est, civilem
non ausus est, quam iste concidit. Sed si verum
adtendamus, deteriora sunt templa ubi haec aguntur
quam theatra ubi finguntur. Unde in his sacris
civilis theologiae has partes potius elegit Seneca
sapienti, ut eas in animi religione non habeat, sed in

---

[1] The reading *lutor* is not in the manuscripts. Most have
lictor, one *luctor*, two *lector*. *Lictor* was evidently the reading
of the archetype, but hardly suits the context, hence *litor*
(" masseur ") and *lutor* (" bather ") have been proposed as
emendations. The last is the choice of Kalb, and seems most
appropriate.

[2] In mythology Jupiter (Zeus) was noted for his affairs with
mortal women. In eastern lands Zeus Ammon, Zeus Belos,
etc., was served by human wives or concubines; at Tralles in
Lydia the practice went on still in the second or third century
of our era (see A. B. Cook, *Zeus* I, 348; II. 2, 959). While

his bather,[1] another his anointer, that is, he gestures
with empty hands to imitate the act of anointing.
There are women who are hairdressers for Juno and
Minerva: while standing far away from the temple
as well as from the image they move the fingers as if
they were dressing the hair, and there are others who
hold a mirror. There are men who summon the gods
to give bond for them, and some who offer them
lawyers' briefs and explain their case. An expert
leading actor in the mimes, now a decrepit old man,
used to act a mime each day in the Capitol—as if the
gods would enjoy the performance of a player when
men had ceased to do so. Every kind of artisan sits
there to devote his time to the immortal gods." A
little further on he continues: " Still these men,
though they offer useless service to the god, offer no
base or indecent service. But there are women who
sit in the Capitol, who imagine that Jupiter is their
lover.[2] They have no fear even of Juno's look,
though she is much given to wrath, if we are to
believe the poets."

Varro did not have this freedom of speech. He
dared to criticize only the poetic theology, and not
the civil, which Seneca slashed so thoroughly. But
to look at the truth of the matter, temples where such
rites are performed in real life are worse than theatres
where they are imaginary. And so in these rites of
the civil theology the role that Seneca prefers the
wise man to adopt is to exclude them from his personal worship, but to go through the motions of

Romans condemned such practices, it here appears that they
flourished amid the superstitions of the mixed population of
the city.

actibus fingat. Ait enim: " Quae omnia sapiens
servabit tamquam legibus iussa, non tamquam diis
grata." Et paulo post: " Quid quod et matrimonia,
inquit, deorum iungimus, et ne pie quidem, fratrum
ac sororum! Bellonam Marti conlocamus, Vulcano
Venerem, Neptuno Salaciam. Quosdam tamen
caelibes relinquimus, quasi condicio defecerit, praesertim cum quaedam viduae sint, ut Populonia vel
Fulgora et diva Rumina; quibus non miror petitorem
defuisse. Omnem istam ignobilem deorum turbam,
quam longo aevo longa superstitio congessit, sic,"
inquit, " adorabimus ut meminerimus cultum eius
magis ad morem quam ad rem pertinere."

Nec leges ergo illae nec mos in civili theologia id
instituerunt quod diis gratum esset vel ad rem
pertineret. Sed iste, quem philosophi quasi liberum
fecerunt, tamen, quia inlustris populi Romani
senator erat, colebat quod reprehendebat, agebat
quod arguebat, quod culpabat adorabat; quia
videlicet magnum aliquid eum philosophia docuerat,
ne superstitiosus esset in mundo, sed propter leges
civium moresque hominum non quidem ageret
fingentem scaenicum in theatro, sed imitaretur in
templo; eo damnabilius quo illa quae mendaciter
agebat sic ageret ut eum populus veraciter agere

---

[1] These three goddesses remain obscure. Populonia would
seem identical with Juno Populonia (or Populona), known
from Macrobius *Saturnalia* 3.11.6 and a number of inscriptions.
Fulgora seems to be the female counterpart of (Jupiter)
Fulgur. Rumina, earlier mentioned as goddess of babes at

feigned conformity. For he says: " The wise man will observe all these rites as being enjoined by the laws, not as being pleasing to the gods." And a little later: " What of the fact that we even join the gods in marriage and dishonourable marriage at that, the marriage of brother and sister? We give Bellona in marriage to Mars, Venus to Vulcan, and Salacia to Neptune. But some we leave unwed, as if no match could be arranged, especially since some are widows, such as Populonia, Fulgora and the goddess Rumina.[1] I am not at all surprised that there has been no suitor for these. As for all this obscure throng of gods, assembled through long years by ancient superstition, we shall invoke them, but with the reservation in mind that their worship belongs rather to custom than to truth."

So neither the laws nor custom instituted anything in the civil theology of a sort to please the gods or conform to truth. But though Seneca was made free, in a sense, thanks to the philosophers, yet because he was a distinguished senator of the Roman people, he worshipped what he rebuked, did what he denounced, invoked what he accused. Philosophy, it is clear, had taught him something important, not to be superstitious as a citizen of the world; yet in support of the laws and customs of men, though he did not take the part of an actor in the theatre, philosophy taught him to imitate that actor in the temple. That was the more reprehensible in that he played his dishonest part in such a way that the people thought that he

the breast (4.11, p. 46 f.), is matched by Jupiter Ruminus (7.11, p. 416). Yet Seneca here describes them as widows (see Wissowa, *RK*², 121 f., 187 f., 242).

existimaret; scaenicus autem ludendo potius delectaret quam fallendo deciperet.

XI

Quid de Iudaeis Seneca senserit

Hic inter alias civilis theologiae superstitiones reprehendit etiam sacramenta Iudaeorum et maxime sabbata, inutiliter eos facere adfirmans quod per illos singulos septenis interpositos dies septimam fere partem aetatis suae perdant vacando et multa in tempore urgentia non agendo laedantur. Christianos tamen iam tunc Iudaeis inimicissimos in neutram partem commemorare ausus est, ne vel laudaret contra suae patriae veterem consuetudinem, vel reprehenderet contra propriam forsitan voluntatem. De illis sane Iudaeis cum loqueretur, ait: "Cum interim usque eo sceleratissimae gentis consuetudo convaluit ut per omnes iam terras recepta sit; victi victoribus leges dederunt." Mirabatur haec dicens et quid divinitus ageretur ignorans subiecit plane sententiam qua significaret quid de illorum sacramentorum ratione sentiret. Ait enim: "Illi tamen causas ritus sui noverunt; maior pars populi facit quod cur faciat ignorat." Sed de sacramentis Iudaeorum, vel cur vel quatenus instituta sint auctori-

was acting sincerely, whereas an actor on the stage plays rather to amuse the people than to deceive them by any cheat.

XI

What Seneca thought of the Jews.

ALONG with other superstitions of the civil theology Seneca also censures the sacred institutions of the Jews, especially the sabbath. He declares that their practice is inexpedient, because by introducing one day of rest in every seven they lose in idleness almost a seventh of their life, and by failing to act in times of urgency they often suffer loss. As for the Christians, however, who were even then most hostile to the Jews, he does not mention them either favourably or unfavourably, not wishing to praise them in defiance of the custom of his country, or to attack them, which would perhaps have been against his own way of thinking. But when speaking of the Jews he says: " Meanwhile the customs of this accursed race have gained such influence that they are now received throughout all the world. The vanquished have given laws to their victors." He shows his surprise as he says this, not knowing what was being wrought by the providence of God. But he adds a statement that shows what he thought of their system of sacred institutions: " The Jews, however, are aware of the origin and meaning of their rites. The greater part of the people go through a ritual not knowing why they do so." But why the rites of the Jews were instituted by divine authority,

tate divina, ac post modum a populo Dei, cui vitae
aeternae mysterium revelatum est, tempore quo
oportuit eadem auctoritate sublata sint, et alias
diximus, maxime cum adversus Manichaeos agere-
mus, et in hoc opere loco oportuniore dicendum est.

XII

*Quod gentilium deorum vanitate detecta nequeat
dubitari aeternam eos vitam nemini posse praestare,
qui nec ipsam adiuvent temporalem.*

NUNC propter tres theologias, quas Graeci dicunt
mythicen physicen politicen, Latine autem dici
possunt fabulosa naturalis civilis, quod neque de
fabulosa, quam et ipsi deorum multorum falsorumque
cultores liberrime reprehenderunt, neque de civili,
cuius illa pars esse convincitur eiusque et ista simil-
lima vel etiam deterior invenitur, speranda est
aeterna vita, si cui satis non sunt quae in hoc volumine dicta sunt, adiungat etiam illa quae in superioribus libris et maxime quarto de felicitatis datore Deo
plurima disputata sunt. Nam cui nisi uni felicitati
propter aeternam vitam consecrandi homines essent,

---

[1] For nine years of his early life, as Augustine tells us
(*Conf.* 4.1.1), he was deceived by the Manichees, and led
others with him into error. After his conversion he sought
to make amends, writing a number of works against the
Manichees. Like many Gnostics of an earlier time, they
attacked the Old Testament as absurd and in contradiction

and for how long, and why at the proper time they were later by the same authority abolished among the people of God to whom the mystery of eternal life was revealed—these are questions that I have discussed elsewhere, especially when arguing against the Manichees, and that I must discuss again at a more convenient point in this work.[1]

XII

Since the pagan gods have been exposed as false, it is clear that they cannot grant eternal life, for they are of no help even for this temporal life.

THERE are three theologies which, if we follow Greek terminology, we may call mythical, physical and political, or by following the Latin they may be termed fabulous, natural and civil. I have shown that we must not expect eternal life either from the fabulous, which even the pagans have censured with the greatest freedom, though they worship gods both many and false, or from the civil, of which the former is proved to be a part. And the civil as a whole is very similar to the fabulous, or even worse. If what has been said in this book is not enough to prove the point to anyone, let him add the extended arguments found in earlier books, especially in the fourth book, on God as the giver of happiness. For if happiness were a goddess, to whom should men consecrate

with the New. The arguments on both sides are most fully set forth in the work *Contra Faustum*. On the Old Testament as a preparation for the New, see 7.32, p. 491 below, and the whole of Book XVII.

si dea felicitas esset? Quia vero non dea, sed munus
est dei: cui deo nisi datori felicitatis consecrandi
sumus, qui aeternam vitam, ubi vera est et plena
felicitas, pia caritate diligimus? Non autem esse
datorem felicitatis quemquam istorum deorum qui
tanta turpitudine coluntur et, nisi ita colantur, multo
turpius irascuntur atque ob hoc se spiritus inmundissimos confitentur, puto ex his quae dicta sunt
neminem dubitare oportere.

Porro qui non dat felicitatem, vitam quo modo
dare posset aeternam? Eam quippe vitam aeternam
dicimus ubi est sine fine felicitas. Nam si anima in
poenis vivit aeternis, quibus et ipsi spiritus crucia-
buntur inmundi, mors est illa potius aeterna quam
vita. Nulla quippe maior et peior est mors quam ubi
non moritur mors. Sed quod animae natura, per id
quod inmortalis creata est, sine qualicumque vita
esse non potest, summa mors eius est alienatio a vita
Dei in aeternitate supplicii. Vitam igitur aeternam,
id est sine ullo fine felicem, solus ille dat qui dat
veram felicitatem. Quam quoniam illi quos colit
theologia ista civilis dare non posse convicti sunt, non
solum propter ista temporalia atque terrena, quod
superioribus quinque libris ostendimus, sed multo
magis propter vitam aeternam, quae post mortem
futura est, quod isto uno etiam illis cooperantibus
egimus, colendi non sunt. Sed quoniam veternosae

themselves in order to gain eternal life except to her alone? But since it is not a goddess, but a gift of a god, to what god should we consecrate ourselves except to the giver of happiness, we who with pious affection cherish eternal life, where true and complete happiness exists? Moreover I maintain that no one who has considered my argument can honestly believe that the giver of happiness is any one of those gods who are worshipped so indecently, and unless they are thus worshipped become angry even more indecently, thereby confessing that they are unclean spirits.

And how can one who is not the giver of happiness be the giver of eternal life? For we call that life eternal in which there is happiness without end. For if a soul is living in eternal torment, with which these unclean spirits shall also be tortured, that is eternal death rather than eternal life. For there is no greater or worse death than where death does not die. For since the soul was created immortal, by its nature it cannot be without some kind of life, hence its greatest death is alienation from the life of God, in eternal punishment. Consequently eternal life, that is, a life happy without end, is given by him alone who gives true happiness. And since this is something which those gods who are worshipped in the civil theology have been proved unable to give, it follows that they should not be worshipped for temporal and earthly blessings, as we showed in the five preceding books, and much less should they be worshipped for the eternal life which is to follow after death. This we have shown in the present book with the help of those preceding as well. But since the

365

consuetudinis vis nimis in alto radices habet, si cui de ista civili theologia respuenda atque vitanda parum videor disputasse, in aliud volumen, quod huic opitulante Deo coniungendum est, animum intendat.

force of ancient custom has struck its roots all too
deep, if it seems to anyone that I have not yet made
good my argument for rejecting and keeping away
from the civil theology, let him give his attention to
another book, which, with the help of God, I must
join to this one.

BOOK VII

LIBER VII

PRAEFATIO

Diligentius me pravas et veteres opiniones veritati pietatis inimicas, quas tenebrosis animis altius et tenacius diuturnus humani generis error infixit, evellere atque exstirpare conantem et illius gratiae qui hoc ut verus Deus potest pro meo modulo in eius adiutorio cooperantem ingenia celeriora atque meliora, quibus ad hanc rem superiores libri satis superque sufficiunt, patienter et aequanimiter ferre debebunt et propter alios non putare superfluum quod iam sibi sentiunt non necessarium. Multum magna res agitur, cum vera et vere sancta divinitas, quamvis ab ea nobis etiam huic quam nunc gerimus fragilitati necessaria subsidia praebeantur, non tamen propter mortalis vitae transitorium vaporem, sed propter vitam beatam, quae non nisi aeterna est, quaerenda et colenda praedicatur.

BOOK VII

PREFACE

Now as I attempt more studiously still to uproot and destroy the old depraved notions, hostile to true piety, which a long-standing error has fixed deeply and tenaciously in the dark places of the heart, and as I co-operate, to the best of my small ability, with the grace of him, the true God, who is able to accomplish this task, while I hope to enjoy his help, readers with quicker and better perceptions who find the preceding books sufficient, and more than sufficient, for the purpose, must bear with me patiently and calmly and, for the sake of others, not regard as superfluous a discussion of which they no longer feel the need themselves. It is a matter of very great importance when we proclaim that the true and truly holy deity, though he provides the helps we need to sustain even this frail life that we now live, should nevertheless not be sought out and worshipped for the sake of the passing vapour of mortal life, but for the sake of the truly happy life, which must be eternal life.

SAINT AUGUSTINE

I

*An cum in theologia civili deitatem non esse constiterit,
in selectis diis eam inveniri posse credendum sit.*

HANC divinitatem vel, ut sic dixerim, deitatem
(nam et hoc verbo uti iam nostros non piget, ut de
Graeco expressius transferant quod illi θεότητα
appellant)—hanc ergo divinitatem sive deitatem non
esse in ea theologia quam civilem vocant, quae a
Marco Varrone sedecim voluminibus explicata est,
id est non perveniri ad aeternae vitae felicitatem
talium deorum cultu quales a civitatibus qualiterque
colendi instituti sunt, cui nondum persuasit sextus
liber, quem proxime absolvimus, cum istum forsitan
legerit, quid de hac quaestione expedienda ulterius
desideret non habebit.   Fieri enim potest, ut saltem
deos selectos atque praecipuos, quos Varro volumine
complexus est ultimo, de quibus parum diximus,
quisquam colendos propter vitam beatam, quae non
nisi aeterna est, opinetur.

Qua in re non dico quod facetius ait Tertullianus
fortasse quam verius: Si dii eliguntur ut bulbi, utique
ceteri reprobi iudicantur.   Non hoc dico; video enim
etiam ex selectis seligi aliquos ad aliquid maius atque
praestantius, sicut in militia, cum tirones electi
fuerint, ex his quoque eliguntur ad opus aliquod
maius armorum; et cum eliguntur in ecclesia qui
fiant praepositi, non utique ceteri reprobantur, cum

---

[1] Tertullian, *Ad Nationes* 2.9.

I

*Though it is clear that there is no true deity in the
civil theology, should we believe that it may
possibly be found in the select gods?*

THIS divinity, or (to adopt a word which Christians
do not hesitate to use, in order more clearly to
translate what the Greeks call *theotes*) this deity, does
not exist in the civil theology described by Marcus
Varro in sixteen books. That is, there is no arriving
at the happiness of eternal life by worshipping such
gods as were set up by the city-states, nor by the kind
of worship that was offered them. If anyone is not
yet convinced of this by the sixth book, which we
have just completed, perhaps when he has read the
present book, he will find that he requires no further
proof to dispose of the question. For possibly someone might suppose that the select and outstanding
gods at least, the subject of Varro's last book, of
which so far I have said little, deserve to be worshipped for the sake of a happy life, which can only
be eternal life.

On this point I will not affirm what Tertullian said,
perhaps with more wit than truth: " If some gods
are selected, like onions, then certainly the rest are
judged unfit." [1] I do not say this, for I see that even
when there is a select group, some are selected from it
for a greater and more important function. Thus in
the army, after recruits have been selected, some of
these are further selected for a more important kind
of armed service. And in the church, when some are
elected to be at the head, the rest are certainly not

373

omnes boni fideles electi merito nuncupentur.
Eliguntur in aedificio lapides angulares, non repro-
batis ceteris, qui structurae partibus aliis deputantur.
Eliguntur uvae ad vescendum, nec reprobantur aliae,
quas relinquimus ad bibendum. Non opus est multa
percurrere, cum res in aperto sit. Quam ob rem
non ex hoc, quod dii ex multis quidam selecti sunt,
vel is qui scripsit vel eorum cultores vel dii ipsi
vituperandi sunt, sed advertendum potius quinam
isti sint et ad quam rem selecti videantur.

II

Qui sint dii selecti, et an ab officiis viliorum deorum
habeantur excepti.

Hos certe deos selectos Varro unius libri con-
textione commendat: Ianum, Iovem, Saturnum,
Genium, Mercurium, Apollinem, Martem, Vulcanum,
Neptunum, Solem, Orcum, Liberum patrem, Tellurem, Cererem, Iunonem, Lunam, Dianam, Minervam, Venerem, Vestam; in quibus omnibus ferme
viginti duodecim mares, octo sunt feminae.

Haec numina utrum propter maiores in mundo administrationes selecta dicuntur, an quod populis magis

---

[1] On the " select gods " see 4.23, p. 84, note 1; on Liber
see 6.9, p. 338, note 1. Though Libera is not among Varro's
select gods, Augustine brings her in (p. 376) with Liber.
Janus, the god of doorways and beginnings, was also first
among the deities of procreation, with the title of Consevius.
All of these deities enjoyed public worship in Rome. Orcus
is identical with Dis Pater, or Pluto. Genius is presumably
not the Genius of household worship, but the Genius Populi

rejected, since all the good and faithful are deservedly called " the elect." And in building a house, corner stones are selected without rejecting the rest of the stones, which are assigned to other parts of the structure. Some grapes are selected to eat without rejecting the rest, which we leave for drinking. There is no need to multiply examples, since the point is clear. Hence the fact that certain gods were selected out of many does not mean that we should denounce either the writer concerned, or the worshippers of those gods, or the gods themselves. Instead, we should notice who these select gods are, and for what purpose they seem to have been selected.

II

Who the select gods are, and whether they are supposed to be relieved of the duties of the lower gods.

At any rate, these are the gods which Varro commends as select, discussing them in the compass of a single book: Janus, Jupiter, Saturn, Genius, Mercury, Apollo, Mars, Vulcan, Neptune, Sol, Orcus, Liber pater, Tellus, Ceres, Juno, Luna, Diana, Minerva, Venus, Vesta. There are twenty altogether, twelve male and eight female.[1]

Are these deities called select because of their more important functions in the world, or because

Romani who had a shrine near the temple of Concord in the Forum, and also an altar in the Capitol where sacrifice was offered on October 9 (Wissowa, *RK*[2], 179).

innotuerunt maiorque est eis cultus exhibitus? Si
propterea quia opera maiora ab his administrantur in
mundo, non eos invenire debuimus inter illam quasi
plebeiam numinum multitudinem minutis opusculis
deputatam. Nam ipse primum Ianus, cum puer-
perium concipitur, unde illa cuncta opera sumunt
exordium minutatim minutis distributa numinibus,
aditum aperit recipiendo semini. Ibi est et Saturnus
propter ipsum semen; ibi Liber, qui marem effuso
semine liberat; ibi Libera, quam et Venerem volunt,
quae hoc idem beneficium conferat feminae ut etiam
ipsa emisso semine liberetur. Omnes hi ex illis sunt
qui selecti appellantur. Sed ibi est et dea Mena,
quae menstruis fluoribus praeest, quamvis Iovis
filia, tamen ignobilis. Et hanc provinciam fluorum
menstruorum in libro selectorum deorum ipsi Iunoni
idem auctor adsignat, quae in diis selectis etiam
regina est et hic tamquam Iuno Lucina cum eadem
Mena privigna sua eidem cruori praesidet. Ibi
sunt et duo nescio qui obscurissimi, Vitumnus et
Sentinus, quorum alter vitam, alter sensus puerperio
largiuntur. Et nimirum multo plus praestant, cum
sint ignobilissimi, quam illi tot proceres et selecti.
Nam profecto sine vita et sensu, quid est illud totum
quod muliebri utero geritur, nisi nescio quid abiectis-
simum limo ac pulveri comparandum?

they are better known to the people and enjoy a greater public worship? If it is because they are charged with higher functions in the world, we ought not to have found them among that plebeian crowd of deities who are assigned trifling little jobs. Yet it is Janus himself who appears first of all at the moment of conception, the moment when all the tasks begin which are minutely divided among minute deities—it is he who opens the way for receiving the seed. Saturn is there too, just because there is seed. Liber, who liberates the male from the seed he expels, is there, and Libera, whom they choose to identify with Venus, is there to confer the same benefit on the woman, that she also may be liberated by the emission of seed. All these deities are among the ones who are called select. But the goddess Mena, who presides over the menstrual flow, is there too, and although she is a daughter of Jupiter, she is still without renown. And this office of governing menstrual flow is also assigned to Juno herself by the same writer, in his book on the select gods. She is even the queen among the select gods, yet here, as Juno Lucina, she presides over the same blood, along with Mena, her step-daughter. Also present are two extremely obscure gods, Vitumnus and Sentinus, of whom one bestows life (*vita*) and the other sensation (*sensus*) on the foetus. And although they are most undistinguished, they surely bestow much more on the child than do those many noble and select gods. For actually, without life and sensation, what is all that burden carried in the mother's womb except some very low substance, comparable to mud and dust?

III

*Quam nulla sit ratio quae de selectione quorundam
deorum possit ostendi, cum multis inferioribus
excellentior administratio deputetur.*

QUAE igitur causa tot selectos deos ad haec opera
minima compulit, ubi a Vitumno et Sentino, quos
" fama obscura recondit," in huius munificentiae
partitione superentur? Confert enim selectus Ianus
aditum et quasi ianuam semini; confert selectus
Saturnus semen ipsum; confert selectus Liber eiusdem seminis emissionem viris; confert hoc idem
Libera, quae Ceres seu Venus est, feminis; confert
selecta Iuno, et hoc non sola, sed cum Mena, filia
Iovis, fluores menstruos ad eius quod conceptum est
incrementum: et confert Vitumnus obscurus et
ignobilis vitam; confert Sentinus obscurus et ignobilis
sensum; quae duo tanto illis rebus praestantiora
sunt quanto et ipsa intellectu ac ratione vincuntur.
Sicut enim quae ratiocinantur et intellegunt profecto
potiora sunt his, quae sine intellectu atque ratione ut
pecora vivunt et sentiunt, ita et illa quae vita sen-
suque sunt praedita his quae nec vivunt nec sentiunt
merito praeferuntur. Inter selectos itaque deos
Vitumnus vivificator et Sentinus sensificator magis
haberi debuerunt quam Ianus seminis admissor et

---

[1] Virgil, *Aeneid* 5.302.
[2] As in the preceding chapter, Libera is identified with
Venus the goddess of love; as in 7.19, p. 443, with Ceres the

III

*No reason can be shown for the selection of some
gods, when higher functions are assigned to
many inferior gods.*

WHAT cause, then, drove so many select gods to
these very minor tasks, where they are put lower than
Vitumnus and Sentinus, whom " an obscure fame has
hidden from view," [1] in the distribution of these gifts ?
For it is the select Janus who offers access, a door
(*ianua*) as it were, to the seed; the select Saturn
bestows the seed itself; the select Liber bestows the
emission of the seed on males, and Libera, who is also
Ceres, or Venus,[2] does the same for women; the select
Juno, not by herself, but with the help of Mena,
daughter of Jupiter, bestows the menstrual flow for the
growth of what has been conceived.   And yet it is the
ignoble and obscure Vitumnus who confers life, and the
obscure and ignoble Sentinus who confers sensation.
These two things are as much superior to the others
as they are themselves inferior to intellect and reason.
For just as those beings that reason and understand
are surely better than those that live like beasts
without intellect and reason, so also those that are
endowed with life and sensation are properly placed
ahead of those that neither live nor feel.   And so
Vitumnus the giver of life and Sentinus the giver of
sensation ought to have been regarded as select gods
rather than Janus who opens the way for the seed and

goddess of grain.   In Roman cult and generally in literature
she is the same as Kore-Proserpina, the daughter of Demeter-
Ceres.

Saturnus seminis dator vel sator et Liber et Libera
seminum commotores vel emissores; quae semina
cogitare indignum est, nisi ad vitam sensumque
pervenerint, quae munera selecta non dantur a diis
selectis, sed a quibusdam incognitis et prae istorum
dignitate neglectis.

Quod si respondetur omnium initiorum potestatem
habere Ianum et ideo illi etiam quod aperitur con-
ceptui non inmerito adtribui, et omnium seminum
Saturnum et ideo seminationem quoque hominis non
posse ab eius operatione seiungi, omnium seminum
emittendorum Liberum et Liberam et ideo his
etiam praeesse quae ad substituendos homines
pertinent, omnium purgandorum et pariendorum
Iunonem et ideo eam non deesse purgationibus
feminarum et partubus hominum, quaerant quid
respondeant de Vitumno et Sentino, utrum et ipsos
velint habere omnium quae vivunt et sentiunt
potestatem. Quod si concedunt, adtendant quam
eos sublimius locaturi sint. Nam seminibus nasci in
terra et ex terra est; vivere autem atque sentire
etiam deos sidereos opinantur. Si autem dicunt
Vitumno atque Sentino haec sola adtributa quae in
carne vivescunt et sensibus adminiculantur, cur non
deus ille qui facit omnia vivere atque sentire etiam
carni vitam praebet et sensum, universali opere hoc
munus etiam partubus tribuens? Et quid opus est
Vitumno atque Sentino?

Saturn the giver of seed, or sower, and Liber and
Libera who set in motion and discharge the seeds—
seeds which are not worth a thought until they
attain to life and sensation. But these gifts do not
come from the select gods, but from some who are
unknown and, when compared with the others in
rank, neglected, not selected.

But the reply may be made that Janus has charge
of all beginnings, and hence the opening made for the
conception is not improperly assigned to him. They
may say that Saturn has charge of all seeds, and
hence the planting also of human seed cannot be
severed from his activity, and that Liber and Libera
have charge of releasing all seeds and so preside also
over those that belong to the reproduction of men,
and that Juno is in charge of all purgations and
births, and so does not fail to assist in the purgations
of women and the delivery of human offspring. Then
let them consider what they should say of Vitumnus
and Sentinus, whether they want them also to have
charge of all things that live and feel. If they grant
this power, let them take note how much higher they
are going to place these gods. For to be born from
seed is to be born on earth and from the earth, but
they hold that life and sensation belong also to the
gods of the heavenly bodies. And if they say that
Vitumnus and Sentinus are assigned only to those
beings who come alive in the flesh and are served by
its senses, why does not that god who makes everything live and feel give life and sensation also to the
flesh, granting, as part of his universal activity, this
gift also to everything born? And then what need
is there for Vitumnus and Sentinus?

Quod si ab illo qui vitae ac sensibus universaliter
praesidet his quasi famulis ista carnalia velut extrema
et ima commissa sunt, itane sunt illi selecti destituti
familia ut non invenirent quibus etiam ipsi ista com-
mitterent, sed cum tota sua nobilitate, qua visi
sunt seligendi, opus facere cum ignobilibus cogerentur? Iuno selecta et regina " Iovisque et soror et
coniunx "; haec tamen Iterduca est pueris et opus
facit cum deabus ignobilissimis Abeona et Adeona.
Ibi posuerunt et Mentem deam, quae faciat pueris
bonam mentem, et inter selectos ista non ponitur,
quasi quicquam maius praestari homini potest;
ponitur autem Iuno, quia Iterduca est et Domiduca,
quasi quicquam prosit iter carpere et domum duci, si
mens non est bona, cuius muneris deam selectores
isti inter selecta numina minime posuerunt. Quae
profecto et Minervae fuerat praeferenda, cui per ista
minuta opera puerorum memoriam tribuerunt.
Quis enim dubitet multo esse melius habere bonam
mentem quam memoriam quantumlibet ingentem?
Nemo enim malus est qui bonam habet mentem;
quidam vero pessimi memoria sunt mirabili, tanto
peiores quanto minus possunt quod male cogitant
oblivisci. Et tamen Minerva est inter selectos deos;
Mentem autem deam turba vilis operuit. Quid de
Virtute dicam? Quid de Felicitate? De quibus in

---

[1] Virgil, *Aeneid* 1.47.

Will they say that the one who presides universally over life and sensation has entrusted to them, as servants, such matters of the flesh, as being base and far removed? Then are those select gods so destitute of servants that they cannot find any to whom they too may assign the menial tasks? With all the nobility which seemed to warrant their selection are they compelled to toil along with the ignoble? Juno is a select goddess and a queen, " both sister and spouse of Jove,"[1] yet she is also Iterduca for children, and does her work with the very obscure Abeona and Adeona. In the same list they have also placed the goddess Mens, to give children a good disposition. And she is not included among the select gods—as if any greater gift could be given to a man! But Juno is included because she is Iterduca and Domiduca, as if it were any advantage to make a journey (*iter*) and get back home (*domum*) if the disposition is not good. Yet the goddess who gives that gift was completely ignored by the selectors who named the select gods. But she should certainly have been preferred even to Minerva, to whom they assign the memory of children in this distribution of petty tasks. For who would doubt that it is much better to have a good disposition than a memory, however vast its capacity? For no one is bad who has a good disposition, but there are some very bad people endowed with a marvellous memory, their character all the worse because they cannot forget their evil designs. And still Minerva is among the select gods, while Mens is lost among the common throng. What shall I say of Virtus? What of Felicitas? Of these I have already spoken at some length in the

quarto libro plura iam diximus; quas cum deas
haberent, nullum eis locum inter selectos deos dare
voluerunt ubi dederunt Marti et Orco, uni effectori
mortium alteri receptori.

Cum igitur in his minutis operibus quae minutatim
diis pluribus distributa sunt etiam ipsos selectos
videamus tamquam senatum cum plebe pariter
operari, et inveniamus a quibusdam diis qui nequaquam seligendi putati sunt multo maiora atque
meliora administrari quam ab illis qui selecti vocantur, restat arbitrari non propter praestantiores in
mundo administrationes, sed quia provenit eis ut
magis populis innotescerent, selectos eos et praecipuos nuncupatos. Unde dicit etiam ipse Varro,
quod diis quibusdam patribus et deabus matribus,
sicut hominibus, ignobilitas accidisset. Si ergo
Felicitas ideo fortasse inter selectos deos esse non
debuit quod ad istam nobilitatem non merito, sed
fortuito pervenerunt, saltem inter illos vel potius
prae illis Fortuna poneretur, quam dicunt deam non
rationabili dispositione, set ut temere acciderit, sua
cuique dona conferre. Haec in diis selectis tenere
apicem debuit, in quibus maxime quid posset
ostendit; quando eos videmus non praecipua virtute,
non rationabili felicitate, sed temeraria (sicut eorum
cultores de illa sentiunt) Fortunae potestate selectos.

Nam et vir disertissimus Sallustius etiam ipsos deos
fortassis adtendit, cum diceret: " Sed profecto

---

[1] 4.21, p. 73, and 4.23, p. 81 f.

fourth book.[1] Although the pagans regarded these as deities, they did not choose to give them a place among the select gods, where they made room for Mars and Orcus, the one a god who causes deaths, the other a god who receives the dead.

And so we see that in these little tasks, which are assigned piecemeal to so many gods, even the select gods, the senate of the gods, so to speak, work side by side with the lower class. And we find that some gods who were by no means thought worthy of selection perform much greater and better tasks than those who are called select. So we are left to conclude that it is not because of their superior functions in the world, but because of winning greater renown among the people that those gods have been called select and outstanding. Hence even Varro himself says that some father-gods and mother-goddesses, like some men, have had obscurity as their lot. So therefore while Felicitas perhaps had no right to a place among the select gods, since these attained their high rank not by merit but by fortune, Fortuna at least should have been given a place among them, or rather before them, for they say that this goddess confers her gifts on each one, not by any rational plan, but by blind chance. Among the select gods she ought to have held the topmost place. It is in their case especially that she showed what she could accomplish, for we see that they have been selected not for outstanding character nor any deserved felicity, but through the power of fortune, arbitrary as their worshippers believe that power to be.

For the excellent writer Sallust was perhaps thinking of gods as well as men when he said: " But

fortuna in omni re dominatur; ea res cunctas ex
libidine magis quam ex vero celebrat obscuratque."
Non enim possunt invenire causam cur celebrata sit
Venus et obscurata sit Virtus, cum ambarum ab istis
consecrata sint numina nec comparanda sint merita.
Aut si hoc nobilitari meruit quod plures adpetunt,
plures enim Venerem quam Virtutem, cur celebrata
est dea Minerva et obscurata est dea Pecunia, cum in
genere humano plures alliciat avaritia quam peritia,
et in eis ipsis, qui sunt artificiosi, raro invenias
hominem qui non habeat artem suam pecuniaria
mercede venalem, plurisque pendatur semper propter
quod aliquid fit, quam id quod propter aliud fit? Si
ergo insipientis iudicio multitudinis facta est deorum
ista selectio, cur dea Pecunia Minervae praelata non
est, cum propter pecuniam sint artifices multi? Si
autem paucorum sapientium est ista distinctio, cur
non praelata est Veneri Virtus, cum eam longe
praeferat ratio?

Saltem certe, ut dixi, ipsa Fortuna, quae, sicut
putant qui ei plurimum tribuunt, in omni re dominatur et res cunctas ex libidine magis quam ex vero
celebrat obscuratque, si tantum et in deos valuit ut
temerario iudicio suo quos vellet celebraret obscura-
retque quos vellet, praecipuum locum haberet in

---

[1] *Catiline* 8.
[2] On the deities of money see 4.21, p. 76 and note. As for
the obscurity of the goddess Pecunia, the satirist Juvenal
(1.112–16) remarks that although she was most highly revered
by the people, she still had no temple in Rome. Evidently

undoubtedly Fortune rules in everything. It is more by caprice than by justice that she brings all things to fame or obscurity." [1] For they cannot find a reason why Venus should be famous and Virtue obscure, though both are consecrated as divinities, and their merits are not to be compared. Or if a deity has won a place of honour because more people seek after him—more, of course, seek after Venus than Virtue—why is the goddess Minerva famous and Pecunia, the goddess of money, obscure? [2] For in all mankind more are allured by greed than by knowledge of the arts, and even among those who are craftsmen a man is rarely found who will not sell his skill for a price in money, and a higher value is always placed on the end for which a thing is done than on the means used to gain that end. If, then, this selection of gods was made by the judgement of the ignorant crowd, why was not the goddess Pecunia preferred to Minerva, since it is to gain money that there are many craftsmen? But if this distinction is due to a few wise men, why was Virtue not preferred to Venus, when reason gives her the preference by far?

At any rate, as I have said, if Fortune herself, according to the view of those who set most store by her, rules in everything and brings all things to fame or obscurity more by caprice than by justice, if she has gained such power over the gods as well that by her capricious judgement she has given fame or obscurity as she wished, she certainly ought to have had an outstanding place among the select gods, since

Pecunia, Aesculanus and Argentinus had no established cult, but remained forgotten names in pontifical books.

selectis, quae in ipsos quoque deos tam praecipuae
est potestatis.   An ut illic esse non posset, nihil aliud
etiam ipsa Fortuna nisi adversam putanda est
habuisse fortunam? Sibi ergo adversata est, quae
alios nobiles faciens nobilitata non est.

IV

*Melius actum cum diis inferioribus, qui nullis
infamentur opprobriis, quam cum selectis, quorum
tantae turpitudines celebrentur.*

GRATULARETUR autem diis istis selectis quisquam
nobilitatis et claritudinis adpetitor et eos diceret
fortunatos, si non eos magis ad iniurias quam ad
honores selectos videret.   Nam illam infimam turbam
ipsa ignobilitas texit, ne obrueretur opprobriis.
Ridemus quidem, cum eos videmus figmentis
humanarum opinionum partitis inter se operibus
distributos, tamquam minuscularios vectigalium
conductores vel tamquam opifices in vico argentario,
ubi unum vasculum ut perfectum exeat per multos
artifices transit, cum ab uno perfecto perfici posset.
Sed aliter non putatum est operantium multitudini
consulendum, nisi ut singulas artis partes cito ac
facile discerent singuli, ne omnes in arte una tarde
ac difficile cogerentur esse perfecti.

Verum tamen vix quisquam reperitur deorum non

she exercises such outstanding power over the very gods to boot. Or are we to think that even Fortune herself has had nothing but bad fortune, to keep her from that position? She has therefore opposed herself, for while ennobling others, she has not been ennobled herself.

IV

That the inferior gods, who have not been disgraced by scandals, have been better treated than the select gods, whose many shameful deeds are publicly celebrated.

EVERYONE who seeks distinction and renown might congratulate these select gods and call them fortunate, if he did not perceive that they were selected more to suffer insults than to receive honours. For that throng of lower gods was protected by its very obscurity from being overwhelmed by scandals. We laugh, to be sure, when we see them assigned, according to the fancies of human beliefs, to the tasks that are shared out among them, as if they were subcontractors for the collection of taxes, or workmen in the silversmiths' quarter where a vessel passes through the hands of many craftsmen before it comes out finished, though it could have been perfected by a single perfect craftsman. But it was supposed that the only way to make good use of a large number of workmen was to have different men learn different parts of the craft quickly and easily, so that all would not be compelled to gain a mastery of the whole craft slowly and with difficulty.

We laugh at this, I say, but still there is hardly one

selectorum qui aliquo crimine famam traxit infamem;
vix autem selectorum quispiam qui non in se notam
contumeliae insignis acceperit. Illi ad istorum
humilia opera descenderunt, isti in illorum sublimia
crimina non venerunt. De Iano quidem non mihi
facile quicquam occurrit quod ad probrum pertineat.
Et fortasse talis fuerit, innocentius vixerit et a faci-
noribus flagitiisque remotius. Saturnum fugientem
benignus excepit; cum hospite partitus est regnum
ut etiam civitates singulas conderent, iste Ianiculum,
ille Saturniam. Sed isti in cultu deorum omnis
dedecoris adpetitores, cuius vitam minus turpem
invenerunt, eum simulacri monstrosa deformitate
turparunt, nunc eum bifrontem, nunc etiam quadrifrontem, tamquam geminum, facientes. An forte
voluerunt ut, quoniam plurimi dii selecti erubescenda perpetrando amiserant frontem, quanto iste
innocentior esset, tanto frontosior appareret?

V

*De paganorum secretiore doctrina physicisque
rationibus.*

SED ipsorum potius interpretationes physicas audia-
mus, quibus turpitudinem miserrimi erroris velut
altioris doctrinae specie colorare conantur. Primum

---

[1] In dividing the land, Janus took the hill on the right bank
of the Tiber which thenceforth was called the Janiculum,
Saturn the one on the left which became the *mons Saturnius,*

of these non-select gods to be found who has con-
tracted an ill-famed fame by any crime, and hardly
one of the select who has not been branded for some
notorious scandal. The select gods have descended
to the low tasks of the obscure, but these have not
risen to the heights of infamy that distinguish the
select. Concerning Janus, to be sure, I cannot
readily think of anything that is of a disgraceful
nature. And perhaps he was such a man as lived a
more innocent life, less infected by crimes and
scandals. He received with kindness the fugitive
Saturn, and divided his realm with his guest on such
terms that each of them founded a city, the one
Janiculum, the other Saturnia.[1] But the pagans,
eager for every kind of impropriety in their worship
of gods, and finding Janus' life free from dishonour,
disfigured him by the monstrous deformity of his
image, making him two-faced, and now even four-
faced, as if he were double. Or was it perchance
their meaning that since most of the select gods had
lost face by perpetrating shameful deeds, Janus
should appear with more faces, to match his greater
innocence?

V

On the more secret teaching of the pagans, and their
physical explanations.

But let us listen, rather, to the physical interpretations with which they try to colour their foul and
miserable error, making it look like a more profound

later the Capitoline (Ovid, *Fasti* 1.235–46; Varro, *On the
Latin Language* 5.42).

eas interpretationes sic Varro commendat ut dicat antiquos simulacra deorum et insignia ornatusque finxisse, quae cum oculis animadvertissent hi qui adissent doctrinae mysteria possent animam mundi ac partes eius, id est deos veros, animo videre; quorum qui simulacra specie hominis fecerunt, hoc videri secutos quod mortalium animus, qui est in corpore humano, simillimus est inmortalis animi; tamquam si vasa ponerentur causa notandorum deorum et in Liberi aede oenophorum sisteretur, quod significaret vinum, per id quod continet id quod continetur; ita per simulacrum, quod formam haberet humanam, significari animam rationalem, quod eo velut vase natura ista soleat contineri, cuius naturae deum volunt esse vel deos.

Haec sunt mysteria doctrinae, quae iste vir doctissimus penetraverat, unde in lucem ista proferret. Sed, o homo acutissime, num in istis doctrinae mysteriis illam prudentiam perdidisti qua tibi sobrie visum est quod hi qui primi populis simulacra constituerunt, et metum dempserunt civibus suis et errorem addiderunt, castiusque deos sine simulacris veteres observasse Romanos? Hi enim tibi fuerunt auctores ut haec contra posteriores Romanos dicere auderes. Nam si et illi antiquissimi simulacra coluissent, fortassis totum istum sensum de simulacris non constituendis, interim verum, timoris silentio pre-

---

[1] See 4.31, p. 119, above.

doctrine. First of all, Varro commends these interpretations by saying that the ancients designed the images, attributes and ornaments of the gods so that men who had approached the mysteries of the doctrine, when they considered these visible things, might gain mental insight into the world and its parts, that is, the true gods. Those who made the images of these gods in human form, he says, appear to have been guided by the thought that the mortal mind that is in the human body is very much like the immortal mind. For example, it is as if vessels were set up to denote the gods, and in the temple of Liber a wine-jar were placed to denote wine, the container standing for the thing contained. Thus the image that has a human form signifies the rational soul, since it is in that sort of vessel, so to speak, that the substance is contained of which they wish to imply that the gods consist.

Such are the mysteries of pagan doctrine, penetrated by that learned man in order to bring these teachings to light. But, O most acute of men, among those mysteries of doctrine did you lose that wisdom whereby you once soberly judged that those who first set up images among the various peoples subtracted fear from their fellow-citizens and added error, and that the ancient Romans had a purer religion when they worshipped the gods without images?[1] Those ancients were your authorities when you dared to bring this charge against the Romans of later times. For if those ancients also had worshipped images, perhaps you would have completely suppressed in timid silence your opinion that images should not have been set up, although that opinion

meres et in huiusce modi perniciosis vanisque
figmentis mysteria ista doctrinae loquacius et elatius
praedicares. Anima tua tamen tam docta et ingeni-
osa (ubi te multum dolemus) per haec mysteria
doctrinae ad Deum suum, id est a quo facta est, non
cum quo facta est, nec cuius portio, sed cuius conditio
est, nec qui est omnium anima, sed qui fecit omnem
animam, quo solo inlustrante anima fit beata, si eius
gratiae non sit ingrata, nullo modo potuit pervenire.

Verum ista mysteria doctrinae qualia sint quan-
tique pendenda, quae sequuntur ostendent. Fatetur
interim vir iste doctissimus animam mundi ac partes
eius esse veros deos; unde intellegitur totam eius
theologian, eam ipsam scilicet naturalem, cui plurimum tribuit, usque ad animae rationalis naturam se
extendere potuisse. De naturali enim paucissima
praeloquitur in hoc libro quem de diis selectis ulti-
mum scripsit; in quo videbimus utrum per interpretationes physiologicas ad hanc naturalem possit
referre civilem. Quod si potuerit, tota naturalis
erit; et quid opus erat ab ea civilem tanta cura distinctionis abiungere? Si autem recto discrimine
separata est, quando nec ista vera est quae illi
naturalis placet (pervenit enim usque ad animam, non
usque ad verum Deum qui fecit et animam), quanto
est abiectior et falsior ista civilis, quae maxime circa
corporum est occupata naturam, sicut ipsae inter-

is true. And you might have proclaimed those
mysteries of doctrine at greater length and with
loftier eloquence, employing these fatal and foolish
fictions. Your soul was learned and naturally gifted,
and for this reason we deeply grieve for you, but that
same soul was quite unable to reach its God through
these mysteries of pagan doctrine—the God, that is,
by whom it was made, not with whom it was made,
the God of whom it is not a part, but the creature, the
God who is not the soul of everything, but who made
every soul, the God by whose light alone the soul
gains happiness, if it is not ungrateful to his grace.

But the discussion which follows will show what
those mysteries of doctrine are, and how high we
should rate them. Meanwhile this learned man
admits that the world soul and its parts are true gods,
hence it is evident that his theology in its fulness, that
is the " natural theology," to which he assigns the
chief place, could extend its range to include the
nature of the rational soul. Concerning natural
theology he speaks very briefly in the preface to his
last book, which was on the subject of the select gods.
We shall see in our study of this book whether he was
able by physical explanations to bring the civil
theology into agreement with the natural theology.
If so, it will all be natural, and what was the need of
so carefully distinguishing the civil from the natural?
But if the distinction was rightly made—since this
natural religion which he favours is not true either,
for it goes only as far as the soul, and not all the way
to the true God who made the soul—how much more
worthless and false is that civil theology which is
concerned chiefly with the nature of bodies! This

pretationes eius, ex quibus quaedam necessaria
commemorare me oportet, tanta ab ipsis exquisitae
et enucleatae diligentia demonstrabunt.

VI

De opinione Varronis qua arbitratus est Deum
animam esse mundi, qui tamen in partibus suis
habeat animas multas quarum divina natura sit.

Dicit ergo idem Varro adhuc de naturali theologia
praeloquens deum se arbitrari esse animam mundi,
quem Graeci vocant κόσμον, et hunc ipsum mundum
esse deum; sed sicut hominem sapientem, cum sit
ex corpore et animo, tamen ab animo dici sapientem,
ita mundum deum dici ab animo, cum sit ex animo et
corpore. Hic videtur quoquo modo unum confiteri
Deum; sed ut plures etiam introducat, adiungit
mundum dividi in duas partes, caelum et terram; et
caelum bifariam, in aethera et aera; terram vero in
aquam et humum; e quibus summum esse aethera,
secundum aera, tertiam aquam, infimam terram;
quas omnes partes quattuor animarum esse plenas, in
aethere et aere inmortalium, in aqua et terra mortalium. Ab summo autem circuitu caeli ad circulum
lunae aetherias animas esse astra ac stellas, eos
caelestes deos non modo intellegi esse, sed etiam
videri; inter lunae vero gyrum et nimborum ac
ventorum cacumina aerias esse animas, sed eas

will be demonstrated by citing the theories themselves which they worked out and explained with such care, some of which I find it necessary to mention.

VI

On the opinion of Varro that God is the world soul,
which nevertheless in its various parts has many
souls which are of divine nature.

THE same Varro, then, still in his introductory remarks about natural theology, says that he thinks that God is the soul of the universe, which the Greeks call *cosmos*, and that this universe itself is God. But just as a wise man, he says, though consisting of body and mind, is called wise because of his mind, so the universe is called God because of its mind, though it likewise consists of mind and body. Varro here seems somehow to confess that there is one true God, but in order to bring in more he adds that the universe is divided into two parts, heaven and earth, and the heaven is two fold, divided into aether and air, and the earth in turn is divided into water and land. Of these the highest is the aether, the second air, the third water and the fourth earth. All these four parts, he says, are full of souls, immortal souls in the aether and the air, mortal souls in the water and on land. From the highest circle of heaven to the circle of the moon are etherial souls, the constellations and the stars, and these are not only known by our intelligence to exist, but are also visible to our eyes as heavenly gods. Then between the circle of the moon and the highest region of clouds and winds are aerial

397

animo, non oculis videri et vocari heroas et lares et genios. Haec est videlicet breviter in ista prae-locutione proposita theologia naturalis, quae non huic tantum, sed multis philosophis placuit; de qua tunc diligentius disserendum est, cum de civili, quantum ad deos selectos adtinet, opitulante Deo vero quod restat implevero.

VII

An rationabile fuerit Ianum et Terminum in duo numina separari.

IANUS igitur, a quo sumpsit exordium, quaero quisnam sit. Respondetur: Mundus est. Brevis haec plane est atque aperta responsio. Cur ergo ad eum dicuntur rerum initia pertinere, fines vero ad alterum, quem Terminum vocant? Nam propter initia et fines duobus istis diis duos menses perhibent dedicatos praeter illos decem quibus usque ad Decembrem caput est Martius, Ianuarium Iano,

---

[1] Compare 8.14, where the daemones are assigned a similar abode midway between the celestial gods and men. Varro seems here, as in Arnobius 3.41, to regard heroes, Lares and Genii as souls of the dead, now occupying these upper regions.

[2] Augustine now devotes four chapters to the discussion of Janus and Terminus, Janus and Jupiter, and the rather fantastic explanations of Janus' double face. As world-god, or sky-god (see next chapter) he is first among the select gods. Some modern scholars have maintained that Janus (*Dianus) was originally a sky-god and essentially a double of Jupiter (see Frazer on Ovid, *Fasti* 1.89). L. A. MacKay presents a summary of modern views and defends the thesis that he was originally the god of the old-and-new moon (*Univ. of Calif. Pub. in Class. Phil.* 15.4, 157–82).

souls, perceived as such by the mind, not by the eyes. They are called heroes and Lares and Genii.[1]   This is, briefly stated, the natural theology that Varro sets forth in his introduction, a theology approved not only by Varro, but by many philosophers.   I shall have occasion to discuss it more carefully after I have, with the help of the true God, finished what remains to be said about the civil theology, so far as it relates to the select gods.

VII

Whether it was reasonable for Janus and Terminus to be separated into two divinities.

Who then, I ask, is Janus, with whom Varro begins his list?[2]   The answer is, " He is the world."   This is certainly a short and clear answer.   Why then is it said that the beginnings of things belong to him, while the ends belong to another whom they call Terminus?   For it is on account of beginnings and ends, they say, that those two gods have two months dedicated to them, outside the ten which run from March to December.[3]   That is, January is dedicated

---

[3] According to the prevalent view in antiquity, the Roman year at first had ten months, beginning with March; January and February were added by Numa or Tarquinius Priscus (see Rose on " Calendars " in *OCD*, 156).   As for the absurdity that January was the beginning and February the ending of the year, Altheim, *History of Roman Religion* 176, takes February to be the end of the old year which began in March, and January to be the beginning of the year in the reformed calendar.   Rose suggests that when Tarquin introduced January, it was intended to be the first month, but that the expulsion of the Tarquin kings stopped this, so that March remained the beginning of the civil year until 153 B.C.

Februarium Termino. Ideo Terminalia eodem
mense Februario celebrari dicunt, cum fit sacrum
purgatorium, quod vocant Februm, unde mensis
nomen accepit. Numquid ergo ad mundum, qui
Ianus est, initia rerum pertinent et fines non pertinent, ut alter illis deus praeficeretur? Nonne
omnia, quae in hoc mundo fieri dicunt, in hoc etiam
mundo terminari fatentur? Quae est ista vanitas, in
opere illi dare potestatem dimidiam, in simulacro
faciem duplam?

Nonne istum bifrontem multo elegantius inter-
pretarentur, si eundem et Ianum et Terminum dicerent atque initiis unam faciem, finibus alteram
darent? Quoniam qui operatur utrumque debet
intendere; in omni enim motu actionis suae qui non
respicit initium non prospicit finem. Unde necesse
est a memoria respiciente prospiciens conectatur
intentio; nam cui exciderit quod coeperit, quo modo
finiat non inveniet. Quod si vitam beatam in hoc
mundo inchoari putarent, extra mundum perfici, et
ideo Iano, id est mundo, solam initiorum tribuerent
potestatem, profecto ei praeponerent Terminum
eumque ab diis selectis non alienarent. Quamquam
etiam nunc cum in istis duobus diis initia rerum
temporalium finesque tractantur, Termino dari debuit
plus honoris. Maior enim laetitia est cum res quaeque perficitur; sollicitundinis autem plena sunt

---

[1] The word *februm*, usually written *februum*, is said to be a
Sabine word for " purification " (Varro, *On the Latin Language*
6.13; see also Ovid, *Fasti* 2.19 and Frazer's note).

to Janus, and February to Terminus. For this reason, they say, the Terminalia are celebrated in the same month, February, when the sacred purification is made which they call Februm,[1] from which the month gets its name. Then do the beginnings of things belong to the world, or Janus, and not the ends, so that a second god was placed in charge of them? Do they not admit that everything that happens in this world also ends in this world? What nonsense, in his work to give Janus only half the job, and in his image to give him a double face!

Would they not give his double face a much more elegant explanation by saying that Janus and Terminus are the same, and assigning one face to the beginnings and the other to the ends? For one who acts must give attention to both, and one who does not at each move in his operation look back to the beginning, does not look forward to the end. Hence it is necessary for the intention that foresees to be linked with the memory that looks back. For one who forgets what he has begun will not find the means to finish it. But if they thought that the happy life is begun in this world and is perfected outside the world, and so assigned to Janus, or the world, only the power over beginnings, then certainly they would put Terminus above him, and would not exclude him from the number of select gods. But even as it is, though in connection with those two gods they have in mind only the beginnings and ends of earthly things, Terminus ought to have received the greater honour. For the joy is greater when anything is finished, while projects begun are fraught with worry until they are carried through to the

coepta donec perducantur ad finem, quem qui aliquid incipit maxime adpetit intendit, expectat exoptat, nec de re inchoata, nisi terminetur, exultat.

VIII

Ob quam causam cultores Iani bifrontem imaginem ipsius finxerint, quam tamen etiam quadrifrontem videri volunt.

SED iam bifrontis simulacri interpretatio proferatur. Duas eum facies ante et retro habere dicunt, quod hiatus noster, cum os aperimus, mundo similis videatur; unde et palatum Graeci οὐρανόν appellant, et nonnulli, inquit, poetae Latini caelum vocaverunt palatum, a quo hiatu oris et foras esse aditum ad dentes versus et introrsus ad fauces. Ecce quo perductus est mundus propter palati nostri vocabulum vel Graecum vel poeticum. Quid autem hoc ad animam, quid ad vitam aeternam? Propter solas salivas colatur hic deus, quibus partim gluttiendis partim spuendis sub caelo palati utraque panditur ianua. Quid est porro absurdius quam in ipso mundo non invenire duas ianuas ex adverso sitas per quas vel admittat ad se aliquid intro vel emittat a se foras, et de nostro ore et gutture, quorum similitudinem mundus non habet, velle mundi simulacrum

end. When a man begins anything, it is the end that he chiefly seeks, aims at, waits for and desires. Nor does he rejoice over a thing begun, unless it be completed.

VIII

Why the worshippers of Janus made his images with two faces, though they also would make him show four faces.

BUT now let the explanation of the two-faced image be produced. They say that he has two faces, one in front and one behind, because the space within our mouth, when it is open, seems similar to the universe. Hence the Greeks call the palate *ouranos*, or sky, and some Latin poets, Varro says, have called the sky *palatum*, or palate. From this hollow space in the mouth there are two passages, one outward toward the teeth, the other inward toward the throat. Now see what they have made of the world because of a word for our palate, whether it be Greek or poetical! But what does this have to do with the soul, or with eternal life? Let us worship this god only for the sake of our saliva, for which a door opens each way from under the " sky " of the palate—one way to swallow it down, the other to spit it out. What, indeed, is more absurd than what they do? In the universe itself we do not find two doors placed opposite each other, through which it lets things come into itself or expels them from itself. But from our mouth and throat, which correspond to nothing in the world, they would produce in Janus a

componere in Iano propter solum palatum, cuius
similitudinem Ianus non habet?

Cum vero eum faciunt quadrifrontem et Ianum
geminum appellant, ad quattuor mundi partes hoc
interpretantur, quasi aliquid spectet mundus foras
sicut per omnes facies Ianus. Deinde si Ianus est
mundus et mundus quattuor partibus constat, falsum
est simulacrum Iani bifrontis; aut si propterea verum
est, quia etiam nomine Orientis et Occidentis totus
solet mundus intellegi, numquid, cum duas partes
alias nominamus Septentrionis et Austri, sicut illi
quadrifrontem dicunt geminum Ianum, ita quisquam geminum dicturus est mundum? Non habent
omnino unde quattuor ianuas quae intrantibus et
exeuntibus pateant interpretentur ad mundi similitudinem, sicut de bifronti quod dicerent saltem in
ore hominis invenerunt, nisi Neptunus forte sub-
veniat et porrigat piscem, cui praeter hiatum oris et
gutturis etiam dextra et sinistra fauces patent. Et
tamen hanc vanitatem per tot ianuas nulla effugit
anima, nisi quae audit veritatem dicentem: *Ego sum
ianua.*

IX

De Iovis potestate atque eiusdem cum Iano comparatione.

Iovem autem, qui etiam Iuppiter dicitur, quem
velint intellegi, exponant. " Deus est," inquiunt,
" habens potestatem causarum, quibus aliquid fit in

---

[1] See John 10.9.

composite image of the world, merely because of the palate, though Janus bears no resemblance to a palate.

But when they make an image with four faces, and call it a " twin Janus," they say this means the four quarters of the universe, as if the universe faced anything outside itself in the way that Janus faces four ways. Then if Janus is the world, and the world consists of four quarters, the two-faced image of Janus is not a true representation. Or if it is true because the expression " Orient and Occident " is used for the whole world, then when we use for two other quarters the names " north " and " south," will anyone then call it a twin world, as they call Janus with four faces a twin Janus? They have no illustration at all to explain four doors, open for entry and exit, as a likeness of the world, corresponding to the interpretation of the two-faced Janus that they did at least find in a man's mouth. Not, that is, unless Neptune were to help them out and toss them a fish. A fish not only has the openings of its mouth and throat, but also has gills that open like jaws to the right and the left. And yet, through all these doors no soul escapes from the empty show here except one that hears Truth saying, " I am the door." [1]

IX

On the power of Jupiter and his likeness to Janus.

Now let them tell us how we should understand Jove, who is also called Jupiter. " He is the god," they say, " who has control of the causes by which

mundo." Hoc quam magnum sit, nobilissimus
Vergilii versus ille testatur:

Felix qui potuit rerum cognoscere causas.

Sed cur ei praeponitur Ianus? Hoc nobis vir ille acutissimus doctissimusque respondeat. " Quoniam
penes Ianum," inquit, " sunt prima, penes Iovem
summa. Merito ergo rex omnium Iuppiter habetur.
Prima enim vincuntur a summis quia, licet prima
praecedant tempore, summa superant dignitate."
Sed recte hoc diceretur si factorum prima discerne-
rentur et summa; sicut initium facti est proficisci,
summum pervenire; initium facti inceptio discendi,
summum perceptio doctrinae; ac sic in omnibus
prima sunt initia summique sunt fines. Sed iam hoc
negotium inter Ianum Terminumque discussum est.
Causae autem, quae dantur Iovi, efficientia sunt, non
effecta; neque ullo modo fieri potest ut vel tempore
praeveniantur a factis initiisve factorum. Semper
enim prior est res quae facit quam illa quae fit.
Quapropter si ad Ianum pertinent initia factorum,
non ideo priora sunt efficientibus causis, quas Iovi
tribuunt. Sicut enim nihil fit, ita nihil inchoatur ut
fiat quod non faciens causa praecesserit.

Hunc sane deum, penes quem sunt omnes causae

---

[1] In Stoic theology Zeus (Jupiter), the primal fire, the world
soul and fate were identical. He was the first cause, and from
him were derived the reasons (*logoi*) or causes (*aitiai*) of all
things (*SVF* I, 27; II, 167; Seneca, *Natural Questions*
2.45.1–2).

anything in the world happens." [1]   How important
this is is shown by the well-known verse of Vergil:

Happy was he who succeeded in seeing the causes
  of all things.[2]

But why is Janus put ahead of him? Let the acute
and learned Varro reply: " Because the beginnings
are in the power of Janus, and their fulfilment in that
of Jupiter. So Jupiter is rightly regarded as king of
all. For beginnings are inferior to fulfilments, since,
though they precede in time, they are surpassed in
dignity by the fulfilment." This statement would be
quite correct if we were making a distinction between
the beginning of acts and their fulfilment. To set
out is the beginning of an act, to arrive is its fulfilment; to set about learning is the beginning of a
process, and the comprehension of what is taught is
its fulfilment. So in all cases the beginnings come
first, and the fulfilment at the end. But this point
has already been discussed in connection with Janus
and Terminus. The causes, however, that are
assigned to Jupiter are efficient causes, not effects,
nor is it in the least possible that they are preceded
even in time by deeds done or by beginnings of
deeds. For that which causes is always prior to the
thing that is caused. Hence, though the beginnings
of deeds may belong to Janus, that is no reason
for putting them ahead of the efficient causes,
which are assigned to Jupiter. For not only is
nothing effected, but nothing starts to be effected,
unless it is preceded by an efficient cause.

If it is this god who has in his power all the causes

[2] Virgil, *Georgics* 2.490.

factarum omnium naturarum naturaliumque rerum,
si Iovem populi appellant et tantis contumeliis
tamque scelestis criminationibus colunt, taetriore
sacrilegio sese obstringunt, quam si prorsus nullum
putarent deum.   Unde satius esset eis alium aliquem
Iovis nomine nuncupare, dignum turpibus et flagi-
tiosis honoribus, supposito vano figmento quod potius
blasphemarent (sicut Saturno dicitur suppositus lapis
quem pro filio devoraret) quam istum deum dicere et
tonantem et adulterantem, et totum mundum
regentem et per tot stupra diffluentem, et naturarum
omnium naturaliumque rerum causas summas habentem et suas causas bonas non habentem.

Deinde quaero quem iam locum inter deos huic
Iovi tribuant, si Ianus est mundus.   Deos enim veros
animam mundi ac partes eius iste definivit; ac per
hoc, quidquid hoc non est, non est utique secundum
istos verus deus.   Num igitur ita dicturi sunt Iovem
animam mundi ut Ianus sit corpus eius, id est iste
visibilis mundus ?   Hoc si dicunt, non erit quem ad
modum Ianum deum dicant, quoniam mundi corpus
non est deus vel secundum ipsos, sed anima mundi
ac partes eius.   Unde apertissime idem dicit deum se
arbitrari esse animam mundi et hunc ipsum mundum
esse deum; sed sicut hominem sapientem, cum sit ex
animo et corpore, tamen ex animo dici sapientem, ita
mundum deum dici ab animo, cum sit ex animo et
corpore.   Solum itaque mundi corpus non est deus,

of all created beings and of all natural things, and the people call him Jupiter and worship him with such vile reproaches and such foul incriminations, the sacrilege in which they are implicated is a fouler thing than if they were to recognize no god at all. Hence it would be better for them to give some other being the name of Jupiter, someone worthy of base and shameful honours, substituting an empty fiction to be the object of their blasphemy, even as they say a stone was substituted for Saturn to devour in place of his son. Better this, than to say that this god is both thunderer and adulterer, one who rules all this world and yet abandons himself to so many base amours, one who has in his power the ultimate causes of all created beings and of all natural things, but does not have good causes motivating his own acts.

Next I ask what place among the gods they assign to this Jupiter, if Janus is the universe. For the true gods, as Varro defined them, are the world soul and its parts; hence according to the pagans whatever is not included in the definition is certainly not a true god. Then will they say that Jupiter is the world soul, while Janus is his body, that is, the visible universe? If they say this, they will have no ground for calling Janus a god, since even by their definition the body of the universe is not a god, for it is the world soul and its parts that are gods. On this point Varro clearly states that he believes that God is the world soul and that the universe itself is a god. But just as a wise man, he continues, though consisting of mind and body, is called wise from his mind, so the world is called a god from its mind, though it consists of mind and body. Therefore the body of the

sed aut sola anima eius aut simul corpus et animus,
ita tamen ut non sit a corpore, sed ab animo deus.
Si ergo Ianus est mundus et deus est Ianus, numquid
Iovem, ut deus esse possit, aliquam partem Iani esse
dicturi sunt?

Magis enim Iovi universum solent tribuere; unde
est: " Iovis omnia plena." Ergo et Iovem ut deus
sit et maxime rex deorum, non alium possunt existimare quam mundum ut diis ceteris secundum istos
suis partibus regnet. In hanc sententiam etiam
quosdam versus Valerii Sorani exponit idem Varro in
eo libro quem seorsum ab istis de cultu deorum
scripsit; qui versus hi sunt:

Iuppiter omnipotens regum rerumque deumque
Progenitor genetrixque deum, deus unus et omnes.

Exponuntur autem in eodem libro ita: cum marem
existimarent qui semen emitteret, feminam quae
acciperet, Iovemque esse mundum et eum omnia
semina ex se emittere et in se recipere: " cum causa,"

---

[1] Virgil, *Eclogues* 3.60.

[2] Jerome preserved a catalogue of Varro's writings, among
which were nineteen essays known as *logistorici*; of these one
bears the title *Curio de cultu deorum*. Augustine mentions it
again in chapter 34, below; it is uncertain whether he used it
elsewhere as a source. The fragments of this essay have been
repeatedly edited, most recently by B. Cardauns, *Varros
Logistoricus über die Götterverehrung* (Diss. Köln, 1958). This
passage appears as fragment 2 in Cardauns. Fragments 3
and 4 are taken from chapters 34 and 35 below, pp. 497–499.
Quintus Valerius Soranus, while serving as tribune of the
people in 82 B.C., fled before the victorious Sulla and was
killed by Pompey in Sicily. Cicero describes him as a neighbour and acquaintance, more distinguished for his literary

universe by itself is not a god, but rather the soul by itself, or body and soul together—viewed in such a way, however, that its being god is due not to its body but to its mind. Then if Janus is the universe, and Janus is a god, will they have to say that Jupiter, in order to be counted as a god, is some part of Janus?

Their custom is rather to assign the universe to Jupiter, whence the saying of the poet: " Of Jupiter all things are full." [1] It follows that, if Jupiter is to be a god, and especially the king of the gods, they must regard him as nought else but the world, so that he may reign over the other gods, which are portions of him, according to their doctrine. In accord with this view Varro also, in a book separate from these, which he wrote, *On the Worship of the Gods*, explains certain verses of Valerius Soranus. The verses run as follows:

> Jupiter, mighty Father of kings and of gods and of all things,
> Mother as well of the gods, one God comprising all others. [2]

The explanation given in the book mentioned is this: the one who emits seed is called male, and the one who receives it, female; Jupiter is the universe, and both emits all seeds and receives them into himself. Hence it is with good reason, Varro says, that

studies than for eloquence. Varro often cites his works, both prose and verse. The two hexameters here quoted seem to be a free translation from an Orphic hymn to Zeus, and set forth a doctrine agreeable also to the Stoic theology (O. Kern, *Orphicorum Fragmenta* 93, frag. 21a; *SVF* 2.316, frags. 1077 f.).

inquit, "scripsit Soranus 'Iuppiter progenitor genetrixque'; nec minus cum causa unum et omnia idem esse; mundus enim unus, et in eo uno omnia sunt."

X

An Iani et Iovis recta discretio sit.

Cum ergo et Ianus mundus sit et Iuppiter mundus sit unusque sit mundus, quare duo dii sunt Ianus et Iuppiter? Quare seorsus habent templa seorsus aras, diversa sacra dissimilia simulacra? Si propterea quod alia vis est primordiorum, alia causarum, et illa Iani, illa Iovis nomen accepit, numquid si unus homo in diversis rebus duas habeat potestates aut duas artes, quia singularum diversa vis est, ideo duo iudices aut duo dicuntur artifices? Sic ergo et unus Deus cum ipse habeat potestatem primordiorum, ipse causarum, num propterea illum duos deos esse necesse est putari, quia primordia causaeque res duae sunt? Quod si hoc iustum putant, etiam ipsum Iovem tot deos esse dicant quotquot ei cognomina propter multas potestates dederunt, quoniam res omnes ex quibus illa cognomina sunt adhibita multae atque diversae sunt, ex quibus pauca commemoro.

Soranus wrote, " Jupiter, mighty Father, and Mother as well," and with equally good reason described him as one God, comprising all others. For the universe is one, and all things are in that one.

X

Whether the distinction between Janus and Jupiter is justified.

THEREFORE, since Janus is the world, and Jupiter is the world, and there is one world, why are there two gods, Janus and Jupiter? Why do they have separate temples, separate altars, different sacred rites, and unlike statues? Is it because power over beginnings is one thing and power over causes another, so that the name Janus is given to the former, Jupiter to the latter? Well, if one man should have two capacities in different fields, or two crafts, should we speak of two judges, or two artisans, because the capacities are different in the two fields? So when one god himself has power over beginnings and over causes, must we then think that he is two gods because beginnings and causes are two things? But if they think that this is right, they should also say that Jupiter himself is as many gods as the number of cult-titles they have given him on account of his many functions. For all together the things that account for those cult-titles are extremely numerous and varied. I shall mention a few of them.

SAINT AUGUSTINE

XI

De cognominibus Iovis, quae non ad multos deos,
sed ad unum eundemque referuntur.

DIXERUNT eum Victorem, Invictum, Opitulum,
Inpulsorem, Statorem, Centumpedam, Supinalem,
Tigillum, Almum, Ruminum et alia quae persequi
longum est. Haec autem cognomina inposuerunt
uni deo propter causas potestatesque diversas, non
tamen propter tot res etiam tot deos eum esse
coegerunt: quod omnia vinceret, quod a nemine
vinceretur, quod opem indigentibus ferret, quod
haberet inpellendi, statuendi, stabiliendi, resupi-
nandi potestatem, quod tamquam tigillus mundum
contineret ac sustineret, quod aleret omnia, quod
ruma, id est mamma, aleret animalia. In his, ut
advertimus, quaedam magna sunt, quaedam exigua;
et tamen unus utraque facere perhibetur. Puto
inter se propinquiora esse causas rerum atque
primordia, propter quas res unum mundum duos
deos esse voluerunt, Iovem atque Ianum, quam
continere mundum et mammam dare animalibus;
nec tamen propter haec opera duo tam longe inter
se vi et dignitate diversa duo dii esse compulsi sunt;
sed unus Iuppiter propter illud Tigillus, propter illud
Ruminus appellatus est.

Nolo dicere, quod animalibus mammam praebere
sugentibus magis Iunonem potuit decere quam

414

XI

*On the cult-titles of Jupiter, which belong, not to
many gods, but to one and the same god.*

THE pagans have called Jupiter by the titles Victor,
Invictus, Opitulus, Impulsor, Stator, Centumpeda,
Supinalis, Tigillus, Almus, Ruminus, and still others
which it would be tedious to enumerate. They have
applied all these names to one god for various reasons and because of his various powers. But they
have not, though there are so many functions, compelled him to become as many different gods. The
functions are that he is victor over all, and invincible,
and brings help to the needy, and has the power of im-
pelling, of causing to stand, of stabilizing, and of lay-
ing flat; because he maintains and sustains the world
like a beam; because he nourishes all things, and
nourishes all animals by the breast (*ruma*). Among
these functions, as we observe, some are important
and some unimportant, yet one god is supposed to
perform both kinds. In my judgement there is a
closer relation between the causes of things and their
beginnings, for which they would have one universe
identical with two gods, Jupiter and Janus, than
there is between maintaining the world and giving
the breast to animals. However, there was no
necessity for having two gods even for two tasks so
different from each other in display of power and
dignity; the one god Jupiter was called Tigillus for
the one task and Ruminus for the other.

I will not say that it would have been more appropriate for Juno than for Jupiter to furnish the breast

Iovem, praesertim cum esset etiam diva Rumina
quae in hoc opus adiutorium illi famulatumve
praeberet. Cogito enim posse responderi, et ipsam
Iunonem nihil aliud esse quam Iovem, secundum
illos Valerii Sorani versus, ubi dictum est:

> Iuppiter omnipotens regum rerumque deumque
> Progenitor genetrixque deum.

Quare ergo dictus est et Ruminus, cum diligentius
fortasse quaerentibus ipse inveniatur esse etiam illa
diva Rumina? Si enim maiestate deorum recte
videbatur indignum ut in una spica alter ad curam
geniculi, altera ad folliculi pertineret, quanto est
indignius unam rem infimam, id est ut mammis
alantur animalia, duorum deorum potestate curari,
quorum sit unus Iuppiter, rex ipse cunctorum, et
hoc agat non saltem cum coniuge sua, sed cum
ignobili nescio qua Rumina, nisi quia ipse est etiam
ipsa Rumina; Ruminus fortasse pro sugentibus maribus, Rumina pro feminis. Dicerem quippe noluisse
illos Iovi femininum nomen inponere, nisi et in illis
versibus " progenitor genetrixque " diceretur, et
inter eius alia cognomina legerem quod etiam Pecunia
vocaretur, quam deam inter illos minuscularios
invenimus et in quarto libro commemoravimus.[1]
Sed cum et mares et feminae habeant pecuniam, cur
non et Pecunia et Pecunius appellatus sit, sicut
Rumina et Ruminus, ipsi viderint.

---

[1] See 4.21, p. 76 and note.

to sucking animals, especially since there was also a
goddess Rumina to furnish her help and service for
this work. For I think the reply can be made that
Juno herself is none other than Jupiter, according
to these verses of Valerius Soranus, where it is said:

Jupiter, mighty Father of kings and of gods and
    of all things,
Mother as well of the gods . . .

Why then was he also called Ruminus, when, if perhaps we were to inquire more carefully, we might find
that he is also identical with the goddess Rumina?
If there was good reason for supposing it unsuitable
to the dignity of the gods, in the case of one stalk of
wheat, that one god should have the care of the knots,
another that of the sheath, how much more unworthy
is it that one low task, namely, to see that animals
get nourishment from the breast, should require the
power of two deities. One of them was Jupiter,
himself king of all things, and he performed this task
not along with his wife, but with some unknown
Rumina. Unless he is himself Rumina—Ruminus
perhaps for suckling males and Rumina for females.
Of course I might say that they were unwilling to
give Jupiter a woman's name, except that it was said
of him in those verses I quoted, " Father and Mother
as well," and except that among his other names I
have read that he was also called Pecunia. I found
this goddess among those petty gods, and have
mentioned her in the fourth book.[1] But since both
males and females have money, why was Jupiter not
called both Pecunia and Pecunius, as he is called
Rumina and Ruminus? I leave the answer to them.

XII

Quod Iuppiter etiam Pecunia nuncupetur.

QUAM vero eleganter rationem huius nominis reddiderunt! "Et Pecunia, inquit, vocatur, quod eius sunt omnia." O magnam rationem divini nominis! Immo vero ille cuius sunt omnia vilissime et contumeliosissime Pecunia nuncupatur. Ad omnia enim quae caelo et terra continentur quid est pecunia in omnibus omnino rebus quae ab hominibus nomine pecuniae possidentur? Sed nimirum hoc avaritia Iovi nomen inposuit ut quisquis amat pecuniam non quemlibet deum, sed ipsum regem omnium sibi amare videatur. Longe autem aliud esset si divitiae vocaretur. Aliud namque sunt divitiae, aliud pecunia. Nam dicimus divites sapientes, iustos, bonos, quibus pecunia vel nulla vel parva est; magis enim sunt virtutibus divites, per quas eis etiam in ipsis corporalium rerum necessitatibus sat est quod adest, pauperes vero avaros, semper inhiantes et egentes; quamlibet enim magnas pecunias habere possunt, sed in earum quantacumque abundantia non egere non possunt. Et Deum ipsum verum recte dicimus divitem, non tamen pecunia, sed omnipotentia. Dicuntur itaque et divites pecuniosi; sed interius egeni, si cupidi.

XII

That Jupiter is also called Pecunia.

How elegantly, indeed, have they given an explanation of this name! " And he is called Pecunia," Varro says, " because all things are his." What a marvellous reason for a god's name! On the contrary, for God, to whom all things belong, it is a base insult to be called Pecunia. For what is money in comparison with all things which are contained in heaven and earth? It is nothing, even if we include all the things that are owned by men and counted as part of their wealth. But doubtless it was greed that gave this name to Jupiter, so that anyone who loves money might flatter himself that he was in love, not with just any god, but with the king of the universe himself. It would be a very different case if he were called " Riches." For riches are one thing, money another. We describe as " rich " men who are wise, just and good, who may have little or no money.[1] They are rich rather because of their virtues, which enable them even in times when material things are lacking to be content with what is at hand. But the greedy, always grasping and needing more, are truly poor. For however large the sums of money they succeed in acquiring, however great its profusion, they cannot escape from suffering want. And we rightly call the true God himself rich, not in money, but in omnipotence. And so, though moneyed people are said to be rich, yet inwardly they are poor,

[1] According to the Stoic paradox only the wise man was rich; see Cicero, *Paradoxa* 6.42 f. and Horace, *Epistles* 1.1.106.

Item dicuntur pauperes pecunia carentes; sed interius divites, si sapientes.

Qualis ergo ista theologia debet esse sapienti, ubi rex deorum eius rei nomen accepit, " quam nemo sapiens concupivit "? Quanto enim facilius, si aliquid hac doctrina quod ad vitam pertineret aeternam salubriter disceretur, deus mundi rector non ab eis Pecunia, sed Sapientia vocaretur, cuius amor purgat a sordibus avaritiae, hoc est ab amore pecuniae!

XIII

Quod, dum exponitur quid Saturnus quidve sit Genius, uterque unus Iuppiter esse doceatur.

Sed quid de hoc Iove plura, ad quem fortasse ceteri referendi sunt, ut inanis remaneat deorum opinio plurimorum, cum hic ipse sint omnes, sive quando partes eius vel potestates existimantur, sive cum vis animae, quam putant per cuncta diffusam, ex partibus molis huius in quas visibilis mundus iste consurgit, et multiplici administratione naturae quasi plurium deorum nomina accepit? Quid est enim et Saturnus? " Unus," inquit, " de principibus deus, penes quem sationum omnium dominatus est." Nonne expositio versuum illorum Valerii Sorani sic se

---

[1] Compare Sallust, *Catiline* 11.3.

if they are greedy for more. Likewise those who lack money are called poor, but inwardly they are rich, if they are wise.

Then what should a wise man think of this theology, where the king of the gods has received the name of that thing " which no wise man ever desired." [1] How much easier it would have been, if there were anything of saving value, related to eternal life, to be learned from this doctrine,—how much easier to have called the God who rules the world not Pecunia, but Sapientia or Wisdom! For the love of wisdom urges the soul from the pollution of greed, that is, from the love of money.

XIII

The accounts that tell what Saturn and Genius are, show that each of them is identical with Jupiter.

But why should I say more about this Jupiter, to whom perhaps all the other gods are to be carried back? In that case the belief in many gods is left without substance, since all are really Jupiter, whether they are held to be parts of him, that is, powers that he has, or whether the vital force, which they believe to be diffused through all things, takes the names of various gods from the parts of this massive structure into which this visible universe expands, and from the manifold operations of nature.

For example, what is Saturn? " He is one of the chief gods," says Varro, " who is lord of the sowing of all seed crops." But was it not the explanation of those verses of Valerius Soranus that Jupiter is the

421

habet, Iovem esse mundum et eum omnia semina ex
se emittere et in se recipere? Ipse est igitur penes
quem sationum omnium dominatus est. Quid est
Genius? " Deus," inquit, " qui praepositus est ac
vim habet omnium rerum gignendarum." Quem
alium hanc vim habere credunt quam mundum, cui
dictum est: " Iuppiter progenitor genetrixque? "
Et cum alio loco genium dicit esse uniuscuiusque
animum rationalem et ideo esse singulos singulorum,
talem autem mundi animum Deum esse, ad hoc idem
utique revocat ut tamquam universalis genius ipse
mundi animus esse credatur. Hic est igitur quem
appellant Iovem. Nam si omnis genius deus et
omnis viri animus genius, sequitur ut sit omnis viri
animus deus; quod si et ipsos abhorrere absurditas
ipsa compellit, restat ut eum singulariter et excel-
lenter dicant deum Genium, quem dicunt mundi
animum ac per hoc Iovem.

XIV

De Mercurii et Martis officiis.

MERCURIUM vero et Martem quo modo referrent ad
aliquas partes mundi et opera Dei quae sunt in
elementis, non invenerunt, et ideo eos saltem
operibus hominum praeposuerunt, sermocinandi et
belligerandi administros. Quorum Mercurius si
sermonis etiam deorum potestatem gerit, ipsi quoque

---

¹ The name Genius is from the root *gen* (*gignere*, *genitus*),
" to beget. " Each man, and especially each paterfamilias,
had his Genius, or power to beget, just as each woman had her

world, and that he emits all seeds from himself and receives them into himself? Then he is the lord who has charge of the sowing of all seed crops. And what is Genius? " The god," Varro says, " who has command and control of everything that is begotten." [1] But what else is there that they think has this power, except the universe, to which were spoken the words, " Jupiter, Father and Mother "?

And in another place he says that a *genius* is the rational soul of each man, so that each individual has one, while the corresponding world soul is a god. Thus he brings us back to the same point, that we should believe the world soul itself to be the universal *genius*. And this is what they call Jupiter. If every *genius* is a god, and the soul of every man is a *genius*, it follows that the soul of every man is a god. But if the very absurdity of this compels its rejection, then they can only say that this Genius, who is uniquely and outstandingly god, is he whom they call the world soul, and hence Jupiter.

XIV

On the duties of Mercury and Mars.

But in the case of Mercury and Mars they could not find a way to assign them to any parts of the world, or activities of God in the elements, and so instead they put them in charge of human activities as helpers in speaking and in waging war. If Mercury exercises power over the speech of gods as well, he

Juno. In the Stoic view this power was a part of the world soul, which has both generative and rational capacity.

regi deorum dominatur, si secundum eius arbitrium
Iuppiter loquitur aut loquendi ab illo accepit facultatem; quod utique absurdum est. Si autem illi
humani tantum sermonis potestas tributa perhibetur,
non est credibile ad lactandos mamma non solum
pueros, sed etiam pecora, unde Ruminus cognomina-
tus est, Iovem descendere voluisse, et curam nostri
sermonis, quo pecoribus antecellimus, ad se pertinere
noluisse; ac per hoc idem ipse est Iovis atque Mercurius.

Quod si sermo ipse dicitur esse Mercurius, sicut ea
quae de illo interpretantur ostendunt (nam ideo
Mercurius quasi medius currens dicitur appellatus,
quod sermo currat inter homines medius; ideo
Ἑρμῆς Graece, quod sermo vel interpretatio, quae
ad sermonem utique pertinet, ἑρμηνεία dicitur; ideo
et mercibus praeesse, quia inter vendentes et ementes
sermo fit medius; alas eius in capite et pedibus
significare volucrem ferri per aera sermonem;
nuntium dictum, quoniam per sermonem omnia
cogitata enuntiantur)—si ergo Mercurius ipse sermo
est, etiam ipsis confitentibus deus non est.

Sed cum sibi deos faciunt eos qui nec daemones
sunt, inmundis supplicando spiritibus possidentur ab
eis qui non dii, sed daemones sunt. Item quia nec
Marti aliquod elementum vel partem mundi invenire
potuerunt ubi ageret opera qualiacumque naturae,

becomes the master of the very king of the gods, that is, if Jupiter speaks according to Mercury's pleasure, or has received from him his faculty of speech. And this is certainly absurd. If, however, it is only over human speech that power is supposed to be assigned to Mercury, it is incredible that Jupiter was willing to come down to the business of giving milk from the breast—not only to children but also to animals,— whence he got the name Ruminus, and was unwilling to take charge of our speech, a faculty in which we excel the animals. Hence it would seem that Jove and Mercury are the same.

But perhaps speech itself is called "Mercury," as the explanation of his name seems to show. For he is said to have been named Mercury as being a middle courier (*medius currens*), because speech runs like a courier between men. Hence he is called Hermes in Greek, since speech, or interpretation, which certainly belongs to speech, is called *hermeneia*. Hence also he is in charge of trade, since between sellers and buyers speech occurs as a medium. The wings on his head and feet mean that speech flies through the air like a bird. He is called a messenger, since language is the messenger that proclaims our thoughts. If therefore Mercury is speech itself, by their own admission he is no god.

But while they make gods for themselves who are not even demons, when they pray to unclean spirits they are seized by those who are not gods, but demons. Likewise, since they could not find any element or part of the world for Mars either, where he could carry on any of the works of nature, no matter what sort, they called him the god of war. That is a

deum belli esse dixerunt, quod opus est hominum et optabilius non est. Si ergo pacem perpetuam Felicitas daret, Mars quid ageret non haberet. Si autem ipsum bellum est Mars sicut sermo Mercurius, utinam quam manifestum est quod non sit deus tam non sit et bellum quod vel falso vocetur deus.

XV

De stellis quibusdam, quas pagani deorum suorum nominibus nuncuparunt.

Nisi forte illae stellae sunt hi dii quas eorum appellavere nominibus. Nam stellam quandam vocant Mercurium, quandam itidem Martem. Sed ibi est et illa quam vocant Iovem, et tamen eis mundus est Iovis; ibi quam vocant Saturnum, et tamen ei praeterea dant non parvam substantiam, omnium videlicet seminum; ibi est et illa omnium clarissima quae ab eis appellatur Venus, et tamen eandem Venerem esse etiam Lunam volunt; quamvis de illo fulgentissimo sidere apud eos tamquam de malo aureo Iuno Venusque contendant. Luciferum enim quidam Veneris, quidam dicunt esse Iunonis; sed, ut solet, Venus vincit. Nam multo plures eam stellam Veneri tribuunt, ita ut vix eorum quisquam reperiatur qui aliud opinetur.

---

[1] Plato speaks of sun, moon, earth, stars and heaven as being gods of many barbarians, and also known to the early Greeks (*Cratylus* 397 CD). Plato, Aristotle and later philosophers regarded the heavenly bodies as " visible gods," superior in constancy of character to the gods of mythology. Following the Chaldaean pattern, the names of well-known gods were

work of men, and not one of the more desirable. So if
Felicitas were to grant perpetual peace, Mars would
have nothing to do. But if war itself is called Mars,
as speech is called Mercury, it is clear that he is no
god. Would it were equally clear that war too did
not exist, to be even falsely called a god!

XV

*Of certain stars, to which the pagans have given the
names of their gods.*[1]

BUT perhaps these gods are identical with the stars
that they have called by their names. For they call
one star Mercury, and another likewise Mars. But
the star that they call Jupiter is there, too, and yet
for them the universe is Jupiter. The star that they
call Saturn is there, and still they assign him a charge
of no small importance, that is, the charge of all the
seeds. There is also that brightest of all stars which
they call Venus, and yet they would have it that this
same Venus is the moon as well. Juno and Venus,
however, are rivals for that brightest of all heavenly
bodies, as they once were for the golden apple. In
fact, the morning star is claimed for Venus by some
and for Juno by others, but Venus comes off winner,
as usual. For the great majority assign the star to
Venus, so that scarcely anyone can be found who
holds the other view.

given to the planets. In Mithraic chapels of Roman times are
found indications of star worship. See Cumont, *Astrology and
Religion* 36–48, and especially Nilsson in *Harvard Theological
Review* 33, 1–8.

Quis autem non rideat, cum regem omnium Iovem dicant, quod stella eius ab stella Veneris tanta vincitur claritate? Tanto enim esse debuit ceteris illa fulgentior quanto est ipse potentior. Respondent ideo sic videri quia illa quae putatur obscurior superior est atque a terris longe remotior. Si ergo superiorem locum maior dignitas meruit, quare Saturnus ibi est Iove superior? An vanitas fabulae quae regem Iovem facit non potuit usque ad sidera pervenire, et quod non valuit Saturnus in regno suo neque in Capitolio, saltem obtinere est permissus in caelo? Quare autem Ianus non accepit aliquam stellam? Si propterea quia mundus est et omnes in illo sunt, et Iovis mundus est et habet tamen. An iste causam suam composuit ut potuit et pro una stella quam non habet inter sidera tot facies accepit in terra?

Deinde si propter solas stellas Mercurium et Martem partes mundi putant, ut eos deos habere possint, quia utique sermo et bellum non sunt partes mundi, sed actus hominum, cur Arieti et Tauro et Cancro et Scorpioni ceterisque huius modi, quae caelestia signa numerant et stellis non singulis, sed singula pluribus constant superiusque istis in summo caelo perhibent conlocata, ubi constantior motus inerrabilem meatum sideribus praebet, nullas aras,

---

[1] According to the Greek myth Cronos (Saturn) was dethroned by his son Zeus (Jupiter). After Saturn found a home in Italy and was established on the Capitoline hill, he

But who can refrain from laughter when they call
Jupiter the king of all, yet his star is far surpassed in
brightness by the star of Venus? His star should
have been as much more resplendent than the rest as
he himself is more powerful. They reply that it
looks as it does because the star that is rated less
bright is higher and far more distant from the earth.
Then if the greater dignity earned the higher place,
why is Saturn higher in the sky than Jupiter? Or
was the foolish myth that makes Jupiter king unable
to spread as far as the stars? Thus, though Saturn
was unable to retain his rank either in his kingdom
or on the Capitol,[1] he was at least allowed to keep it
in the sky. Moreover, why did Janus not receive
some star? Was it because he is the universe,
including all the stars that are in it? But Jove, too,
is the universe, and still has a star. Or did Janus
make the best bargain he could, and exchange the
one star that he does not have in heaven for the extra
face that he has on earth?

Again, if it is only as stars that Mercury and Mars
are regarded as parts of the universe and so considered gods—for of course speech and war are not
parts of the universe, but activities of men,—why
have they not established any altars or sacred rites or
temples for Aries and Taurus and Cancer and Scorpio
and the rest of their kind? These are counted as
celestial signs, consisting not of one star but of several
stars each. And they say that they are placed in the
highest heaven, higher than the planets, where a
more constant motion gives the stars an invariable

was again displaced to make way for Jupiter's temple (see 7.4,
p. 390 and note 1).

nulla sacra, nulla templa fecerunt, nec deos, non dico inter hos selectos, sed ne inter illos quidem quasi plebeios habuerunt?

XVI

De Apolline et Diana ceterisque selectis diis quos partes mundi esse voluerunt.

APOLLINEM quamvis divinatorem et medicum velint, tamen ut in aliqua parte mundi statuerent, ipsum etiam solem esse dixerunt, Dianamque germanam eius similiter lunam et viarum praesidem (unde et virginem volunt quod via nihil pariat), et ideo ambos sagittas habere quod ipsa duo sidera de caelo radios terras usque pertendant. Vulcanum volunt ignem mundi, Neptunum aquas mundi, Ditem patrem, hoc est Orcum, terrenam et infimam partem mundi. Liberum et Cererem praeponunt seminibus, vel illum masculinis, illam femininis; vel illum liquori, illam vero ariditati seminum. Et hoc utique totum refertur ad mundum, id est ad Iovem, qui propterea dictus est " progenitor genetrixque " quod omnia semina ex se emitteret et in se reciperet. Quando quidem etiam Matrem Magnam eandem Cererem volunt, quam nihil aliud dicunt esse quam terram, eamque perhibent et Iunonem, et ideo ei secundas

---

[1] The identification of Apollo with the sun and Diana (Artemis) with the moon was a Stoic commonplace; see Cicero, *On the Nature of the Gods* 2.68 and Pease's notes. From the time of Ennius, Diana was also known as Trivia, the

course. Why were they not held in esteem as gods,
if not among the select, at least among those of the
common sort?

XVI

*Of Apollo and Diana and the other select gods, whom
they have chosen to regard as parts of the world.*

ALTHOUGH they choose to make Apollo the god of
divination and medicine, still, to give him a place in
some part of the world, they say that he is also the
sun god, and that his sister Diana is likewise the
moon, and the guardian of roads.[1] Hence they will
also have her a virgin, because a road produces nothing. Both of them have arrows because the two
heavenly bodies shoot their rays from heaven as far
as the earth. They would have it that Vulcan is the
fire of the world, Neptune the water of the world, Dis
Pater (that is, Orcus) the earthy and lowest part of
the world. They put Liber and Ceres in charge of
seeds, either putting him in charge of male seeds and
her of female, or him in charge of the moist class and
her of the dry class of seeds. And of course all this is
a subdivision of the whole universe, that is, of Jupiter,
who was called " Father and Mother " because he
emitted all seeds from himself and received them into
himself. Sometimes they also identify Ceres with
the Great Mother, and say that she is nothing else
but the earth, and that she is also Juno, and that is
why they assign the secondary causes of things to

goddess of the crossroads, like the Greek Artemis-Hekate
(Wissowa, *RK*² 251).

causas rerum tribuunt, cum tamen Iovi sit dictum
" progenitor genetrixque deum," quia secundum eos
totus ipse mundus est Iovis. Minervam etiam,
quia eam humanis artibus praeposuerunt nec invenerunt vel stellam ubi eam ponerent, eandem vel
summum aethera vel etiam lunam esse dixerunt.
Vestam quoque ipsam propterea dearum maximam
putaverunt, quod ipsa sit terra, quamvis ignem mundi
leviorem qui pertinet ad usus hominum faciles, non
violentiorem qualis Vulcani est ei deputandum esse
crediderunt.

Ac per hoc omnes istos selectos deos hunc esse
mundum volunt, in quibusdam universum, in quibusdam partes eius; universum sicut Iovem, partes eius,
ut Genium, ut Matrem Magnam, ut Solem et
Lunam, vel potius Apollinem et Dianam. Et
aliquando unum deum res plures, aliquando unam
rem deos plures faciunt. Nam unus deus res plures
sunt, sicut ipse Iuppiter; et mundus enim totus
Iuppiter, et solum caelum Iuppiter, et sola stella
Iuppiter habetur et dicitur; itemque Iuno secun-
darum causarum domina et Iuno aer et Iuno terra et,
si Venerem vinceret, Iuno stella. Similiter Minerva
summus aether et Minerva itidem luna, quam esse

---

[1] While Jupiter is regularly taken to represent the sky, Juno
is sometimes the air, sometimes the earth (see 4.10, p. 37,
above). Here she is made to represent secondary causes,
Jupiter, of course, having the primary causes (see 7.30, p. 487,
below). Such refinement of interpretation is more charac-
teristic of Neoplatonic than of Stoic allegory. Compare
Plotinus, *Ennead* 3.5.8, where Zeus is Nous, the principle of
causation, and Aphrodite (who is the same as Hera, his wife) is
Soul, his companion.

her.[1] However, it is Jupiter to whom the words are
addressed, " Father and Mother of gods," because
in their view the whole universe itself is his. As for
Minerva, since they have put her in charge of the
crafts and have not even found a star to put her on,
they have said that she is either the highest realm of
aether, or even the moon. And they have also supposed Vesta to be the greatest of the goddesses,[2] for
the reason that she is the earth. Yet they have also
thought that the gentler fire of the world, which is
suited to human use, should be assigned to her,
though not the more violent fire, which belongs to
Vulcan.

And so the pagans will have it that all those select
gods are nothing but this universe, some identical
with the whole world and some with portions of it.
The whole world, for instance, is Jupiter, while such
gods as Genius, the Great Mother, Sol and Luna (or
rather, Apollo and Diana) are equated with portions
of it. And sometimes they create of several things
one god, and sometimes they create of one thing
several gods. Several things are one god in the case
of Jupiter himself, for the whole universe is regarded
and is called Jupiter, and so is the sky by itself, and
the planet Jupiter by itself. So also Juno is mistress
of secondary causes and is the air and the earth, and
if she could win over Venus, she would also be a star.
Likewise Minerva is the highest realm of aether and
also the moon, which they think is at the lowest

[2] Or perhaps *dearum maximam* should be translated, " eldest
of the goddesses." Hestia (Vesta) was the first of the children
of Kronos (*Homeric Hymns* 5.22, 32). On Vesta, compare
4.10, p. 40 and note 2.

in aetheris infimo limite existimant. Unam vero
rem deos plures ita faciunt: Et Ianus est mundus et
Iuppiter; sic et Iuno est terra et Mater Magna et
Ceres.

XVII

Quod etiam ipse Varro opiniones suas de diis
pronuntiarit ambiguas.

Et sicut haec, quae exempli gratia commemoravi,
ita cetera non explicant, sed potius inplicant; sicut
impetus errabundae opinionis inpulerit, ita huc atque
illuc, hinc atque illinc insiliunt et resiliunt, ut ipse
Varro de omnibus dubitare quam aliquid adfirmare
maluerit. Nam trium extremorum primum de diis
certis cum absolvisset librum, in altero de diis
incertis dicere ingressus ait: " Cum in hoc libello
dubias de diis opiniones posuero, reprehendi non
debeo. Qui enim putabit iudicari oportere et
posse, cum audierit, faciet ipse. Ego citius perduci
possum ut in primo libro quae dixi in dubitationem
revocem quam in hoc quae perscribam omnia ut ad
aliquam dirigam summam." Ita non solum istum de
diis incertis, sed etiam illum de certis fecit incertum.

In tertio porro isto de diis selectis, postea quam
praelocutus est quod ex naturali theologia prae-

---

[1] This seems to make clear Varro's plan: Book XIV De dis
certis dealt with gods of whose nature Varro was certain, and
Book XV with the rest.

boundary of the aether. But they also make one thing into several gods. For example, the world is both Janus and Jupiter; likewise the earth is both Juno and the Great Mother and Ceres.

XVII

Even Varro himself declared that his views of the gods were uncertain.

THE remaining points that Varro makes are like those that I have cited as examples; they result not in explanations but in complications. As the impulse of their vagrant beliefs drives them, just so, hither and thither, back and forth they bound and rebound, so that Varro himself preferred to be sceptical about everything rather than to affirm anything. For when he had finished the first of the last three books, on the subject of the certain gods, in the next book, when taking up the uncertain gods, he says: " If in this book I set down uncertain views of the gods I should not be reproved. For if anyone thinks that a definite verdict should and can be given, he will produce one for himself after hearing what I say. As for me, I can sooner be brought to withdraw and leave doubtful what I have said in the first book, than to bring everything that I shall write in this book to any onec onclusion."[1] Thus he renders uncertain not only what he says about the uncertain gods, but also what he says about the certain gods.

Then in the third book, which treats of the select gods, after a preliminary discussion of such matters as he thought fit in natural theology, he takes up the

loquendum putavit, ingressurus huius civilis theologiae vanitates et insanias mendaces, ubi eum non solum non ducebat rerum veritas, sed etiam maiorum premebat auctoritas: " De diis," inquit, " populi Romani publicis, quibus aedes dedicaverunt eosque pluribus signis ornatos notaverunt, in hoc libro scribam, sed ut Xenophanes Colophonios scribit, quid putem, non quid contendam, ponam. Hominis est enim haec opinari, dei scire." Rerum igitur non conprehensarum nec firmissime creditarum, sed opinatarum et dubitandarum sermonem trepidus pollicetur dicturus ea quae ab hominibus instituta sunt. Neque enim, sicut sciebat. esse mundum, esse caelum et terram, caelum sideribus fulgidum, terram seminibus fertilem, atque huius modi cetera, sicut hanc totam molem atque naturam vi quadam invisibili ac praepotenti regi atque administrari certa animi stabilitate credebat, ita poterat adfirmare de Iano quod mundus ipse esset, aut de Saturno invenire quo modo et Iovis pater esset et Iovi regnanti subditus factus esset et cetera talia.

XVIII

Quae credibilior causa sit, qua error paganitatis inoleverit.

De quibus credibilior redditur ratio, cum perhibentur homines fuisse et unicuique eorum ab his

---

[1] Xenophanes migrated, perhaps about 545 B.C., from Colophon to Sicily, where he distinguished himself as a poet and critic of Homer, Hesiod and the traditional religion (see Diels, *Vorsokratiker* I, 137, frag. 34; Cicero, *Academica* 2.74).

follies and false ravings of the civil theology. On
this topic he was not only without the guidance of
truth, but was also under the pressure of the weight
of tradition. Thus he writes: " In this book I shall
write about the official gods of the Roman people,
gods to whom they have dedicated temples, gods that
they have honoured and made famous by the number
of their statues. But, as Xenophanes of Colophon
writes, I will set down what I think, but not what I
am prepared to insist on. For in these matters man
has opinions, but only God has knowledge." [1] Thus
it is a discourse about things not understood, nor
firmly believed, but matters of opinion subject to
doubt, that Varro timidly promises us, when he faces
the prospect of describing the institutions set up by
men. There were things that he knew: that there is
a world, that heaven and earth exist, heaven resplendent with stars, earth productive when seeded,
and the rest of this sort. He also believed with sure
conviction that this whole material and natural
world is ruled and controlled by some invisible and
overruling power. But he could make no sure statement that Janus is himself the world. Nor could he
discover how Saturn was both the father of Jupiter
and yet had become a subject of Jupiter who was
king. And so it was for all the rest.

XVIII

On the probable reason why the pagan error took root.

THE most reasonable explanation of these beliefs is
that the gods were once men, and that for each of

qui eos adulando deos esse voluerunt, ex eius ingenio
moribus, actibus casibus sacra et sollemnia constituta
atque haec paulatim per animas hominum daemonibus similes et ludicrarum rerum avidas inrependo
longe lateque vulgata, ornantibus ea mendaciis
poetarum et ad ea fallacibus spiritibus seducentibus.
Facilius enim fieri potuit ut iuvenis impius vel ab
impio patre interfici metuens et avidus regni patrem
pelleret regno quam id quod iste interpretatur, ideo
Saturnum patrem a Iove filio superatum quod ante
est causa quae pertinet ad Iovem quam semen quod
pertinet ad Saturnum. Si enim hoc ita esset, numquam Saturnus prior fuisset nec pater Iovis esset.
Semper enim semen causa praecedit nec umquam
generatur ex semine. Sed cum conantur vanissimas
fabulas sive hominum res gestas velut naturalibus
interpretationibus honorare, etiam homines acutissimi
tantas patiuntur angustias ut eorum quoque vanitatem dolere cogamur.

XIX

De interpretationibus quibus colendi Saturni ratio
concinnatur.

" Saturnum," inquit, " dixerunt quae nata ex eo
essent solitum devorare quod eo semina unde
nascerentur redirent. Et quod illi pro Iove gleba

them sacred rites and festivals suited to his genius, character, actions and destiny were set up by those whose adulation chose to regard them as gods. These rites, gradually infiltrating men's souls—souls like the demons in their craving for theatrical shows— spread far and wide, for the poets adorned them with lying fancies, and deceitful spirits enticed men to accept them. It could easily have happened that a young man without filial piety, or one who was afraid of being killed by a wicked father, should have driven his father from a throne that he craved for himself. This is a more probable account than the explanation Varro offers, namely, that Saturn the father was overcome by Jupiter his son because the first cause that belongs to Jupiter takes precedence over the seed that belongs to Saturn. If this were so, Saturn could never have been first, nor could he be the father of Jupiter. For the cause always precedes the seed, and is never begotten from the seed. But whenever they try to exalt foolish fables or events of men's lives by treating them as allegories of nature, even the cleverest men are caught in such straits that we are forced to lament their foolishness too.

XIX

Of the explanations by which an argument for worshipping Saturn is contrived.

I QUOTE Varro's words: "They have said that Saturn was wont to devour his offspring, because seeds return to the place from which they spring. And the fact that instead of Jupiter he was given a

obiecta est devoranda, significat," inquit, " manibus
humanis obrui coeptas serendo fruges, antequam
utilitas arandi esset inventa." Saturnus ergo dici
debuit ipsa terra, non semina; ipsa enim quodam
modo devorat quae genuerit, cum ex ea nata semina
in eam rursus recipienda redierint. Et quod pro
Iove accepisse dicitur glebam, quid hoc ad id valet
quod manibus hominum semen gleba coopertum est ?
Numquid ideo non est, ut cetera, devoratum quod
gleba coopertum est ? Ita enim hoc dictum est
quasi qui glebam opposuit semen abstulerit, sicut
Saturno perhibent oblata gleba ablatum Iovem, ac
non potius gleba semen operiendo fecerit illud
diligentius devorari. Deinde isto modo semen est
Iuppiter, non seminis causa, quod paulo ante dice-
batur. Sed quid faciant homines qui, cum res stultas
interpretantur, non inveniunt quid sapienter dicatur ?

" Falcem habet," inquit, " propter agriculturam."
Certe illo regnante nondum erat agricultura, et ideo
priora eius tempora perhibentur, sicut idem ipse
fabellas interpretatur, quia primi homines ex his
vivebant seminibus quae terra sponte gignebat. An
falcem sceptro perdito accepit ut qui primis temporibus rex fuerat otiosus filio regnante fieret opera-
rius laboriosus ?

Deinde ideo dicit a quibusdam pueros ei solitos
immolari, sicut a Poenis, et a quibusdam etiam
maiores, sicut a Gallis, quia omnium seminum

---

[1] Augustine elsewhere follows the usual account, that
Saturn was given a stone to swallow in place of Jupiter (7.9,
p. 409; Hesiod, *Theogony* 485). Varro apparently took the
lump of earth (*gleba*) as better suited to his allegory at this
point.

lump of earth [1] to swallow means that before the
advantage of ploughing was discovered, when grains
were first sown, they were buried by human hands."
In this case the name Saturn should have been given
to the earth itself, not to the seeds, for it is the earth
that somehow devours what she has produced, since
the seeds that spring from her return to be received
again into her bosom. And as for his receiving a
lump of earth instead of Jupiter, what does this have
to do with the seed being covered with earth by the
hands of men? Did that prevent it being devoured
like the rest, because it was covered with a lump of
earth? The interpretation implies that the one who
placed the clod took away the seed, as Jupiter in the
tale was stolen from Saturn when the clod was placed
before him. In fact, the clod that conceals the seed
causes it to be devoured the more thoroughly. And
next, by this explanation, Jupiter is the seed, not the
cause of the seed, as they said shortly before. But
what are men to do when they are explaining foolish
things and cannot find any wise thing to say?

" He has a sickle," Varro says, " because of agriculture." Surely when he was king, agriculture did
not yet exist, and to follow once more Varro's interpretation of the fables, his times were regarded as
the earliest for the reason that the first men lived on
such seeds as the earth bore untilled. Or did he get
the sickle after he lost his sceptre, so that he who in
the earliest times had been a king sitting at ease now
in his son's reign became a toiling workman?

Next he says that the reason why certain peoples,
like the Carthaginians, made a practice of sacrificing
children to him, and others, like the Gauls, even

optimum est genus humanum. De hac crudelissima
vanitate quid opus est plura dicere? Hoc potius
advertamus atque teneamus, has interpretationes
non referri ad Deum verum, vivam, incorpoream
incommutabilemque naturam, a quo vita in aeternum
beata poscenda est; sed earum esse fines in rebus
corporalibus, temporalibus, mutabilibus atque mortalibus.

" Quod Caelum," inquit, " patrem Saturnus
castrasse in fabulis dicitur, hoc significat penes
Saturnum, non penes Caelum semen esse divinum."
Hoc propterea, quantum intellegi datur, quia nihil
in caelo de seminibus nascitur. Sed ecce, Saturnus
si Caeli est filius, Iovis est filius. Caelum enim esse
Iovem innumerabiliter et diligenter adfirmant. Ita
ista, quae a veritate non veniunt, plerumque et nullo
inpellente se ipsa subvertunt.

Chronon apellatum dicit quod Graeco vocabulo
significat temporis spatium, sine quo semen, inquit,
non potest esse fecundum. Haec et alia de Saturno
multa dicuntur, et ad semen omnia referuntur. Sed
saltem Saturnus seminibus cum tanta ista potestate
sufficeret; quid ad haec dii alii requiruntur, maxime
Liber et Libera, id est Ceres? De quibus rursus,
quod ad semen adtinet, tanta dicit quasi de Saturno
nihil dixerit.

---

[1] Human sacrifice was practised both in Carthage and in
Gaul until it was forbidden by the Romans. There were
emergencies when it was practised in Rome also in historical
times, but it was regarded as a very un-Roman rite (*minime
Romano sacro*, Livy 22.57.6). The Punic deity honoured by
the sacrifice of children was regularly identified with Kronos,
or Saturn. See Tertullian, *Apology* 9.2; Minucius Felix,

adults,[1] is because the best of all seeds is mankind. What need is there to say more about this cruellest of absurdities? Rather, let us observe and remember this principle, that these explanations have nothing to do with the true God. He is a living, incorporeal, and immutable being, and from him must that life be sought which is happy forever, while their goals are in material, temporal, mutable and mortal things.

Again he says: " The fact that Saturn in the myth castrated his father Caelus, or Heaven, means that the divine seed is in Saturn's keeping, not in that of Caelus." The reason for this is that, so far as can be known, nothing in the sky springs from seed. But lo and behold! If Saturn is the son of Caelus, he is the son of Jupiter. For countless writers are careful to state times without number that Jupiter is Caelus, or the sky. In this way their theories, which do not proceed from truth, generally overthrow each other even when no one attacks them.

Varro says that Saturn was called Chronos, the Greek word for a space of time, without which a seed cannot be fruitful. These statements and many others are made about Saturn, and all refer to seed. With all this power Saturn should at least be enough to care for seed. But why are other gods required for this work, especially Liber and Libera, who is also known as Ceres? But concerning these gods and their relation to seed Varro says all over again quite as much as if he had said nothing at all about Saturn.

30.3; Dionysius of Halicarnassus, *Roman Antiquities* 1.38.2; Wissowa, *RK*² 420; and Rose on " Kronos " in *OCD*. On Varro's treatment of Saturn, see 4.10, p. 38 f.; 6.8, p. 334 f. and notes.

XX

De sacris Cereris Eleusinae.

In Cereris autem sacris praedicantur illa Eleusinia
quae apud Athenienses nobilissima fuerunt. De
quibus iste nihil interpretatur, nisi quod adtinet ad
frumentum, quod Ceres invenit, et ad Proserpinam,
quam rapiente Orco perdidit; et hanc ipsam dicit
significare fecunditatem seminum; quae cum de-
fuisset quodam tempore eademque sterilitate terra
maereret, exortam esse opinionem quod filiam
Cereris, id est ipsam fecunditatem, quae a proser-
pendo Proserpina dicta esset, Orcus abstulerat et
apud inferos detinuerat; quae res cum fuisset luctu
publico celebrata, quia rursus eadem fecunditas
rediit, Proserpina reddita exortam esse laetitiam et
ex hoc sollemnia constituta. Dicit deinde multa in
mysteriis eius tradi, quae nisi ad frugum inventionem
non pertineant.

XXI

De turpitudine sacrorum quae Libero celebrabantur.

Iam vero Liberi sacra, quem liquidis seminibus ac
per hoc non solum liquoribus fructuum, quorum
quodam modo primatum vinum tenet, verum etiam
seminibus animalium praefecerunt, ad quantam

---

[1] On Liber, see 6.9, p. 338, note 1. Wissowa, *RK*[2] 299, finds
in Varro's description a view of the native Italian Liber before
his identification with Dionysus-Bacchus in 493 B.C. Altheim,
on the contrary, argues that all the details of the Italic cult
point to an origin in the rites of Dionysus (*Terra Mater* 20 f.).

XX

On the rites of Ceres at Eleusis.

AMONG the rites of Ceres those performed at Eleusis are especially praised, and were formerly most highly renowned among the Athenians. Varro gives no explanation of these except in relation to grain, which Ceres discovered, and to Proserpina, whom she lost when Orcus carried her off. He says that Proserpina represents the reproductiveness of seed. When at one time this productiveness failed, and Earth was sad with the same sterility, the notion arose that the daughter of Ceres, that is, this fertility which had been named Proserpina (from the verb *proserpere*, " to creep forth "), had been carried off by Orcus and detained in the lower world. This event was commemorated by public mourning. Then because the same fertility came back, there was a joyful celebration for Proserpina's return, and from this the annual rites were instituted. Varro adds that there are many traditions in her mysteries, all related to the discovery of grain.

XXI

On the shameful nature of the rites which are performed for Liber.

I COME now to the rites of Liber,[1] a god whom they have put in charge of moist seeds; this includes not only the juice of fruits, among which wine somehow holds first place, but also the semen of animals. It

turpitudinem pervenerint, piget quidem dicere
propter sermonis longitudinem; sed propter istorum
superbam hebetudinem non piget. Inter cetera
quae praetermittere quoniam multa sunt cogor in
Italiae compitis quaedam dicit sacra Liberi celebrata
cum tanta licentia turpitudinis ut in eius honorem
pudenda virilia colerentur, non saltem aliquantum
verecundiore secreto, sed in propatulo exultante
nequitia. Nam hoc turpe membrum per Liberi dies
festos cum honore magno plostellis inpositum prius
rure in compitis et usque in urbem postea vectabatur.
In oppido autem Lavinio unus Libero totus mensis
tribuebatur, cuius diebus omnes verbis flagitiosissi-
mis uterentur, donec illud membrum per forum
transvectum esset atque in loco suo quiesceret. Cui
membro inhonesto matrem familias honestissimam
palam coronam necesse erat inponere. Sic videlicet
Liber deus placandus fuerat pro eventibus seminum,
sic ab agris fascinatio repellenda ut matrona facere
cogeretur in publico quod nec meretrix, si matronae
spectarent, permitti debuit in theatro.

Propter haec Saturnus solus creditus non est
sufficere posse seminibus, ut occasiones multipli-
candorum deorum inmunda anima reperiret, et ab
uno vero Deo merito inmunditiae destituta ac per
multos falsos aviditate maioris inmunditiae prostituta

is tedious to relate the degree of filth to which these rites sank, for it is a long story; but because the pagans are so arrogant in their stupidity, it is not too tedious. Among other points that I am compelled to pass over because of their number, Varro says that at the crossroads of Italy certain rites of Liber were celebrated with such shameless abandon that phallic symbols were worshipped in his honour. And this was not even done in secret to preserve some modesty, but with an unconcealed parade of lewdness. For this obscene member was set up with great honour on little carts for the days of the festival of Liber, being first displayed at the crossroads in the country and later conveyed even into the city. In the town of Lavinium one whole month was assigned to Liber, and during the days of that month everyone was expected to use the most shameful words, until the member was finally conveyed across the forum and allowed to rest in its own place. Moreover it was required that the most honourable matron of the city should publicly place a crown on this most dishonourable member. We must understand that the god Liber had to be appeased in this way to ensure the success of the crops and to avert evil influences from the fields: a matron had to do in public what not even a courtesan should have been allowed to do in the theatre, if there were matrons in the audience.

Here we find an explanation for the belief that Saturn could not by himself do enough for the seeds. It was to give the impure soul opportunities to multiply the number of gods. Abandoned by the one true God as a punishment for its impurity, and

ista sacrilegia sacra nominaret seseque spurcorum
daemonum turbis conviolandam polluendamque
praeberet.

XXII

De Neptuno et Salacia ac Venilia.

Iam utique habebat Salaciam Neptunus uxorem,
quam inferiorem aquam maris esse dixerunt. Ut
quid illi adiuncta est et Venilia nisi ut sine ulla causa
necessariorum sacrorum sola libidine animae prosti-
tutae multiplicaretur invitatio daemoniorum? Sed
proferatur interpretatio praeclarae theologiae quae
nos ab ista reprehensione reddita ratione compescat.
"Venilia," inquit, "unda est, quae ad litus venit;
Salacia, quae in salum redit." Cur ergo deae fiunt
duae, cum sit una unda quae venit et redit? Nempe
ipsa est exaestuans in multa numina libido vesana.
Quamvis enim aqua non geminetur quae it et redit,
huius tamen occasione vanitatis duobus daemoniis
invitatis amplius commaculatur anima, quae it et
non redit.

Quaeso te, Varro, vel vos, qui tam doctorum hominum talia scripta legistis et aliquid magnum vos
didicisse iactatis, interpretamini hoc, nolo dicere
secundum illam aeternam incommutabilemque naturam, qui solus est Deus, sed saltem secundum animam mundi et partes eius, quos deos esse veros

prostituted to the many false gods by its greed for greater impurity, it called these sacrileges sacred, and offered itself to the throngs of unclean demons to be violated and defiled.

XXII

On Neptune, Salacia and Venilia.

It is well known that Neptune already had a wife, Salacia, whom they explained as being the lower water of the sea. Then for what end was Venilia also joined to him? Without any reason suggested by the prescribed ritual, surely it was only the lust of a prostituted soul that more and more demons might be invited to be its guests. But let us hear the explanation of their renowned theology, giving its due account to set our fault-finding at rest. " Venilia," says Varro, " is the wave that comes (*venit*) to the shore, Salacia the one that goes back out to sea (*in salum*)." But why are there two goddesses, when it is the same water that comes in and goes back? Obviously we have here boiling up the same frenzied lust for many gods. For though the water that comes in and goes back does not become two waters, still when two demons are invited in on this foolish pretext, more spots infect the soul; and that goes and does not return.

I beg you, Varro, or you pagans who have read such writings of such learned men and boast that you have gained some great knowledge, interpret this mystery. I will not ask you to reconcile it with that eternal and unchangeable Being who alone is God, but at least reconcile it with the world soul and its

existimatis. Partem animae mundi, quae mare permeat, deum vobis fecisse Neptunum utcumque tolerabilioris erroris est. Itane unda ad litus veniens et in salum rediens duae sunt partes mundi aut duae partes animae mundi? Quis vestrum ita desipiat ut hoc sapiat? Cur ergo vobis duas deas fecerunt, nisi quia provisum est a sapientibus maioribus vestris, non ut dii plures vos regerent, sed ut ea quae istis vanitatibus et falsitatibus gaudent plura vos daemonia possiderent? Cur autem illa Salacia per hanc interpretationem inferiorem maris partem, qua viro erat subdita, perdidit? Namque illam modo, cum refluentem fluctum esse perhibetis, in superficie posuistis. An quia Veniliam pelicem accepit, irata suum maritum de supernis maris exclusit?

XXIII

De Terra, quam Varro deam esse confirmat eo quod ille animus mundi, quem opinatur deum, etiam hanc corporis sui infimam partem permeet eique vim divinam inpertiat.

Nempe una est terra, quam plenam quidem videmus animalibus suis, verum tamen ipsam magnum corpus in elementis mundique infimam partem. Cur eam volunt deam? An quia fecunda est? Cur ergo non

parts, which you think are true gods. When you
take the god Neptune as the part of the world soul
that permeates the sea, we can at least have some
patience with your mistake. Will you say in the
same way that the wave that comes to the shore and
goes back out to the open sea is two parts of the
world, or two parts of the world soul? Which of you
is so unreasonable as to think this reasonable?
Then why have they made two goddesses for you?
Did your wise ancestors make provision, not for more
gods to rule you, but for more demons to possess you,
demons that rejoice in these absurdities and false-
hoods? And according to the explanation, why was
it that Salacia lost the lowest part of the sea, where
she was placed under her husband? For now, when
you say that she is the receding wave, you have put
her on the surface. Does that mean that she is
angry with her husband for taking Venilia as a
mistress, and has excluded him from the upper waters
of the sea?

XXIII

*Of the earth, which Varro declares is a goddess, since the
world soul, which he takes as a god, permeates even
this lowest part of his own body and imparts
to it a divine force.*

No doubt there is a single earth, the one we see
full of its own living creatures, yet it is at the same
time a great mass of matter among the world's
elements, and is the lowest part of the universe.
Why do they choose to make it a goddess? Is it
because the earth is fruitful? Then why are not

magis homines dii sunt, qui eam fecundiorem faciunt
excolendo; sed cum arant, non cum adorant? Sed
pars animae mundi, inquiunt, quae per illam permeat,
deam facit. Quasi non evidentior sit in hominibus
anima, quae utrum sit nulla fit quaestio; et tamen
homines dii non habentur et, quod est graviter dolendum, his qui dii non sunt et quibus ipsi meliores sunt
colendis et adorandis mirabili et miserabili errore
subduntur. Et certe idem Varro in eodem de diis
selectis libro tres esse adfirmat animae gradus in
omni universaque natura: unum, quod omnes partes
corporis quae vivunt transit et non habet sensum,
sed tantum ad vivendum valetudinem; hanc vim in
nostro corpore permanare dicit in ossa, ungues,
capillos; sicut in mundo arbores sine sensu aluntur
et crescunt et modo quodam suo vivunt: secundum
gradum animae, in quo sensus est; hanc vim pervenire in oculos, aures, nares, os, tactum: tertium
gradum esse animae summum, quod vocatur animus,
in quo intellegentia praeminet; hoc praeter hominem
omnes carere mortales. Hanc partem animae
mundi dicit Deum, in nobis autem genium vocari.
Esse autem in mundo lapides ac terram, quam
videmus, quo non permanat sensus, ut ossa, ut
ungues Dei; solem vero, lunam, stellas, quae sentimus quibusque ipse sentit, sensus esse eius; aethera
porro animum eius; cuius vim, quae pervenit in astra,

---

[1] On the three grades of soul, compare 7.29, p. 483, below.
See also Cicero, *On the Nature of the Gods* 2.33 f. with Pease's
note, where parallels from Aristotle and the Stoics are cited.

human beings rather divine, who render the earth more fruitful by cultivation—that is, by ploughing the earth, not worshipping her? But they say that it is the part of the world soul that permeates the earth that makes her a goddess. As if soul were not more conspicuous in man, where its existence is unquestioned! Yet men are not regarded as gods. And what is most deplorable, by a strange and pitiable error they are subjected to beings who are not gods, beings worse than themselves who demand worship and adoration.

To be sure, the same Varro in the same book about the select gods states that there are three grades of soul in the whole of nature:[1] first, that which is found in every part of a living body, having no sensation, but only enough power to enable life to go on. This force in our bodies spreads to the bones, nails and hair. Elsewhere in the world the trees are similarly without sensation, but they are nourished and grow and live in a certain way proper to them. The second grade of soul is that which has sensation, a power that extends to the eyes, ears, nose, mouth and sense of touch. The third grade is the highest grade of soul, and is called mind. There intelligence is dominant, a trait lacking in all mortal creatures except men. This part of the world soul is called God, according to Varro, while in us it is called *genius*. Moreover, in the world the stones and the earth that we see, to which there comes no flow of sensation, are like bones and nails of God. But the sun, moon and stars that we perceive, and by which he perceives, are his senses. The aether, in turn, is his mind. Its force extending to the stars makes them

ea quoque facere deos, et per ea quod in terram permanat, deam Tellurem; quod autem inde permanat in mare atque oceanum, deum esse Neptunum.

Redeat ergo ab hac quam theologian naturalem putat, quo velut requiescendi causa ab his ambagibus atque anfractibus fatigatus egressus est; redeat, inquam, redeat ad civilem; hic eum adhuc teneo, tantisper de hac ago. Nondum dico, si terra et lapides nostris sunt ossibus et unguibus similes, similiter eos intellegentiam non habere, sicut sensu carent; aut si idcirco habere dicuntur ossa et ungues nostri intellegentiam quia in homine sunt qui habet intellegentiam, tam stultum esse qui hos in mundo deos dicit quam stultus est qui in nobis ossa et ungues homines dicit. Sed haec cum philosophis fortassis agenda sunt; nunc autem istum adhuc politicum volo. Fieri enim potest ut, licet in illam naturalis theologiae veluti libertatem caput erigere paululum voluisse videatur, adhuc tamen hunc librum versans et se in illo versari cogitans, eum etiam inde respexerit et hoc propterea dixerit ne maiores eius sive aliae civitates Tellurem atque Neptunum inaniter coluisse credantur.

Sed hoc dico: pars animi mundani, quae per terram permeat, sicut una est terra, cur non etiam unam fecit deam, quam dicit esse Tellurem? Quod si ita fecit, ubi erit Orcus, frater Iovis atque Neptuni,

also gods. What flows through them and reaches the earth makes the goddess Tellus, while any that flows farther, into the sea and ocean, makes the god Neptune.

Let Varro return now from this kind of theology, which is called natural in his system. He retired to it for a holiday when he was weary with the circumlocutions and perplexities of his argument. Now, I say, let him return to business, to the city and its theology. Here I must detain him and discuss this point for a moment. I might argue that if earth and stones are like our bones and nails, they must resemble them in having no intelligence, just as they have no sensation. Or if our bones and nails are said to have intelligence because they are in a man who has intelligence, then the man who says that these parts of the world are gods is as foolish as one who says that in us the bones and nails are men. But perhaps these points should be discussed with philosophers of nature—for the moment I want to argue with him as a Roman citizen. Although it seems that he wished to lift his head for a moment, as it were, into the freedom of the natural theology, it may be that while still occupied with this book and reflecting on that occupation, he looked down from his vantage point and made this statement to prevent anyone supposing that his ancestors, or other city-states, had been merely silly when they worshipped Tellus and Neptune.

Here is the point I would make: if there is a part of the world soul that permeates the earth, and there is only one earth, why not also have a single goddess, the one that he calls Tellus? In that case, where will Orcus be, the brother of Jupiter and Neptune,

quem Ditem patrem vocant? Ubi eius coniux
Proserpina, quae secundum aliam in eisdem libris
positam opinionem non terrae fecunditas, sed pars
inferior perhibetur? Quod si dicunt animi mundani
partem, cum permeat terrae partem superiorem,
Ditem patrem facere deum; cum vero inferiorem,
Proserpinam deam, Tellus illa quid erit? Ita enim
totum quod ipsa erat in duas istas partes deosque
divisum est ut ipsa tertia quae sit aut ubi sit invenire
non possit; nisi quis dicat simul istos deos Orcum
atque Proserpinam unam deam esse Tellurem et non
esse iam tres, sed aut unam aut duos; et tamen tres
dicuntur, tres habentur, tres coluntur aris suis, de-
lubris suis, sacris, simulacris, sacerdotibus suis, et per
haec etiam fallacibus prostitutam animam constu-
prantibus daemonibus suis.

Adhuc respondeatur quam partem terrae permeet
pars mundani animi ut deum faciat Tellumonem?
Non, inquit, sed una eademque terra habet geminam
vim, et masculinam, quod semina producat, et
femininam, quod recipiat atque nutriat; inde a vi
feminae dictam esse Tellurem, a masculi Tellumonem.
Cur ergo pontifices, ut ipse indicat, additis quoque
aliis duobus quattuor diis faciunt rem divinam,
Telluri, Tellumoni, Altori, Rusori? De Tellure et

---

[1] For Varro, Tellus was " Mother Earth," from which all
life springs and to which it returns (compare Lucretius, 5.259).
It has been argued (St. Weinstock, in *RE* 5A.1, 791–806) that
Tellumo and her male counterpart Tellumo were primitive
Roman deities of vegetation, whose connection with Mother
Earth was late and due to Greek influence. In any event, her
connection with Ceres goes back to very early times, and
Greek conceptions of both must have prevailed from the time

whom they call Dis Pater? Where will his wife
Proserpina be? According to another view stated
in the same work of Varro's she is held to be, not the
fertility of the earth, but its lowest part. And if they
say that a part of the world soul, in permeating the
upper part of the earth, constitutes the god Dis
Pater, and in permeating the lower part constitutes
the goddess Proserpina, then what will Tellus be?
For the whole of which she consisted was divided
into two parts and into two gods in such a way that
no one can find out any third part, Tellus, or any place
for her. That is, unless someone says that the two
deities Orcus and Proserpina, taken together, constitute the one goddess Tellus. Then there are no
longer three, but either one or two. But still they
have three names; they are regarded as three and
worshipped as three, with their own altars, shrines,
rituals, images and priesthoods, and hence their own
deceiving demons to debauch the prostituted soul.

Again let them answer: What part of the earth is
permeated by a part of the world soul to make the
god Tellumo? None, Varro says, but one and the
same earth has a double faculty, the male power to
produce seeds and the female power to receive and
nourish them. Hence from the female power she
is called Tellus and from the male Tellumo. Then
why did the pontiffs, as Varro relates, add two more,
and offer sacrifice to four gods: Tellus, Tellumo,
Altor and Rusor?[1] Enough has already been said

when Ceres was equated with Demeter (493 B.C.). Altor and
Rusor appear to be pontifical inventions; as against Varro,
Weinstock takes the original meanings to be " Feeder " and
" Ploughman." Compare Rose on " Tellus " in *OCD*.

Tellumone iam dictum est. Altori quare? Quod
ex terra, inquit, aluntur omnia quae nata sunt.
Rusori quare? Quod rursus, inquit, cuncta eodem
revolvuntur.

XXIV

*De Telluris cognominibus eorumque significationibus,
quae etiamsi erant multarum rerum indices, non
debuerunt multorum deorum firmare opiniones.*

DEBUIT ergo una terra propter istam quater-
geminam vim quattuor habere cognomina, non
quattuor facere deos; sicut tot cognominibus unus
Iuppiter et tot cognominibus una Iuno, in quibus
omnibus vis multiplex esse dicitur ad unum deum vel
unam deam pertinens, non multitudo cognominum
deorum etiam multitudinem faciens. Sed profecto
sicut aliquando etiam ipsas vilissimas feminas earum,
quas libidine quaesierunt, taedet paenitetque tur-
barum, sic animam vilem factam et inmundis
spiritibus prostitutam deos sibi multiplicare, quibus
contaminanda prosterneretur, sicut plurimum libuit,
sic aliquando et piguit. Nam et ipse Varro quasi de
ipsa turba verecundatus unam deam vult esse
Tellurem.

"Eandem," inquit, "dicunt Matrem Magnam;
quod tympanum habeat, significari esse orbem
terrae; quod turres in capite, oppida; quod sedens
fingatur, circa eam cum omnia moveantur, ipsam non

about Tellus and Tellumo. But why sacrifice to
Altor? Because it is from the earth, he says, that
things born are nourished (*aluntur*). And why to
Rusor? Because all things, he says, return again
(*rursus*) to the same place.

XXIV

*The names of the earth-goddess and their meaning;
though they designated many things, they should not
have been used to support the notion of many gods.*

WELL, this fourfold power might have justified four
titles for a single earth, but it could not justify the
creation of four gods. The one Jupiter and the one
Juno each have many titles, or epithets, in all of
which the manifold powers belonging to a single
god or goddess are said to be expressed; yet the
plurality of epithets does not create an equal number
of gods. But just as the basest women sometimes
grow weary and repentant of the throngs of lovers
that they have gained by lust, so the soul that is
debased and prostituted to unclean spirits, though
generally glad to multiply gods for itself before
whom it may fall in vile prostration, yet at times it
has grown weary of them. For even Varro, as if he
were ashamed of the crowd of deities, decided in
favour of a single earth-goddess, Tellus.

" The same goddess," he says, " is called the Great
Mother. The timbrel which she carries means that
she is the circle of earth, the towers on her head
stand for fortified towns, and she is represented as
seated because, while all things move about her, she

459

moveri. Quod Gallos huic deae ut servirent fecerunt, significat qui semine indigeant terram sequi oportere; in ea quippe omnia reperiri. Quod se apud eam iactant, praecipitur, inquit, qui terram colunt ne sedeant; semper enim esse quod agant. Cymbalorum sonitus ferramentorum iactandorum ac manuum motum [1] et eius rei crepitum in colendo agro qui fit significant; ideo aere, quod eam antiqui colebant aere, antequam ferrum esset inventum. Leonem, inquit, adiungunt solutum ac mansuetum, ut ostendant nullum genus esse terrae tam remotum ac vehementer ferum quod non subigi colique conveniat."

Deinde adiungit et dicit Tellurem matrem et nominibus pluribus et cognominibus quod nominarunt, deos existimatos esse complures. "Tellurem," inquit, "putant esse Opem, quod opere fiat melior; Matrem, quod plurima pariat; Magnam, quod cibum pariat; Proserpinam, quod ex ea proserpant fruges; Vestam, quod vestiatur herbis. Sic alias deas," inquit, "non absurde ad hanc revocant." Si ergo una dea est, quae quidem consulta veritate nec ipsa est, interim quid itur in multas? Unius sint ista multa numina, non tam deae multae quam nomina. Sed errantium maiorum auctoritas deprimit et eundem Varronem post hanc sententiam trepidare

----

[1] motum *is not found in the MSS.*

----

[1] *Numina* (" divine powers ") is the reading of two Munich manuscripts of the tenth century, adopted by Dombart and Kalb. All others have *nomina* (" names "), which seems to give equally good sense, and should perhaps be preferred as having the best manuscript support.

herself is unmoved. They have created emasculate Galli to serve this goddess, meaning that those who lack seed should follow after the earth, for in her all things are found. They leap about before her, teaching those who till the earth not to sit idle, says he, for there is always something for them to do. The sound of the cymbals signifies the movement of iron tools in men's hands and the clatter produced by all the work done in agriculture. The cymbals are of bronze because the ancients tilled the earth with bronze before the use of iron was invented. She is accompanied by a lion, which is unleashed and tame, to show that there is no kind of land so remote or so exceedingly wild that it is not suitable for subduing and cultivating."

Then Varro adds that because they have given many names and epithets to mother earth, men have thought that there were many earth deities. I quote again: "They think that the earth (*tellus*) is Ops because she is made better by work (*opus*); Mater, or mother, because she brings forth many things; Magna, or great, because she gives birth to food; Proserpina, because the crops creep forth (*proserpant*) from her; Vesta, because she is clothed (*vestiatur*) with grass. And there are other goddesses also who are not unreasonably held to hark back to her." Then if the earth is a single goddess (if truth were considered it would not be even that), why do men in the meantime run after many? Let those many divine powers [1] belong to one goddess, and not to as many goddesses as there are names. But the authority of ancestors, mistaken as they were, puts pressure on Varro and compels him to waver after writing the

compellit. Adiungit enim et dicit: " Cum quibus opinio maiorum de his deabus, quod plures eas putarunt esse, non pugnat." Quo modo non pugnat, cum valde aliud sit unam deam nomina habere multa, aliud esse deas multas? " Sed potest," inquit, " fieri ut eadem res et una sit et in ea quaedam res sint plures." Concedo in uno homine esse res plures, numquid ideo et homines plures? Sic in una dea esse res plures, numquid ideo et deas plures? Verum sicut volunt, dividant conflent, multiplicent replicent inplicent.

Haec sunt Telluris et Matris Magnae praeclara mysteria, unde omnia referuntur ad mortalia semina et exercendam agriculturam. Itane ad haec relata et hunc finem habentia tympanum, turres, Galli, iactatio insana membrorum, crepitus cymbalorum, confictio leonum vitam cuiquam pollicentur aeternam? Itane propterea Galli abscisi huic Magnae deae serviunt ut significent qui semine indigeant terram sequi oportere; quasi non eos ipsa potius servitus semine faciat indigere? Utrum enim sequendo hanc deam, cum indigeant, semen adquirunt, an potius sequendo hanc deam, cum habeant, semen amittunt? Hoc interpretari est an detestari? Nec adtenditur quantum maligni daemones praevaluerint, qui nec aliqua magna his sacris polliceri ausi sunt, et tam crudelia exigere potuerunt.

statement quoted above. For he adds the following words: "With these views the opinion of our ancestors about the plurality of these goddesses is not in conflict." How can it not be in conflict? Surely it is a very different thing for one goddess to have many names, and for many goddesses to exist. "It is possible," Varro says, "for the same thing to be one, and to have many things contained in it." I grant that there are many things in one man, but are there for this reason many men? Granting that there are many things in one goddess, are there for this reason many goddesses? But let them go on as they like, let them divide or combine, multiply or simplify, and complicate the list of gods.

These are the famous mysteries of Tellus and the Great Mother, in which everything relates to perishable seeds and the work of agriculture. Then is it possible that the features which belong to this cult and have that function—the timbrel, the towers, the Galli, the wild tossing of the limbs, the banging of the cymbals, and the lions depicted—give anyone the promise of eternal life? They say that the mutilated Galli serve this great goddess to indicate that those who lack seed should follow after the earth—as if it were not rather their own slavery that caused them to be without seed! For do they by following the goddess acquire seed when they lack it, or do they rather by following her lose the seed that they have? Is this an explanation or a denunciation of the rites? Nor do people observe how far malignant demons have got the upper hand, in that they have been able to exact such cruel service without promising any great reward to be gained by the rites.

Si dea terra non esset, manus ei homines operando
inferrent ut semina consequerentur per illam, non et
sibi saeviendo ut semina perderent propter illam; si
dea non esset, ita fecunda fieret manibus alienis ut
non cogeret hominem sterilem fieri manibus suis.
Iam quod in Liberi sacris honesta matrona pudenda
virilia coronabat spectante multitudine, ubi rubens et
sudans, si est ulla frons in hominibus, adstabat
forsitan et maritus, et quod in celebratione nuptiarum
super Priapi scapum nova nupta sedere iubebatur,
longe contemptibiliora atque leviora sunt prae ista
turpitudine crudelissima vel crudelitate turpissima,
ubi daemonicis ritibus sic uterque sexus inluditur ut
neuter suo vulnere perimatur.   Ibi fascinatio timetur
agrorum, hic membrorum amputatio non timetur.
Ibi sic dehonestatur novae nuptae verecundia ut non
solum fecunditas, sed nec virginitas adimatur; hic ita
amputatur virilitas ut nec convertatur in feminam
nec vir relinquatur.

XXV

Quam interpretationem de abscisione Attidis
Graecorum sapientium doctrina reppererit.

Et Attis ille non est commemŏratus nec eius ab
isto interpretatio requisita est, in cuius dilectionis

---

[1] See 6.9 p. 344 f., above, with note.

If the earth were not a goddess, men would lay hands on her in toil to obtain seeds by means of her. They would not with mad violence also lay hands on themselves in order to lose their seed for her sake. If the earth were not a goddess, she would become fruitful by the hands of others, without compelling a man to become sterile by his own hands. Scandalous it is that in the rites of Liber an honorable matron used to place a crown on the phallic symbol while the crowd looked on, and perhaps her husband also was standing there, red and covered with sweat, if there is any shame in mankind. Scandalous, too, that in the celebration of a wedding the new bride was asked to sit on the rod of Priapus.[1] But such practices are far more trivial and more easily disregarded, when compared with this most cruel obscenity, or obscene cruelty. In them both sexes were mocked by rites truly devilish, although neither sex was destroyed by its wound. In them men feared evil influence on their fields; in this they do not fear the amputation of their members. In that the modesty of a bride is deflowered, but not so as to rob her of fecundity, or even of virginity; in this a man's virility is cut away, so that neither is he changed into a woman, nor does he remain a man.

XXV

The explanation of the mutilation of Attis that has been discovered by the learning of Greek philosophers.

It is in memory of the love of Attis that the Galli mutilate themselves. Yet though Attis is well

memoriam Gallus absciditur. Sed docti Graeci
atque sapientes nequaquam rationem tam sanctam
praeclaramque tacuerunt. Propter vernalem quippe
faciem terrae, quae ceteris est temporibus pulchrior,
Porphyrius, philosophus nobilis, Attin flores significare perhibuit, et ideo abscisum quia flos decidit ante
fructum. Non ergo ipsum hominem vel quasi
hominem, qui est vocatus Attis, sed virilia eius flori
comparaverunt. Ipsa quippe illo vivente deciderunt;
immo vero non deciderunt neque decerpta, sed plane
discerpta sunt; nec illo flore amisso quisquam postea
fructus, sed potius sterilitas consecuta est. Quid
ergo ipse reliquus, et quidquid remansit absciso?
Quid eo significari dicitur? Quo refertur? Quae
interpretatio inde profertur? An haec frustra
moliendo nihilque inveniendo persuadent illud potius
esse credendum quod de homine castrato fama
iactavit litterisque mandatum est? Merito hinc
aversatus est Varro noster, neque hoc dicere voluit;
non enim hominem doctissimum latuit.

XXVI

De turpitudine sacrorum Matris Magnae.

ITEMQUE de mollibus eidem Matri Magnae contra
omnem virorum mulierumque verecundiam con-

---

[1] Porphyry was a disciple of Plotinus who edited his master's
works about A.D. 300, and was himself a versatile writer on
philosophical and religious subjects. In spite of his sharp
attack on the Christian faith and defence of the pagan cults,
Augustine respected him as a philosopher, and frequently cites
him in the later books of the *City of God*. This fragment is
preserved also in Eusebius, *Preparation for the Gospel* 3.11.12.

known, Varro does not mention him, nor seek out any interpretation of his myth. But learned Greeks and philosophers have not failed to speak of so holy and glorious a matter. Because the aspect of the earth in spring is more beautiful than in the other seasons, Porphyrius, the famous philosopher, declared that Attis symbolized the flowers, and was mutilated because the flower falls before the fruit.[1] Then it is not the man, or what passes for a man named Attis, that was compared with a flower, but rather his virile parts. These fell to earth, of course, while he went on living. Or rather, they did not fall, nor were they picked off, but were obviously ripped off. And when that flower was lost, there was no fruit afterwards, but rather sterility followed. What then is the meaning of the remnant of the man, whatever was left of him after his mutilation? What is supposed to be symbolized by this? To what does it refer? What interpretation is offered for it? Or did they make a vain attempt and, finding no answer, simply persuade men that it was better to believe what rumour reported and books recorded about the castrated man? Varro had good reason to turn his back on the story and to refuse to speak of it. For a man of his learning was surely not ignorant of it.

XXVI

On the shamefulness of the rites of the Great Mother.

VARRO was likewise unwilling to speak of the effeminate persons consecrated to the same Great

Augustine here shows his acquaintance with Neoplatonic allegorical explanation, as well as the Stoic kind used by Varro.

secratis, qui usque in hesternum diem madidis capillis
facie dealbata, fluentibus membris incessu femineo
per plateas vicosque Carthaginis etiam a propolis
unde turpiter viverent exigebant, nihil Varro dicere
voluit nec uspiam me legisse commemini. Defecit
interpretatio, erubuit ratio, conticuit oratio. Vicit
Matris Magnae omnes deos filios non numinis
magnitudo, sed criminis. Huic monstro nec Iani
monstrositas comparatur. Ille in simulacris habebat
solam deformitatem, ista in sacris deformem crudeli-
tatem; ille membra in lapidibus addita, haec in
hominibus perdita.

Hoc dedecus tot Iovis ipsius et tanta stupra non
vincunt. Ille inter femineas corruptelas uno Gany-
mede caelum infamavit; ista tot mollibus professis et
publicis et inquinavit terram et caelo fecit iniuriam.
Saturnum fortasse possemus huic in isto genere
turpissimae crudelitatis sive conferre sive praeferre,
qui patrem castrasse perhibetur; sed in Saturni sacris
homines alienis manibus potius occidi quam suis
abscidi potuerunt. Devoravit ille filios, ut poetae
ferunt, et physici ex hoc interpretantur quod volunt;
ut autem historia prodit, necavit; sed quod ei Poeni

Mother in defiance of all male or female modesty.
Even till yesterday you could still see them, with oily
hair and whitened faces and soft limbs, passing with
feminine gait through the squares and streets of
Carthage, demanding even from hucksters the means
to continue their shameful life. Varro chose to say
nothing of these people, nor do I recall reading
about them elsewhere. Interpretation failed, reason
blushed and eloquence fell silent. It was not the
greatness of the deity, but the greatness of her
crimes, in which the Great Mother outstripped all
the gods, her children. Not even the monstrosity of
Janus is to be compared with this monster. Janus
had his only deformity in his image, but she had a
deformity in her cruel rites. Janus had extra
features added in stone, while she had men with
missing organs.

This infamy is not surpassed by all the guilty
amours of Jupiter himself, great as they were.
Though he seduced so many women, it was by Gany-
mede alone that he brought ill fame to heaven. She
by her thousands of male effeminates, who make
public profession of themselves, has defiled the earth
and done a wrong to heaven. Perhaps we might
compare Saturn with her in this utterly obscene kind
of cruelty, or even put him ahead of her, for it is
said that he mutilated his father. But in the rites
of Saturn men, though they had to be slain by the
hands of others, did not have to castrate themselves
with their own hands. Saturn devoured his children,
as the poets tell the story; and the physical philosophers make of the story what they will. As history
relates it, he killed them, yet the Carthaginian

suos filios sacrificati sunt, non recepere Romani. At vero ista Magna deorum Mater etiam Romanis templis castratos intulit atque istam saevitiam moremque servavit, credita vires adiuvare Romanorum exsecando virilia virorum.

Quid sunt ad hoc malum furta Mercurii, Veneris lascivia, stupra ac turpitudines ceterorum, quae proferremus de libris nisi cotidie cantarentur et saltarentur in theatris? Sed haec quid sunt ad tantum malum, cuius magnitudo Magnae Matri tantummodo competebat? Praesertim quod illa dicuntur a poetis esse conficta, quasi poetae id etiam finxerint quod ea sint diis grata et accepta. Ut ergo canerentur vel scriberentur, sit audacia vel petulantia poetarum; ut vero divinis rebus et honoribus eisdem imperantibus et extorquentibus numinibus adderentur, quid est nisi crimen deorum, immo vero confessio daemoniorum et deceptio miserorum? Verum illud, quod de abscisorum consecratione Mater deum coli meruit, non poetae confinxerunt, sed horrere magis quam canere maluerunt.

Hisne diis selectis quisquam consecrandus est ut post mortem vivat beate, quibus consecratus ante mortem honeste non potest vivere, tam foedis super-

practice of sacrificing their children to him was not adopted by the Romans. Yet this Great Mother of the gods has brought her eunuchs even into the Roman temples, and has preserved that savage custom, since it is believed that she adds to the power (*vires*) of the Romans by cutting off the virile powers of her men (*virorum*).

In comparison with this evil, what are the thefts of Mercury, the wanton escapades of Venus, the debaucheries and base deeds of the others? We could produce such stories from books, if they were not daily portrayed by song and dance in the theatre. But what are these to compare with so great an evil, whose enormity was matched only by the greatness of the Great Mother? Especially since those deeds are said to be the inventions of poets, as if poets had also invented the fact that they are pleasing and acceptable to the gods. Suppose it is due to the poets and their shameless boldness that these songs were sung or written; still when they were added to the divine institutions and divine honours at the demand and insistence of the same deities, what is this, if not crime on the part of the gods? Or rather, it is a confession on the part of the demons and a deception of wretched men. But as for the cult of the Mother of the gods, and the right she won to be worshipped by eunuch priests, this the poets did not invent. They shrank from it in horror rather than sing about it.

Can anyone then be consecrated to serve these select gods in order to live a happy life after death? He cannot live honourably before his death if he is consecrated to them, for he will be subject to foul

stitionibus subditus et inmundis daemonibus obli-
gatus? Sed haec omnia, inquit, referuntur ad
mundum. Videat ne potius ad inmundum. Quid
autem non potest referri ad mundum, quod esse
demonstratur in mundo? Nos autem animum
quaerimus qui vera religione confisus non tamquam
deum suum adoret mundum, sed tamquam opus Dei
propter Deum laudet mundum, et mundanis sordibus
expiatus mundus perveniat ad Deum qui condidit
mundum.

XXVII

De figmentis physiologorum, qui nec veram
divinitatem colunt, nec eo cultu quo colenda
est vera divinitas.

Istos vero deos selectos videmus quidem clarius
innotuisse quam ceteros, non tamen ut eorum
inlustrarentur merita, sed ne occultarentur opprobria;
unde magis eos homines fuisse credibile est, sicut non
solum poeticae litterae, verum etiam historicae
tradiderunt. Nam quod Vergilius ait:

Primus ab aetherio venit Saturnus Olympo,
Arma Iovis fugiens et regnis exul ademptis,

et quae ad hanc rem pertinentia consequuntur, totam
de hoc Euhemerus pandit historiam, quam Ennius in

---

[1] Virgil, *Aeneid* 8.319 f. The story of Saturn in Latium is
often mentioned by both Roman and late Greek writers.
How much of it was derived from Euhemerus, or from Ennius'

superstitions and in bondage to unclean demons. But, we are told, all this is related to the universe. To a universal uncleanness, I fear. What is shown to be in the universe that is not related to the universe? But we seek a mind that will rely on true religion and not worship the universe as its god, but will praise the universe for God's sake, as a work of God. Then, cleansed from the uncleanness of this world, the soul will find its way, all clean (*mundus*), to God who created the world (*mundus*).

XXVII

On the fanciful explanations of philosophers who do not worship the true God, nor practise the cult by which the true God should be worshipped.

WE see, then, that these select gods became better known than the rest, not, however, in order to glorify any merits of theirs, but rather in order not to conceal their shameful deeds. Hence it is all the more credible that they were once men. This tradition is preserved not only in poetry but also in history. For Virgil writes:

Saturn was first to descend from the heavenly heights of Olympus,
Fleeing the bolts of Jove, an exile robbed of his kingdom.[1]

Virgil goes on with the story, a story related in full by Euhemerus and translated into Latin by Ennius.

translation of his work is uncertain. See Jacoby in *RE* VI, 956.

Latinum vertit eloquium; unde quia plurima posuerunt qui contra huius modi errores ante nos vel
Graeco sermone vel Latino scripserunt, non in eo
mihi placuit inmorari.

Ipsas physiologias cum considero quibus docti et
acuti homines has res humanas conantur vertere in
res divinas, nihil video nisi ad temporalia terrenaque
opera naturamque corpoream vel etiamsi invisibilem,
tamen mutabilem potuisse revocari; quod nullo
modo est verus Deus. Hos autem si saltem religiosi-
tati congruis significationibus ageretur, esset quidem
dolendum non his verum Deum adnuntiari atque
praedicari, tamen aliquo modo ferendum tam foeda
et turpia non fieri nec iuberi; at nunc cum pro
Deo vero, quo solo anima se inhabitante fit felix,
nefas sit colere aut corpus aut animam, quanto magis
nefarium est ista sic colere ut nec salutem nec decus
humanum corpus aut anima colentis obtineat!
Quam ob rem si templo sacerdote sacrificio quod vero
Deo debetur colatur aliquod elementum mundi vel
creatus aliquis spiritus, etiamsi non inmundus et
malus, non ideo malum est quia illa mala sunt quibus
colitur, sed quia illa talia sunt, quibus solus ille
colendus sit cui talis cultus servitusque debetur.

Si autem stoliditate vel monstrositate simulacrorum, sacrificiis homicidiorum, coronatione virilium pu-
dendorum, mercede stuprorum, sectione membrorum,

But since a great deal has been set down on this subject by those who have written before us, either in Greek or in Latin, against errors of this sort, I have decided not to dwell on the topic.

When I consider the natural explanations by which learned and ingenious men try to turn these human things into divine, I find nothing except what can be referred to temporal and earthly affairs, and to corporeal beings, invisible perhaps, but still mutable, whereas the true God is immutable. Now if this symbolism were set forth in a way suited to the religious mind, it would indeed be regrettable that the true God is not thereby announced and proclaimed; but we might somehow endure it, if only such foul and shameful deeds were not done or commanded. But as it is, since it is a crime to worship either a body or a soul in place of the true God, by whose indwelling alone the soul is made happy, how much more criminal it is to worship them in such a manner that neither the body nor the soul of the worshipper gains either salvation or honour among men! Hence if some element of the world, or some created spirit, though it be no unclean or evil spirit, is worshipped with temple, priest and sacrifice such as is due to the true God, the worship is an evil not because those means of worship are evil, but because they are such as should be used only in worshipping him to whom such worship and service is due.

But if anyone contends that he is worshipping the one true God, that is, the creator of soul and body, when he employs for worship lifeless or monstrous images, human sacrifices, the crowning of phallic symbols, prostitution for a fee, the slashing of limbs, amputation

abscisione genitalium, consecratione mollium, festis inpurorum obscenorumque ludorum unum verum Deum, id est omnis animae corporisque creatorem, colere se quisque contendat, non ideo peccat quia non est colendus quem colit, sed quia colendum non ut colendus est colit. Qui vero et rebus talibus, id est turpibus et scelestis, et non Deum verum, id est animae corporisque factorem, sed creaturam quamvis non vitiosam colit, sive illa sit anima sive corpus sive anima simul et corpus, bis peccat in Deum, quod et pro ipso colit quod non est ipse, et talibus rebus colit qualibus nec ipse colendus est nec non ipse.

Sed hi quonam modo, id est quam turpiter nefarieque, coluerint, in promptu est; quid autem vel quos coluerint esset obscurum, nisi eorum testaretur historia ea ipsa quae foeda et turpia confitentur numinibus terribiliter exigentibus reddita; unde remotis constat ambagibus nefarios daemones atque inmundissimos spiritus hac omni civili theologia invisendis stolidis imaginibus et per eas possidendis etiam stultis cordibus invitatos.

XXVIII

*Quod doctrina Varronis de theologia in nulla sibi
parte concordet.*

QUID igitur valet quod vir doctissimus et acutissimus Varro velut subtili disputatione hos omnes deos in caelum et terram redigere ac referre conatur?

of genitals, consecration of effeminate men, and the celebration of impure and obscene shows—if this is his contention, his sin is not in worshipping the wrong God, but in worshipping the God who deserves worship in the wrong way. But if a man chooses such means of worship as are foul and criminal, not to worship the true God but to worship some creature, even if it is not a bad creature, he sins twice against God, first, because he worships something that is not God, whether it be soul or body or a union of soul and body; and second, he uses means of worship that are wrong whether for the worship of God himself or of any other.

As for the manner of the pagan worship, it is clear how foul and abominable it is. As for the object or the persons that they worship, this might be obscure if their history did not bear witness that the very rites which are admittedly foul and base were instituted because the deities demanded them with threats. Hence all doubt is removed, and it is clear that it is evil demons and unclean spirits who have been invited in all this civil theology to visit the lifeless statues, and through them also to take possession of the foolish hearts of men.

XXVIII

That Varro's teaching about theology is nowhere self-consistent.

WHAT is the result, then, when Varro with all his learning and acumen undertakes by a supposedly fine-drawn argument to reduce and refer all these

Non potest; fluunt de manibus, resiliunt, labuntur et decidunt.   Dicturus enim de feminis, hoc est deabus: " Quoniam," inquit, " ut primo libro dixi de locis, duo sunt principia deorum animadversa de caelo et terra, a quo dii partim dicuntur caelestes, partim terrestres, ut in superioribus initium fecimus a caelo, cum diximus de Iano, quem alii caelum, alii dixerunt esse mundum, sic de feminis scribendi facimus initium a Tellure."

Sentio quantam molestiam tale ac tantum patiatur ingenium.   Ducitur enim quadam ratione verisimili, caelum esse quod faciat, terram quae patiatur, et ideo illi masculinam vim tribuit, huic femininam, et non adtendit eum potius esse qui haec facit, qui utrumque fecit.   Hinc etiam Samothracum nobilia mysteria in superiore libro sic interpretatur eaque se quae nec suis nota sunt scribendo expositurum eisque missurum quasi religiosissime pollicetur.   Dicit enim

---

[1] That is, Book IV of his *Antiquitates Rerum Divinarum*. See 6.3, p. 299, above.

[2] The mysteries of Samothrace, an island in the north-eastern Aegean, gained a fame in Roman times second only to those of Eleusis.   The gods there worshipped were known as Cabiri, or, more vaguely, " the great gods " (*magni di*), and were commonly identified with the Penates that Aeneas brought from Troy to Italy; these, in turn, are explained by Varro as being none other than the great gods of the Capitoline temple.   As Macrobius and Servius report his words, Jupiter is the middle aether, Juno the air and earth below and Minerva the highest part of the aether, corresponding to the reasoning faculties of the soul.   These, we are told, were established on the Capitol by Tarquin, who had been initiated into the Samothracian mysteries (the texts are collected and discussed by Wissowa, *Gesammelte Abhandlungen*, 95–128, esp. pp. 101, 117).   For the Stoics (*SVF* II, 305; III, 217)

gods to sky and earth? He cannot do it; these
creatures spill from his hands, they leap away, they
slip and fall. When about to speak of females,
that is, the goddesses, he says: "As I have said
in the first book about places,[1] there is a double
origin of the gods, the sky and the earth. Hence
some gods are called celestial and some terrestrial.
In the previous book we began with the sky, speaking
of Janus, whom some identify with the sky, others
with the universe. So now as we begin to write
about the female deities, we start with Tellus, the
earth."

I realize how much perplexity a man so great and
so talented must have suffered. For a certain plausi-
bility leads him to think that the sky is that which
acts, while the earth is passive. Hence he ascribes a
male power to the former and a female to the latter,
without noticing that both powers belong to him who
made them both. Hence also in the preceding book
Varro similarly explains the famous mysteries of
Samothrace,[2] and promises most solemnly that he
will expound in writing matters unknown even to the
Samothracians,[3] and send them his exposition. For
he says that in Samothrace he gathered many proofs

Minerva was the ruling part, or intelligence, of the aether.
In this fragment, however, Varro seems, rather surprisingly, to
abandon his usual Stoic allegory to bring in Platonic "Ideas."

[3] Instead of *suis* ("to their own people," that is, "to the
Samothracians") Wissowa (*op. cit.* 117) proposed the emendation *Sais* ("to the Sai"). The emendation is approved by
Kern, *RE* 10.2, 1447. It depends in turn on Lobeck's emendation of the expanded Servius on *Aeneid* 2.324, where the Sai
are described as high priests (*antistites*) of the Samothracian
gods.

se ibi multis indiciis collegisse in simulacris aliud
significare caelum, aliud terram, aliud exempla
rerum, quas Plato appellat ideas; caelum Iovem,
terram Iunonem, ideas Minervam vult intellegi;
caelum a quo fiat aliquid, terram de qua fiat, exem-
plum secundum quod fiat. Qua in re omitto dicere,
quod Plato illas ideas tantam vim habere dicit ut
secundum eas non caelum aliquid fecerit, sed etiam
caelum factum sit.

Hoc dico, istum in hoc libro selectorum deorum
rationem illam trium deorum, quibus quasi cuncta
complexus est, perdidisse. Caelo enim tribuit
masculos deos, feminas terrae; inter quas posuit
Minervam, quam supra ipsum caelum ante posuerat.
Deinde masculus deus Neptunus in mari est, quod
ad terram potius quam ad caelum pertinet. Dis
pater postremo, qui Graece Πλούτων dicitur, etiam
ipse masculus frater amborum terrenus deus esse
perhibetur, superiorem terram tenens, in inferiore
habens Proserpinam coniugem. Quo modo ergo
deos ad caelum, deas ad terram referre conantur?
Quid solidum quid constans, quid sobrium quid
definitum habet haec disputatio?

Illa est autem Tellus initium dearum, Mater scilicet
Magna, apud quam mollium et abscisorum seseque
secantium atque iactantium insana perstrepit turpitudo. Quid est ergo quod dicitur caput deorum
Ianus, caput dearum Tellus? Nec ibi facit unum

that one of their statues signified the sky, another the earth and another the patterns of things which Plato calls ideas. He identifies the sky with Jupiter, the earth with Juno and the ideas with Minerva— the sky by which a thing is made, the earth of which it is made, and the pattern according to which it is made. I pass over the fact that Plato says that his ideas have a power so great that even the heavens were made after their pattern; it was not the sky that made anything patterned on the ideas.

But I will point out that in this book on select gods Varro has quite forgotten the system of three gods in whom, so to speak, he includes all things. For he assigned the male gods to the sky and the female to the earth, placing Minerva between them, though formerly he had put her above the sky itself. Then the male deity Neptune is in the sea, which belongs to the earth rather than to the sky. Finally Dis Pater, called Pluto by the Greeks, is a male deity and brother of the other two, yet is considered an earth god, holding the upper earth and having a wife Proserpina in the lower earth. Then how is it that they attempt to put the male gods in the sky and the goddesses in the earth? What is there in this whole discussion that is solid, firm, sensible or clear-cut?

So this Tellus is the source of all the goddesses, the Great Mother, that is, before whom the throng raise their mad and shameful cries, the throng of effeminate and mutilated and of those who slash themselves and toss their limbs about. Why then is Janus called the head of the gods and Tellus the head of the goddesses? Error makes him more than one head, and

caput error, nec hic sanum furor. Cur haec frustra referre nituntur ad mundum? Quod etsi possent, pro Deo vero mundum nemo pius colit; et tamen eos nec hoc posse veritas aperta convincit. Referant haec potius ad homines mortuos et ad daemones pessimos, et nulla quaestio remanebit.

XXIX

Quod omnia quae physiologi ad mundum partesque ipsius rettulerunt ad unum verum Deum referre debuerint.

NAMQUE omnia quae ab eis ex istorum deorum theologia velut physicis rationibus referuntur ad mundum, quam sine ullo scrupulo sacrilegae opinionis Deo potius vero, qui fecit mundum, omnis animae et omnis corporis conditori, tribuantur, advertamus hoc modo: Nos Deum colimus, non caelum et terram, quibus duabus partibus mundus hic constat; nec animam vel animas per viventia quaecumque diffusas, sed Deum, qui fecit caelum et terram et omnia quae in eis sunt; qui fecit omnem animam, sive quocumque modo viventem et sensus ac rationis expertem, sive etiam sentientem, sive etiam intellegentem.

frenzy robs her of her sanity. Why do they strive in vain to make all this refer to the universe? Even if they could, no religious man worships the universe in place of the true God. But in any case the obvious truth proves that they cannot do it. Let them attribute all this rather to dead men and to wicked demons, and every difficulty will disappear.

XXIX

That all the powers that the philosophers have ascribed to the universe and its parts should be ascribed to the one true God.

LET us consider everything that they ascribe to the world by physical explanations in accord with the theology that deals with their gods, and notice how much easier it would be, without any fear of sacrilegious belief, to ascribe it all to the true God who made the world, the Creator of every soul and body. We worship God, not heaven and earth, the two parts of which the universe consists. Nor do we worship the soul or souls that are diffused through all living things, but God who made heaven and earth and all things that are in them, who made every soul, no matter what the measure of life that it has, whether it lacks both sensation and reason, or possesses only sensation, or also has intelligence.

XXX

*Qua pietate discernatur a creaturis Creator, ne pro
uno tot dii colantur quot sunt opera unius auctoris.*

Et ut iam incipiam illa unius et veri Dei opera
percurrere, propter quae isti sibi, dum quasi honeste
conantur sacramenta turpissima et scelestissima
interpretari, deos multos falsosque fecerunt, illum
Deum colimus, qui naturis a se creatis et subsistendi
et movendi initia finesque constituit; qui rerum
causas habet, novit atque disponit; qui vim seminum
condidit; qui rationalem animam, quod dicitur
animus, quibus voluit viventibus indidit; qui sermonis
facultatem usumque donavit; qui munus futura
dicendi quibus placuit spiritibus inpertivit et per
quos placet ipse futura praedicit et per quos placet
malas vlaetudines pellit; qui bellorum quoque
ipsorum, cum sic emendandum et castigandum est
genus humanum, exordiis progressibus finibusque
moderatur; qui mundi huius ignem vehementissi-
mum et violentissimum pro inmensae naturae
temperamento et creavit et regit; qui universarum
aquarum creator et gubernator est.

Qui solem fecit corporalium clarissimum luminum
eique vim congruam et motum dedit; qui ipsis
etiam inferis dominationem suam potestatemque non
subtrahit; qui semina et alimenta mortalium, sive
arida sive liquida, naturis competentibus adtributa

XXX

With what piety the Creator is distinguished from his
creatures, lest instead of one God as many gods be
worshipped as there are works of the one Creator.

AND now I shall begin to enumerate those works of
the one true God on which they have based the
invention of many false gods, trying to interpret
their shameful and wicked rites as if they were
honourable. We worship the God who assigned to
all beings that he created the beginning and the ending of their existence and motion. He holds in his
hands the causes of all things; he knows them and
disposes them. He gives seeds their germinal
power. He placed the rational soul which is called
mind in such living beings as he wished, and bestowed
the faculty and use of speech. He imparted the gift
of foretelling the future to such spirits as he thought
fit, and he himself foretells the future through those
whom he thinks fit, and drives out sickness through
those whom he thinks fit. He also regulates the
beginning, the progress and the end even of wars,
when mankind must thus be corrected and chastised.
He first created and now he rules the vehemence
and violence of the universal fire, to preserve the due
balance of the boundless natural world; he is also
creator and director of all waters.

He made the sun to be the brightest of all corporeal
lights, and gave it suitable power and movement. He
has not withdrawn his overlordship and power even
from the souls below. He has supplied seeds and foods
for mortals, both dry and moist, assigning each to its

485

substituit; qui terram fundat atque fecundat; qui
fructus eius animalibus hominibusque largitur; qui
causas non solum principales, sed etiam subsequentes
novit atque ordinat; qui lunae statuit modum suum;
qui vias caelestes atque terrestres locorum muta-
tionibus praebet; qui humanis ingeniis, quae
creavit, etiam scientias artium variarum ad adin-
vandam vitam naturamque concessit; qui coniunc-
tionem maris et feminae ad adiutorium propagandae
prolis instituit; qui hominum coetibus, quem focis et
luminibus adhiberent, ad facillimos usus munus
terreni ignis indulsit.

Ista sunt certe quae diis selectis per nescio quas
physicas interpretationes vir acutissimus atque
doctissimus Varro, sive quae aliunde accepit, sive
quae ipse coniecit, distribuere laboravit. Haec
autem facit atque agit unus verus Deus, sed sicut
Deus, id est ubique totus, nullis inclusus locis, nullis
vinculis alligatus, in nullas partes sectilis, ex nulla
parte mutabilis, implens caelum et terram praesente
potentia, non indigente natura. Sic itaque administrat omnia, quae creavit, ut etiam ipsa proprios
exserere et agere motus sinat. Quamvis enim nihil
esse possint sine ipso, non sunt quod ipse. Agit
autem multa etiam per angelos; sed non nisi ex se
ipso beatificat angelos. Ita quamvis propter aliquas
causas hominibus angelos mittat, non tamen ex

natural producer. He gives the earth its foundation and its fecundity; he bestows its products on animals and men. He knows and ordains not only primary causes, but also secondary. He established the course of the moon; he provides paths in the sky and on earth for all movements in space. To the human intelligence that he created he granted also the knowledge of the various arts which minister to life and advance nature. He instituted the union of male and female to contribute to the propagation of offspring. He granted the gift of earthly fire, to be employed in the homes of men as a ready source of warmth and light.

These are precisely the functions which Varro, the supremely keen-witted and learned, has endeavoured to distribute among the select gods by some physical explanation or other, whether he borrowed explanations from another source or made up his own conjectures. But all these things are made and done by the one true God, acting, however, as God. That is, he is everywhere wholly present, not enclosed in any place nor bound by any chains, not divisible into parts or changeable in any part. He fills heaven and earth with a power that is present everywhere and with a nature that is deficient in nothing. And so he manages everything that he created in such a way as to allow each creature to initiate and carry through its own movements. For although they can do nothing without him, they are not what he is. He does many things also through angels, but he makes angels happy only through himself. And so though he sends angels to men for some reasons, yet he does not make men happy through the presence of angels,

angelis homines, sed ex se ipso, sicut angelos, beatificat. Ab hoc uno et vero Deo vitam speramus aeternam.

XXXI

Quibus proprie beneficiis Dei excepta generali largitate sectatores veritatis utantur.

HABEMUS enim ab illo praeter huiusce modi beneficia, quae ex hac de qua nonnulla diximus administratione naturae bonis malisque largitur, magnum et bonorum proprium magnae dilectionis indicium. Quamquam enim quod sumus, quod vivimus, quod caelum terramque conspicimus, quod habemus mentem atque rationem qua eum ipsum qui haec omnia condidit inquiramus, nequaquam valeamus actioni sufficere gratiarum, tamen quod nos oneratos obrutosque peccatis et a contemplatione suae lucis aversos ac tenebrarum, id est iniquitatis, dilectione caecatos non omnino deseruit misitque nobis Verbum suum, qui est eius unicus filius, quo pro nobis adsumpta carne nato atque passo, quanti Deus hominem penderet nosceremus atque illo sacrificio singulari a peccatis omnibus mundaremur eiusque spiritu in cordibus nostris dilectione diffusa omnibus difficultatibus superatis in aeternam requiem et contemplationis eius ineffabilem dulcedinem veniremus, quae corda, quot linguae ad agendas ei gratias satis esse contenderint?

but through himself, as when he makes angels happy. It is from this one true God that we hope for life eternal.

XXXI

What special benefits, besides the bounties conferred on all, the seekers of truth enjoy.

BESIDES the benefits of this sort which God bestows on both good and evil in accordance with his regulation of nature, of which we have said a few words, we have a great proof of his great love for us, and one that is reserved for the good. To be sure, we can never sufficiently thank him for the fact that we exist, that we live, that we behold the heaven and the earth, that we have a mind and power to reason, by which we seek out him who made all this. But more than that, when we were laden and overwhelmed by sins, turning away from the contemplation of his light and blinded by the love of darkness, that is, of iniquity, he then did not utterly desert us, but sent us his Word, who is his only Son, in order that when he had been born in the flesh, which he put on for us, and had suffered, we might discover how highly God valued man, and might be cleansed from all our sins by that unique sacrifice, and with his love shed abroad in our hearts by his Spirit and all our difficulties now overcome, might enter into eternal rest and the unspeakable sweetness of contemplating him. What hearts, what tongues could claim to be equal to the task of returning thanks to him for this?

XXXII

*Quod sacramentum redemptionis Christi nullis retro
temporibus defuerit semperque sit diversis
significationibus praedicatum.*

Hoc mysterium vitae aeternae iam inde ab exordio
generis humani per quaedam signa et sacramenta
temporibus congrua, quibus oportuit, per angelos
praedicatum est. Deinde populus Hebraeus in
unam quandam rem publicam quae hoc sacramentum
ageret congregatus est, ubi per quosdam scientes,
per quosdam nescientes id quod ex adventu Christi
usque nunc et deinceps agitur praenuntiaretur esse
venturum; sparsa etiam postea eadem gente per
gentes propter testimonium scripturarum, quibus
aeterna salus in Christo futura praedicta est. Omnes
enim non solum prophetiae quae in verbis sunt, nec
tantum praecepta vitae quae mores pietatemque
conformant atque illis litteris continentur, verum
etiam sacra, sacerdotia, tabernaculum sive templum,
altaria, sacrificia, ceremoniae, dies festi et quidquid
aliud ad eam servitutem pertinet quae Deo debetur
et Graece proprie λατρεία dicitur—ea significata et
praenuntiata sunt, quae propter aeternam vitam
fidelium in Christo et impleta credimus et impleri
cernimus et implenda confidimus.

XXXII

*That the mystery of Christ's redemption was never
lacking in past times, but was always declared
by various signs.*

THIS mystery of eternal life was announced from
the very beginning of the human race, through certain signs and symbols suited to the times, to those
who were to know it, through the ministry of angels.
Then the Hebrew people were gathered into a single
commonwealth to carry on the mystery. To them it
was foretold, sometimes by men who spoke with
knowledge, sometimes by men in ignorance, that
events would come to pass as they have from the
coming of Christ up till now, and as they are still
going on. The same Hebrew people have since been
scattered among the nations to spread the witness of
their Scriptures, which foretold the eternal salvation
that was to come in Christ. For not only all the
prophecies which are stated in words, not only the
precepts for living which go to form morality and
religion and are found in those writings, but also the
worship, the priestly offices, the tabernacle or temple,
the altars, sacrifices, ceremonies, feast days and
whatever else belongs to the service due to God that
is properly called *latreia* in Greek, are prophecies.
They all symbolized and foretold a series of events
leading up to eternal life for the faithful in Christ.
These prophecies we either believe to have been
fulfilled, or we see them in process of fulfilment, or
we confidently look to see them fulfilled.

XXXIII

*Quod per solam Christianam religionem manifestari
potuerit fallacia spirituum malignorum de
hominum errore gaudentium.*

PER hanc ergo religionem unam et veram potuit
aperiri deos gentium esse inmundissimos daemones,
sub defunctarum occasionibus animarum vel creatura-
rum specie mundanarum deos se putari cupientes et
quasi divinis honoribus eisdemque scelestis ac
turpibus rebus superba inpuritate laetantes atque ad
verum Deum conversionem humanis animis invi-
dentes. Ex quorum inmanissimo et impiissimo
dominatu homo liberatur cum credit in eum qui
praebuit ad exsurgendum tantae humilitatis exem-
plum quanta illi superbia ceciderunt.

Hinc sunt non solum illi de quibus multa iam
diximus, et alii atque alii similes ceterarum gentium
atque terrarum, sed etiam hi de quibus nunc agimus,
tamquam in senatum deorum selecti; sed plane
selecti nobilitate criminum, non dignitate virtutum.
Quorum sacra Varro dum quasi ad naturales rationes
referre conatur, quaerens honestare res turpes, quo
modo his quadret et consonet non potest invenire,
quoniam non sunt ipsae illorum sacrorum causae
quas putat vel potius vult putari. Nam si non
solum ipsae, verum etiam quaelibet aliae huius
generis essent, quamvis nihil ad Deum verum
vitamque aeternam, quae in religione quaerenda est,

XXXIII

*That only by the Christian religion could the lies of
the evil spirits who rejoice in human error be exposed.*

It is by this religion, therefore, the only true
religion, that the gods of the heathen could be
exposed as unclean demons. Under the guise of the
spirits of the dead, or taking the form of mundane
creatures, they wish to pass for gods. Proud of their
uncleanness they take pleasure in supposedly divine
honours which are really crimes and shameful deeds,
and they envy the souls of men who are converted
to the true God. From their most barbarous and
unholy rule man is freed when he believes on him
who, to raise man up, offered an example of humility
as great as the pride by which the demons fell.

Among their number are found not only those gods
of whom we have already written at length, and other
Roman gods, and other similar gods of other nations
and lands, but also those which we are discussing now,
selected, as it were, to form a senate of the gods, but
obviously selected for their notoriety in crime and
not for their worth of character. When Varro tries
to relate the rites of these gods to his so-called
natural explanations, seeking to make shameful
things seem decent, he is unable to find any way to
square and harmonize the two. For the real reasons
for those rites are not what he thinks, or rather,
wishes others to think. For if either these or any
other explanations of the same kind were true,
although they had nothing to do with the true God
or with that eternal life which should be sought in

pertinerent, tamen qualicumque de rerum natura
reddita ratione aliquantulum mitigarent offensionem,
quam non intellecta in sacris aliqua velut turpitudo
aut absurditas fecerat; sicut in quibusdam theatrorum fabulis vel delubrorum mysteriis facere conatus
est, ubi non theatra delubrorum similitudine absolvit,
sed theatrorum potius similitudine delubra damnavit;
tamen utcumque conatus est ut sensum horribilibus
rebus offensum velut naturalium causarum reddita
ratio deleniret.

XXXIV

*De libris Numae Pompilii, quos senatus, ne sacrorum
causae, quales in eis habebantur, innotescerent,
iussit incendi.*

SED contra invenimus, sicut ipse vir doctissimus
prodidit, de Numae Pompilii libris redditas sacrorum
causas nullo modo potuisse tolerari nec dignas habitas
quae non solum lectae innotescerent religiosis, sed
saltem scriptae reconderentur in tenebris. Iam
enim dicam quod in tertio huius operis libro me suo

---

[1] See 3.9, vol. I, 291. In 181 B.C., according to Livy 40.29,
two stone chests were found at the foot of the Janiculum, with
inscriptions marking one as the coffin of Numa, the other as
containing his books. The first was empty, but the second
contained two bundles of books (which appeared to be quite
new, *recentissima specie*), seven in Latin on pontifical law,
seven in Greek on philosophy, recognized as Pythagorean.
Other accounts with variations in detail are found in Pliny,
Natural History 13.84–8 and Plutarch, *Numa* 22. Such "dis-
coveries" were common in antiquity, and their genuineness
was seldom questioned. This was evidently a Pythagorean

religion, still, by offering any sort of explanation derived from nature they might have mitigated to some slight degree the offence caused by any shameful or absurd features of the rites whose meaning was not understood. Such was Varro's purpose in attempting to explain certain fables of the theatre or mysteries performed in the temples. In this Varro did not justify the theatre by showing its similarity to the temples, but rather condemned the temples because they were like the theatres. Still he tried as best he could to give an explanation of natural causes that would soothe the sensibilities offended by the horrors of the pagan cult.

XXXIV

On the books of Numa Pompilius, which the Senate ordered to be burned, lest the explanations that they contained of the sacred rites should become common knowledge.

BUT on the other hand we learn from the report of the same scholar that the explanations of the sacred rites given in the books of Numa Pompilius were rejected as intolerable. They were judged unworthy, not only of being read and known by religious people, but even of being preserved in writing in some dark place. I shall now quote what I promised in the third book of this work [1] to quote at the proper

attempt to make Numa a sponsor for their doctrines, and perhaps even to reform the Roman cult according to those doctrines. Compare K. Latte, *Römische Religionsgeschichte*, 269 and the work of A. Delatte there cited.

loco dicturum esse promiseram. Nam sicut apud eundem Varronem legitur in libro de cultu deorum, " Terentius quidam cum haberet ad Ianiculum fundum et bubulcus eius iuxta sepulcrum Numae Pompilii traiciens aratrum eruisset ex terra libros eius, ubi sacrorum institutorum scriptae erant causae, in Urbem pertulit ad praetorem. At ille cum inspexisset principia, rem tantam detulit ad senatum. Ubi cum primores quasdam causas legissent, cur quidque in sacris fuerit institutum, Numae mortuo senatus adsensus est, eosque libros tamquam religiosi patres conscripti, praetor ut combureret, censuerunt."

Credat quisque quod putat; immo vero dicat, quod dicendum suggesserit vesana contentio, quilibet tantae impietatis defensor egregius. Me admonere sufficiat sacrorum causas a rege Pompilio Romanorum sacrorum institutore conscriptas nec populo nec senatui nec saltem ipsis sacerdotibus innotescere debuisse ipsumque Numam Pompilium curiositate inlicita ad ea daemonum pervenisse secreta, quae ipse quidem scriberet ut haberet unde legendo commoneretur; sed ea tamen, cum rex esset, qui minime quemquam metueret, nec docere aliquem nec delendo vel quoquo modo consumendo perdere auderet. Ita quod scire neminem voluit ne homines nefaria doceret, violare autem timuit ne daemones

place. These words of Varro are found in his book, *On the Worship of the Gods*: " A certain Terentius had a field on the Janiculum, and his ox-driver was ploughing near the tomb of Numa Pompilius. The plough turned up from the ground the books of the king in which were written down the explanations of reasons for his religious institutions. Terentius took them to the praetor in the city, who examined the first part, and submitted so important a matter to the Senate. But when the leading senators had read some of the reasons given why each item of the cult had been established, the Senate voted their agreement with Numa now dead, and so, as Conscript Fathers with due respect for religion, ordered the praetor to burn these same books."

Let each man believe what he likes; nay more, let any distinguished defender of such impiety speak up and say whatever his perverse love of controversy may suggest. I think it enough to point out that the treatise on the causes of the rites, written down by king Pompilius, the founder of the rites, was not fit to become known to the people, the Senate or even the priests themselves. Numa Pompilius himself, enticed by an unlawful curiosity, had penetrated these secrets of the demons and had himself written them down in order to have a means to refresh his memory. But though he was a king, the last person who had anyone to fear, he still did not dare to teach these things to anyone, nor yet to dispose of them by destroying the books or by using them up in any way. It was a thing he did not choose to let anyone know, for fear of teaching men abominable secrets; but he was afraid to tamper with it, lest he should thereby

iratos haberet, obruit ubi tutum putavit, sepulcro suo
propinquare aratrum posse non credens. Senatus
autem cum religiones formidaret damnare maiorum
et ideo Numae adsentiri cogeretur, illos tamen libros
tam perniciosos esse iudicavit ut nec obrui rursus
iuberet, ne humana curiositas multo vehementius
rem iam proditam quaereret, sed flammis aboleri
nefanda monumenta ut, quia iam necesse esse
existimabant sacra illa facere, tolerabilius erraretur
causis eorum ignoratis quam cognitis civitas tur-
baretur.

XXXV

De hydromantia, per quam Numa visis quibusdam daemonum imaginibus ludificabatur

NAM et ipse Numa, ad quem nullus Dei propheta,
nullus sanctus angelus mittebatur, hydromantian
facere compulsus est ut in aqua videret imagines
deorum vel potius ludificationes daemonum a quibus
audiret quid in sacris constituere atque observare
deberet. Quod genus divinationis idem Varro a
Persis dicit allatum, quo et ipsum Numam et postea
Pythagoram philosophum usum fuisse commemorat;

---

[1] Although magic, divination and necromancy were
practised by the Greeks before the time of Homer, the Persian
lore in this field is said to have been introduced by Ostanes,
one of the Magi who accompanied Xerxes on his invasion of
Greece in 480 B.C. Pythagoras is supposed (presumably before
that date) to have learned magic from the Magi; it is not clear
how Numa, who lived still earlier, learned anything from the

anger the demons. So he buried it where he thought it safe, thinking that no plough could come near his tomb. As for the Senate, though they feared to condemn the religion of their forefathers, and so felt compelled to approve of Numa, still they judged those books so pernicious that they would not even order them to be buried again, lest men's curiosity should be much more eager to search for a thing once brought to light. Instead, they ordered the cursed documents to be destroyed by fire. Thus, since they thought it now a necessity to maintain those rites, they considered it the lesser evil that men should continue their error without knowing the causes, rather than by learning the causes bring turmoil in the state.

XXXV

Of hydromancy, by which Numa was deluded when he saw certain demonic images.

For even Numa himself, to whom no prophet of God and no holy angel was sent, was forced to practise hydromancy, whereby he saw in the water the forms of gods, or rather, the mocking illusions of demons, from whom he heard what rites he should establish and observe. Varro says that this kind of divination was introduced from the Persians, and records its use by Numa himself and later by Pythagoras.[1] He says that when blood was employed, the shades of the

Persians. The lore of Ostanes was published by Hellenistic writers and so reached Varro, Pliny and Tertullian (see F. Cumont, *Les Mages Hellénisés* I, 168–207, esp. p. 184, and fragments, *ibid*. II, 267, 287).

ubi adhibito sanguine etiam inferos perhibet sciscitari
et νεκυομαντείαν Graece dicit vocari, quae sive
hydromantia sive necromantia dicatur, id ipsum est,
ubi videntur mortui divinare. Quibus haec artibus
fiant, ipsi viderint. Nolo enim dicere has artes etiam
ante nostri Salvatoris adventum in ipsis civitatibus
gentium legibus solere prohiberi et poena severissima
vindicari. Nolo, inquam, hoc dicere; fortassis enim
talia tunc licebant. His tamen artibus didicit sacra
illa Pompilius, quorum sacrorum facta prodidit,
causas obruit (ita timuit et ipse quod didicit),
quarum causarum proditos libros senatus incendit.

Quid mihi ergo Varro illorum sacrorum alias nescio
quas causas velut physicas interpretatur, quales si
libri illi habuissent, non utique arsissent, aut et istos
Varronis ad Caesarem pontificem scriptos atque
editos patres conscripti similiter incendissent?
Quod ergo aquam egesserit, id est exportaverit,
Numa Pompilius, unde hydromantian faceret, ideo
nympham Egeriam coniugem dicitur habuisse, quem
ad modum in supradicto libro Varronis exponitur.
Ita enim solent res gestae aspersione mendaciorum
in fabulas verti. In illa igitur hydromantia curio-
sissimus rex ille Romanus et sacra didicit, quae in
libris suis pontifices haberent, et eorum causas,

---

¹ Egeria was originally the spirit of a spring in the grove of
Diana at Aricia. In Rome her name was attached to the
spring of the Camenae near the Porta Capena, where the
Vestals drew water for ritual purposes; hence her name was
explained from the Vestals' "carrying out" the water (Egeria
from *egerere*). The Camenae were regarded as water nymphs,
or Muses, like those known to the Greeks, and so Egeria was
able to inspire and direct Numa in his dealings with the gods,

dead were also summoned, a practice called *nekyo-mantia* in Greek. But whether called hydromancy or necromancy, it is the same thing, where the dead appear to prophesy. As for the arts by which this is accomplished, I leave that to the pagans, for I will not affirm that these arts were forbidden by law in heathen cities even before the coming of our Saviour, and punished by severe penalties. This, I say, I will not affirm, for perhaps such things were then lawful. However, it was by these arts that Pompilius learned those sacred rites whose action he revealed, while at the same time he buried the explanations, such was even his fear of what he had learned. And when the books containing these causes were produced, the Senate burned them.

Then why does Varro offer other explanations of some sort for those rites, explanations supposedly based on nature? If Numa's books had explanations of that sort, they would surely not have been burned, or else the conscript fathers would likewise have burned Varro's books as well, even after they were dedicated to Caesar, the Pontifex Maximus, and published. Well, it was because Numa Pompilius drew, that is, carried out the water to perform hydromancy, that he is said to have had the nymph Egeria as a wife—an explanation given in the book of Varro previously cited.[1] Thus it is that real events are turned into fables by sprinkling them with lies. Hence it was by hydromancy that the Roman king, filled with curiosity, learned the rites, which the pontiffs were to preserve in their books, along with

and he in turn became a kind of " medicine man," or magician (see Ovid, *Fasti* 3.275–348, with Frazer's notes).

quas praeter se neminem scire voluit. Itaque eas
seorsum scriptas secum quodam modo mori fecit,
quando ita subtrahendas hominum notitiae sepe-
liendasque curavit. Aut ergo daemonum illic tam
sordidae et noxiae cupiditates erant conscriptae ut
ex his tota illa theologia civilis etiam apud tales
homines execrabilis appareret qui tam multa in ipsis
sacris erubescenda susceperant; aut illi omnes nihil
aliud quam homines mortui prodebantur, quos tam
prolixa temporis vetustate fere omnes populi gentium
deos inmortales esse crediderant, cum et talibus
sacris idem illi daemones oblectarentur, qui se
colendos pro ipsis mortuis, quos deos putari fecerant,
quibusdam fallacium miraculorum adtestationibus
supponebant.

Sed occulta Dei veri providentia factum est ut et
Pompilio amico suo illis conciliati artibus quibus
hydromantia fieri potuit, cuncta illa confiteri permitterentur, et tamen ut moriturus incenderet ea
potius quam obrueret admonere non permitterentur;
qui ne innotescerent nec aratro quo sunt eruta
obsistere potuerunt, nec stilo Varronis quo ea quae
de hac re gesta sunt in nostram memoriam pervenerunt. Non enim possunt quod non sinuntur efficere;
sinuntur autem alto Dei summi iustoque iudicio pro
meritis eorum quos ab eis vel adfligi tantum, vel etiam
subici ac decipi iustum est. Quam vero perniciosae

their causes, which he would have no one know but
himself. Thus he had them written down separately,
intending them to die with him, so to speak, when he
took care to have them withdrawn from the knowledge of men and buried. These books either contained an account of the foul and hurtful passions of
the demons, such as to make the whole civil theology
appear abominable even to such men, who had
adopted so many shameful practices in their worship,
or else all the gods were there revealed as nothing
but dead men whom for so long a time almost all the
heathen nations had believed to be immortal gods.
For even by such rites they pleased those same
demons who, by using false miracles as evidence,
had substituted themselves as objects of worship for
the actual dead men whom they had caused to be
regarded as gods.

But by the secret providence of the true God it
came to pass that the demons were won over to their
friend Pompilius by the arts of hydromancy and were
allowed to confess all these matters. However, they
were not allowed to warn him to burn the books
before he died, rather than bury them. And they
were not allowed to prevent their discovery by
stopping either the plough that turned them up or
the pen of Varro, by which the record of these events
has come down to our time. For they are unable to
do what they are not permitted to do; and permission
is granted only by the sublime and righteous judgement of the supreme God. He acts according to the
deserts of men, who are sentenced either to be only
afflicted by demons, or also to be mastered and
deceived by them. But we can understand how

vel a cultu verae divinitatis alienae illae litterae
iudicatae sint hinc intellegi potest, quod eas maluit
senatus incendere, quas Pompilius occultavit, quam
timere quod timuit, qui hoc audere non potuit.
Qui ergo vitam nec modo habere vult piam, talibus
sacris quaerat aeternam; qui autem cum malignis
daemonibus non vult habere societatem, non superstitionem qua coluntur noxiam pertimescat, sed
veram religionem qua produntur et vincuntur
agnoscat.

harmful these writings were judged to be, how inconsistent with the worship of a true deity, by the fact that the Senate preferred to burn what Pompilius had hidden, rather than fear what he feared when he did not dare to burn them.   And so let the man who refuses even now to lead a pious life seek eternal life by those rites!   But let him who refuses to associate with malignant demons have no fear of the harmful superstition by which they are worshipped.   Let him rather recognize the true religion, by which they are exposed and vanquished.